W

Web Design

Richard Tammadge

Gill & Macmillan

Gill & Macmillan Ltd

Hume Avenue

Park West

Dublin 12

with associated companies throughout the world

www.gillmacmillan.ie

© Richard Tammadge 2001

0 7171 3216 1

Index compiled by Patrick Roberts

Design by Graham Thew Design, Dublin

Print origination in Ireland by O'K Graphic Design

Contents

The concept of hotspots and how they can be used for navigation

How style sheets work
Designing and coding simple and complex style sheets
Applying style sheets to Web pages
The concept of block level elements and canvas space
HTML core attributes

The differences between HTML editors and fully featured Web
authoring software
A brief look at freeware, shareware and commercial Web authoring
packages
Advantages and disadvantages of using Web authoring software
Other utilities for Web content production

Part 2 - Designing a site for the World Wide Web

Basic design concepts
Deciding and implementing site objectives
Defining and targeting a site audience
Establishing key messages
The hierarchical approach to planning a site
Managing files and folders for maximum efficiency
Using content to determine design
Drawing up initial site plans

The concept of design consistency
The use of appropriate style and colour schemes
Using templates to achieve consistent design
Balancing text and graphic content
How to grab an audience's attention
Inventing good titles and headlines
The importance of page length

An introduction to active and interactive content

INTRODUCTION

This book is intended as a practical text book for students wanting to learn HTML — the mark-up language used to create pages for the World Wide Web. It also covers the complexities of Web site design and maintenance, as well as providing background information on Internet terminology and the technologies which drive the Web.

The book is intended to help at four levels of study:

1. Post Junior Certificate students who are studying HTML authoring and Web authoring as part of their computer studies.
2. Students taking the NCVA Level 2 module in Web authoring.
3. Students taking the NCVA Level 3 module in Web authoring.
4. Students at Third Level who need a text on HTML and Web design for degrees/diplomas in computing.

I hope that it will also prove useful for "civilians" who need to get to grips with Web design for their work or who simply have an interest in this rapidly developing medium. Not all of the book will apply to every level of study. Some students might well find that it goes beyond the range of their syllabus, while others might need to progress to more specialised books. I am confident, however, that this book will provide you with all the skills you need to create interesting and effective sites on the World Wide Web.

The book is divided into two sections. Section one deals with the basic mechanics of HTML coding, while section two develops that practical knowledge into a logical method of designing and building a Web site. Chapters contain detailed explanations of the HTML code and techniques in question, a series of short practical assignments and screen shots to show how completed assignments should appear in a Web browser. Where new HTML elements are introduced, the chapter closes with a table explaining the tags which have been used.

At the end of the book, you will find a series of appendices which provide a complete listing of all the common HTML tags and their usage, hexadecimal RGB values and names for all Web-safe colours, and the codes to create special characters such as the Irish fada.

I have attempted a cheerful tone throughout this book, but have not avoided using technical terms where they were necessary. Computing — perhaps more than any other subject — is riddled with jargon, and I thought it important that students should be able to understand and use the correct terminology. The more complicated terms are explained in footnotes within the chapters.

Finally, I would like to acknowledge the help and support I have received from fellow teachers and lecturers, and to thank my long-suffering students on whom most of this book was tried out. In particular I would like to thank those three tireless teachers/lecturers who took on the thankless task of reading the first draft. Their comments and suggestions were invaluable.

Richard Tammadge

Part **1**

Coding With HTML

Chapter 1
An Introduction to the Web

Brief contents:

1. Origins of the World Wide Web.

2. How the Web relates to the Internet.

3. Who controls the Web.

4. The concept of Client/Server computing.

5. The origins of Hypertext.

6. HyperText Transfer Protocol and how it works.

7. Universal Resource Locators.

8. HyperText Mark-up Language and its limitations.

9. How to read the rest of this book.

An Introduction to the Web

The Internet and the World Wide Web

These days the Internet is everywhere. The press is full of it. We are bombarded with adverts from .com[1] businesses trying to sell us everything from books to on-line banking. Politicians sing its praises or curse its flaws in equal measure. We are still discovering new uses for the Internet. Certainly it is the greatest storehouse of information mankind has ever created, but we can also use it to chat to our friends, to send personal and business messages, to book tickets and to buy those hard-to-find videos and CDs.

---

[1] **.com:** pronounced "dot com". A .com company is a **com**mercial organisation doing business on the Web, so called because most Web businesses have an address like www.microsoft.com. (Registering a name on the Web is quite complicated and your Web address will often depend on which country you register from. We will be looking at this in detail later in the book.)

The Internet may be the most important development in human communications since the invention of the printing press, but how it will affect our lives in the future cannot be predicted. One of the reasons why the Internet has become so significant is that everyone can be a part of it. Each time you fire up your browser and connect, the computer you are sitting at becomes a tiny part of that trans-national network. You join a global community of millions of other Internet users.

For many individuals and organisations, simply using the Internet is not enough. They want, or sometimes need, to be a part of it. Businesses see the Internet as a new, almost unlimited marketplace in which to sell their goods and services. Governments and public bodies wish to use it to broadcast information. Private individuals with something to say about their hobbies, politics, fantasies or aspirations want others to share their opinions. Lonely people want to make friends. The list is endless.

Figure 1.1: The World Wide Web – Oceanfree.net's opening page

This book is intended to teach you how to create a presence on the Internet. There are several ways of doing this, but we will concern ourselves with authoring for the World Wide Web – the fastest growing and surely the most exciting aspect of the Internet. Before we can get down to creating Web pages and eventually Web sites, it is important that we understand how the Web relates to the Internet itself, and how the Web actually works.

People often confuse the Internet with the World Wide Web, but they are not the same thing. The Internet is simple enough. It is a collection of millions of computers all round the world, all connected to each other and all talking the same language.

But if the Internet itself is a thing of machines and wires, the World Wide Web is more like an idea. It has been described as "an abstract space with which people can interact, populated chiefly by interlinked pages of text, images and animations, with occasional sounds, three-dimensional worlds and videos". This doesn't help much. It has also been described more poetically as "a pair of soft pyjamas clothing the hard metal body of the Internet itself". This helps even less.

Up until recently, the easiest way to think of the Web was as a collection of shared information, stored all over the world and connected by software links which allowed you to move from place to place. It is a library which contains almost anything that anyone could ever want to know, and that information is available as text, images, sounds and video. In the same way that the books in a library rely on the shelves to hold them, the passages between the shelves to provide access for readers, and the library building itself to protect them from the elements, so the Web relies on the Internet to store and protect that information and deliver it to its users. But the Web never closes, you don't pay a fine if you hold onto the information for too long and no-one ever tells you to keep quiet!

Today the Web is much more than this. As well as a library, the Web has become an interactive medium where you can communicate with other people, bargain and auction, hunt down obscure facts and run programs on computers on the other side of the world. Pages are no longer static, but alive with animations and video shows. Access speeds are increasing, which brings the possibility of Web video and real-time Web TV. The next few years may see the Internet change beyond recognition. Already the old ISPs (*Internet Service Providers*[2]) are being joined by ASPs (Application Service Providers), Web-based organisations which provide all the software you currently run on your local machine. New programming languages are being developed which will allow you to interact directly with Web databases. And all these possibilities are opening up on a communications medium which remains outside the control of nations, corporations or any group of individuals.

The birth of the World Wide Web

We will start our exploration by considering the ideas and technologies behind the World Wide Web. The software that allows communication across the Web is largely the work of one man. In 1989 Tim Berners-Lee, while working at the European Laboratory for Particle Physics (CERN) in Geneva, Switzerland, developed a system that allowed physicists to share their research results over the Internet. He and his colleagues at CERN hacked together a simple way to display information on screen and to move from place to place by clicking "hypertext links" – active pieces of text which linked the user to other pieces of information stored on the Internet. But rather than keeping this idea to themselves, or trying to make money from it, Berners-Lee and his team posted the code on the Internet, allowing everyone to make use of it.

---

[2] **Internet Service Providers**: ISPs are companies which provide their clients with a connection to the Internet. In Ireland there is a choice of ISPs, including Eircom, Oceanfree, Ireland-on-Line and Indigo. For this book, we assume that you already have an Internet connection at home or via your school or college.

Although this code allowed users to combine words, pictures and sounds on pages which would display on the Internet, it was another two years before Marc Andreesen and a team of students at the National Center for Supercomputing Applications (NCSA) in Illinois, USA, developed the first graphical *Web browser*[3]. Launched in 1993, Mosaic was the ancestor of all of today's browsers. They are so easy to use that nobody needs to type in commands to use the Internet as they were obliged to do in the early days. But it is worth remembering that underneath the Web browser's graphical interface (the "soft pyjamas" we mentioned earlier), the Internet still exists and still does the essential work of moving data from place to place.

"The World Wide Web is conceived as a seamless world in which all information, from any source, can be accessed in a consistent and simple way." The quote is from Tim Berners-Lee and sums up the basic concept behind the Web. The World Wide Web Consortium (WWWC or W3C) that Berners-Lee and his colleagues founded is the body responsible for overseeing the development of the software which allows the Web to function. From its beginnings, the WWWC has adhered to six fundamental principles:

1. *That the Web's information system must be able to link data stored in an arbitrary fashion in different locations.*

2. *That users must be able to move around the Web independently, without following a predetermined linear path from one computer to the next. (Think of the difference between driving from one village to the next along the roads and walking there across the fields. You will get there either way, but the roads force you to travel in certain directions, while if you walk across the fields, you can twist and turn as you please.)*

3. *That the Web must work in the same way for every user regardless of that user's make of computer, operating system or native language.*

4. *That it must be possible to access information from every type of computer and operating system – including ones that have not yet been developed. (This is called "future-proofing", and the fact that it was designed into the Web at the very beginning explains how the Web has continued to grow and prosper despite all the new technologies that have emerged since.)*

5. *That users must be able to set up their computers' information systems and use them on the Web in any way that they wish; there should not be one fixed model to which every connected machine must conform.*

6. *That updating and correcting information on the Web should be a simple and straightforward operation.*

From the outset, the Web was intended to be independent and uncontrolled. Its architects did not want a formal, rigid structure. Remember that the World Wide

---

[3] **Web browser:** the software that allows you to access the World Wide Web. The most common browser in use today is Microsoft's Internet Explorer, followed by Netscape. There are many others such as Opera, KatieSoft and HotJava. We will be looking at some of them later in the book.

Web was grafted onto the Internet which itself had grown up in a completely random and disorganised fashion[4]. Author Bruce Sterling summed it up perfectly: "The Internet is a rare example of a true, modern, functional anarchy. There is no 'Internet Inc'. There are no official censors, no bosses, no board of directors, no stockholders." Although the WWWC has overall responsibility for developing the Web's software, it exercises no control over the information that is posted to the Web and does not try to influence how the Web is used.

And almost every day, new uses for the Web are discovered. If the original Internet was seen as an infinite storehouse for information, the second generation of users were taking things much further. In 1999, well over a billion dollars changed hands in the Internet shopping malls. "Vanity sites" – private sites created for their owners' pleasure – are springing up everywhere. (Many of these sites were never intended to be accessible to all and thus contradicted one of the cornerstones of Web philosophy.) It seems as if every business in the world, from the tiniest cheese maker in the wilds of Killarney to the biggest multinational, just has to have a Web site. The age of the Internet has arrived in style.

Key Facts

1 The Internet and the World Wide Web are NOT the same thing. In simple terms, the Internet is the hardware (and software) that transfers data from place to place. The World Wide Web is a vast collection of inter-linked data stored on computers around the world and accessible via a Web browser.

2 In 1989, Tim Berners-Lee and a team working at CERN in Switzerland posted on the Internet some basic code which allowed text and graphics to display on a computer screen. This code allowed pieces of text to become 'active' – when clicked the user was redirected to other information stored on the Internet.

3 In 1993, the first graphical Web browser was launched. Mosaic had been developed by Marc Andreesen and a team at NCSA. It was the prototype for all the Web browsers which are currently available and allowed the user to access Web content in a simple, intuitive way.

4 The World Wide Web Consortium (WWWC) oversees the development of the software which drives the Web. Their guiding principles include independence for Web users, access to the Web regardless of the computer and operating system being used, and that information held on the Web must be simple to update.

5 The Web itself (like the Internet) is not controlled or managed by anyone. It is an open system which anyone can use in any way they wish to, limited only by the restrictions imposed by the Web's own architecture.

[4] **growth of the Internet:** the growth and development of the Internet itself is not strictly relevant to the subject of Web Authoring. For those who are interested, we have included a brief history of the Internet as Appendix 1 at the back of this book.

How the World Wide Web works

The relative ease of clicking on links, buttons or images has made the World Wide Web accessible to everyone. The ordinary user does not **need** to know how Web content is delivered to his computer, any more than the ordinary driver **needs** to know how his car works, but effective Web Authoring means understanding exactly how the Web operates. A good Web author is a good Web mechanic. Understanding a system's strengths and weaknesses means that you can tailor your own pages to take advantage of all the resources the Web provides while avoiding most of the problems.

The Web can be looked at as a two-sided system. At the user end (the **client**, in computer terminology) there are resources to handle the requesting of data, its input and display. Your Web browser is the key component here. At the remote end (the **server**), there are resources to handle storage and retrieval. This approach to handling information flow is called **client/server computing**. Figure 1.2 shows a simplified model.

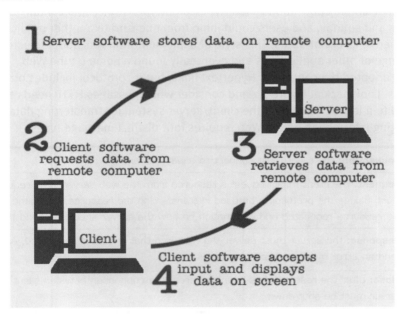

1 Server software stores data on remote computer

2 Client software requests data from remote computer

3 Server software retrieves data from remote computer

Server

Client

4 Client software accepts input and displays data on screen

Figure 1.2: A simplified model of client/server computing

There are several reasons why this client/server approach has proved so successful on the Web. Because it divides the job of delivering Web pages between client and server, the client can concentrate on managing the user interface (the browser), while the server looks after handling requests for data. By storing data on the server, information providers maintain control of their systems and can protect their data, control access to it and keep an accurate record of how often it is requested. To sum up, the World Wide Web makes use of client/server computing by linking powerful, graphical clients (Web browsers) with fast, efficient servers.

HyperText Transfer Protocol – the language of the Web

Before two computers can communicate, they have to agree a set of rules and formats. In computer terminology, an agreed system of communications between two computers is called a **Protocol**. Before the World Wide Web came into existence, the commonest protocol used for accessing remote data on the Internet was the File Transfer Protocol (FTP). FTP was too slow for the Web and did not allow the additional features the Web designers wanted, so a new protocol was developed and christened **HyperText Transfer Protocol (HTTP)**.

To understand HTTP, it is first necessary to understand the concept of Hypertext. The idea of Hypertext has been around for quite a while. The name was first coined by a computer scientist called Ted Nelson way back in 1965. He was trying to invent a way to link all the documents in a library and came up with a system where references in one document would lead the reader to connected references in other documents. The idea was good, but it would be another 20 years before the technology to implement his ideas became available. In 1987, Apple Computers launched a simple application called Hypercard. Hypercards could contain text, graphics and sounds, and users could jump from one card to another by clicking underlined links or hot-spots. This style of implementation was adopted across a wide range of other applications and eventually found a home on the Web.

HTTP adopted the concept of Hypertext links, but its protocol includes other methods. Look back at Figure 1.2 and consider what messages HTTP needs to respond to if it is to implement the client/server system for transferring data. Exchanging information on the Web requires four distinct message types:

1. **Connection:** the client must connect to a web server.

2. **Request:** the client must request a resource from the web server. (The request must include the protocol to be used in transferring the resource, the name of the resource requested and information on how the server should respond.)

3. **Response:** the server must deliver the resource that has been requested, or send an error message explaining why it cannot.

4. **Close:** after the resource has been delivered, the connection between client and server must be shut down.

At the end of this process, HTTP has done its job and it is up to your browser (or other software on the client computer) to take on the resource and handle its display or storage.

So why do we need to understand HTTP when designing for the Web? Remember that HTTP **is** the Web protocol and every page we create will be handled by HTTP. When a client downloads a page we have written, it is HTTP which handles the transfer. When a Web user clicks a hypertext link that we have installed, it is HTTP which will move him to that link's target. When something goes wrong, it is HTTP which generates the error messages which explain the problem encountered. We will be looking at how HTTP handles Web pages later in the book. For now it is enough to remember that everything we produce for the Web will rely on HyperText Transfer Protocol.

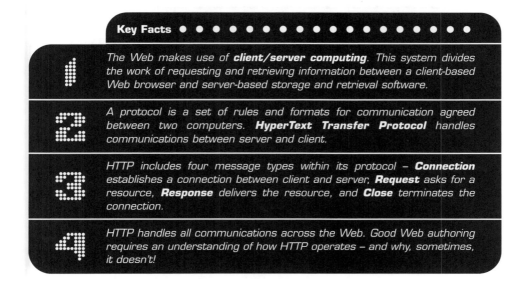

Key Facts ● ● ● ● ● ● ● ● ● ● ● ● ● ● ● ● ● ● ●

1 *The Web makes use of **client/server computing**. This system divides the work of requesting and retrieving information between a client-based Web browser and server-based storage and retrieval software.*

2 *A protocol is a set of rules and formats for communication agreed between two computers. **HyperText Transfer Protocol** handles communications between server and client.*

3 *HTTP includes four message types within its protocol – **Connection** establishes a connection between client and server, **Request** asks for a resource, **Response** delivers the resource, and **Close** terminates the connection.*

4 *HTTP handles all communications across the Web. Good Web authoring requires an understanding of how HTTP operates – and why, sometimes, it doesn't!*

Universal (or Uniform!) Resource Locators

The Web is a big place and getting bigger by the minute. With billions of documents stored on computers all round the globe, how does HTTP (or any other Web protocol, for that matter) know how to find the Web page you are interested in reading? In simple terms, HTTP understands URLs.

URL stands for **Universal Resource Locator** or sometimes **Uniform Resource Locator**, depending on the book you are looking at. A URL is an address on the Web – not necessarily the address of a page or a Web site. A URL can just as well point to an image or a video file. All of these things in Web-speak are resources. If you've ever used the Web, you have used URLs – maybe without even knowing it. When you visit a site, for example, the string of words divided by slashes that appears in the browser's address box is that site's URL. We will be looking at URLs in greater detail later in this book, but for the moment, we should understand how a URL works.

A URL has at least two parts and sometimes as many as six. The type of URL you will often met might look like this:

http://www.rte.ie

This is the Web address of RTE television and consists of two parts – the protocol and the address itself. To understand what each part of a URL means, look at the example below:

http://www.flywithus.com:8080/holidays/florida.html#miami

This URL contains every part that a URL can contain. Most URLs are a lot less complicated. Let's take each part in order and see how it works:

1. **http://** – the first part of the URL specifies the protocol used to access the resource. **http** usually points to a hypertext document, and most of the URLs you encounter will look like this, but there are other *protocols on the Internet*[5].

2. **www.flywithus.com** – the site address of the Web server storing the resource. (We will look at site addressing later in the book.)

3. **:8080** – the port address. (You will not usually see a port address, but we are including it for the sake of completeness. If a port address appears in a URL, it is important that you include it.)

4. **holidays/** – the directory path to the resource requested. This could have several parts: **holidays/America/expensive/** for example.

5. **florida.html** – the name of the resource requested. This will often be a Web page, but could be an image, a video file etc.

6. **#miami** – if the resource requested is a Web page, this part directs the browser to an anchor – a specific location on the page.

Most URLs you deal with will be much shorter than our example. Modern browsers do not require the **http://** bit for example, but as a Web author (don't worry, you **will** be!) you need to understand how to construct a complete URL. The most important thing to remember with URLs is they must be entered accurately. Not only must the words be spelled correctly, but all the letters must be in the right case. Many computers on the Internet are case-sensitive – Holidays/Florida.html is **not** the same as holidays/florida.html.

Hypertext Mark-Up Language (HTML)
Before we can learn anything at all, we have to learn language. HTML is the language in which almost all of the Web's billions of pages are written. There are others, but they are mostly varieties of HTML modified to provide additional facilities. HTML is a text mark-up language, whose function is to tell Web browsers how to display Web pages. HTML is itself a version of SGML (Standard Generalized Mark-Up Language), but you don't need to know anything about SGML to create documents for the Web.

You have met text mark-up before, probably without even realising it. At school, you probably had one or two assignments returned to you decorated with your teacher's comments in red ink. The comments suggested ways you could improve or correct your work, but the notes in red were not a part of the assignment itself. In the same way, HTML is separate from the actual contents of a Web page.

[5] **protocols on the Internet**: other protocols you might meet include **ftp://** a file accessible through the File Transfer Protocol, **gopher://** a file system index accessible through the Gopher protocol, **mailto://** links to an application from which you can send an email message, **news://** links to a Usenet group, and **file:///** indicating that the resource is stored locally (probably on your own computer).

The World Wide Web Consortium we encountered earlier is primarily responsible for standardising HTML. It is continuously being improved and expanded, and this ongoing process gives Web authors one of their biggest headaches. The current standard is HTML 4, and this is the standard that all the latest browsers are supposed to support, but older browsers cannot cope with some of HTML 4's features and do not display their pages properly. Web authors are always looking backwards, trying to match their designs to the abilities of older browsers. We will be looking at compatibility issues later in the book.

Let us close this section by looking at some of the things HTML is **not**. This might sound odd, but HTML was **not** intended for Web page design. We use it, because we have to, but other technologies, such as style sheets, handle page layout much better. HTML is **not** finished. The WWWC's work continues and new modifications to the standard mean that Web authors need to continuously update their work. Finally, HTML is **not** all you need to know to create good Web pages. While HTML is the language you must use to express your designs, authoring for the Web involves a whole range of other skills. Good graphic and text design, the ability to match colour, the use of space, grammar and spelling, awareness of hardware and software limitations, even some programming ability are all part of Web authoring: but at its heart is an understanding of HTML. We like the opinion of Thomas A Powell in his excellent *HTML: The Complete Reference* – "HTML [is] the bedrock upon which the information superhighway is built."

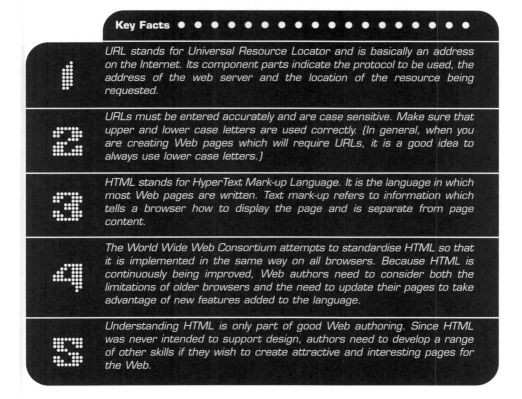

Key Facts ●

1 URL stands for Universal Resource Locator and is basically an address on the Internet. Its component parts indicate the protocol to be used, the address of the web server and the location of the resource being requested.

2 URLs must be entered accurately and are case sensitive. Make sure that upper and lower case letters are used correctly. (In general, when you are creating Web pages which will require URLs, it is a good idea to always use lower case letters.)

3 HTML stands for HyperText Mark-up Language. It is the language in which most Web pages are written. Text mark-up refers to information which tells a browser how to display the page and is separate from page content.

4 The World Wide Web Consortium attempts to standardise HTML so that it is implemented in the same way on all browsers. Because HTML is continuously being improved, Web authors need to consider both the limitations of older browsers and the need to update their pages to take advantage of new features added to the language.

5 Understanding HTML is only part of good Web authoring. Since HTML was never intended to support design, authors need to develop a range of other skills if they wish to create attractive and interesting pages for the Web.

Understanding the rest of this book

Before we start looking at HTML code and how it works, you need to be aware of the conventions we will be using in the following chapters. The box below explains how we will be making use of certain styles of text to indicate special information.

HOW TO READ THIS BOOK:

Technical terms are printed in italics and explained in a footnote. So when you see things like *cross-platform*[1], look to the bottom of the page where the term will be explained.

When you see **words printed like this**, they need to be entered from your keyboard exactly as they are printed on the page. Be careful to copy the exact punctuation and make sure you don't add or ignore any spaces between the letters.

It is good policy to type all HTML code in capital letters as we have done in this book. It is not strictly necessary, but it makes life much easier when you are correcting errors. As we mentioned earlier, because some computers handle letter case differently, it is also a good idea to name all files in lower case letters and not leave any spaces in the name. Name your files in this format: **myfile_one.html** rather than **My File One.HTML**.

When we ask you to click on buttons, icons or menu items, we will print the instructions like this. So if you see "click **start > programs > accessories > notepad**". This means click on the <u>Start</u> button, then click <u>Programs</u> on the menu that appears, then click <u>Accessories</u> on the next menu, then click <u>Notepad</u> on the final menu.

There's one other thing to note before we begin. In the first part of this book, you will meet three special icons. This is what they mean:

Whenever you see this icon, expect a chunk of technical information. Sorry... but it's stuff you really should know.	*This icon flags something that you need to remember if you are to work successfully in Web authoring.*	*This icon indicates a clever trick or a shortcut that might save you a whole heap of time and trouble.*

QUICK REVISION QUESTIONS

1. What is the difference between the Internet and the World Wide Web?
2. What was Tim Berners-Lee's contribution to the start of the Web?
3. What is the World Wide Web Consortium and what is its principal responsibility?
4. Who controls the World Wide Web?
5. What was the first graphical Web browser called and who designed it?
6. What is client/server computing and what part does it play in the operation of the World Wide Web?
7. What is a computer protocol?
8. What are the four message types included in the HyperText Transfer Protocol which handle the transfer of data between computers?
9. What does URL stand for and what are its possible component parts?
10. What does HTML stand for, what is it and what are its limitations in Web authoring?

Chapter 2
The Basics of Web Authoring

Brief contents:

1. Web authoring involves both good design and the correct use of HTML mark-up.

2. The concept of text mark-up.

3. Some of HTML's shortcomings.

4. The ways in which different browsers handle HTML.

5. The different versions of HTML standardisation.

6. The difference between page content and HTML code.

7. Different types of page content and how a Web browser handles them.

8. The software required for this book.

9. Organising your computer workspace ready for the exercises in the remainder of this book.

The Basics of Web Authoring

This chapter looks at the fundamentals of authoring for the World Wide Web. The first point we must make is that Web authoring involves much more than just typing in text, throwing in a few pictures and formatting it all with HTML. Instead there are two distinct aspects we will need to look at — **HTML coding** and **Web design**, and although these two connect at every point, you will need to understand both before you can call yourself a Web author.

A good analogy here is building a house. Before a single block is laid, someone — probably an architect — has to draw up the plans. He or she has to work out how the various rooms and features will fit together, and how all the components will merge into a single, attractive whole. Only when everything has been worked out in the finest detail will the architect hand over the plans to a builder. The builder brings a different range of skills to the project. His job is to turn the architect's ideas into reality. Sometimes this may not be possible, and the builder will have to modify the design to suit the limitations of the materials he has to work with. On occasions, the builder will find a more efficient way of doing something. The architect might have to be called in again to make changes. To be a Web author, you must be both architect and builder. Figure 2.1 shows a simplified model of the Web design process.

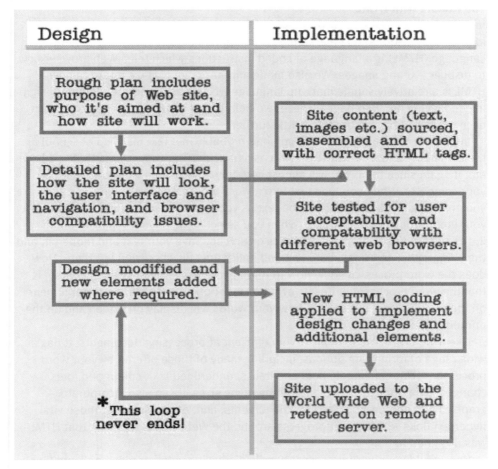

Figure 2.1: A simplified model of the design process

In this book, we are going to start with the building blocks — the basic HTML tags you will be using to create your Web pages. Although this chapter deals with a number of design issues, most of Part 1 is about HTML and how it is used. We will take you through all the tags you will need to create pages for the Web, but don't forget, these are just the builder's skills. In Part 2, you will become an architect. We will look at the design skills you will need as a Web author, and the constraints that HTML and the Web itself will impose on you. It might seem as if we are going about this the wrong way round. After all, the diagram above clearly shows that design comes first. Think again about our house building analogy. Before the architect can draw up his plans, he needs to know all about the materials he can use. He needs to understand how houses are put together; what brick, concrete and wood are capable of, and how they can be combined to create an attractive and efficient home. This is why we are starting from the ground up.

The trouble with HTML

In Chapter 1, we looked at how the World Wide Web operates and introduced the idea of Hypertext and text mark-up. Just to remind ourselves: Hypertext Mark-up Language (HTML) is a language of coded instructions which tell a Web browser how to display text and images. We also made another point that we return to now. HTML is a relatively simple mark-up language which was never intended for designing and laying out Web pages. These two points might sound as if they contradict each other, so let's explore this a little further.

In Chapter 1 we suggested that you had probably met text mark-up at school as the comments a teacher wrote on your assignments. The chances are that you have met it again since then. You will almost certainly have used a word processor on your computer. When you type text into a word processing application, the software you are using will usually format the text as you type. When you hit the **Return** key, your input drops to the next line. When you select some of your typing and italicise it, the selected text changes into italics on screen. Save your text and reopen it, and the paragraphs, new lines, bold text and italics are still where you left them. How does the word processor know how to format your text? The answer, of course, is that the word processor writes its own text mark-up — code that does not appear on the printed page, but defines how your words will display on screen and on the printed page.

Like a word processor, HTML is very efficient at processing documents. It has a wide range of formatting options, including many of those offered by your word processor. HTML can handle bold and italics, underlined text, colour and font changes, paragraphs, line-breaks and headline sizes. It can also incorporate graphics and photographs into text documents, and, of course insert those vital hypertext links which power progress around the Web. This is the work that HTML was designed to do.

How would your word processor handle displaying video or playing sound files while you sat back and reviewed your work? It couldn't, of course, because that is not what it has been designed for. In the same way, HTML was never intended to be a tool for graphic designers. It was not created to handle complex page layouts, multimedia content, interactive content or even elaborate colour schemes. But all of these are now common features on the Web, because Web authors (and Web authoring software designers) have both deliberately **misused** HTML and extended its capabilities in new directions. Misused? This sounds unlikely, but let us give you a single example — you will meet others as you work through this book.

The designers of HTML thought it would be useful if Web authors could create tables to display information in neat little boxes, so they included mark-up code to allow this. Think what happens if you use HTML to create a table with several columns and just one row, like this...

...and then fill your columns with text and reduce the table's border width to o so it becomes invisible, like this...

Look! You now have a three-column layout on your page — similar to the layout you might find in a magazine. If we use the centre column to display an image, like this:

...we have effectively created a complex page layout of text and integrated graphics by using HTML in a way it was never intended to be used. Now you see what we mean!

Although we will be covering laying out pages with tables later in the book, this seems an ideal opportunity to introduce these little Tricks of the Trade notes. Most of the best sites use this trick with tables to create multiple columns on a page. It's never too early to start thinking in terms of Web design!

HTML has many other shortcomings we will be examining later in the book, but for now it seems that we have a problem. We want to design pages that look professional and make use of all the resources available to us, and before we even start, we discover that the mark-up language we are going to be using is not designed to do what we want it to do. We can help avoid this problem by bearing the following points in mind:

1. We can try to ensure that our designs for the Web stay within the limitations HTML imposes, but at the same time...

2. ...we can follow the example of other Web authors and adapt existing HTML code to suit our own needs, and if that fails...

3. ...we can extend HTML by bringing in elements from compatible languages such as JavaScript and DHTML. (Don't worry about these for the moment, we will introduce them when we need them later in the book.)

In order to see exactly what is available to us, it's time we took a closer look at HTML itself.

What is HTML?

Let's start by reviewing what we already know. HTML is **H**yper**T**ext **M**ark-**u**p **L**anguage and, like a programming language, it consists of a range of text commands that tell your computer what to do. Unlike a programming language, HTML doesn't communicate directly with the operating system. Instead its commands are interpreted by your Web browsing software. Internet Explorer, Netscape, NeoPlanet, Opera, NetCaptor, HotJava and every other browser you might find are all *HTML-aware*[1]. In theory, they all display HTML in exactly the same way; in practice it doesn't quite work like that. Some browsers are much better at displaying Web pages than others, and some are much more forgiving of mistakes in the HTML code.

We also noted in Chapter 1 that HTML is a continuously developing language. The current standard, HTML 4, includes code for a whole range of new features. Unfortunately because HTML keeps moving forward, older Web browsers get left behind. Early versions of Internet Explorer and Netscape Navigator (prior to Version 4.0 of each) don't understand a lot of the new code included in HTML 4.0. They either ignore it or make a mess of displaying it. Worse still, the various companies which distribute browser software cannot agree on a common standard. Different browsers offer different features, require different code and even respond to the same code in different ways. We will be looking at some of these problems later in the book.

HTML has gone through a series of versions since it was first designed. In each case, the new version has included additional features to suit the changing demands of Web authors. The table below lists the various versions of HTML, known as Standardisation Levels.

HTML Standardisation Levels:	
Version:	**Description:**
0	The original mark-up language developed by Tim Berners-Lee and his team at CERN. It could only handle text — no graphic content. This version was never released to the general public
1.0	The first public implementation of HTML. It now had the ability to handle graphic content — some browsers still operate at this level of HTML.
2.0	The first "official" implementation of HTML which now included the tags to handle interactive forms. Graphical Web browsers (Mosaic, Internet Explorer, Netscape Navigator etc.) operate at this level or higher.
3.0	The second official version of HTML, which again included elements to handle new Web content. HTML 3.2 is the base level at which most browsers operate today and it is not practical to design for browsers which cannot handle this implementation of the language.
4.0	The current official version of HTML, which includes a number of improvements including the ability to handle style sheets and frames.

[1] **HTML-aware**: If a Web browser responds correctly to HTML code, it is said to be *HTML-aware*.

Creating a Web page — that is a page which will display in a Web browser — requires no more skill than does using a word processor. Provided you can type and enter the necessary HTML code accurately, you can create Web pages. Please focus on the word "accurately". Accuracy is everything when it comes to writing HTML — a single word misspelled, even a single bracket out of place, and the whole document can turn into gibberish when it is displayed in a browser.

One good thing to remember is that there is nothing complicated in writing HTML. A Web page consists of:

1. **Content:** the words and images that appear in your browser window, AND

2. **HTML Code:** the commands which tell the browser how to display your text, where to place your graphics, when to play your sound files etc.

Here is a very simple example:

<B>Hello!</B>

The HTML code is **<B>** and **</B>**, and the content is **Hello!**. In this case the code tells a browser to display the word "Hello!" in bold text.

So HTML is simple, but it is also surprisingly powerful. We noted above that HTML was not originally designed to handle multimedia or active content, but it was designed to handle hypertext, and hypertext can link to a whole range of different resources. Let us imagine that an HTML page on the Web includes a link to a music file you want to listen to. Once the link has been made and HTTP has *downloaded*[2] the resource you have requested, your own computer's installed software takes over. Provided you have an application which can play that type of music file, the application starts up and out comes the song. Add-on software to handle specific types of Web content are often called **plug-ins** and we will be looking at several of these in the book. We will examine how a Web browser and its plug-ins work together to handle Web content later in this chapter.

It is important to remember that most of the Web's actual resource handling takes place inside your own computer. You make a link and are connected to whichever server is holding the Web resource you have requested. As soon as the resource has been downloaded, you are immediately disconnected from that server. What you see on your screen or hear over your speakers is now stored on your own machine and is handled by your browser, installed applications, or plug-in software. (Even audio and video content works like this, although the latest players will start playing the sound or showing the video before it has all downloaded.)

---

[2] **downloaded**: remember client/server computing? Items moved from your own computer (the client) to a remote server on the Web, are said to be uploaded. Items moved from server to client are said to be downloaded. Strictly speaking, HTTP doesn't handle the download itself, that is the function of TCP.

Hypertext is certainly the most powerful feature of HTML. Links can be created to different parts of the same document, to different documents on a Web site or to documents on a different Web site altogether. All that is required is that the HTML code points to the correct URL, and your visitor will be whisked to his or her destination as quickly as the Internet can manage the transfer.

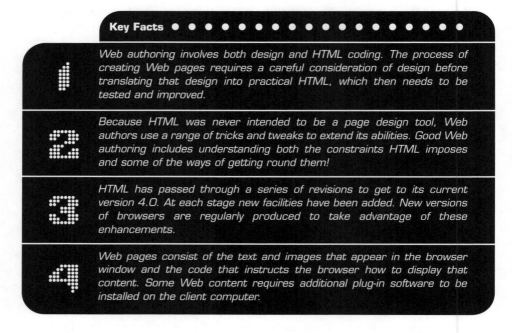

Key Facts

1. Web authoring involves both design and HTML coding. The process of creating Web pages requires a careful consideration of design before translating that design into practical HTML, which then needs to be tested and improved.

2. Because HTML was never intended to be a page design tool, Web authors use a range of tricks and tweaks to extend its abilities. Good Web authoring includes understanding both the constraints HTML imposes and some of the ways of getting round them!

3. HTML has passed through a series of revisions to get to its current version 4.0. At each stage new facilities have been added. New versions of browsers are regularly produced to take advantage of these enhancements.

4. Web pages consist of the text and images that appear in the browser window and the code that instructs the browser how to display that content. Some Web content requires additional plug-in software to be installed on the client computer.

Web page content

We have mentioned *page content*[3] several times, so let us look at what a Web page can contain. As we said above, pages written in HTML consist only of content and mark-up, with the mark-up telling a Web browser how to display the content. Only the actual text content is written into the page itself. We know that pages on the World Wide Web are full of graphics, photographs, animations and video, so how is such non-textual content handled? Let's look at some of the different types of Web page content and see how each is managed:

---

[3] **page content:** of interest, but not vital to know, is how the Web delivers all the different types of non-text content in a single bundle. MIME (Multipurpose Internet Mail Extensions) was originally designed to allow e-mails to carry different attachments, but is now used by Web servers to bundle different file types together and deliver them to your computer. The text part of the message arrives first and starts to format the page, then the other content arrives and is slotted into the page according to the HTML code employed. When a page first opens, you will often see little graphic "placeholders" — icons which show where the graphics will eventually appear.

1. **Text:** Text itself is simple enough. The words that appear in a browser window are actually a part of the HTML-coded page. They can be typed in (or cut and pasted) as in any word processor, then formatted with the required HTML tags.

2. **Images:** Images — whether graphics or photographs — are not a physical part of the HTML-coded page. Instead the page contains a link (**NOT** a hypertext link) to the URL of the file containing the image and instructions within the code that tell the browser how and where to display it on the page. This means, of course, that the images included in a Web page can be stored anywhere on the Internet. The quality of the image displayed depends on both the format it is stored in and the settings on the client computer's monitor and graphics software. Different image formats and their advantages and disadvantages are looked at in detail in Chapter 7.

3. **Animations:** Animations are used widely — some would say **too** widely — on the Web. Because an animation is simply a series of graphic images displayed one after the other, HTML treats them like static images, referencing them via a URL. Most browsers know how to handle animations. Once all the frames have been downloaded, the browser displays them in sequence, according to the instructions stored in the animation file itself.

4. **Sounds:** Sounds on the Web can be anything from simple sound effects up to full music tracks or spoken commentaries. Like images, they are not a part of the Web page, but are linked to it via their URLs. Almost all modern computers contain software that can handle the common types of sound file, although some of the new types require additional plug-ins. The original model for handling sound required the whole of the sound file to be downloaded before it could be played, but as Internet delivery has improved with faster modems and better connections, some audio formats have been designed that can deliver sound in a constant stream which can be played as it is received. This is known as **streaming** data, or playing in **real time**. The problem with this approach is that the Internet itself is subject to traffic jams and dropped connections which can interfere with the smooth delivery of a data stream. We will be looking at the problems of delivering audio content in Chapter 13.

5. **Video:** Almost all of the previous paragraph applies to motion-video, but more so! Video files are much larger than audio files, even when they are designed to play in a tiny window on your computer screen. The possibility of real time playing is pretty remote as the following figures show. Subject to the smooth running of the Internet, a 56.6Kbps modem will usually receive about 4 Kilobytes of data per second, while even a low specification video requires its player to process around 27 Megabytes of data per second — and that's without sound. As you might have guessed, we will be looking at video content later in the book.

Finally in this section, let's look briefly at the way in which a browser and a plug-in application co-operate to deliver non-text content within a page. The process works like this:

1. HTML code within the Web page is interpreted by the Web browser to create an **active** region as a hypertext link to the multimedia resource.

2. The user clicks the link and the browser sends a request for the multimedia resource, which is subsequently delivered from the Web server which stores it.

3. The browser checks the type of resource. If it can handle it internally, it does so; if not, the browser calls on a suitable application to handle the resource. (This application might be installed separately on the client computer, or it might be a special browser plug-in.)

4. The application or plug-in takes over the resource and plays it, displays it or whatever else is required.

5. After it is finished, the application closes and the browser reasserts control, allowing the user to carry on.

There is no doubt that visual and audio content is what makes the World Wide Web an interesting place to visit, but the wise Web author should always remember two things. Firstly, not all browsers can handle advanced content — indeed some users turn graphics off altogether to improve download speeds; and secondly, all non-text content takes up a lot of *bandwidth*[4], so an excess of graphics or multimedia content can slow up a download to such an extent that users get irritated or give up altogether. As a general rule, keep graphics files small and use them sparingly, and only include multimedia content where it is relevant.

Finally, while we have been discussing the commonest resources available on the Web, it is worth remembering that any type of file can be linked to a Web page for downloading. While recognised Web content is handled by the browser and its plug-ins, linking to other file types causes most browsers to open a special download box asking the user where he wishes to store the file on his own computer. Once the file has been downloaded, it is available to the user to handle with his own installed software.

One point to remember (which we shall return to later) is that wherever possible, you should make non-text content voluntary, rather than compulsory for the user. Rather than integrating an extensive sound effect or music track into your page, give the user a chance to access it via a hypertext link. If you want to provide access to large detailed images, display small low-resolution versions on your pages and allow the user to click on them to obtain the full-size version.

---

[4] **bandwidth:** bandwidth is defined as the range of frequencies that a communications channel can carry. The bandwidth of a digital signal is measured in bits per second (bps) and can be considered to be a measure of its carrying capacity. Since the overall bandwidth of a channel is determined by the band-width of the slowest part of that channel, the ability of the Internet to move data is limited by bottlenecks and slow connections. These translate to slow responses from a Web site.

Key Facts ● ● ● ● ● ● ● ● ● ● ● ● ● ● ● ● ● ● ●

 Web page content can include text, images, audio and video elements. Apart from the basic text, all of these are stored as linked files and are then incorporated into the page as specified by the page's HTML code.

 New audio technology means that audio files (sound effects, speech and music) can be streamed — that is played in real time, but hold-ups on the Internet can affect the process. Streaming video is far more difficult since a video file contains so much more data. At present only very fast Internet connections can stream very low resolution video, but the technology continues to develop.

A Web browser and other software installed on the client computer co-operate to handle some types of page content. Provided the client computer is equipped with an application which can recognise and handle the resource, any type of file can be linked to a Web page.

Requirements for Web authoring

Most of this chapter has been concerned with Web authoring concepts and theory, so we will close by looking at some of the practical issues involved in Web authoring. The only software you need to write for the Web is a text editor such as Windows Notepad or SimpleText on the Apple Macintosh. UNIX users can try vi or pico. Since all HTML consists of typed text and tags, there is not a page on the Web which could not have been created with the humblest of text editors. Some excellent Web authors still prefer to work at this level, claiming that it gives a greater degree of control over the finished work and produces far less bloated code.

There are, of course, a wide range of dedicated HTML editors — some for free on the Web — which simplify the authoring process by writing much of the code for you. Beyond these, there are *WYSIWYG*[5] Web authoring applications which effectively hide the code altogether, allowing you to concentrate on the look of your pages. Some of these are excellent products, if very expensive, but they take away a lot of the Web author's control.

Since this book is designed to teach HTML as well as Web design, we will be coding by hand using a text editor. For this, we suggest you use the simplest text editor you have installed. In Windows, this usually means Notepad and in MacOS, SimpleText. If you prefer to, you can use a word processor, but remember to save your pages as plain text files. In fact, we would discourage you from using a word processor because of the confusion between text formatting and HTML coding. A word processor will format your text as bold, but save the text as a Web page and the formatting will disappear. Stick to a humble text editor and you will not have any problems.

---

[5] **WYSIWYG:** (pronounced "whizzywig") What You See Is What You Get! WYSIWYG software lets you see on screen exactly what your finished product will look like when printed or, in this case, displayed on the Web. Your word processor is a good example of WYSIWYG software.

Then you need a browser, or rather, access to several different browsers since you will need to make sure your pages work properly whatever the browser being used. As we stated above, the commonest Web browser is Microsoft's Internet Explorer and the next most widely used is Netscape, which used to be known as Netscape Navigator (this is part of Netscape Communicator). After these two giants come a wide range of others including NeoPlanet, KatieSoft, NetCaptor, Opera and HotJava. You will certainly need to test your pages in the big two, but try and get one or two others as well. Most are available free of charge on magazine cover disks or on the Web itself.

Later in the book, you will need access to graphic and photographic software, to a GIF animation package, to an FTP application for transferring files onto the Web, to video and audio players, and several other applications. We will discuss these in detail at the start of the first chapter for which you will need them.

While we will provide as much support as we can for readers using other operating systems, this book will concentrate on the Microsoft Windows® operating system and the software it supports. We do this for two reasons. Firstly, over 90% of Web pages are designed on computers running Windows, and secondly almost all Irish schools and colleges teach on this platform. Our apologies to those using MacOS, Linux, BeOS, UNIX etc. We salute your enthusiasm and are confident that this book will still provide all the information you need to author good Web pages.

We also suggest you organise space on your computer to accommodate the various files you will be creating and using. Our recommendation is:

1. On your computer's hard drive, create a new folder called **Web Works** to contain everything you need for the assignments in this book.

2. Within **Web Works** create the following folders:

    a. **web_pages:** this will contain the Web pages you create to upload to the Web itself. We recommend the use of lower case names with no spaces in them for all folders and files which you might eventually wish to upload.

    b. **test_pages:** this is for trying ideas out and for storing some of the exercises you will complete as you work through this book.

    c. **downloads:** this is for storing pages and images you download from the Web.

    d. **cabinet:** this is for storing materials you might wish to use on your own Web site — scraps of text, notes, logs, scanned images, sound files etc.

3. Within **Web_pages**, create a new folder called **resources**. This will store any images, sound files etc. that appear in your pages.

4. Within **test_pages**, also create a new folder called **resources**.

It is extremely important that whenever you type in the name of a folder or a file, you spell it correctly. It is also vital that you give any files you create the correct **extension**. If you are familiar with Windows software, you will be familiar with file extensions — that sequence of letters after the dot, which tells your software which application the file is associated with. In MacOS and UNIX-based operating systems, file extensions, while perfectly legal, are far less common. Every page you create for the Web should have the extension **.html** (as in **my_file.html**). Windows-based servers can also recognise **.htm**, because until Windows 95 was launched, Windows and MSDOS files could only have three letter extensions. To be sure that every server and every browser recognises your pages as HTML-coded, it is safest always to use the full **.html** extension.

This naming convention might cause a problem, depending on the text editor you are using. Notepad tries to name all files it creates as **something.txt,** while the Mac's SimpleText doesn't add an extension at all. When saving the pages you have created in Notepad, type in your file name to include the **.html** extension. With SimpleText, just remember to add the **.html** extension to all your file names.

We emphasised that any files you create for the Web MUST have a .html extension. This can cause problems because you are creating a file in one application (Notepad) that is associated by Windows with another application (your Web browser). If you open Notepad again and try to reopen a .html file you have created, it may not appear to be where you saved it. This is because Notepad looks for files with a .txt extension and doesn't list any others. To find it you will need to change Files of Type: *to* All Files *in Notepad's "Open" window. Remember also that if you double-click any file with a .html extension, Windows will automatically open it in your browser — fine if you wish to view it, but not so useful when you wish to edit it!*

QUICK REVISION QUESTIONS

1. Why is HTML not suitable for designing Web pages?
2. What is meant by text mark-up?
3. What is meant by the term HTML-aware?
4. What are the two components of a page written in HTML?
5. What is a browser plug-in?
6. What is meant by Web content and what are the commonest types of Web content?
7. Which types of Web content are physically included in a Web page, and which are linked to it as external files?
8. What is meant by streaming data and why doesn't it always work?
9. What software is essential to create pages for the World Wide Web?
10. Why should all pages created for the Web be saved with a **.html** extension?

Chapter 3
Starting with HTML

Brief contents:

1. Understanding that HTML tags represent the code element of a Web page.

2. Using HTML tags to create a Web page.

3. Using HTML tags for simple text formatting.

4. The importance of correct HTML syntax.

5. How to nest HTML tags correctly.

6. Using text formatting tags with caution.

7. Understanding the concept of an attribute.

8. The workings of a tag table.

Starting with HTML

After two chapters of theory, it is something of a relief to get around to some practical work. In this chapter we are going to look at how Web pages are constructed, we are going to examine the different HTML elements used to define a page's structure, and we are going to do some basic text formatting using simple HTML tags.

We know from the last chapter that a Web page consists only of page content and HTML code and that the code is there to tell a Web browser how to display the content. Now we want to introduce the idea of HTML tags. The easiest way to explain this is to create a simple Web page and see exactly how it works.

Exercise One

1. Open a text editor – Notepad will do perfectly (click **Start > Programs > Accessories > Notepad**) as will SimpleText if you are working on a Mac.

2. Type in the following exactly as printed:

<HTML>

<HEAD>

<TITLE> This is a Web page </TITLE>

</HEAD>

<BODY>

**I am a genius.
**

I have just created my first Web page!

</BODY>

</HTML>

3. Save this file to your **test_pages** folder as **first_page.html** — remember that you MUST type the .html extension so that your Web browser knows that this file is intended for display on the Web.

4. Close your text editor and find the file you have just saved in Windows Explorer. It will have your Web browser's icon next to it. Double click it. (If you are working on a Mac, you will need to load your browser first, then click **File > Open File** and browse to where it is stored on the Macintosh Hard Drive.)

5. Internet Explorer or Netscape (or whatever is your default browser) will·open and display your page. It should look like Figure 3.1.

Figure 3.1: A simple Web page (Microsoft Internet Explorer).

Check the tags

Although the page you have just created is a very simple one, it is a genuine Web page. Upload it to a *Web-server*[1] and it would be perfectly at home on the Web. To understand exactly how this page has been created, let's break the exercise down into content and code:

CODE:	CONTENT:
<HTML>	
<HEAD>	
<TITLE>...</TITLE>	This is a Web page
</HEAD>	
<BODY>...	I am a genius.
 ...	I have just created my first Web page!
</BODY>	
</HTML>	

Note: the content for each line replaces the dots in the code column.

The content – in this case, the words which actually appear in the browser's window and title bar – is surrounded by HTML tags which tell the browser how to display it. Most of the tags for this page are in pairs – **<HTML>** and **</HTML>**, **<TITLE>** and **</TITLE>** etc. When tags are paired like this, the first tag, for example **<TITLE>**, turns something on. The second tag, preceded by a slash, **</TITLE>**, turns it off again. (These used to be called HTML **containers** – a good word since it explained exactly how tag pairs **contain** content, but the term seems to have fallen into disuse!) Let's look at each tag individually.

❑ The first tag on the page is the **<HTML>** tag. This tells a browser that the document which follows is intended to be displayed in a Web browser.

❑ Next comes the **<HEAD>** tag which is turned off again by **</HEAD>** two lines later. This pair contains information about the page, but none of this information appears in the browser window itself. **<HEAD> ... </HEAD>** tags only enclose information about the page.

---

[1] **Web-server:** We have already discussed client/server computing. Clearly, Web-servers are computers that are used to store and provide access to Web sites. Note that they are usually "hard-wired" to the Internet. This means that they are permanently connected, unlike most computers which are connected only when someone dials in on a phone line. (See the note below.)

 Two terms we have already met are **"server"** and **"client"**. Things that happen on the server are often described as **"server-side"**. If they happen on the client computer, they are described as **"client-side"**. We will be using both of these terms later in the book.

- ❏ Nested within the **<HEAD> ... </HEAD>** tags appear the **<TITLE> ...</TITLE>** tags. These surround the page's title **"This is a Web page."** Note that the title appears in the browser's title bar and not on the page. Check this by looking at the top of Figure 3.1. In the title bar it announces **"This a Web page — Microsoft Internet Explorer."**

- ❏ The only text that actually appears in the window of the browser is surrounded by the **<BODY> ... </BODY>** tags.

- ❏ After the first line of text there is a single **
** tag. This tells the browser to start a new line. The **
** tag does not require a **</BR>** closing tag

- ❏ Finally there is a **</HTML>** tag to tell the browser that the page is finished.

Look again at the HTML code you have created. Note that the file you saved consists entirely of text. There is no programming language, no special characters, no binary data. It is because all HTML documents, however complex, are written entirely in straight text that they can be read and understood by every computer platform.

If all this seems like a lot of code just to get a browser to display two short lines of text, keep in mind that the same tags, with a few more **
** tags to create breaks, could just as easily enclose several hundred lines of text. We will use a Key Facts box to set down some of the basic rules for using HTML:

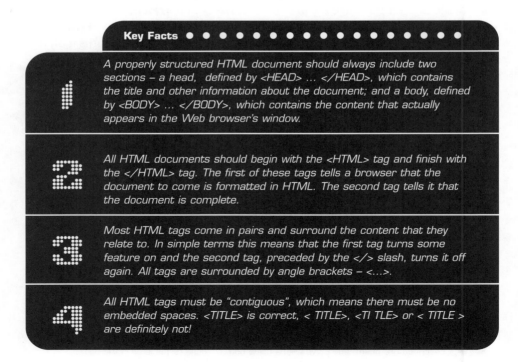

Key Facts ● ● ● ● ● ● ● ● ● ● ● ● ● ● ● ● ● ● ●

1. *A properly structured HTML document should always include two sections – a head, defined by <HEAD> ... </HEAD>, which contains the title and other information about the document; and a body, defined by <BODY> ... </BODY>, which contains the content that actually appears in the Web browser's window.*

2. *All HTML documents should begin with the <HTML> tag and finish with the </HTML> tag. The first of these tags tells a browser that the document to come is formatted in HTML. The second tag tells it that the document is complete.*

3. *Most HTML tags come in pairs and surround the content that they relate to. In simple terms this means that the first tag turns some feature on and the second tag, preceded by the </> slash, turns it off again. All tags are surrounded by angle brackets – <...>.*

4. *All HTML tags must be "contiguous", which means there must be no embedded spaces. <TITLE> is correct, < TITLE>, <TI TLE> or < TITLE > are definitely not!*

HTML is very unforgiving

You simply cannot afford to make mistakes when typing in HTML code. Silly little errors will make a complete mess of your pages. Sometimes Web browsers are clever enough to work out what you meant to put and display your pages properly, but you can't rely on them to help you out. Let's make a deliberate mistake and see how easily things can go wrong.

Exercise Two

1. Open your text editor again and reopen your **first_page.html** file. (If you are using Windows, don't forget to change the **File of Type:** box to read **All Files (*.*)** in Notepad's **Open** window, otherwise you will not see the file at all.)

2. Make one tiny change. Delete the slash (/) from the **</TITLE>** tag.

3. Save the file and open **first_page.html** again in your Web browser. (Or click the Web browser's **Refresh** button if you left if open.)

4. Your text has disappeared from the page. Without a properly formatted **</TITLE>** tag, the browser doesn't know that the title is complete and assumes that everything else you have written is part of the page's title.

5. Open the file for a third time and reinsert the slash before saving the file once more. Reopen it in your browser or click the **Refresh** or **Reload** button.

6. Hopefully, everything is back as it should be. If it isn't, check your code again.

Every Web page should have a title, and the title should be chosen with some care. When you open a page in a browser, the title is the first content that appears. Use it to tell a viewer what is coming and to clearly identify content. The most important reason for this is that when a Web user bookmarks a page – or in Microsoft terms, when he or she adds it to a list of favourites – it is the page's title which is added to the list. To see what we mean, open your browser and check the bookmarks or favourites menu. The items listed there are page titles.

To save time when working through future exercises, it is worth noting that most browsers contain a link to your text editor which allows you to check and modify your HTML directly. In Internet Explorer, clicking **View > Source** *will open your text editor preloaded with the HTML source code for the page you are viewing. If you are using Netscape, click* **View > Page Source**. *Most other browsers have a similar feature.*

When you are using a text editor to create your HTML code, it is a good idea to keep both your text editor and your Web browser open on the desktop. You can switch between them on the task bar or by clicking on the relevant window. This means that you can keep checking your code as you write it. Remember that you must SAVE your work in the text editor and Refresh or Reload your browser if you want to see the changes you have made.

Simple text mark-up tags

Now we have examined the basic tags required to create a Web page, we will move on to look at some basic text formatting using HTML. Perhaps the easiest tags of all are the tags used to mark-up text in the same way that any word processor can. If you have ever used a word processor, you will know that you can select a number of words on a page and click a button or select from a menu to turn them into bold text, italic text or underlined text. HTML works in a similar way but you need to type in the tags to create the formatting your require. As always, they need to be entered very precisely. The simple trick to making sure that you apply text mark-up tags correctly, is to think of them as start and stop signs which surround the text they are being applied to.

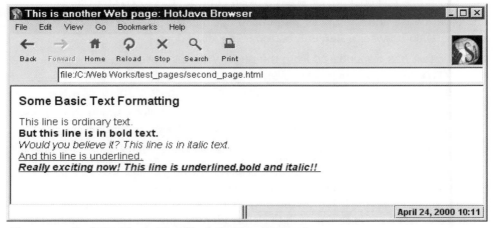

Figure 3.2: Basic text formatting (Sun's HotJava Browser)

Exercise Three

1. Open your text editor just as before, start a new document and type in the following:

    <HTML>

    <HEAD>

    <TITLE> This is another Web page </TITLE>

    </HEAD>

    <BODY>

    <H2> Some Basic Text Formatting </H2>

    <P>

    **This line is ordinary text.
**

    **<B> But this line is in bold text.</B>
**

    **<I> Would you believe it? This line is in italic text.</I>
**

    **<U> And this line is underlined.
**

<I> <B> Really exciting now!

This line is underlined, bold and italic!! </B> </I> </U>

</BODY>

</HTML>

2. Save this file in your **test_pages** folder as **second_page.html**, then open it in your Web browser. It should look like Figure 3.2.

Check the tags

Again, let us begin by breaking the exercise down into code and content:

CODE:	CONTENT:
<HTML>	
<HEAD>	
<TITLE>...</TITLE>	**This is another Web page**
</HEAD>	
<BODY>	
<H2>...</H2>	**Some Basic Text Formatting**
<P>...	**This line is ordinary text.**
** **	
<B>...</B>	**But this line is in bold text.**
** **	
<I>...</I>	**Would you believe it? This line is in italic text.**
** **	
<U>...	**And this line is underlined.**
** **	
<I><B>...</B></I></U>	**Really exciting now! This line is underlined, bold and italic!!**
</BODY>	
</HTML>	

Note: the content for each line replaces the dots in the code column.

Look back at the code you've typed in. There's quite a lot going on there. First of all, you have created a heading for the page. Note that this isn't the title. Your title is **"This is another Web page"** and just as before, that has appeared in the browser's title bar. Your heading is **"Some Basic Text Formatting"** and that goes within the

\<BODY\> ... \</BODY\> tags and therefore appears on the page itself.

You've defined the title with the **\<H2\> ... \</H2\>** tags. These are heading tags and the number 2 defines the size of the heading. There are six predefined sizes with **\<H1\>** as the largest and **\<H6\>** as the smallest. In fact, **\<H5\>** and **\<H6\>** are not much use as headings since they usually appear smaller than normal text does – try changing the code in Exercise 2 and see the size headings these produce. They can be quite handy for producing contrasting text.

Headings can be used to add structure to page content. They provide what is often called a hierarchy of information. An **\<H1\>** heading might introduce your page content. Below that an **\<H2\>** heading might introduce a section, with an **\<H3\>** heading opening each paragraph. We will come back to page structuring later in the book, but for now remember that Web users prefer to receive information in short bite-sized chunks. Use headings to break up your text into manageable pieces.

If you look at the page in your browser, you will notice a line space between the heading and the first line. Although the heading tag creates space below it, you have also included **\<P\>,** the paragraph tag. Like **\<BR\>,** the line break tag, **\<P\>** does not require a closing tag, although it is often a good idea to put one in after the paragraph – we'll explain why later. Note the difference between **\<BR\>** and **\<P\>**. **\<BR\>** stops the text and starts it again on the line below, while **\<P\>** stops the text, leaves one line blank and starts it again on the following line. (If you think about it, this means that typing two line breaks **\<BR\> \<BR\>** has the same effect as typing **\<P\>**. But some browsers ignore more than one **\<BR\>** and in any event, why type eight characters when you can get away with typing three?)

Tags within tags within tags

Now look at the lines of text themselves. The first line below the heading is just standard text. On the second line your text is in bold because you have turned on bold with **\<B\>** and turned it off at the end of the line with **\</B\>**. The third line is much the same; you have turned italic text on and off with **\<I\>** and **\</I\>**.

The fourth line is underlined. You have turned the underline on with **\<U\>**, but you have not turned it off again at the end of the line because we want the fifth line underlined as well. Instead, at the start of the fifth line you have turned bold and italic on again, and it is not until the end of the fifth line that you have turned everything off with **\</B\> \</I\> \</U\>**. (Just for the record, it is not a good idea to underline text on a Web page. Remember that hypertext links are usually underlined, and if you underline other text, readers may get confused and start clicking ordinary content.)

The technique of enclosing one pair of tags within another pair is called nesting, and quite a number of tags can be nested in this way as we will see later in the book.

\<B\> \<I\> \<U\> Wow! \</U\> \</I\> \</B\>

...is good coding because it follows the golden rule "last on, first off". In the code, as you move left and right away from the word "Wow!" the on and off tags are in pairs. By way of contrast the following line is badly coded:

<B> <I> <U> Wow! </B> </U> </I>

Although it will work, it is not logically structured. When the code starts getting complicated – and believe us, it will – using this simple nesting rule makes it easier to find and correct errors.

As well as the three text formatting elements detailed above there are several others which most browsers support. All of these operate in exactly the same way. For simplicity, they are listed in the tag table at the end of the chapter along with examples of how they would be rendered on a Web page. We include them for the sake of completeness, but most of them are very seldom used today.

Using text formatting in Web Pages

Having looked at the tags HTML uses to format text, we need to consider how text styles should be used within a Web page. The first thing we should note is that they involve quite a lot of code to create very simple effects. (In fact, in HTML 4.0 many of the text formatting tags are "deprecated", which means that eventually they will be removed from the language altogether in favour of a better method of formatting text using style sheets. We will be looking at style sheets later in the book.)

One of the problems with text formatting is that Web authors sometimes feel that they have to use lots of it, just because it is available. On the Web you will find many documents which are awash with headings and bold and italic text, and often look a mess because of it. The best Web pages use text formatting very sparingly – just enough to create impact. Big blocks of text should be divided up with headlines, but not too many or the page looks fragmented. Occasional words or phrases that require special emphasis can be set in bold, but use too much bold and the impact is lost. Many people are unsure when to use italics. Italics are simply a way to draw attention to text or to let the reader know that the text contains something different. If you must emphasise a lot of text, italics are less aggressive than bold, but like bold, they should only be included when there is a good reason for doing so.

Learn to think in terms of good proportions. A size 1 heading is very large, and if the text it introduces is standard size, it can look completely out of scale. Look at Figure 3.3 to see what we mean.

One final thought on text formatting. Try to avoid typing in capitals unless there is a good reason for doing so. We have used capitals for our heading in Figure 3.3 and the effect is as if the page is trying to shout at us! A good Web page is neat and compact, using only the minimum amount of formatting required for impact and readability.

Figure 3.3: Headlines can look out of proportion

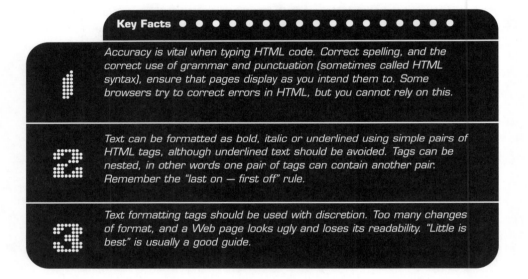

Key Facts

1 Accuracy is vital when typing HTML code. Correct spelling, and the correct use of grammar and punctuation (sometimes called HTML syntax), ensure that pages display as you intend them to. Some browsers try to correct errors in HTML, but you cannot rely on this.

2 Text can be formatted as bold, italic or underlined using simple pairs of HTML tags, although underlined text should be avoided. Tags can be nested, in other words one pair of tags can contain another pair. Remember the "last on – first off" rule.

3 Text formatting tags should be used with discretion. Too many changes of format, and a Web page looks ugly and loses its readability. "Little is best" is usually a good guide.

Understanding tag tables

As we move on along the highways and byways of HTML we will be meeting any number of tags. At the end of each chapter you will find a table like the one below listing all the tags covered in the chapter. (There is also a complete listing of all the common HTML tags arranged alphabetically in Appendix 2 at the back of the book.) Since this is the first one, let's take this opportunity to explain how these tables work.

As we noted above, most tags operate in pairs; the opening tag to turn some feature on and the closing tag to turn it off again. But there are tags, like **
**, which do not require a closing tag. (These are more correctly known as "empty" tags.) The first column in our table lists the opening tag and the second column lists the closing tag. Where there is no closing tag listed, do not put one in. The fourth column explains how the tag is used, what it does and, sometimes, gives examples.

We didn't forget about the third column, but it is the most complicated and gets a paragraph and an exercise all to itself. The third column lists **attributes** – an awkward word, but we're stuck with it. You can think of an attribute as an option that decides how the tag will operate. (For example, the **<BODY>** tag that we met earlier can contain an attribute that changes the colour of all the text in the body of the page.) An attribute is always enclosed in the opening tag's angle brackets and requires an equals sign (=) giving the value of the attribute which is contained in quotes ("...").

This often confuses people, so let us look at one more example before going on to the table itself.

Exercise Four

1. Open your text editor and reload your **second_page.html** file.

2. Find the **<BODY>** tag and change it to read

    <BODY TEXT="Red">

3. Save this file and load it (or refresh it) in your Web browser. All the text on your Web page has turned red.

That's enough about attributes for the time being. Let's look at the table for the tags we have met in the course of this chapter.

Opening Tag	Closing Tag	Attributes	Description
<HTML>	</HTML>		These tags enclose the entire HTML document and should appear first and last on any page you create. They tell a Web browser that the text between them is formatted in HTML.
<HEAD>	</HEAD>		These tags should appear in all HTML documents, straight after the opening <HTML> tag. They enclose information about the page and its title but NOT page content.
<TITLE>	</TITLE>		These tags must appear between <HEAD> and </HEAD>. They enclose a title for the page which the Web browser displays in its title bar.

<BODY>	</BODY>		These tags enclose page content — the words, images etc. which actually appear in the Web browser's window. All HTML documents should have just one pair of body tags. In most cases, the <BODY> tag should come straight after the </HEAD> tag.
		TEXT="value"	The TEXT attribute allows you to set the colour of the text that appears in the body of the page. It takes a value which is either the RGB value of a colour (don't worry about this at the moment) or the name of a colour. Most common colours (red, green, blue etc.) work fine. The correct syntax is: <BODY TEXT="Yellow"> .... </BODY>
 			This tag creates a line break – equivalent to starting a new line when word processing.
<P>	</P>		This tag creates a new paragraph, leaving a blank line after the previous paragraph. The closing tag is optional but can be useful to define the extent of a paragraph if you are applying formatting to it.
<H1> to <H6>	</H1> to </H6>		These tags set the headline size for the text they enclose. <H1> is the largest size, <H6> is the smallest. Note that a headline tag automatically inserts a blank line below the heading.
<B>	</B>		These tags cause the text they enclose to be displayed in bold.

<I>	</I>		These tags cause the text they enclose to be displayed in italic.
<U	</U>		These tags cause the text they enclose to be underlined. (Note: try not to use them!)
<TT>	</TT>		These tags cause the text they enclose to be monospaced. Example – `monospaced`.
<STRIKE> or <S>	</STRIKE> or </S		These tags cause the text they enclose to be struck through. Example – ~~struck through.~~
<BIG>	</BIG>		These tags cause the text they enclose to be rendered larger. Example – `bigger`. (Note: by nesting a series of <BIG> elements, you can continue to make text larger.)
<SMALL> (As	</SMALL>		These tags cause the text they enclose to be rendered smaller. Example – `smaller`. in <BIG> above, <SMALL> elements can be nested.)
[	]		These tags cause the text they enclose to be displayed as superscript. Example – `superscript`.
_			These tags cause the text they enclose to be displayed as subscript. Example – `subscript`.

QUICK REVISION QUESTIONS

1. What are HTML tags and how are they used on a Web page?

2. What is contained between the **<HEAD> ... </HEAD>** tags?

3. What is contained between the **<BODY> ... </BODY>** tags?

4. What is the difference between a page's title and its heading?

5. What are the first and last tags which should appear on a Web page?

6. What tags would you use to create large and small headings?

7. What is the golden rule for nesting tags?

8. Why is it a bad idea to underline text in Web pages?

9. Why should text formatting tags be used sparingly in a Web document?

10. What is an "attribute" and what is the correct syntax for including one?

Chapter 4
Advanced Text Formatting

Brief contents:

1. The concept of typography and why it's important in
    designing for the Web.

2. The difference between printer and system fonts.

3. The importance of selecting the correct fonts.

4. Understanding absolute and relative text sizes
    and how to apply them to your Web pages.

5. How to change the colour of your text.

6. Logical formatting elements and preformatted text.

7. How to insert special characters including the Irish fada.

Advanced Text Formatting

In the previous chapter we looked at the basics of text formatting. We noted that text formatting in HTML was similar to applying text formats in a word processing package. In this chapter we will be looking at text for the Web from a different point of view – that of the typographer. The Concise Oxford Dictionary defines typography as "the style and appearance of printed matter". A typographer is usually employed by a publisher or design house to look after all aspects of printed text. He (or she) will select fonts for a project, considering their readability, impact and suitability for the subject matter. He will decide text size and colour, where to apply formatting, and how to lay the text out on the page.

If you are familiar with a word processing package such as Microsoft Word® or Corel WordPerfect®, you will already know a fair bit about typography. We can sum up the most important aspects of typography in the following table:

Aspect:	Typography:
Font	Selecting suitable font(s) for the page.
Style	Deciding the appropriate use of bold and italic formatting. (Remember from last chapter why we prefer not to use underlining on Web pages.)
Colour	Choosing suitable colour(s) for the text, headlines, captions etc.
Size	Deciding the correct sizes for text, headlines, captions etc.
Alignment	Deciding how the text will be placed on a page – whether it will line up on the left or right hand margins, or whether it will be justified. (Justified text has extra spaces added between words so it lines up on both margins – like the text in this paragraph.)
Spacing	Deciding how much space to leave between lines, paragraphs, sections etc.
Indentation	Deciding whether paragraphs are to be indented.

Essential aspects of typography

Most of the typographical aspects listed above can be handled within HTML and are managed by using the correct HTML tags. But, as always, we need to consider the overall design of our pages and how they are going to be viewed in a Web browser. Alignment, spacing and indentation are considered in the next chapter. We will begin this chapter by looking at how to choose fonts for the Web.

Fonts for the Web
Take a look at the fonts installed on your computer – you can check them from within your word processor if it helps. You will probably find dozens of them from formal text fonts like Times New Roman, through casual fonts like Comic Sans MS®, to fonts which generate symbols and tiny graphics like WingDings®. These are **printer** fonts. You can use them in word processing or DTP and your printer will faithfully reproduce them on paper. On the Web, things are different.

Remember in Chapter 1 we noted that Web content was downloaded to a client computer and then interpreted by a Web browser. While it is possible to use HTML tags to specify any font you like, unless that font is installed on the client computer, the text will not be displayed in that font. Instead the browser will use the *default*[1] font which may look nothing at all like what you intended. (Of course, if the font you specified **is** installed, then your text will appear in the browser just as you wanted it to.)

So how can you be sure that the Web pages you design display as you intended? You could always use the default font by never specifying a font at all, and you will find many pages on the Web that do just that. Of course page after page of identical text can look very uninteresting. A better solution is to play percentages and specify only those fonts which the majority of client computers will recognise. In a perfect world, there would be an agreed range of what we could call **Web-safe fonts**, but different platforms install different fonts. Here is a list of some of the system fonts usually installed on Windows®, Macintosh® and UNIX computers:

Windows:	Macintosh:	UNIX:
Arial	Chicago	Courier
Comic Sans MS	Courier	Helvetica
Courier New	Monaco	Sans Serif
Times New Roman	Helvetica	Times
Verdana	Times	Utopia

Fonts with similar names will usually appear the same in browsers on different computers. For example, text in Courier New in Windows® will look very similar to text in Courier on Macintosh® and UNIX computers, but there are some differences. (We should also note here that different browsers often display a particular font slightly differently as well!)

Choosing a suitable font.

Even if we stick to using the limited number of fonts which we can reasonably assume our readers will have installed, we still have to decide on an appropriate

---

[1] **default:** You have probably met the concept of a default before, but just in case... We can define a default as what happens if nothing else is specified. When you open your word processor and start typing, text appears on your screen. You haven't specified a font – or even a type size and style; instead your word processor uses its default font, and will continue to use it until you specify something else.

font for our page content. Look at the list below:

- This line is printed in Arial.
- This line is printed in Comic Sans MS.
- This line is printed in Courier New.
- This line is printed in Times New Roman.
- This line is printed in Verdana.

Note the differences between these five standard Windows® fonts. Arial and Verdana, for example, are modern, casual fonts, Times New Roman is an older, more formal font, while Courier New is a monospaced font (all the letters are the same width) which resembles old style typewriting. Times New Roman and Courier New are also "serif" fonts. If you look closely at the letter "l" in each line, you will see little strokes at the top and bottom. These are serifs and some people believe that they help readers to concentrate on the text by drawing their eyes along the line.

One important consideration in choosing a font is its suitability to the subject matter. If you were designing a Web site for a firm of solicitors, you might feel that a formal font such as Times New Roman was appropriate. On the other hand, if your site was concerned with dance music, a very casual font like Comic Sans MS might be better. It is always a mistake to use too many fonts. One style for headlines and another for text is often the most effective choice -– you might add in a third for quotations or special emphasis.

Before we move on to consider the tags we need to specify fonts, let's sum up the key points so far:

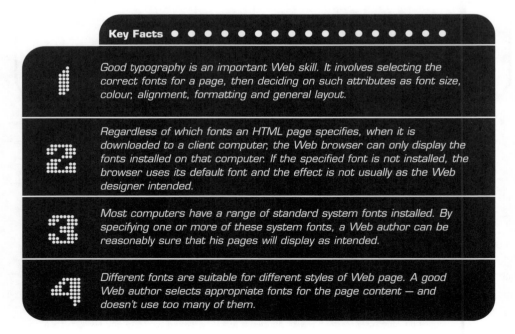

Key Facts ● ● ● ● ● ● ● ● ● ● ● ● ● ● ● ● ● ● ●

1   *Good typography is an important Web skill. It involves selecting the correct fonts for a page, then deciding on such attributes as font size, colour, alignment, formatting and general layout.*

2   *Regardless of which fonts an HTML page specifies, when it is downloaded to a client computer, the Web browser can only display the fonts installed on that computer. If the specified font is not installed, the browser uses its default font and the effect is not usually as the Web designer intended.*

3   *Most computers have a range of standard system fonts installed. By specifying one or more of these system fonts, a Web author can be reasonably sure that his pages will display as intended.*

4   *Different fonts are suitable for different styles of Web page. A good Web author selects appropriate fonts for the page content — and doesn't use too many of them.*

Specifying fonts in a Web page

We need to keep all of the above in mind when using fonts in our pages. There are several ways of specifying which font a browser should use and some of them we will look at later in the book. In this chapter we will concentrate on simple HTML tags. Here is the code you used in the first exercise of the previous chapter:

```
<HTML>
<HEAD>
<TITLE> This is a Web page </TITLE>
</HEAD>
<BODY>
I am a genius. <BR>
I have just created my first Web page!
</BODY>
</HTML>
```

Notice that it does not contain any tags which specify which font the browser should use, but it still produces readable text. Without contrary instructions, the browser uses its default font. Let's try specifying the fonts.

Exercise One

1. Open your text editor and type in the following code:

```
<HTML>
<HEAD>
<TITLE> This Web page specifies fonts</TITLE>
</HEAD>
<BODY>
<H3>Font Tests</H3>
<FONT FACE="Comic Sans MS">This line is in Comic Sans
    MS.</FONT><BR>
<FONT FACE="Courier New">This line is in Courier New.</FONT><BR>
<FONT FACE="Verdana">This line is in Verdana.</FONT>
</BODY>
</HTML>
```

2. Save this file to your **test_pages** folder as **font_page.html**, then open it in your browser. It should look like Figure 4.1.

We have achieved this result by wrapping the text we want to appear in a particular font face in a pair of HTML tags — **<FONT> ... </FONT>** and within the opening tag, we have included an attribute to specify the particular font we required — **FACE="Verdana"**. You will recall that this is exactly how we handled italics, for

Figure 4.1: Different fonts displayed in a browser

example, in the previous chapter. Note also that although we have specified the fonts for entire lines, we could just as easily have wrapped the font tags around a single word, or even a single letter. Go ahead and try it...

What if we wanted to specify the font for an entire document? To save ourselves having to wrap pages of text in the font tags, HTML allows us to specify an overall font using the **<BASEFONT>** tag. This should be placed within the **<HEAD> ... </HEAD>** tags, although it doesn't have to be as long as it comes before any text in the document. So to specify Verdana as the font to use in the example above, we would include the following code:

```
<HTML>
<HEAD>
<TITLE> This Web page specifies fonts</TITLE>
<BASEFONT FACE="Verdana">
</HEAD>
```

Note that even though we have specified Verdana as our base font, the font changes we have made within the page text itself will still apply as *in-line formatting* [2] takes precedence.

Earlier in this chapter we discussed the difficulty of coding for computers with different fonts installed. The example above illustrates this problem. We have specified Verdana, and that font should be available on most Windows-based computers, but as our table indicated, it is not so likely to be installed on Macs or UNIX systems. If you wish to ensure that your choice of fonts will work on all platforms, it is safest to include a series of fonts within the **FACE** attribute, using code like this:

---

[2] **In-line formatting**: Essentially, there are two ways to format items in HTML. You can use tags which apply to the whole page, like the **<BASEFONT>** tag used here, or you can apply formatting to individual elements like words, lines or paragraphs. Where such formatting is used within the lines of text, this is known as in-line formatting, as opposed to document-wide formatting.

<BASEFONT FACE="Verdana, Chicago, Helvetica">

Regardless of the platform it is running on, a browser which encounters this tag will check the first face against its list of installed fonts and use it if it can. If not, it will check the second and so on.

Text sizing

In the same way that HTML provides for a default font, it also provides a default text size. **SIZE=".."** is another attribute of the **<FONT>** element and is used in exactly the same way that **FACE=".."** is used. HTML provides for seven **absolute** sizes of text numbered from **1** to **7**, with **1** as the smallest. (Note that this is the reverse of Headline sizing, where **1** is the largest.) The default size, if you don't specify something else, is **3**. To see how these sizes look on the page, work through the following exercise.

Exercise Two

1. Open your text editor and type in the following code:

   <HTML>

   <HEAD>

   <TITLE> This Web page compares font sizes</TITLE>

   </HEAD>

   <BODY>

   <H3>Font Sizes</H3>

   **<FONT SIZE="1">This is as small as it gets.</FONT>
**

   **<FONT SIZE="2">Getting larger</FONT>
**

   **<FONT SIZE="3">and larger</FONT>
**

   **<FONT SIZE="4">and larger </FONT>
**

   **<FONT SIZE="5">and larger </FONT>
**

   **<FONT SIZE="6">and larger </FONT>
**

   <FONT SIZE="7">and this is as big as it gets.</FONT>

   </BODY>

   </HTML>

2. Save this file to your **test_pages** folder as **font_size.html**, then open it in your browser. It should look like Figure 4.2.

This would be a useful file to print out and save as it gives you a reference document for when you are deciding which text size would suit a particular project. Click **File > Print** in your browser. (We won't keep reminding you to print out reference pages, but you should consider putting together a file of useful material like this.)

There are two other design considerations to be kept in mind when choosing a size. Firstly, remember that different visitors to your pages may have their monitors set to different screen resolutions. We will look at this in more detail later in the

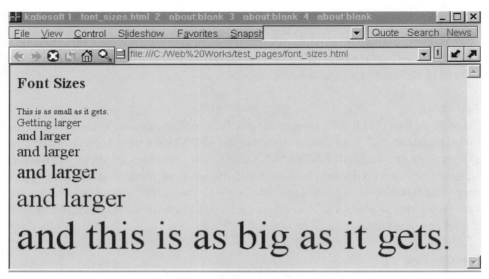

Figure 4.2: Different font sizes displayed in the KatieSoft browser.

book, but for now keep in mind that a screen resolution of say 1024 x 768 pixels will display text considerably smaller than a resolution of 640 x 480 pixels. On the other hand, many beginners to Web authoring make their text far too big, thinking that it will make it easier to read. The solution – as usual – is to check your pages in different browsers and see how they look to you.

In the same way that you can specify a font face using the **<BASEFONT>** tag, you can also specify a default font size. Extending our previous example, to specify that all your text appears in the Verdana font at size **2**, you would use the following code:

```
<HTML>
<HEAD>
<TITLE> This Web page specifies fonts</TITLE>
<BASEFONT FACE="Verdana" SIZE="2">
</HEAD>
```

The use of the **<BASEFONT>** tag to specify an overall text size gives us an extra resource which can prove quite useful. Instead of using **<FONT SIZE="1-7">** to change the size of individual paragraphs, lines or words, we can now specify a font size **relative** to the size we set up with the **<BASEFONT>** tag. For example, if our base font size is set to **2**, the tag:

```
<FONT SIZE="+2">Two sizes larger.</FONT>
```

...will render the words "Two sizes larger." in text size **4**. Remember that there are still only 7 sizes to play with, so if you specify a size of, say, **+10**, the browser will ignore this and render your text at size **7**.

Colouring your text

The final font attribute that we are concerned with at this point is colour, and you will not be surprised to learn that it is handled in exactly the same way as face and size. We look at the whole realm of colour for the Web in a later chapter, so for now we will just consider the fundamentals. The first thing you **must** do, is read the Vital Information note below.

Always remember that HTML uses American *spellings. At present we are considering colour which is spelled* color *in the USA. If your HTML includes code such as* Colour="red", *it simply will not work! There are other American spellings we will meet later, but this is the one which always causes the most trouble.*

Colours in HTML can be defined in two ways. There are 16 common colours which can be referenced by name and these are the ones we are concerned with at this point. (For the full range of colours, you will need to understand colour hex (hexadecimal) values which are explained in Chapter 6.) The 16 common colour names are:

Aqua	**Black**	**Blue**	**Fuchsia**
Grey	**Green**	**Lime**	**Maroon**
Navy	**Olive**	**Purple**	**Red**
Silver	**Teal**	**White**	**Yellow**

To set any part of your text in one of these colours, you simply use the **COLOR** attribute within a **<FONT>** tag, so to render the word "Banana" in yellow, the code would read:

```
<FONT COLOR="Yellow">Banana</FONT>
```

Just as before, a colour for all the text in the document can be set using the **COLOR** attribute of the **<BASEFONT>** element. (You will remember from the previous chapter that this can also be achieved by using the **TEXT="..."** attribute of the **<BODY>** element.)

In the same way that using too many different fonts spoils the look of a Web page, so can an indiscriminate use of coloured text. However, it is possible to use the **COLOR** attribute to create some interesting effects.

Exercise Three

1. Open your text editor and type in the following code:

```
<HTML>
<HEAD>
<TITLE> Colourful Headlines</TITLE>
<BASEFONT SIZE="7" FACE="Comic Sans MS">
</HEAD>
<BODY>
```

```
<FONT COLOR="Red">R</FONT>
<FONT COLOR="Fuchsia">A</FONT>
<FONT COLOR="Yellow">I</FONT>
<FONT COLOR="Green">N</FONT>
<FONT COLOR="Olive">B</FONT>
<FONT COLOR="Blue">O</FONT>
<FONT COLOR="Purple">W</FONT>
</BODY>
</HTML>
```

2. Save this file to your **test_pages** folder as **font_colour.html**, then open it in your browser. What do you think?

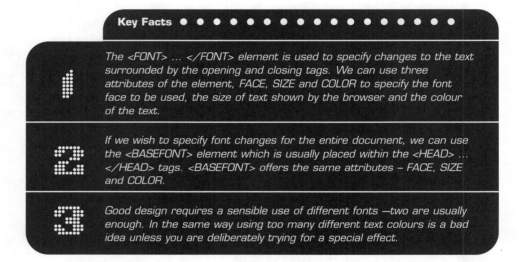

Key Facts

1   The <FONT> ... </FONT> element is used to specify changes to the text surrounded by the opening and closing tags. We can use three attributes of the element, FACE, SIZE and COLOR to specify the font face to be used, the size of text shown by the browser and the colour of the text.

2   If we wish to specify font changes for the entire document, we can use the <BASEFONT> element which is usually placed within the <HEAD> ... </HEAD> tags. <BASEFONT> offers the same attributes – FACE, SIZE and COLOR.

3   Good design requires a sensible use of different fonts —two are usually enough. In the same way using too many different text colours is a bad idea unless you are deliberately trying for a special effect.

Logical Formatting Elements

Remember that HTML was first designed to display text without images. Its designers were aware that long passages of identical text were neither visually attractive nor easy to read, so they included a series of special elements to display text in different ways. These elements are called logical elements -— although there is nothing particularly logical about them. They work in exactly the same way as the **<FONT>** element described above, and the best way to understand them is to use them:

Exercise Four

1. Open your text editor and type in the following code:

```
<HTML>
<HEAD>
```

```
<TITLE>Logical Elements</TITLE>
<BASEFONT SIZE="4" COLOR="Navy">
</HEAD>
<BODY>
<H2>Formatting with Logical Elements</H2>
<EM>This text is emphasised.</EM><BR>
<STRONG>This text is strong.</STRONG><BR>
<CITE>This text is citation.</CITE><BR>
<CODE>This text is code.</CODE><BR>
<DFN>This text is a definition.</DFN><BR>
<KBD>This text is keyboard.</KBD><BR>
<SAMP>This text is sample.</SAMPLE><BR>
<VAR>This text is variable.</VAR>
</BODY>
</HTML>
```

2. Save this file to your **test_pages** folder as **logical.html**, then open it in your browser. It should look like Figure 4.3.

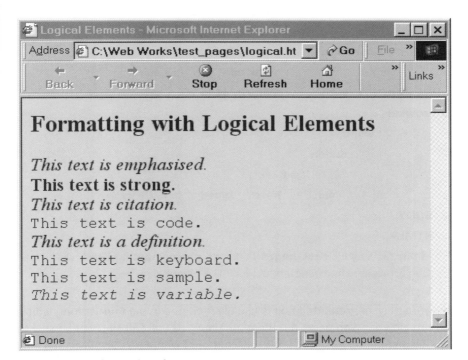

Figure 4.3: Logical formatting elements.

If you look at this page as it appears in your browser you will notice that the text produced by the **<EM>**, **<CITE>** and **<DFN>** elements is identical, as is the text produced by the **<KBD>** and **<SAMP>** elements. Despite this, logical elements are useful on occasions. They offer a simple way to vary the look of a document.

Preformatted text

The last text effect we shall consider in this chapter is the **<PRE>** (**Preformatted Text**) element which allows us to force a browser to show text exactly as we have typed it in. Again, the easiest way to explain this is to see how it works.

Exercise Five

1. Open your text editor and type in the following code (Note: create spaces with the spacebar and NOT with the tab key):

    <HTML>

    <HEAD>

    <TITLE>Preformatted Text</TITLE>

    <BASEFONT SIZE="4" COLOR="Navy">

    </HEAD>

    <BODY>

    Normally   HTML   ignores   spaces and

    carriage

    returns.

    <PRE>But   with   preformatted   text a browser

    will

    render

    text

    just   as   you   have   typed   it!</PRE>

    </BODY>

    </HTML>

2. Save this file to your **test_pages** folder as **preformatting.html**, then open it in your browser. The result should look like Figure 4.4.

Unfortunately, preformatted text is usually rendered in the Courier font, which might not suit your Web page, but there are times, as you will see, when using the **<PRE>** element is very useful for precise control of where text displays on a page.

Special Characters

Anyone who has ever tried to type text in Irish or French using a word processor

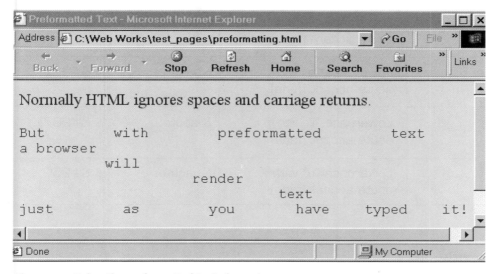

Figure 4.4: Using the preformatted text element.

knows the difficulties of trying to produce the *fada*[3] or acute and grave accents. The standard ASCII character set is firmly based in English. To overcome this limitation, HTML includes a set of special codes to generate special characters. All of these have a code and the most common ones also have a name – either can be used within your text.

One example is the copyright symbol ©. To include this symbol within an HTML document, you type either **©** (the symbol's name) or **©** (its code). Note that these character codes must begin with the ampersand (&) and end with a semicolon (;). The fada itself is not supported, so the accepted way to produce it is to use the code for the French accented letter. Thus **Seán** would be coded as **Seán.** Since all special character codes are preceded with the ampersand (**&**), this should never be used in place of the word "and". There are several hundred of these special character codes and the most useful ones are listed in Appendix 4 of this book. The following table lists some examples you will need for the next exercise:

Character	Description	Name	Code
©	Copyright symbol	&copy;	&#169;
É	Uppercase "E" with acute accent (fada)	&Eacute;	&#201;

[3] **Fada**: For students who are not familiar with Irish, the *fada* is the accent which appears over certain vowels in Irish to change the sound of the word. For example, **bird** in Irish is éan.

Ó	Uppercase "O" with acute accent (fada)	&Oacute;	&#211;
á	Lowercase "a" with acute accent (fada)	&aacute;	&#225;
í	Lowercase "i" with acute accent (fada)	&iacute;	&#237;
ú	Lowercase "u" with acute accent (fada)	&uacute;	&#250;

Exercise Six

Create a simple Web page containing the following text (Note: from here onwards we assume you are familiar enough with HTML elements to include the correct tags to format the page as HTML, to create Head and Body sections, to insert a title and to format any text as required):

The new book "An Éan" is © Pádraig Ó Súilleabhán and Síobhán ní Líodán 2001.

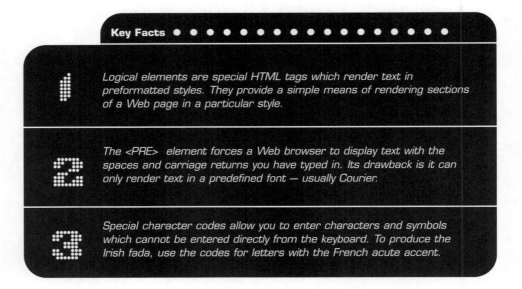

Key Facts ●

1 Logical elements are special HTML tags which render text in preformatted styles. They provide a simple means of rendering sections of a Web page in a particular style.

2 The <PRE> element forces a Web browser to display text with the spaces and carriage returns you have typed in. Its drawback is it can only render text in a predefined font — usually Courier.

3 Special character codes allow you to enter characters and symbols which cannot be entered directly from the keyboard. To produce the Irish fada, use the codes for letters with the French acute accent.

The HTML tags used in this chapter are laid out in the following tag table.

Opening Tag	Closing Tag	Attributes	Description
<FONT>	</FONT>		These tags enclose content to which the various <FONT> attributes are to be applied.
		FACE=".."	Specifies the font to be used for the enclosed text. Any font can be specified, but only those available on the client computer will be effective.
		SIZE=".."	Specifies the text size to be used for the enclosed text. Values from 1 to 7 are valid with 7 as the largest. (Where <BASEFONT> has been used to specify an overall text size, relative values such as +2 or –3 may be substituted.)
		COLOR=".."	Specifies the colour in which the text should be rendered. Some colours may be specified by name.
<BASEFONT>			<BASEFONT> should appear between the <HEAD> and </HEAD> tags. It specifies how all the text in the document should be rendered.
		FACE=".." SIZE=".." COLOR=".."	Usage as in <FONT> above, but SIZE must reference an absolute value from 1 to 7.
<EM>	</EM>		These tags render the enclosed text as emphasised.
<STRONG>	</STRONG>		These tags render the enclosed text as strong.

<CITE>	</CITE>		These tags render the enclosed text as a citation.
<CODE>	</CODE>		These tags render the enclosed text as code.
<DFN>	</DFN>		These tags render the enclosed text as a definition.
<KBD>	</KBD>		These tags render the enclosed text as if typed from a typewriter keyboard.
<SAMP>	</SAMP>		These tags render the enclosed text as a sample.
<VAR>	</VAR>		These tags render the enclosed text as a variable.
<PRE>	</PRE>		These tags cause the browser to render the enclosed text with any spaces and carriage returns you have included.

QUICK REVISION QUESTIONS

1. What is typography and why is it important in designing for the Web?

2. What should be borne in mind when selecting fonts for a Web page?

3. What is meant by a Web browser's default font?

4. What is meant by absolute and relative text sizes? What is the range of absolute text sizes and what are relative text sizes relative to?

5. What is the **<BASEFONT>** element used for and where should it appear in an HTML coded page?

6. What is wrong with this code: **<FONT COLOUR="Red">**Hello!**</FONT>** ?

7. Why should you restrict the number of text colours used in a Web page?

8. What are logical formatting elements and how are they used?

9. What is preformatted text?

10. How would you create the Irish fada in a Web page?

Chapter 5
Laying out text and using lists

Brief contents:

1. The concept of text alignment and how to align sections of a page in HTML.

2. One or two tricks for indenting paragraphs, and creating indented first lines.

3. The differences between ordered and unordered lists.

4. Using HTML code to create lists.

5. Modifying the look of lists by changing the numbers, letters or bullets used to introduce them.

6. The benefits that a logical use of lists brings to Web page design.

Laying out text and using lists

We have spent the last two chapters looking at ways of formatting text. In this chapter we will consider two further aspects of typography: text alignment and indentation. We shall then go on to look at creating and using lists – one of the most important aspects of good Web design.

We will begin by looking at how HTML handles blocks of text. As usual, there is a default mechanism. Unless we specify otherwise, a Web browser renders text starting at the left-hand margin of the browser window. Because it knows the width of that window, as the line of text approaches the right-hand margin, the browser automatically wraps the text onto the next line, making the break between words. When you change the size of the browser window, the text is immediately reformatted to fit the new window.

If you think about it, this is exactly the way in which your word processor operates when you enter text. Since lines are seldom exactly the same length, this leaves the text "ragged" against the right-hand margin – just as it is in this paragraph. We introduced the concept of "justification" at the start of the previous chapter. You will remember that it means inserting spaces between words in a line, so all the lines in a paragraph appear to be the same length.

We will start this chapter by looking at how to align paragraphs.

Aligning text

Within a Web document it is often useful to break the text up into sections so that we can specify particular alignments for each of them. The HTML *element* which handles this is **<DIV>**, short for Division and the **<DIV> ... </DIV>** tags must surround each section of text we wish to handle individually. The **<DIV>** element takes the attribute **ALIGN=".."** with the values **Left**, **Right**, **Justify** and **Center**.

This is another American spelling to remember. The value Center *will have an effect, but* Centre *will be ignored by a browser. Later in this chapter we will meet the value* Disc, *which is often spelled* Disk *on this side of the Atlantic. HTML always uses American English spellings.*

Exercise One

1. Open your text editor and create an HTML page using the correct tags.
2. Type in the first paragraph of this chapter three times (or type it once, and copy and paste it twice), separating them with the paragraph tag.
3. Wrap each paragraph in turn with the following tags:

   <DIV ALIGN="Right"> ... </DIV>

   <DIV ALIGN="Justify"> ... </DIV>

   <DIV ALIGN="Centre"> ... </DIV>

4. Save this file to your **test_pages** folder as **aligning_text.html** and open it in your Web browser. Change the size of your browser window (drag the bottom right hand corner) and see what happens to your text.

You will notice that however you change the size of the browser window, the text adapts by wrapping to the new size. The first paragraph ranges from the right hand margin, the second paragraph rejustifies itself to remain square to both margins, and the third paragraph ... is not centred to the window unless you noticed the error in the third line of code! Go back and correct your code, resave it and refresh your browser. (This is a subtle way of making our point about spellings although we are told it isn't "pedagogically sound".)

---

[1] **Element**: In case there is any confusion, now would seem to be a good time to explain the difference between an HTML element and HTML tags. An element is a coded instruction to a browser which is embedded in a page. HTML elements consist of tags, often in pairs.

Indenting lines and paragraphs

Another problem with laying out text is that HTML does not recognise tabs. You probably know that in word processing the **Tab** key moves the text insertion point a regular number of spaces across the page. Many people still prefer to indent the start of their paragraphs with a tab. We learnt in Chapter 3 that almost all the standard techniques for laying out text require special HTML tags if they are to be recognised by a browser. You already know, for example, that unless a line is terminated with the **
** line break tag, a browser will simply ignore any break you make from your keyboard and will tack the next line of text on to the end of the previous one. You also know that without the **<P>** paragraph tag, you cannot create paragraphs that a browser will recognise.

So what do we do if we want to indent the first line of a paragraph, or even a whole paragraph? As so often when working in HTML, there are several ways of getting round such problems. One way is to use the additional resources available in style sheets, but we won't be looking at these until Chapter 12. A second way is to create a tiny image the same colour as the page background and use that to push the text around. We will be looking at this in Chapter 7. This still leaves us with two techniques to consider here.

At the end of the previous chapter, we looked at a number of special codes used to create non-standard characters like the © symbol. One special character we can use here is the non-breaking space character ** ** (Note: the semi-colon (;) at the end of the code is an essential part of it.)

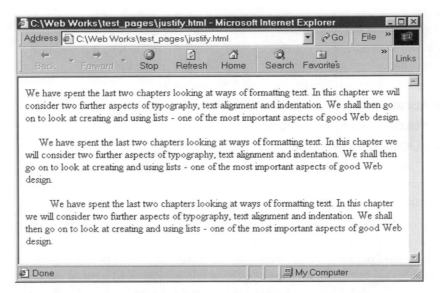

Figure 5.1: Indenting paragraphs using a special character.

Exercise Two

1. Reopen the file **aligning_text.html** and change all the **<DIV ALIGN= ".."></div>** tags to the value **Left**.

Insert five blank spaces in front of the first word of the first paragraph.

Insert the following code in front of the first word of the second paragraph:

**   **

Insert the following code in front of the first word of the third paragraph:

**   **

2. Save this file again and reload it into your browser. It should look like Figure 5.1.

Notice that inserting spaces in front of the first paragraph has had no effect at all. We noted in the previous chapter that HTML does not support multiple spaces – it doesn't even support a single space at the start of a line. The first line of the second paragraph has been indented by five spaces – one for each ** ** character. In the third paragraph we have done even better. By inserting blank spaces between each ** ** character, we have fooled the browser into creating an even larger indent. HTML treats ** ** as a character and we are allowed to leave spaces between characters – even if they are invisible!

The second trick described here we can use to indent whole paragraphs. This time we are going to fool the browser into thinking that each paragraph is actually an item in a list, but before we do this, we are going to have to look at lists in general.

Lists

Lists are everywhere on the Web and very useful they are too. A list is the accepted way to lay out a number of related items. Look at the contents pages in the front of this book and think how awkward it would be if the information there had simply been printed in paragraphs. As well as being useful, lists can help with the effective lay-out of a Web page. They can break up long chunks of information and, as we will see later, can be used to add style to a page.

HTML supports three different kinds of lists – ordered lists, using the element **<OL>**, unordered lists, using the element **<UL>** and definition lists, using the element **<DL>**. (There are two other kinds, menu lists **<MENU>** and directories **<DIR>**, but these are not well supported by browsers and are seldom used.) Ordered lists are used for items that need to be numbered in some way, although the numbers can just as easily be letters. Here are some examples of ordered lists:

List 1	List 2	List 3
1. Blood	a. egg	i. Ulster
2. Sweat	b. beans	ii. Leinster
3. Tears	c. chips	iii. Munster
4. Bananas	d. sausages	iv. Connaught

The HTML syntax for an ordered list is very precise, requiring the **<OL> ... </OL**
tags. Take List 1 above as an example and follow the code and explanations in the
box below

Code and Content:	Explanation:	Rendered in a browser as:
<OL>	Tells the browser that a list follows.	
<LI>Blood	Precedes a list item.	1. Blood
<LI>Sweat	Precedes the next item.	2. Sweat
<LI>Tears	Etc.	3. Tears
<LI>Bananas	Etc.	4. Bananas
</OL>	Tells the browser that the list is complete.	

You will notice that the list items in the table above are introduced **1, 2, 3** etc. This
is the default setting, but the **<OL>** tag can carry an attribute **TYPE=".."** which can
specify a different numbering system. The following list gives the range:

> **<OL TYPE="a">** produces lower case letters – **a, b, c** etc.
> **<OL TYPE="A">** produces upper case letters – **A, B, C** etc.
> **<OL TYPE="i">** produces lower case Roman numerals – **i, ii, iii** etc.
> **<OL TYPE="I">** produces upper case Roman numerals – **I, II, III** etc.
> **<OL TYPE="1">** produces ordinary (Arabic) numbers – **1, 2, 3** etc.

The **TYPE** attribute can also be used within the **<LI>** tag itself if, for any reason,
you wish to change your numbering system mid-list.

Unordered lists

Unordered lists, defined by the **<UL>** element, are used when the order of the items
they contain is not important. They also offer an additional resource – they can be
nested. We met the concept of nesting in Chapter 3, when we looked at nested
tags. A nested list is a list within a list as in the example below:

○ **Jobs for the Garden:**

    ◆ **Dig up potatoes**

    ◆ **Mow the lawn**

○ **Jobs in the house:**

    ◆ **Paint the back door**

    ◆ **Build bookshelves**

        ○ **Buy timber**

        ○ **Buy screws**

A simple unordered list uses similar code to an ordered list, except that the list items, each introduced by the **<LI>** tag, are wrapped in the unordered list tags **<UL>** ... **</UL>**. Unordered list items are preceded by bullets and, as in the list above, the bullet style changes for each level of nesting. The code to create the nested list above is explained in the table below. This will produce a page in your browser similar to Figure 5.2.

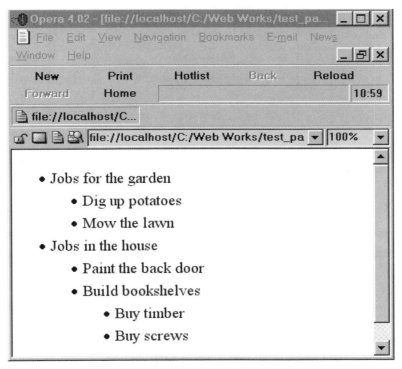

Figure 5.2: Nested unordered lists in the Opera browser.

Code and Content:	Explanation:	Rendered in a browser as:
<UL> (B)	Tells the browser that an unordered 1st level list follows.	
<LI>Jobs for the garden	Precedes 1st level item.	○ Jobs for the garden
<UL>	Tells the browser to start a 2nd level list.	
<LI>Dig up potatoes	Precedes 2nd level item.	◆ Dig up potatoes
<LI>Mow the lawn	Precedes 2nd level item.	◆ Mow the lawn
</UL>	Tells the browser to close the 2nd level list.	
<LI>Jobs in the house	Precedes 1st level item.	○ Jobs in the house
<UL>	Tells the browser to start another 2nd level list.	
<LI>Paint the back door	Precedes 2nd level item.	◆ Paint the back door
<LI>Build bookshelves	Precedes 2nd level item.	◆ Build bookshelves
<UL>	Tells the browser to start a 3rd level list.	
<LI>Buy timber	Precedes 3rd level item.	○ Buy timber
<LI>Buy screws	Precedes 3rd level item.	○ Buy screws
</UL>	Tells the browser to close the 3rd level list.	
</UL> (A)	Tells the browser to close the 2nd level list	
</UL> (B)	Tells the browser that the 1st level list is complete.	

Code to set up a nested unordered list. (Letters (A) and (B) are not part of the code.)

At first sight this code table looks very complicated, but when you stop to analyse it, it's quite logical. Look first at the boxed area across three columns. This is a properly coded list in its own right. It is wrapped in the correct tags – **<UL>...</UL>** and contains two list items preceded by the **<LI>** tags. This list is contained within a second level list. Note that the closing tag for the second level list – marked **(A)** – comes after the closing tag of the third level list. All three nested lists are wrapped in the first level list tags – marked **(B)**. To understand in practice how this operates, work your way through the next exercise.

Exercise Three

1. Create an HTML page in your text editor and carefully enter the code from the first column of the table above. (Remember **not** to include the **(A)** and **(B)** notations.)

2. Save the page as **ul_list.html** and open it in your browser. Check that it looks like Figure 5.2 above. If it doesn't, check and edit your code to correct it.

    As with modifying numbering styles in ordered lists, it is possible to force a browser to use your choice of bullets. Again the **TYPE=".."** attribute can be used in either the **<UL>** or **<LI>** elements. The following list gives the range of values:

    <UL TYPE="Square"> produces square bullets.

    <UL TYPE="Disc"> produces solid disc bullets.

    <UL TYPE="Circle"> produces circular bullets.

Key Facts ● ● ● ● ● ● ● ● ● ● ● ● ● ● ● ● ● ●

*HTML does not generate any alignment or indentation directly from typed input. It requires the use of the correct tags to lay out page content. Sections of text can be aligned by use of the <DIV> element which takes the attribute ALIGN="..", with valid values of **Left**, **Right**, **Center** and **Justify**.*

*Indentation of text is not supported, but space can be created at the start of (or anywhere else within) a paragraph, by inserting any number of ** ** special characters.*

HTML includes the facility to create several different kinds of lists. Ordered lists are used where the sequence of items is significant. They are created with the <OL> element and generate sequential numbers or letters for list items. Unordered lists use the <UL> element and generate bullets for list items. In both cases the characters which precede the list items are generated automatically.

In both ordered and unordered lists the character which precedes each list item can be specified using the TYPE=".." attribute.

Indenting paragraphs as unordered list items

We mentioned above that it was possible to indent paragraphs by making a browser believe they are items in an unordered list. Strictly speaking, the browser thinks they are the headings for lists. Wrapping a paragraph (or several paragraphs) in the **<UL> ... </UL>** tags has the effect of indenting that paragraph. Do it several times — **<UL> <UL> <UL> ... </UL> </UL> </UL>** and the paragraph will be further indented. This kind of misuse of HTML is frowned on by some purists, but it is a useful trick and well worth remembering!

One trick of the trade is to remember that there ARE tricks of the trade. As we have mentioned several times, HTML was never designed to handle all the layout we require for the Web. If you find yourselve facing a brick wall, try to think around the problem. Ask yourself how else you could achieve the result you are looking for. The   trick is so obvious once you've been told about it, but there are always other tricks waiting to be discovered!

Definition lists

A definition list (sometimes called a glossary list) is a list of paired items which relate to each other. The best example is a dictionary which pairs a word with its definition. The **<DL>** element does not add numbers or bullets and lays out the first item (the term) against the left hand margin, then indents the second item (the definition). The end result produces a list like this:

> **Definition**
> > **A word beginning with D.**
>
> **List**
> > **A word ending with T.**

The code for the above list is:

```
<DL>
<DT>Definition
<DD>A word beginning with D.
<DT>List
<DD>A word ending with T.
</DL>
```

(Note: Although they are not required, when writing long definitions, it is often useful to add the closing tags **</DT>** and **</DD>** after the list items.)

Using lists for Web design

Although lists in HTML were intended originally as a way of displaying information, over the years they have become an important design tool. Listing information makes it easier to read and more attractive visually. Lists help to break up pages into manageable chunks. They vary the placement of text on a page and with a wise choice of font style and colour can add impact and interest.

Exercise Four

1. Create a Web page in your own style, but bearing in mind what we have said so far about good design, to convey the information below. You may change the text as much as you like as long as the meaning remains the same. You

should ensure that your page is designed for maximum impact and readability. Use any of the HTML elements we have listed so far in the book.

A recipe for tomato sauce

Making the perfect tomato sauce requires three things: 1. top quality ingredients, 2. care and attention to detail, and 3. endless patience.

You will need a big splash of olive oil, one finely chopped onion, several cloves of minced garlic, a tin of chopped tomatoes, a tin of tomato puree, a pinch of dried oregano, half a teaspoon of sugar, and salt and pepper.

Here's how to do it. Fry the garlic in the olive oil, then drop in the chopped onions. Continue to fry until the onions are soft and have started to colour. Add both tins, the dried oregano and the sugar. Lower the heat and cook for a very long time until most of the water has evaporated and the olive oil starts to appear round the edge of the pan. Finish with salt and pepper to taste.

Enjoy on pasta or poured over sausages.

2. Save the exercise as **tomato_sauce.html** and open it in your browser.

3. Now take a long critical look at it. Does it look interesting and well-balanced on the page? Could the information be presented more effectively? Are the fonts too big? (If the recipe is longer than a single screen, they certainly are!) If you are not satisfied, change your code, save it and refresh your browser, then take another look.

Our attempt at this exercise is shown in Figure 5.3

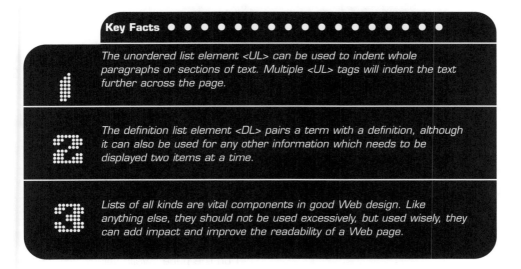

Key Facts

1. The unordered list element <UL> can be used to indent whole paragraphs or sections of text. Multiple <UL> tags will indent the text further across the page.

2. The definition list element <DL> pairs a term with a definition, although it can also be used for any other information which needs to be displayed two items at a time.

3. Lists of all kinds are vital components in good Web design. Like anything else, they should not be used excessively, but used wisely, they can add impact and improve the readability of a Web page.

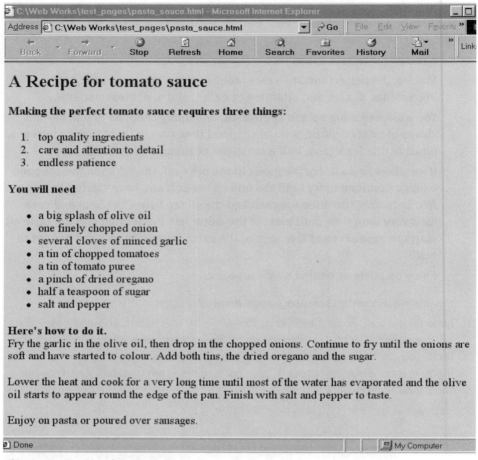

Figure 5.3: A recipe for tomato sauce.

The following tag table gives details of all the HTML elements used in this chapter:

Opening Tag	Closing Tag	Attributes	Description
<DIV>	</DIV>		The <DIV> element allows you to divide a page into sections and apply different alignments to each.
		ALIGN=".."	This attribute specifies how the enclosed section should be aligned on the page. Valid values are: Left, Right, Center and Justified.

<OL>	</OL>		These tags enclose an ordered list – one in which the list items are numbered or marked with a sequence of letters.
		TYPE=".."	This attribute defines what style of numbers or letters should be used to introduce list items. Valid values are: a, A, i, I, and 1.
<UL>	</UL>		These tags enclose an unordered list – one in which the order of the list items is not important. List items are introduced with a bullet.
		TYPE=".."	This attribute defines the style of bullet that is used to introduce list items. Valid values are: Square, Disc and Circle.
<LI>			This tag introduces a list item in either an ordered or an unordered list.
<DL>	</DL>		These tags enclose a definition list – one in which a term is matched with its definition. List items are not numbered or marked in any way.
<DT>			This tag introduces the term to be defined in a definition list.
<DD>			This tag introduces the definition of the term in a definition list.

QUICK REVISION QUESTIONS

1. What is meant by aligning text?

2. What is meant by justification? How would you justify a paragraph in HTML?

3. How might you use special character codes to indent the start of a paragraph?

4. What are the differences between ordered lists, unordered lists and definition lists?

5. What code would you use to add a list item to an ordered list?

6. What code would you use if you wished items in an unordered list to be preceded by a square bullet?

7. How would you use the unordered list element to indent a whole paragraph?

8. What benefits do lists bring to the concept of Web page design?

Chapter 6
Adding colour to Web pages

Brief contents:

1. How HTML defines colours.

2. Creating a Web-safe colour scheme.

3. Defining colours in terms of their RGB values using the hexadecimal system.

4. The importance of co-ordinating colour schemes for maximum readability and impact.

5. Changing the background colour of a Web page.

6. The importance of white space as a design tool.

7. How to insert invisible comments into HTML code.

Adding colour to your Web pages

Without colour, the Web would be a dismal place. Colour brings the Web to life. It adds interest and excitement to site content. It is also probably the most misused resource that HTML offers authors. The most important lesson to learn when adding colour to your Web pages is not how to do it, but when and where to apply it. We will discuss this further later in the chapter. Let us begin with the basics.

Colour can be applied to Web documents in a number of ways. One of them we have looked at already – setting text into colour. We can also colour the page background, use a coloured image as a page background or insert a coloured image into the page itself. We can even apply special effects like regularly changing the background colour or flashing coloured graphics on and off, but these require advanced techniques which are beyond the scope of this book.

Software required for handling colour images

Until now we have managed quite nicely with just a simple text editor and a Web browser. There is still a lot we can do with just those tools, and some Web authors never use anything else, but this chapter introduces the use of images on the Web – a subject which is explored in more detail in the following chapter. It is possible to be a very effective Web designer without ever creating or modifying graphics. You can use freely available Web clip-art for all your illustrations, but in our opinion this would seriously hamper your ability to design good Web pages.

Of course, we do not expect you to be a digital artist, but even the ability to create a coloured square and use it on your Web pages will allow you to generate some useful effects. To build even the most basic colour graphics, you will require some form of graphics software. Our choice would always be Adobe Photoshop®, but this is a very expensive option. An excellent package is JASC's PaintShop Pro® which is widely available on computer magazine cover discs as *shareware*. Any of the digital art packages like CorelDraw®, Macromedia Fireworks® or Adobe Illustrator® will do the job, but these are *vector-based* drawing packages and you will need to export your illustrations in a suitable format for the Web. There are even a number of *freeware* packages available on cover discs or direct from the Internet.

As far as this book is concerned, this is what we require from your graphics package. Whichever software you choose (or are obliged) to use, it must be able to:

Create an image of an exact size in pixels. (Pixels is short for "picture elements" — the resolution of your monitor is measured in pixels. To check this out on a Windows-based computer, right-click on your desktop, go to **Properties > Settings**, and look at the box marked **Screen Area**.)
Create simple shapes such as squares, rectangles, circles etc.
Fill these shapes with exact colours. (We'll explain about Web-safe colours in the following section.)
Add text to an image.
Save that image to your hard disc as a **.gif** or **.jpg** file. (Again, we will explain what these file types are in the next chapter.)
It would also be helpful if your software allowed you to measure distances on graphics in terms of pixels.

---

[1] **Shareware**: Shareware is simply try-before-you-buy software. You install it on your computer, test it out for a few days and if it meets your requirements, you pay for it. Often you can do this over the Internet by credit card and receive your registration code immediately. Enter the code and the software is yours to keep. We should stress how important it is to register your shareware within the stated trial period. Shareware authors rely on people's honesty!

[2] **Vector-based**: Graphics can be defined in two ways. Bitmaps — the technique used for most Web graphics at present — define an image as a pattern of coloured dots. It is also possible to define an image in terms of curves and angles. These are vectors. In most cases, vector-based graphics must be converted into bitmaps before they can be included in Web pages, although this is changing with the development of new graphic formats such as Flash and SVG.

Because we don't know which software you will be using for graphics work, we cannot give precise instructions on how to complete the various tasks we will be assigning. But the tasks will be relatively simple, we will be giving general instructions and with most graphics software working in a similar way, this should be enough to get you through. Let us stress once more that home-made graphics and image manipulation are not essential for good Web design, but they do add extra dimensions to your abilities.

Note for those of you who are already familiar with graphic software. When you are creating or modifying images for the Web, you should always work in RGB colour mode rather than CMYK mode. RGB files use the same colour model as a monitor screen. CMYK files need to dither[4] colours to produce screen colours. They also tend to be larger in size.

Colours for the Web

An understanding of how colour relates to Web content is vital if you are to use colour effectively. A **bit** is a single binary digit -– a piece of information that can be set to carry a **0** or a **1**. A black and white computer display can be generated by defining a single **bit** for each pixel on your monitor screen – a **1** to indicate white and a **0** to indicate black. So this range of colour, black and white, is known as 1-bit colour. Early computers used 4-bit colour. Four bits allow you to define sixteen colours. (If you want proof, here is the range of different definitions four **1**'s or **0**'s can generate: **0000, 0001, 0010, 0011, 0100, 0101, 0110, 0111, 1000, 1001, 1010, 1011, 1100, 1101, 1110, 1111**.)

The more bits you use, the wider the range of colours you can display. 8-bit colour provides for 256 colours. (We won't list all the combinations.) The latest standard is 32-bit colour which provides for millions of colours – certainly more than the eye can see. Let's drop back to the 8-bit colour range for a moment which was the working range when the Web first came into being. And let's say that the colour we're looking at is red. Who decides what red is? There are probably a dozen different reds around you while you are reading this. Different computer platforms use different ranges of colour, called colour palettes. A red on a Macintosh might be several shades different from a red on a Windows-based computer. So code that called for a piece of text to be printed in red might achieve different results on different platforms.

---

[3] **Freeware**: Some software authors are just naturally generous people. They design programs, then give them away for nothing. In many cases, freeware is just as good as — and sometimes better than — commercial software. It's certainly cheaper.

[4] **Dither:** a strange word which means using a pattern of coloured dots to create the illusion of extra colours. For example, if you print a series of blue and yellow dots near to or even overlapping each other, the eye will see the area as green. This technique is used in almost all colour printing where just four colours are used to create a whole spectrum.

There are a total of 216 colours on which the three major platforms (Macintosh, UNIX and Windows/PC) agree, and these colours comprise what is called the **Web-safe palette**. To ensure that colour was consistent across platforms, it was agreed that these colours would be specified using the **RGB** model (see the note below). The Web-safe palette uses a hexadecimal (hex) value to determine how much of each colour should be mixed.

There are several ways in which colour can be specified. A very common one is the CMYK model used by most ink jet printers. CMYK refers to the amounts of Cyan, Magenta, Yellow and blacK which are overlaid on a page to produce the final colour. The RGB model is used by monitors, and defines the levels of Red, Green and Blue light which are mixed on the screen to give the desired shade.

Working in hex is complicated. Instead of counting in tens, as we normally do, hex counts in sixteens. Luckily, we don't need to master the hexadecimal system to make use of it. Here are the first sixteen "numbers" in hex listed against their everyday equivalents:

0	1	2	3	4	5	6	7	8	9	10	11	12	13	14	15
0	1	2	3	4	5	6	7	8	9	A	B	C	D	E	F

The **RGB** model uses a simple formula to specify colour — **#RRGGBB**, where **RR** represents a two digit hex value for red, **GG** represents a two-digit hex value for green, and **BB** represents the hex value for blue. **00** would therefore represent none of a colour, while **FF**, the highest value, would represent all of a colour. The table below explains how this system works in practice:

Hexadecimal RGB Value:	Explanation:	Resulting Colour:
#000000	None of any of the three colours makes black.	Black
#FFFFFF	The maximum amount of each colour makes white.	White
#FF0000	Maximum red and no other colours gives red.	Red
#800080	Moderate amounts of red and blue and no green makes purple.	Purple
#FFFF00	Maximum red and green with no blue gives yellow.	Yellow
#32CD32	Small amounts of red and blue with a lot of green makes a light green.	Lime

A full listing of colour hex values and their resulting colours is given in Appendix 3 at the back of this book.

Using hexadecimal colour values to specify colours
Earlier in the book, we used the names of certain colours in the code we created to change text colour. Let us now develop that code to make use of hex values. At the same time, let's introduce some new code to specify the background colour of the page.

In Chapter 3, we noted that the **<BODY>** element is used to define the actual content which appears on a Web page. We also described the **TEXT=".."** attribute which defines the colour of the text on that page. The code we used for this was **<BODY TEXT="Red">** ... **</BODY>**. If we wish to, we can substitute the hex value for red, and render the code as **<BODY TEXT="#FF0000">** ... **</BODY>**. This would be safer code since we could then be certain that all browsers would render exactly the same colour – in theory. Like most elements, **<BODY>** can handle a series of attributes. The one we are interested in now is the attribute which sets the background page colour. This is the **BGCOLOR=".."** attribute. Work through the exercise below to see how this attribute can be used.

Exercise One

1. Open your text editor and load the code you previously saved as **second_page.html**. It should look like this:

    ```
    <HTML>
    <HEAD>
    <TITLE> This is another Web page </TITLE>
    </HEAD>
    <BODY TEXT="Red">
    <H2> Some Basic Text Formatting </H2>
    <P>
    This line is ordinary text. <BR>
    <B> But this line is in bold text.</B> <BR>
    <I> Would you believe it?  This line is in italic text.</I> <BR>
    <U> And this line is underlined. <BR>
    <I> <B> Really exciting now!
    This line is underlined, bold and italic!! </B> </I> </U>
    </BODY>
    </HTML>
    ```

2. Change the code so that the **<BODY>** tag now reads:
    ```
    <BODY TEXT="#FF0000" BGCOLOR="#808080">
    ```

3. Save this file and open it in your browser. You should have your text in red

while your page background is now mid-grey.

4. Using the colour table above where necessary, change the code to produce white text on a black background. (Remember to save your code and refresh your browser to see the effect.) How effective do you think this colour scheme is? How good is its readability?

5. Make further changes to your code to produce white text on a yellow background, then lime text on a purple background. For each change, consider the effectiveness of the colour scheme you have produced.

6. Finally, try inserting a random hex value into both the text and background colour attributes. (Remember that any "number" from **0** to **F** is valid in any of the six places in the hex value.) Again evaluate the result.

Effective Web colour schemes

What was your opinion of the various colour schemes you created in the above exercise? To assess a colour scheme, we need to consider at least four aspects – its readability, its suitability for the subject matter, the impact the scheme has on a reader and its artistic value. (We call this the **RSIA** test – Readability, Suitability, Impact and Artiness, and will be returning to it later.) Let's consider one or two examples, remembering always that we are dealing here with matters of opinion, and that your opinion might not match ours.

1. **White text on a black background**: this is a highly readable colour scheme – indeed for many years it was all that was available to computer readers. White on black (or black on white) provides the maximum colour contrast. It also has a powerful impact on readers who have grown used to multi-coloured images. We think white on black looks slightly sinister, even depressing –- not the colour scheme you might choose for a Web site devoted to the beauty of nature!

2. **White text on a yellow background**: this, you will agree, is worse than useless. It's almost unreadable.

3. **Lime text on a purple background**: artistically this is quite striking, but its readability is only moderate. We feel that after pages of this scheme, the reader might start to get a headache. It does not provide a very formal look to the page, and while, in moderation, it might suit a site on 1960s psychedelia, it would hardly be suitable for a government department's Web site.

4. How would you rate the colour scheme you created using random hex values?

We will be looking at colour schemes in more detail in Part 2 of this book, but from here onwards we want you to get into the habit of assessing the Web pages you are creating from a designer's perspective. After every exercise, we want you to ask yourself four questions:

1. **R. Is this page easy to <u>Read</u>?**
2. **S. Is the style of this page <u>Suitable</u> to its contents?**
3. **I. Does this page make an immediate <u>Impact</u> on the reader?**
4. **A. <u>Artistically</u>, is this page interesting and stimulating?**

You should also consider any limitations your readers might bring with them. Remember that many Web users are partially sighted and some might be colour-blind. We have deliberately put readability at the top of our list of questions, since we believe that this must be the Web author's first priority. Always aim for high contrast between the text and the background and let your artistic inclinations take second place.

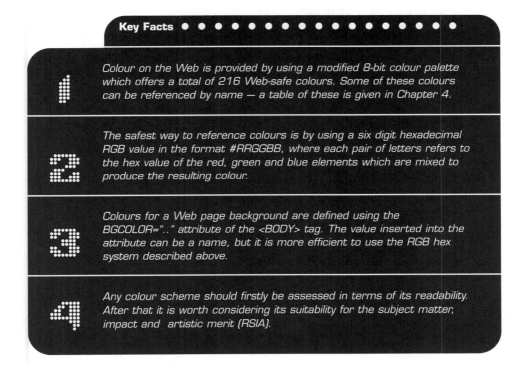

Key Facts

1. Colour on the Web is provided by using a modified 8-bit colour palette which offers a total of 216 Web-safe colours. Some of these colours can be referenced by name — a table of these is given in Chapter 4.

2. The safest way to reference colours is by using a six digit hexadecimal RGB value in the format #RRGGBB, where each pair of letters refers to the hex value of the red, green and blue elements which are mixed to produce the resulting colour.

3. Colours for a Web page background are defined using the BGCOLOR=".." attribute of the <BODY> tag. The value inserted into the attribute can be a name, but it is more efficient to use the RGB hex system described above.

4. Any colour scheme should firstly be assessed in terms of its readability. After that it is worth considering its suitability for the subject matter, impact and artistic merit (RSIA).

White space

Strangely enough, from a designer's viewpoint white space doesn't need to be white. White space refers to the unoccupied areas of the page – clear space above, below and to either side of your text. It might be white, if white is your background colour, but it's just as likely to be pale blue, grey or even black. White space is an important design consideration. If text is crammed onto a page, it becomes difficult to read and all sense of style is lost. Give your text room to breathe.

HTML's **<P>** element does this easily by leaving a blank line before a new paragraph. The use of lists is also recommended since lists are automatically indented from the margin, thus leaving space to the left of the text.

As an example of the creative use of white space, work through the following exercise:

Exercise Two

1. Open your text editor and type in the following code

```
<HTML>
<HEAD>
<TITLE> Creating white space. </TITLE>
</HEAD>
<BODY BGCOLOR="#COCOCO TEXT="#000080">
<!- - The above code sets the background colour to silver and the text
to navy. - ->
<H2> A headline automatically creates space above and below it.
</H2>
This paragraph has not been specially formatted. It wraps at the right
hand margin in the normal way. The paragraph tag that comes next
creates a blank line below this paragraph.<P>
<DIV ALIGN="Center"><B> Central alignment creates space on either
side.</B></DIV><P>
<UL>"Abusing" the unordered list element allows us to indent a
paragraph and creates space to the left.</UL><P>
<UL><UL>And doubling the abuse allows us to indent even further.
</UL></UL><P>
        Finally,      use of the
     non-breaking space character code,  
   allows us to space a line      in a very
strange way!
</BODY>
</HTML>
```

2. Save this file as **white_space.html** and open it in your browser. It should look like Figure 6.1. (We're showing it in Sun's HotJava browser, and we've taken out the text and background colours for better visibility.)

While the page in this example is too short to require much in the way of white space, it does show how laying out your text with room around it improves both the readability and the impact of the page content.

You will also have spotted a new element we have dropped into this exercise. The **comment** element **<!- - ... - ->**, which has no closing tag, allows us to add in notes on our code which we do not wish to appear in the browser window. Comments replace the dots. In this case, we have defined colours for the text and background as hex values, and to remind ourselves what they will actually appear as, we have noted their real names as a comment.

Including comments in your code is a very good idea. You can drop in explanations of what your code was intended to do, and if the effect needs to be changed later, you will know what you were originally aiming for. You can drop in dates and times to remind you of when you completed a section of code. You can mark sections you will need to come back to. In general, whenever your code is not straightforward — and it will get complicated, trust us — it's an excellent idea to put in a comment. It may save you a lot of time later on.

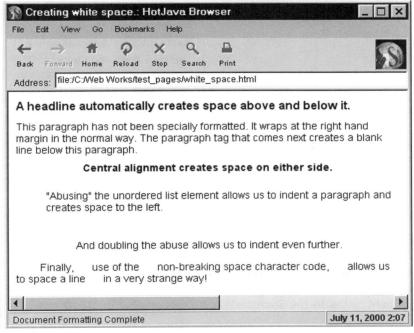

Figure 6.1: Using white space to improve readability.

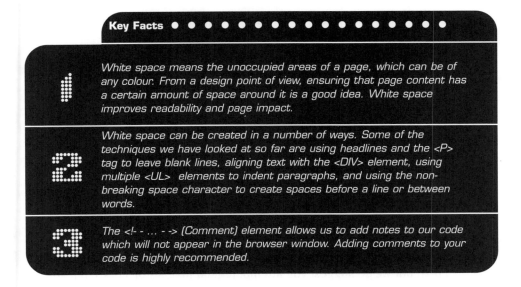

Key Facts

1. White space means the unoccupied areas of a page, which can be of any colour. From a design point of view, ensuring that page content has a certain amount of space around it is a good idea. White space improves readability and page impact.

2. White space can be created in a number of ways. Some of the techniques we have looked at so far are using headlines and the <P> tag to leave blank lines, aligning text with the <DIV> element, using multiple <UL> elements to indent paragraphs, and using the non-breaking space character to create spaces before a line or between words.

3. The <!- - ... - -> (Comment) element allows us to add notes to our code which will not appear in the browser window. Adding comments to your code is highly recommended.

The following table lists the HTML tags used in this chapter.

Opening Tag	Closing Tag	Attributes	Description
<BODY>	</BODY>	BGCOLOR=".."	New attribute: Specifies a colour for the page background. Some colours may be referenced by name, but a safer method is to reference them by their hexadecimal RGB value in the format: #RRGGBB. A complete table of RGB hex values is given in Appendix 3.
<!- - ... - ->			The comment element allows you to insert any comments you wish to make within a page's code. Comments replace the dots in the tag and are not displayed by the browser.

 QUICK REVISION QUESTIONS

1. What is meant by the terms Shareware and Freeware?
2. In computer terms, what is a bit? How many different colours would an 8-bit colour system define?
3. What is meant by the Web-safe palette? How many colours does it contain?
4. What is the difference between the CMYK and the RGB colour models? Suggest output devices which might make use of each model.
5. In HTML, the RGB colour model uses the hexadecimal system to define the value for each colour component. What is the hexadecimal system and how is it applied to the formula #RRGGBB?
6. A high-contrast colour scheme helps to ensure the readability of Web pages. What is meant by a high-contrast colour scheme? Can you give an example?
7. What is meant by white space and why is it important in Web design?
8. What code would you use to add a comment which would not appear in a Web browser?

REVISION PROJECT: Chapters 3 – 6

Every few chapters, we will be providing a major revision project. If you are study-ing this book to help with your own Web design project, you might prefer to use your own text, but we do suggest you attempt regular major projects so that you can apply the Web authoring skills you have learnt.

For each project we will provide some suggestions on technique. Since this is the first one, we will be more generous and propose a logical approach to creating your exercise pages. This is not, incidentally, the approach we will suggest later in the book for designing a full Web site. This is just for these projects. We propose that you follow these steps:

1. Read through the text we provide to get a feeling for its style and tone. Is it light-hearted? Is it serious or even sombre in tone? Decide from this reading whether you will present the material in a cheerful, breezy style or whether it requires a more formal presentation. You should already be thinking in terms of a colour scheme, possible choice of font(s), text size and the overall look of the layout.

2. Create a simple page *template*[5]. We shall be looking at templates in detail later in the book, but for the time being, the following code will probably be enough:

```
<HTML>
<HEAD>
<TITLE>Replace this text with your page title.</TITLE>
</HEAD>
<BODY>
Replace this with your headlines, graphics, text etc.
<P>
<FONT SIZE="3"><B>Your name goes here.<BR>
Time and date go here<BR>
Your course, module, exercise number etc. go here.</B></FONT>
</BODY>
</HTML>
```

Save this template as **template1.html**. Now every time you need to create an exercise page, you simply open this template, change the text and code as necessary, and save it under a new name.

3. Open **template1.html** in your text editor and type in all the text for the exercise before worrying about any kind of formatting. Save the page as a **.html** file and open it in your browser. From here on keep both your text editor and your browser open on the desktop. As you make changes, save the file and refresh your browser. You can then see the effect of each change as you make it.

---

[5] **Template**: in engineering terms, a template is a pattern usually of thin board or metal plate, used as a guide in cutting or drilling metal, stone, wood, etc. When we talk about Web page templates we mean pre-prepared pages containing the standard HTML tags which can then be modified and added to as required by the exercise.

4. Keeping in mind the ideas you had in Point 1 above, start applying text formatting. Think about your headlines, whether any of the text would look better in bold or italic type, and whether any of the information would be better displayed as a list.

5. Ask yourself whether the page would look better with a few sub-headings. These can act to divide up page content into sections which are easier to read. Sub-headings would be smaller than your main headline, but larger than the text they introduce.

6. Consider text alignment and indentation. Think about white space and whether the text looks crowded on the page. At all times, try to put yourself into the mind of your reader. Remember the importance of readability, followed by suitability for the page content, impact and artistic effect. (RSIA)

7. Finally, when the page looks balanced and professional, and when you have checked the text for spelling and grammatical errors, consider applying colour to your exercise. Remember the guidelines about colour. Be artistic, but at the same time be cautious and remember that the main purpose behind a Web page is to pass on information.

Of course, these are just suggestions. You are free to adopt any approach that suits your style, but try to be logical in your methods. Whatever your approach, we suggest that after your first shot at the page, you flick back through the previous four chapters and check the **Key Facts** boxes. These contain all the information you need and will serve as a checklist to make sure that you have considered all the options available to you as a Web author.

Here is the text for the first revision project:

An Exercise in non-verbal communication
Thinking in terms of hand signals

You are to design a method of conveying the following messages to a person who is deaf, does not speak English and comes from another European country. You can assume that he will understand internationally accepted hand signals (hello, goodbye etc)...

Basic Level

1. Good morning. Please come in and sit down. Would you like a cup of coffee?

2. I am extremely tired and need a place to sleep. Can I get an alarm call at 7am?

3. You look ill. Have you had an accident? Where does it hurt? I will call an ambulance. Stay here and wait until I come back.

4. Can you direct me to the station? How far away is it? Can I walk there? Do you have the time?

Advanced level

5. I am looking for a little girl who is lost. She is wearing a green dress and a red sweater. Have you seen her?

6. Are you lost? Where are you staying? Can you talk? Are you here on your own?

7. Please leave me alone. I am not in the mood for company. I don't want to buy whatever you're selling. Leave me alone or I'll call for help.

8. You stupid fool! You ran straight into me! Would you pick up the rest of my bags?

9. I agree. I'll see you in half an hour. Let's meet up under the bridge. Remember to bring an umbrella.

© 2001 Seán Laffey, Centre for Disabled Studies, Dublin

Chapter 7
Graphics for the Web

Brief contents:

1. The different graphic formats that can be used on the Web.

2. How and when to use graphics in Web pages.

3. Where to look for clip-art to use in your pages.

4. How images can be used as page backgrounds.

5. The "single-pixel graphic trick" to align text.

6. How to use horizontal rules in Web pages.

7. How Web animations are generated.

8. Why the use of animation should be limited.

Graphics for the Web

In this chapter we begin to examine the use of graphics on the Web. "Graphics" is one of those confusing terms which can mean different things to different people. We will define graphics as non-textual page content, excluding video and audio content. This definition would therefore include photographic images, coloured drawings, black and white line drawings, cartoons, icons, logos, lines, boxes and buttons etc. We will also include animated graphics.

We hope that following the advance warning we gave you at the start of the last chapter, you now have some sort of graphics software installed. You will be needing it for some of the exercises in this chapter.

In its early days, the Internet was entirely text-based, but today's users have been programmed by television and magazines to expect information to be presented graphically. It is also widely recognised that we absorb information much better when it is offered visually. But graphics have a downside as well. They can slow up the download speed of a Web page, they can distract us from a site's real purpose, and, badly used, they can easily turn a page into a complete mess.

From the very start it's important to realise what images can do. They can:

- Present information that cannot be given as text.

- Illustrate points made in the text.

- Decorate a page and improve its accessibility to readers.

- Provide a visual navigation system around a site.

On the other hand, they cannot:

- Make up for poor page content

Before we can look at the mechanics of using images in your pages, we need to know something of the file types available and their advantages and disadvantages.

Image file types

An image file is just like any other type of *binary*[1] file. The software that transfers data over the Internet is not bothered with the file contents. It will download an image file, an executable program or a virus with equal enthusiasm. As we noted in Chapter 2, when a Web page's HTML code references any type of file that is not plain ASCII text in HTML format, it is downloaded from the Internet, and only as it arrives does the client computer software decide what to do with that file. You will remember that there are basically three options:

1.   If the client's Web browser can handle the file type internally, it will insert it into the page as the HTML code instructs.

2.   If the browser has access to a plug-in application which can handle the file type, it passes the file onto the plug-in which then manages the file.

3.   Otherwise it asks the user where he would like to store the file on his or her hard drive. It then saves the file and leaves the user to manage it.

It follows from this that if we want graphics to appear on our Web pages, we must use image file types that a browser can recognise and display. There are several file types that fit this requirement, and new ones are being developed, but at present there are only two which are widely supported on the Web – the **GIF** (pronounced "jiff") and **JPEG** (pronounced "jaypeg") image formats. We will look at each in turn.

The GIF format

GIF stands for Graphics Interchange Format. Originally designed by Compuserve®, GIF files are still the most widely used for graphics other than photographs. One

---

[1] **Binary file**: as you already know, computers translate data into digital code — a string of 1's and O's. A file containing digitally encoded data is referred to as a binary file. In Web terms we also talk about binary objects, meaning digitally encoded file types which can be embedded in a Web document. Binary objects include graphics, sound and video files.

drawback of the format is that it can only display 256 colours or *greyscale*[2] variations. When you save a graphic in GIF format, the software finds the 256 colours
which best represent the colours in the image and creates a palette of them which
is stored in the image's *file header*[3]. GIF files have a **.gif** file extension (for example:
my_picture.gif) and are heavily compressed for faster downloads. 256 colours is a
very restricted palette, making the GIF format unsuitable for photographs.

The GIF format comes in two versions, GIF78 and GIF89a. GIF89a is the current
format and brings two great advantages. Firstly, one of the colours in its palette can
be made transparent, and if this seems less than earth-shattering, look at Figure 7.1
and you will see why Web designers like this benefit so much.

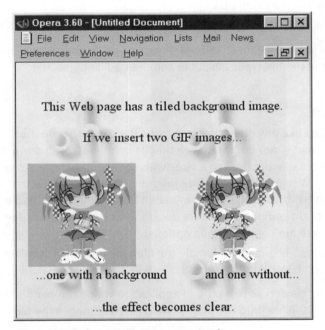

Figure 7.1: Using a GIF's transparent colour.

In the screen shot above, we have used two versions of the same image. The first
one has a rectangular grey background. This is not necessarily a bad thing, but it
does separate the image from the rest of the page. In the second version, we have
used the GIF89a format to render the grey background transparent. Now the image
of the little girl is much better integrated into the page. Instead of a separate
image, it has become a design feature. It could be part of a company's *logo*[4] or
used to attract readers to a particular piece of text.

---

[2] **Greyscale:** refers to all the variations in shade between white and black. The GIF89a format allows for
254 different shades between pure white and pure black.
[3] **File Header:** We have already met the concept of Head and Body in Web pages. Many other file types
operate in a similar way. Information on the file (meta information) is separated from the actual file content and stored at the top of the file in a file header.
[4] **Logo:** short for logotype, is an image or graphic used to identify a business in its display material. Good
examples are the Nike® tick, or the Shell Petroleum® yellow shell symbol.

A second advantage of the GIF89a format is that it can produce an **interlaced** image. Normally, when a browser loads a graphic, it starts to appear from the top and steadily unfolds downwards. When a graphic has been interlaced, the whole image appears in very low resolution after just one-eighth of the image has loaded. This builds up to the full resolution as the rest of the graphic downloads. Again this is best illustrated with an example. Figure 7.2 shows three stages in the loading of an interlaced GIF in a browser window. Although an interlaced graphic downloads at exactly the same speed as a normal one, it appears faster because the viewer has something to watch as the image appears.

Stage One:
A very low resolution image loads. This version, at only 9 pixels per inch, loads into the browser very quickly and marks a place for the full image.

Stage Two:
The graphic builds up progressively in the browser. At 37 pixels per inch, the image is becoming clearer.

Stage Three:
The final image appears at 75 pixels per inch. As the GIF has downloaded, the viewer has, at least, been "entertained"!

Figure 7.2: An interlaced GIF graphic downloads

Finally, note that the GIF89a format supports animation. We will be looking at animated GIFs later in the chapter.

JPEG – the photographic format

The second graphics format we are concerned with is the **JPEG**, short for Joint Photographic Experts Group, the consortium which originally designed the format. A JPEG file has the extension **.jpg**, as in **my_picture.jpg**. The format was designed specially for photographs and can display up to 16.7 million colours (24-bit). It uses a compression technique known as "lossy", because when the graphic is compressed, some of the information it contains gets lost. With JPEG files the amount of information lost in the compression can be controlled. There is a trade-off here. High compression gives a smaller file size, faster downloads and poorer image quality, while low compression means a larger file size, slower downloads and better image quality.

While the JPEG format is clearly more suited to photographic images, it does not support transparent colours and cannot be interlaced. With modern graphics software able to quickly convert one format into another, which should the Web author choose? The answer is both. If your graphic needs a wide range of colours – and remember that it is not only photographs that use millions of shades – select the JPEG format. If, on the other hand, your graphic uses a limited palette, the GIF format brings other advantages.

There are several other formats on the Web, but they are not all supported by different types of browser. A new one that is gaining popularity is the **PNG** (Portable Network Graphic) format. The PNG format produces smaller, and therefore faster loading, files than the GIF format. You might also see **.pic** files – these are in Apple's® proprietary format, or **.bmp** and **.wmf** files on Windows-based computers.

Choosing images for a Web page

Now we are clear about the formats we can use, we can consider the wider question of sourcing images for our Web pages. But before we start grabbing images at random and planting them in our work, we need to agree some guidelines for using graphics. The first and most important thing to consider is download speed. A Web page that consists of nothing but text downloads quickly, even through slower modems. As soon as we start inserting graphics, download times start to rocket. The mathematics is very convincing.

Look again at Figure 7.1. The text part of that Web page creates a file size of just 1 Kilobyte and if we assume that a modern modem downloads at 5 Kilobits per second, the text part would load in less than one second. But the page includes three graphics – the background image is 23KB, and the two GIFs are 8KB each. Our loading time has just risen to seven seconds. This figure assumes that the whole of the "pipe" delivering the graphic from server to client is operating at the speed of the modem. If there are any traffic jams on the Internet, that figure could easily double. Count to 14 slowly and imagine that you are waiting for a page to load. How much patience do you think the average Web user has?

The example we are looking at is a very small page with very small graphics. A large colour graphic could weigh in at 60KB or even 100KB. Drop a few of those into your page and its access time becomes ridiculous. Our first rule when using graphics is to keep them small. Of course there are times when graphics cannot be kept small. If, for example, you were designing a site on the works of a great artist, presenting that artist's paintings to your visitors would be the whole point of the site. In cases like this, we can use another trick. We can load small, low resolution versions of the images and give our visitors the choice of viewing the full-sized, high resolution versions. We will look at this technique of "thumbnailing" in detail in Chapter 9.

Our second rule will be to keep them relevant. Given the wealth of images freely available to the Web designer, there is always a temptation to use them just because they're there. Unnecessary decorations are often referred to as "eye-candy", and the term fits very well. "Art for art's sake" does not apply to Web design. Every graphic we include must have a specific purpose.

Now that we have agreed our rules, we can consider sources for Web graphics. There is a huge amount of free clip-art available. A selection is often supplied with commercial graphics software, on the free cover discs that come with computer magazines, or on the Web itself. Unfortunately, much of this is of very poor quality. Remember that you are only looking for GIFs or JPEGs. Clip-art is often supplied in other formats like WMFs (Windows® MetaFiles) or BMPs (BitMaPs), and these would need to be converted if you wished to use them. Most graphics software includes a conversion utility.

Tricks Of The Trade

Almost any graphic you view on the Web can be stored on your own computer. Windows users can Right-click on the graphic, and select Save As from the menu that appears, specify the folder you wish to use for storage and click OK. Macintosh users should hold down the single mouse button to access the save menu. But remember that many graphics are copyright, and while no-one will object to you keeping a copy on your own machine, you might run into trouble if you use the graphic in your own Web pages without the author's approval. For safety's sake, you should only use graphics that are clearly marked as copyright free. If in doubt, don't use the graphic!

Later in the book we will consider how graphics can fit into our overall Web site design, but in the meantime you should consider starting a collection of images that you can use in your Web pages. At the end of Chapter 2, you created a series of folders to store your work in. One of them was **Web Works\downloads**, and this is a good place to store any graphics you download from the Web itself. A second folder, **Web Works\cabinet** is intended for any images you obtain from other sources. You may not realise it, but you probably have a lot of different graphics already stored on your computer. It would be useful at this point to move some of these into your **cabinet** folder so that they are available for future exercises. To do this, work through the following exercise:

Exercise One

1. If you are using a Windows-based computer, start up **Windows Explorer** (click **Start > Programs > Windows Explorer**). [Mac users should open the hard drive and use **Sherlock** to find files whose **Name – contains — .gif**.] Scroll down to your **Web Works** folder and open your **Cabinet** folder.

2. On the **Tools** menu, click **Find > Files or Folders**. In the **Named** box type in ***.gif**, and in the **Look In** box type **C:**. Click **Find Now**.

3. The program will now scan your computer and find all files with a **.gif**

extension. These will be listed in the window at the bottom. Depending on the software you have installed on your computer, there might be very few or there might be a lot. Double click on some of the **.gif**'s listed and, again depending on your software, they should open in a graphics package. (If they don't, look at the **Tricks of the Trade** box below.)

4. Find 10 or so examples which appear no larger than one-eighth the size of your monitor screen, and holding down the Control key (**Ctrl**), drag them from the **Find** window into your **Cabinet** folder. This will copy them rather than move them. Try to pick those with a relatively small file size – less then 20KB would be ideal, but you might have little choice.

5. Repeat this process using ***.jpg** as the file mask in the **Finder**. All being well, you should now have a selection of GIFs and JPEGs in your **Cabinet** folder.

Tricks Of The Trade

Not many people realise that you can use most Web browsers to view graphic files. Internet Explorer works very well. To use it, open it alongside the File Finder, click on the graphic you wish to view and drag it into the browser window where it will be displayed.

Key Facts ●

1 *Photographic images and illustrations are a vital part of Web content but must only be used when they make a valid contribution to the page. They enhance but do not replace good page content.*

2 *The preferred graphic file types for the Web are GIFs and JPEGs, each of which has different advantages. GIFs are compressed images that can show 256 colours, one of which can be made transparent to allow the background to show through. They also support interlacing and animation. The JPEG format is also compressed. It supports over 16 million colours and is best used for photo-quality images.*

3 *Whenever graphics are to be included in a Web page, thought must be given to the time they will take to download to the client computer. Web users – like all of us – have limited patience and will move elsewhere if they are obliged to wait a long time for pages to build.*

4 *Graphics are freely available from pre-installed software, magazine cover discs or even the Web itself, but not all graphics are copyright free. A Web designer must never use someone else's copyrighted work in his or her pages.*

Inserting graphics into Web pages

The actual code required to insert a graphic into a page could not be simpler. The **<IMG>** element, which does not require a closing tag, is used with the compulsory attribute **SRC="‥"** (**Source**) to tell the browser where the graphic file is stored. Here is an example:

<IMG SRC="my_picture.jpg">

Correct use of the **SRC="‥"** attribute is vital. Unless it points directly to the graphic's location, the element will not work, and your page will probably display a little box with a red cross in it, called a placeholder. The **SRC="‥"** attribute must point to the **URL** of the graphic file. We looked at **URL**s back in Chapter 1 and we will be using them continuously from here onwards, so it is worth reminding ourselves what they are.

A **URL** is an address on the Web. It can also be an address on your own computer. **URL**s can be **relative** or **absolute**. A relative **URL** gives directions to a file relative to the page it appears in. An absolute **URL** gives directions which are valid no matter where you start from. If you are not clear about all this, turn back to Chapter 1 now and check the details.

As far as HTML is concerned, there are four possible locations for a graphics file – in the same folder as the Web page that uses it, in a sub-folder of the folder containing the Web page, in another folder on the same (local) computer or somewhere else on the Web. (This also applies to other binary objects we will be looking at later in the book.) Each of these require a slightly different use of the **SRC="‥"** attribute and we will look at each in turn:

1. **The graphic is stored in the same folder as the Web page**.

   When the browser sees a properly coded **<IMG>** tag calling for an image with no information on where it is stored, it looks to see if that graphic is located in the same folder as the page itself. If it finds it, it inserts it into the page.

   Code: **<IMG SRC="my_picture.jpg">**

2. **The graphic is stored in a sub-folder**.

   You will remember that when you set up your workspace, you created a **test_pages** folder with a sub-folder called **resources**. To insert a graphic from this folder (which will be our standard way of working in future), you must tell the browser to look in a named sub-folder.

   Code: **<IMG SRC="resources/my_picture.jpg">**

3. **The graphic is stored elsewhere on your local computer**

   Here we need to use an absolute **URL** for the graphic. We cannot expect the browser to navigate up and down our folders structure looking for a specific file. HTML includes code to allow for an absolute **URL** on a local computer. Let's say the graphic is stored in a folder called images which is a sub-folder of **My Documents**.

   Code: **<IMG SRC="file:///C:/My documents/images/my_picture.jpg">**

   Note that this code uses a special (false) protocol called **file:///** in place of the usual **http://**. It requires three slashes (**///**) instead of the normal two.

4. The graphic is stored elsewhere on the Web

A Web page can include a graphic file that is stored anywhere on the Web –
although this could make for very slow downloads. Here the **URL** must
include the full Web address.

Code: **<IMG SRC="http://www.elephant.com/images/my_picture.jpg">**

It is important that you appreciate the difference between these four types of location. Later in the book you will find that similar code is used to include other types
of Web content. For the moment let's put some of this into practice.

Exercise Two

1. Use Windows Explorer to copy (not move) three of your graphics from your
    Cabinet folder to your **test_pages\resources** folder. We will refer to these
    files as **picture1.jpg, picture2.jpg** and **picture3.jpg**, but you must
    substitute the actual names of the files. It doesn't matter whether you use
    JPEGs or GIFs in this exercise, but remember to give them the correct
    extensions.

2. Open your text editor, load the exercise template you created for the earlier
    revision exercise and type the following code into the body section:

    **This page illustrates the right and wrong way to include graphics in
    your Web pages.
**

    <IMG SRC="picture1.jpg">

    <IMG SRC="resources/picture2.jpg">

    <IMG SRC="file:///C:/Web Works/Cabinet/picture3.jpg">

3. Save this in your **test_pages** folder as **images.html** and open it in your
    browser. It should look like Figure 7.3.

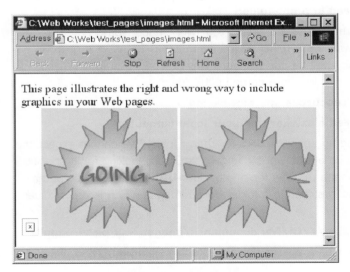

Figure 7.3: Inserting images into a Web page

There are three graphics referenced by the code, but the first one has not displayed correctly. This is because the code tells the browser to look for the graphic in the same folder that the page itself is stored in, and there is no graphic there. The other two graphics have appeared because each of them has been properly addressed. The first one has been addressed using a relative URL which points the browser to the subfolder **/resources**, while the second addresses the same folder but uses an absolute URL defining the complete path on your local computer.

Although JPEG graphics cannot be interlaced, there is a useful technique which produces a similar result. Most browsers support the LOWSRC attribute of the <IMG> element. Like SRC, LOWSRC points to the URL of an image, but the image located here should be a very low resolution or even a black-and-white version of the graphic that the SRC attribute is referencing. It should, however, be of exactly the same dimensions. The LOWSRC image downloads much faster and appears on the page, giving the user something to look at while the high resolution version is loading. This technique is explained in detail in Chapter 9.

When inserting graphics, it is important to remember that a small proportion of Web users prefer to browse with image rendering turned off; still others use text-only browsers. It is therefore good manners to provide some text that will display in place of the graphic and this is done using the **ALT="..."** attribute of the **<IMG>** element. It is also worth noting that this text will display if, for any reason, the Web browser cannot find the graphic being called for. A third good reason for including alternative text is that more and more blind or visually impaired Web users are taking advantage of voice synthesising software which will read the alternative text out loud. To see how the **ALT="..."** attribute operates, work through the following exercise.

Exercise Three

1. Open your text editor and reload **images.html**. Find the line of code which pointed to the wrong address for its image:

   <IMG SRC="picture1.jpg">

   and change it to read:

   <IMG SRC="picture1.jpg" ALT="This text will be displayed if image rendering is turned off, or if the browser cannot find the image.">

2. Save this again and reload it or refresh it in your browser. The **ALT**ernative text has replaced the missing image.

Aligning graphics

Earlier in the book we noted the difficulties of aligning text on a Web page. Aligning graphics can be just as awkward. The **<IMG>** element has a further attribute **ALIGN= "..",** which instructs the browser how to integrate the graphic into the surrounding text. This attribute has a range of possible values, best listed in a table. (In each case we assume that the **<IMG>** element has been inserted at the start of a paragraph of text.)

ALIGN="..'"	Explanation:
Top	The graphic is placed against the left margin. The first line of text is aligned with the top of the graphic, the rest of the text appears below the graphic.
Bottom	The graphic is placed against the left margin. The first line of text is aligned with the bottom of the graphic, the rest of the text appears below the graphic.
Middle	The graphic is placed against the left margin. The first line of text is aligned with the middle of the graphic, the rest of the text appears below the graphic.
Left	The graphic appears against the left margin. The text is aligned to the right at the top of the graphic and flows down and around the graphic.
Right	The graphic appears against the right margin. The text is aligned to the left at the top of the graphic and flows down and around the graphic.

Note: there are additional values for the **ALIGN=".."** attribute, but since these are only supported by certain browsers, they are not included here.

Exercise Four

1. Open your text editor, create an HTML page or load a template and type the first paragraph of this chapter into the body. In front of the first word of the paragraph, insert the following code:

   <IMG SRC="resources/picture2.jpg" ALT="If you can see this text, you have done something wrong!" ALIGN="Top">

2. Save this to your **test_pages** folder as **image_alignment.html** and load it into your browser. Leave your text editor open. Note how the image and text have been aligned.

3. Return to your text editor, and replace the value **Top** with the value **Middle**. Save the file and refresh your browser. Do the same for each of the other values listed in the table above. Note how the text behaves after each change you make.

There are two further attributes of the **<IMG>** element we need to consider, **HSPACE=".."** and **VSPACE=".."**. These are used to create **H**orizontal space to the left and right of the graphic and **V**ertical space above and below the graphic. These attributes take a value of a number of pixels. To see how this works, reopen **image_alignment.html** in your text editor and add the following attributes to the **<IMG>** tag:

VSPACE="25" HSPACE="25"

If you load or refresh the page in your browser you will see that a border of 25 pixels has been created around your graphic. When using these attributes, note that the browser sees the border as part of the graphic and will flow the text around it. This can create awkward spaces.

Sizing graphics

All computer graphics are rectangular. If you see any that appear to have a different shape, it is because part of the graphic has been rendered transparent. This means, of course, that all graphics have a width and a height. It is possible to resize a Web graphic *on the fly*[5] using the **<IMG>** element's **HEIGHT=".."** and **WIDTH=".."** attributes. If your page includes a graphic which is 100 pixels wide and 100 pixels high, setting the values of both these attributes to 200 would enlarge the graphic by a factor of four. This would be a bad idea for two reasons. Firstly, anything other than a very minor modification of the graphics size will almost certainly distort it and secondly if a Web browser is forced to recalculate the size of a graphic, it will add considerably to the time it takes for the page to display. If a graphic you wish to use is the wrong size, it is much better to modify it in a suitable graphics program such as Photoshop® or PaintShop Pro®.

Despite this you should consider always using the **HEIGHT=".."** and **WIDTH=".."** attributes, but with their values set to the actual size of the graphic to be displayed. There is a very good reason for doing this. We know that the text content of a Web page is displayed in a browser before the graphics start to load. By including the **HEIGHT=".."** and **WIDTH=".."** values, the browser is forced to create the correct space for the graphics before they arrive and to wrap the text around those spaces. This speeds up the loading time because the browser doesn't have to recalculate the page layout to fit in the graphics when they finally download.

There is only one time when you could use the **HEIGHT=".."** and **WIDTH=".."** attributes to resize a graphic, and that is when the graphic is all of a single colour, and if this makes no sense at all, move onto the next section and all will be revealed.

The single pixel image trick

We mentioned back in Chapter 5 that we had a further trick up our sleeve to help with the alignment of text on a Web page. Here it is.

---

[5] **On the fly:** If your computer processes something as it happens, or in "real time", this is often described as processing on the fly.

Exercise Five

1. For this exercise you will need to use your graphics software to create an image that is just one pixel square and filled with white. We will list the instructions for doing this in Photoshop®. You will need to modify these if you are working in another graphics package. From the **File** menu, click **New**. In the window that opens, set the **Width** and **Height** to **1** pixel, make sure that **Contents** is set to **White** and click **OK**. On the **Image** menu, click **Mode** and then **Indexed Color** and click **OK**. Save this image as **white_pixel.gif** in your **test_pages\resources** folder.

2. Reopen the file **image_alignment.html** in your text editor. Change the **<IMG>** tag, so the body section of the page reads as follows:

   <IMG SRC="resources/white_pixel.gif" ALIGN="Left" WIDTH="1" HEIGHT="1">In this chapter we begin to examine the use of graphics on the Web. Graphics is one of those confusing terms which can mean different things to different people. We will define graphics as non-textual page content, excluding video and audio content. This definition would therefore include photographic images, coloured drawings, black-and-white line drawings, cartoons, icons, logos, lines, boxes and buttons etc. We will also include animated graphics.

3. Save this file as **pixel_trick.html** in your **test_pages** folder and open it in your browser. Note that the first line of text has been indented slightly. It has wrapped around the single pixel graphic, but since that graphic is the same colour as the page background, it remains invisible.

4. Now change the **<IMG>** tag so that it reads:

   <IMG SRC="resources/white_pixel.gif" ALIGN="Left" WIDTH="50" HEIGHT="50">

5. Save the file and refresh your browser. This has created a much bigger block of white space and again the text is wrapped around it. To see what has actually happened, change the **<BODY>** tag to read:

   <BODY BGCOLOUR="Aqua">

   Save and refresh and now you can see the white block against the aqua background.

6. Finally, change the **<IMG>** tag to read:

   <IMG SRC="resources/white_pixel.gif" ALIGN="Left" WIDTH="1" HEIGHT="1" HSPACE="25">

7. Save and refresh as usual. The white block has disappeared since one pixel is too small to see. Instead you have created a good indent to the first line of the paragraph. (It is actually indented by 51 pixels – the single pixel of the image and 25 pixels on each side created by the **HSPACE=".."** attribute. Your final page should look like Figure 7.4.

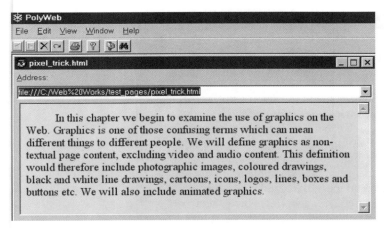

Figure 7.4: Using a single pixel graphic to indent text in the PolyWeb browser.

Using graphics to create page backgrounds

As well as inserting graphics into Web page content, we can also use them as backgrounds for our pages. To do this we use one of the **<BODY>** element's attributes, **BACKGROUND="..."**. The attribute's value can be set to the URL of any GIF or JPEG file, using the same addressing methods described earlier in the chapter. The selected graphic is then "tiled" or repeated across and down the page continuously. If the selected graphic is "seamless", in other words if the graphic can be tiled without visible joins, this gives the impression of a smooth background. To see how a tiled graphic works, reopen **pixel_trick.html** in your text editor, and change the **<BODY>** tag to read:

<BODY BACKGROUND="resources/picture2.jpg">

Save the file and check it in your browser. You should see **picture2.jpg** tiled across the page background. Unless you've been lucky in your choice of graphics, it will probably look a right mess and the text will be very hard to read. The first lesson in choosing background images is to make sure that all the colours they contain contrast well with your text colour.

The difference between good and bad background images is demonstrated in Figures 7.5 and 7.6. The same text colour and content has been used in each.

In these two examples, the top one uses a totally unsuitable background graphic. Its wide range of colours means that the text is difficult – even irritating – to read. The bottom example uses a subtle graphic of intertwined birds. It creates an impression without interfering with the readability of the text.

Once again we must consider the size of the graphic file we intend using as our background. This will, of course, have to be downloaded.

In addition to providing stylish page backgrounds, there is another trick we can use the **BACKGROUND="..."** attribute for. We can create a very small image of, say, five pixels in height and 1200 pixels in width, and colour the first 200 pixel width in black and the rest in white. A section of it might look like this:

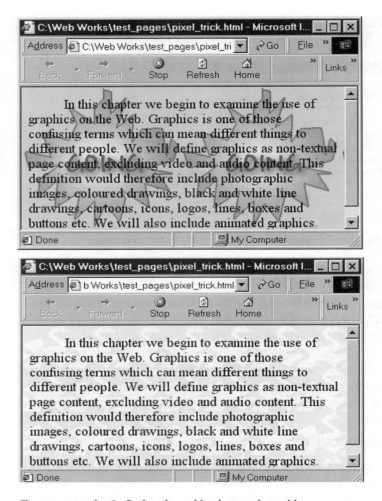

Figures 7.5 and 7.6: Bad and good background graphics.

Our 1200 pixel width was chosen because it is wider than most of the screen resolutions that are currently in use. If our background image is too narrow, it will tile across the page as well as down it and this will ruin the effect we are trying to achieve. At 1200 pixels wide, if we tile this as a background graphic, it is too wide to repeat across the page, but will repeat down the page, giving us a black column on the left of the screen with the remainder white. Look at Figure 7.7 to see this in action.

The same trick can be used with multi-coloured rather than two-toned strips. Tiling multi-coloured strips will produce a series of coloured bars up and down the page. It can be difficult to align text with these bars, but there is a way of doing it by using tables – an idea we will develop in Chapter 10. Vertical strips can also be used, but care must be taken to ensure that the strip is longer than the maximum possible length of the page. If the strip is too short, the graphic will repeat further down the page and the darker colour might obscure part of the text.

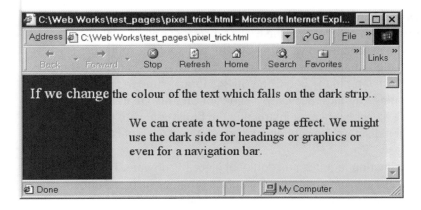

Figure 7.7: A two-tone graphic strip used as a tile.

Horizontal rules

HTML does provide for one graphic element which does not need to be downloaded. The **<HR>** (horizontal rule) element provides a simple way to divide pages into sections. It does not require a closing tag. Inserting the **<HR>** tag between paragraphs creates a bar almost the full width of the page and adds a shadow to give it a 3D effect.

The **<HR>** element takes several attributes to control the way it appears on the page. **WIDTH="..."** and **SIZE="..."** set the bar's height and thickness. Both attributes take a value which is the number of pixels. The **ALIGN="..."** attribute takes values of Left, Right and Center, and operates the same as the **ALIGN="..."** attribute for other elements. Finally, in some browsers, the **NOSHADE** attribute renders that bar without a shadow. Figure 7.8 shows the various ways in which the **<HR>** element can be used.

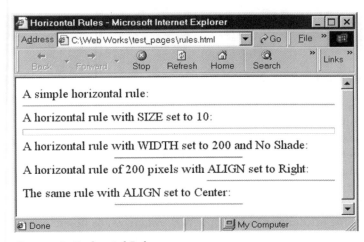

Figure 7.8: Horizontal Rules

Animated GIFs

We noted earlier in this chapter that the GIF89a format supports animation. Animations can be assembled in various ways, for example Macromedia's Flash® software creates high-quality animations which are now very common on the Web. We will look at Flash later in the book. The GIF89a format supports a very simple method of animating graphics. Basically, a series of GIFs are created and assembled into a single file with a header instructing the browser how to play the animation. They are then displayed in sequence to create the illusion of continuous motion.

Building an animation requires an additional piece of software. The individual graphics, known as cells, are created in a graphics program such as Adobe Photoshop®, then imported into an animation program like GIF Movie Gear® or Alchemy Mindworks' GIF Construction Set® where they are sequenced. The resulting file appears to be an ordinary **.gif** file but contains additional instructions in its header which tell the Web browser how long to show each cell for.

Figure 7.9 shows an animation of a talking mouth being assembled in GIF Movie Gear.

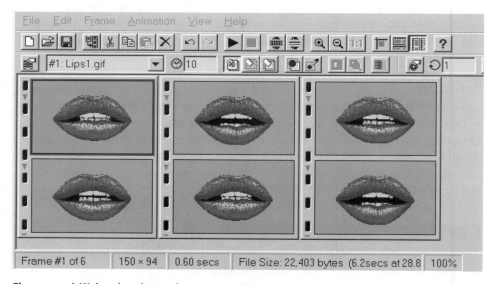

Figure 7.9: A Web animation under construction.

Many people feel that there are too many animations on the Web. Certainly they can get irritating and distract visitors from more important page content, but used wisely, they can add interest and a bit of action to an otherwise static page. As with all graphics files, thought must be given to file size and subsequent download times.

Animated GIFs are inserted into a Web page in exactly the same way as any other graphic and the same attributes can be applied. Browsers which do not support animation, or in which animation rendering has been turned off, display the first frame of the animation as a static image.

Key Facts ● ● ● ● ● ● ● ● ● ● ● ● ● ● ● ● ● ● ●

 Graphics are inserted into a Web page using the <IMG> element, which requires the SRC=".." attribute taking the graphic's absolute or relative URL as its value. Other attributes offer control over alignment, size and alternative text.

 Tiny graphics the same colour as the page background allow fine control over text placement on a Web page. By specifying the size of the graphic and the width of a white space border around it, text can be "reshaped" to suit the Web designer's layout.

 Graphics can be tiled as a page background. Care must be taken to ensure that the text remains readable. Background images should be subtle and unobtrusive. The use of tiled multi-coloured strips can create a series of coloured columns or rows on a page.

 The <HR> (horizontal rule) element provides a simple way to create section divisions across a page. The height, width and alignment of the rule can be specified.

The GIF89a format supports animated GIFs. A sequence of individual cells are played one after the other to create an animated effect. Care must be taken not to overuse animations which can prove intrusive and distracting.

The following table lists all the HTML tags used in this chapter.

Opening Tag	Closing Tag	Attributes	Description
<IMG>			This tag inserts a GIF or JPEG graphic into a Web page.
		SRC=".."	This attribute MUST appear in every <IMG> tag. Its value is the relative or absolute URL of the graphic to be displayed.
		ALT=".."	This attribute should always be used. Its value is a text string which is displayed when the browser is unable to show the graphic.
		ALIGN=".."	This attribute specifies how the graphic is aligned on the Web page. Valid values are: Top, Bottom, Middle, Left and Right.

		VSPACE="..."	This attribute specifies how much space should be created above and below the graphic in pixels.
		HSPACE="..."	This attribute specifies how much space should be created to the left and right of the graphic in pixels.
		HEIGHT="..."	This attribute specifies the height at which the graphic should be displayed in pixels.
		WIDTH="..."	This attribute specifies the width at which the graphic should be displayed in pixels.
<BODY>	</BODY>		New attribute:
		BACKGROUND="..."	This attribute specifies the URL of an image to use as a tiled back ground to a page.
<HR>			This tag inserts a horizontal rule.
		WIDTH="..."	This attribute specifies the width of the rule in pixels.
		SIZE="..."	This attribute specifies the height of the rule in pixels.
		ALIGN="..."	This attribute specifies how the rule should be aligned on the page. Valid values are: Left, Right and Center.
		NOSHADE	This attribute removes the shadow from the rule.

QUICK REVISION QUESTIONS

1. What are the benefits of including graphics in a Web page? Are there any disadvantages?

2. Which graphic formats can be used on the Web and what are the major differences between them?

3. In Web graphics terms, what is meant by a transparent colour and interlacing?

4. Why is the size of an image file important when it comes to selecting graphics for Web pages?

5. The **<IMG>** element has one compulsory attribute. What is it, and how is it used?

6. Which attribute of the **<IMG>** element can be used to determine where a graphic appears on a page? What are the values it can take and how do they affect text flow around the graphic?

7. Why should the **HEIGHT** and **WIDTH** attributes of the **<IMG>** element not be used to resize a graphic? What would you use them for?

8. How would you instruct a browser to use a graphic as a page background?

9. What code would you use to insert a horizontal rule aligned to the right of a page?

10. What should be kept in mind when deciding on animations for a Web page?

Chapter 8
Hyperlinks

Brief contents:

1. Understanding the workings of hyperlinks on the Web.

2. How hyperlinks use absolute and relative URLs to reference a range of different Web resources.

3. How to insert hypertext links into your pages.

4. How to use graphic images as hyperlinks.

5. The design benefits of using a graphical navigation system on a Web site.

6. The concept of a Graphical User Interface (GUI).

Hyperlinks

It has taken us seven chapters to get here, but we have finally arrived at the heart of the World Wide Web. Let us be honest. Almost everything we have done so far could equally well have been done with a good desktop publisher — and probably with a great deal less effort. It is the operation of hyperlinks that lifts Web pages onto a higher plane than mere printed documents. Hyperlinks give us the ability to cruise through a world of information by clicking words or images that appear on our screen.

We looked at the concept of **hypertext** and **HTTP** (HyperText Transfer Protocol) in some detail back in Chapter 1. Since that was quite a way back, it would be a good idea if you would read through those sections again so that the operation of hypertext is fresh in your mind. If you want to see an example of hypertext operating locally, click on the **Start** button then click **Help** in Windows 95/98/2000 or click on the **Help** menu in MacOS. On the help pages which open, you will see various topics in underlined blue text. Click these and you are transported to linked topics. These in turn link to further information. Hypertext is an essential component of modern software design.

As we look at the idea of hyperlinks and discover how to implement them in HTML, it is important that you remember the actual mechanics of viewing documents on the Web. To review the key point, keep in mind that you do not actually move from computer to computer across the Internet. Instead, by clicking a hyperlink, your computer (the client) sends a request to a remote computer (the server), which responds by sending back the page you have requested.

Hypertext, you will recall, is text that links to other information. On today's Web, a large percentage of those links are graphics rather than text. Even many clickable words are in fact just parts of larger graphics such as navigation bars and image maps. So rather than talk about "hypertext", we will be accurate and discuss "hyperlinks" – a term which includes both textual and graphical links.

In Chapter 7, we talked at some length about absolute and relative URLs. We will be using both for our hyperlinks, and it is even more crucial that we get them accurate here. Using the wrong URL for a graphic just means that the image won't display on your Web page. Using the wrong URL in a hyperlink will either cause a browser to bring up its problem page, or, worse still, call up the wrong site on the Internet. Either way, your visitors will curse you.

You will notice another, more important, change in this chapter. For the first time we are moving on from considering simple Web pages, and starting to talk about Web sites instead. Of course you know already that a Web site is a collection of pages which are hyperlinked together. Creating your own Web site is the ultimate aim of this book. Instead of users, we will start talking about visitors – those Web citizens who we are going to attract to our site.

Site addressing

In Chapter 1, we provided an example of a complete URL. The example we used was:

http://www.flywithus.com:8080/holidays/florida.html#miami

..and we broke this down into its various components. If we inserted a hyperlink into a page which referenced this URL, we would be issuing the instructions in the following table:

Component:	Explanation:
http://	Use the HyperText Transfer Protocol to down load this resource.
www.flywithus.com	Look for a server whose name on the World Wide Web is "flywithus", and which has been registered as a commercial organisation.

:8080	Access that site via port 8080.
/holidays	Look in a folder called "holidays".
/florida.html	Download a document named "florida.html".
#miami	Find and display the part of the document marked with an anchor called "miami".

As we explained in Chapter 1, most of the time a URL would be simpler than this. Very often a link would only point to a site address like **http://www.flywithus.com**. When a site is addressed in this way, the remote server would send us the page which has been defined as its default page. Often this would be called either **home.html**, **default.html** or **index.html**.

Technical Stuff

Because servers expect a site to have an entry page called* home.html *or* index.html, *it is a good idea to make one of these the first page of any site you design. Further pages can be called anything you like -- keeping in mind the naming conventions we described earlier in the book. (Use lower case letters and don't leave spaces between words.* mypage.html *is good,* My Page.html *is not.)

Because the Internet originated in the United States, sites registered there tend to have different naming conventions from those registered elsewhere in the world. Note, however that we are only referring to sites <u>registered</u> in a particular country. There is no reason why a site registered in Korea cannot actually reside on a server in Germany. On the Internet, most site addresses are **Fully Qualified Domain Names (FQDN**s). FQDNs in the US take the format:

machine name.domain name.domain type

An example of this would be Adobe's® Web site at **www.adobe.com**, where **www** specifies the name of a machine at the domain called **adobe**, a **com**mercial organisation. Outside the United States, an additional component is added which defines the country in which the site was registered:

machine name.domain name.domain type.country code

Country codes are two-letter extensions such as **ie** for Ireland or **ca** for Canada. In recent times FQDNs have become less important and arbitrary URLs like **flyto.mybusiness** or **me.righthere.net** have become more common. FQDNs are only a convention. In theory, a site can be called anything at all -- in fact **anything.at.all** could be a valid address provided HTTP understands where the site is located. Site names are convenient and help people remember where to go, but a server's <u>real</u> address is its **Internet Protocol (IP)** address, a string of four numbers between 0 and 255, separated by dots – **223.156.27.190**, for example. Before a site can be accessed, its written (symbolic) name must be "mapped" or translated into its proper IP address. This is handled by a series of Internet servers which provide a **Domain Name Service** (**DNS**). So the mechanics are: you request a site by name, the request is passed along the internet to a DNS server which translates your request into an IP address, this IP address is then added to your request which is passed to the correct server.

At this point we have to introduce a new protocol. Earlier in the book we explained HTTP as the protocol used for accessing information on the Internet. In fact, we only gave you half the story. HTTP is the protocol which allows the client computer's browser to communicate with the server, but the actual transportation of files across the Internet is handled by another network protocol, **TCP/IP** or **Transmission Control Protocol/Internet Protocol.**

Let us put some simple examples into practice before moving on to more complicated URLs.

Exercise One

1. Create a new HTML page or open a suitable template in your text editor.
2. Give the page the title "**Hyperlinks**", and in the **BODY** section type in the following code:

   \<H2\>Creating Hyperlinks\</H2\>

   To connect to the Google search engine \<A HREF="http://www.google.com"\>CLICK HERE\</A\>\<BR\>

   To connect to Microsoft's home page \<A HREF="www.microsoft.com"\>CLICK HERE\</A\>\<BR\>

   To connect to the last exercise I completed \<A HREF="image_alignment.html"\>CLICK HERE\</A\>\<BR\>

3. Save this file to your **test_pages** folder as **hyperlinks.html**; it should look like Figure 8.1. (Our page is shown in the KatieSoft® browser.)

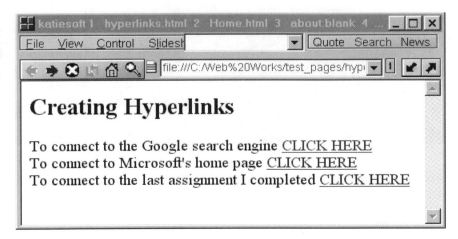

Figure 8.1: An example of hyperlinks

4. If you have an Internet connection, try clicking the hyperlink to Google. If your code is correct, Google's default page will open in your browser. Use your browser's **Back** button and click the link to Microsoft. If that works, come back again and click the final link. Your **image_alignment.html** page should load.

You have been using the **<A> (Anchor)** element and its attribute **HREF.** (Note that from here onwards we will not be listing an attribute in the format **HREF="..".** By now you will have enough experience to know how to use an attribute. If you need to find out whether an attribute takes a value, and the range of valid values, you should check the Tag Table at the end of the chapter.) The **HREF** attribute takes as its value any valid URL, absolute or relative. The first two links on the page use an absolute URL to define a site on the Web. The third uses the relative URL of a document stored in the same folder on your local computer.

Note also that HTML has formatted your links according to its default settings. The words "CLICK HERE" have changed colour – usually to blue, but this can vary – and been underlined. Traditionally on the Web, blue underlined text indicates a clickable link. If you have clicked any of these links, they have probably changed colour again – usually to purple. HTML uses a different default colour for links that have been visited. This is very convenient for a site visitor who can then tell where he has and hasn't been.

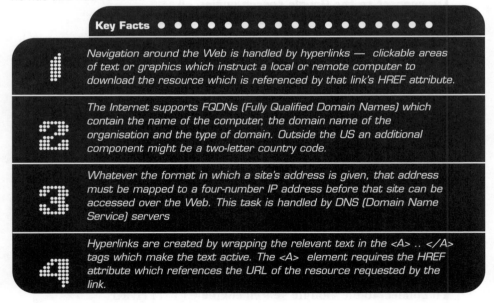

Key Facts

1. Navigation around the Web is handled by hyperlinks — clickable areas of text or graphics which instruct a local or remote computer to download the resource which is referenced by that link's HREF attribute.

2. The Internet supports FQDNs (Fully Qualified Domain Names) which contain the name of the computer, the domain name of the organisation and the type of domain. Outside the US an additional component might be a two-letter country code.

3. Whatever the format in which a site's address is given, that address must be mapped to a four-number IP address before that site can be accessed over the Web. This task is handled by DNS (Domain Name Service) servers

4. Hyperlinks are created by wrapping the relevant text in the <A> .. </A> tags which make the text active. The <A> element requires the HREF attribute which references the URL of the resource requested by the link.

Links to other resources
As well as pointing to other pages on the Web, hyperlinks can reference a wide range of other resources. They can also point to images such as GIFs or JPEGs which will be displayed by the browser, to those file types which can be handled by a browser's plug-in applications, to files for downloading, to programs which can be

run or even to an e-mail application.

The following exercise uses an invented company Earpop Records to show how different types of hyperlink might be used. (Don't bother clicking any of the links, since none of them will work!)

Exercise Two

1. Create a new HTML page or open a suitable template in your text editor.

2. Give the page the title **"Earpop Records"**, and change the **<BODY>** tag to read:

   <BODY BGCOLOR="Black" TEXT="White" LINK="Yellow" ALINK="Aqua" VLINK="White">

   in the **BODY** section, type in the following code:

   <DIV ALIGN="Center">

   <H2>EARPOP RECORDS</H2>

   <H4>Welcome to Earpop Records, home of the finest Indy artists around!</H4>

   Use the links below to find what you are looking for..<P>

   **<A HREF="listing.html"><B>Click here</B></A> to check out our range of artists.
**

   **<A HREF="http://www.earwax_records.com/listing.html"><B>Click here</B></A> to check the artists listed by our sister company, Earwax Records.
**

   **<A HREF="images/dead_balloons.jpg"><B>Click here</B></A> to see a photo of Dead Balloons recording their latest CD.
**

   **<A HREF="listing.html#dead_balloons"><B>Click here</B></A> to read about Dead Balloons on our listings page.
**

   **<A HREF="ftp://ftp.earpop.ie/orderform.pdf"><B>Click here</B></A> to download the order form you will need to buy from our catalogue.
**

   **<A HREF="mailto:info@earpop.ie"><B>Click here</B></A> to send us an email.
**

   </DIV>

3. Save this to your **test_pages** folder as **earpop_home.html**, open it in your browser and check that it looks like Figure 8.2

This is the most complicated bit of coding we have tried so far, so let us go through it with some care.

1. We are looking for a cool and modern design so we have decided to use a white on black colour scheme. We set this up as previously using the **<BODY>** element. Unfortunately, the default colour for a hyperlink is blue,

which doesn't stand out very well from our black background. We have therefore changed it to yellow, using the **<BODY>** element's **LINK** attribute. For the same reason we have changed the link's active colour — the colour it changes to when we roll the mouse pointer over it — to aqua, using the **ALINK** attribute, and its visited colour to white, using the **VLINK** attribute. All of these three attributes take colour values in the same way that the **BGCOLOR** attribute did in Chapter 6.

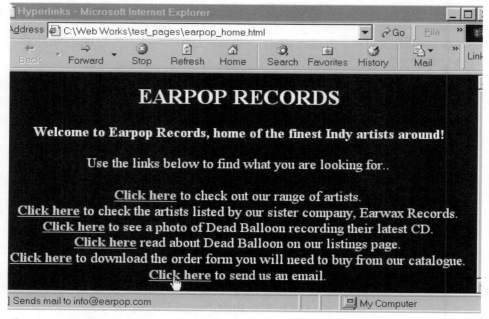

Figure 8.2: Earpop Records uses hyperlinks for navigation

2. To centre our content on the page, we have used the **<DIV>** element.

3. We have included six hyperlinks, each of which operates in a slightly different way. Without clicking the links, park your mouse pointer on each one in turn. As well as showing up our rather sexy aqua text, most browsers will indicate somewhere on screen what will happen when you click the link. In Internet Explorer this usually appears in the bar at the bottom of the browser window. We will look at each one it turn:

   a. **<A HREF="listing.html">** This link will open another page called **listing.html** which is stored in the same folder as our home page.

   b. **<A HREF="http://www.earwax_records.com/listing.html">** This link opens the page called **listing.html** from another site altogether. In this case, the site is www.earwax_records.com which could be stored on the same server or on another server halfway across the world.

   c. **<A HREF="images/dead_balloons.jpg">** This link loads a JPEG image called **dead_balloons.jpg** which is stored in a sub-folder named **images**.

d. **<A HREF="listing.html#dead_balloons"">** This link, like link (a) above, also opens the page called **listing.html**, but in this case it opens at a particular part of that page which is marked with an anchor named **dead_balloons**. If listing.html was a very long page and our visitor was looking for a particular section of it, this would save him from having to scroll down to find it.

e. **<A HREF="ftp://ftp.earpop.ie/orderform.pdf">** We looked at the File Transfer Protocol in a footnote in Chapter 1. It is an older Internet protocol but still highly efficient at moving files. In this case Earpop maintains a file archive on an FTP server, and this link will download a file called **orderform** in the Adobe® PDF format.

f. **<A HREF="mailto:info@earpop.ie">** This final link triggers the user's default e-mail program with the **Send To**: box already loaded with Earpop's e-mail address. This is the one link which might work on your computer, so try clicking it and see what happens.

Technical Stuff

We have mentioned before that it is important not to leave spaces in the names of any files or documents which might be accessed on the Web. A space is considered to be an unsafe character in a file name because it might cause a server's operating system to misbehave. If you must use a file name which contains spaces, the safest thing to do is to replace each space with its ASCII Hex value — %20, *so a file called* history of space.pdf *would be mapped to* history%20of%20space.pdf. *Other unsafe characters include* / $? : ; ! + and *.

Using graphics as links

There are several reasons why you might consider using graphics as hyperlinks.

- Modern computer operating systems have accustomed us to clicking on-screen buttons. We can carry the same "metaphor" onto the Web and make our sites easier to navigate.

- Graphic links can add an attractive design element to our pages.

- Remember the discussion in Chapter 7 on the problems with downloading large graphic files? One good solution is to create a tiny version of the larger graphic for our page, to link that small version to the large version, and give a visitor the opportunity of loading the full-sized image if he or she wants to. (This technique, using **thumbnails** is described in detail in Chapter 9.)

The use of buttons as hyperlinks is very widespread. You might have noticed from your own Web cruising that on many sites, buttons appear to move in when clicked. This is a technique we will look at later in the book. Here we will content ourselves with simple two-dimensional buttons as part of a site's navigation system. The following exercise creates a working navigation page for some of the contents of your **test_pages** folder:

Exercise Three

1. Using your graphics software, create four plain white GIF images 50 pixels square and within each create a 50 pixel diameter circle. Fill the circles with light blue, yellow, light green and pink respectively. Save them to your **test_pages\resources** folder as **button1.gif**, **button2.gif** etc. (The following instructions will achieve this in Adobe Photoshop®; you will need to modify them for other graphics software. Click **File > New**. Set the **Name**: to **button1**, the **Width**: to 50 pixels, the **Height**: to 50 pixels, the **Mode**: to **RGB Color** and the **Contents**: to **White**. Click **OK**. Select the **Circular Marquee Tool** (top left on the toolbar) click on the top left-hand corner of the image and drag a circle to the bottom right-hand corner. Select a light blue colour in the **Color Picker** and use the **Paint Bucket Tool** to fill the circle with the chosen colour. Click **Image > Mode > Indexed Color**, and **Save** the image as **button1.gif**. Follow the same procedure for each of the other three graphics, changing the colour as required.)

2. Create a two-toned background strip like the one we described in Chapter 7. (Again these instructions are for Photoshop and will need to be modified to suit your own graphics software. Click **File > New**. Set the **Name**: to **background.gif**, the **Width**: to 1200 pixels, the **Height**: to 10 pixels, the **Mode**: to **RGB Color** and the **Contents**: to **White**. Click **OK**. Select the **Rectangular Marquee Tool** (top left on the toolbar) click on the top left-hand corner of the image and drag a rectangular marquee **65** pixels across from the left of the image. Make sure that the marquee comes right to the bottom of the image. Click **Select > Inverse**. Select a light blue colour in the **Color Picker** and use the **Paint Bucket Tool** to fill the rectangular marquee. Click **Image > Mode > Indexed Color**, and **Save** the image as **background.gif** in your **test_pages/resources** folder.)

3. Make sure that the following HTML pages are present in your **test_pages** folder: **earpop_home.html**, **hyperlinks.html**, **pixel_trick.html** and **image_alignment.html**. These are the pages our buttons will link to.

4. Create a new HTML page or open a suitable template in your text editor.

5. Give the page the title "**Navigator**", and change the **<BODY>** tag to read:

   ```
   <BODY TEXT="Navy" BACKGROUND="resources/background.gif">
   ```

6. Insert the following code into the **BODY** section.

   ```
   <H2><FONT COLOR="Red"> My Navigator</FONT></H2>
   <A HREF="earpop_home.html"><IMG SRC="resources/button1.gif"
   HEIGHT="50" WIDTH="50" BORDER="0" ALT="This should be a
   button!"></A> Click this button for Earpop! <BR>
   <A HREF="hyperlinks.html"><IMG SRC="resources/button2.gif"
   HEIGHT="50" WIDTH="50" BORDER="0" ALT="This should be a
   button!"></A> Click this button for Hyperlinks! <BR>
   <A HREF="pixel_trick.html"><IMG SRC="resources/button3.gif"
   ```

**HEIGHT="50" WIDTH="50" BORDER="0" ALT="This should be a button!"></A> Click this button for Pixel Trick!
**

**<A HREF="image_alignment.html"><IMG SRC="resources/button4.gif" HEIGHT="50" WIDTH="50" BORDER="0" ALT="This should be a button!"></A> Click this button for Image Alignment!
**

Save this to your **test_pages** folder as **navigator.html** and open it in your browser. If everything has been coded correctly, it should look like Figure 8.3 (except in living colour!). Click the links and make sure it all works.

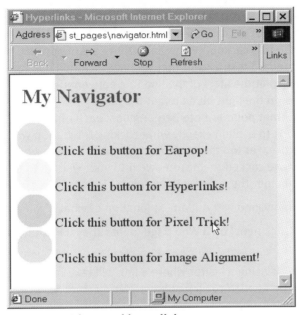

Figure 8.3: Using graphics as links.

The exercise above assumes that you have access to some sort of graphics software. If you do not, see if you can find some ready-made buttons to use instead. You already know how to scan your own hard drive for GIFs. Check a few of those out and see if they could be used as buttons. Try the Web itself. Remember you can right-click on any image you find and save it on your own computer. Store any you can find in your test_pages/resources folder and remember to modify the code above to reflect the names of the buttons you are using. The background strip we created for the exercise looks stylish, but the page works just as well without it. Try a different background image.

You must admit we are beginning to create pages that look as good as those you see on the Web. At the same time, our code is getting a lot more complicated. Always try to analyse code logically, then you will be able to work out exactly what is happening. We'll take just one of the links from the exercise and break it down:

```
<A HREF="earpop_home.html"><IMG SRC="resources/button1.gif"
HEIGHT="50" WIDTH="50" BORDER="0" ALT="This should be a
button!"></A> Click this button for Earpop! <BR>
```

The first section of code **<A HREF="earpop_home.html">** is similar to the code we have used in the previous exercise. The tags **<A> .. </A>** are making the enclosed content active and clickable, while the **HREF** attribute is referencing the relative URL of the page we wish to access. Between these tags we have included not text, but the **<IMG>** element **<IMG SRC="resources/button1.gif" HEIGHT="50" WIDTH= "50" BORDER="0" ALT="This should be a button!">** which we have used with four of its attributes to specify height, width etc. In effect, we have turned the image into a clickable hyperlink. Our text ** Click this button for Earpop!** is standard text, except that we have included the non-breaking space character (** **) at the start of the line to create enough space to move the rest of the text onto the light blue area of the page.

There is one more important point to note here. Against each of our four buttons, we have added text to explain exactly what clicking the button will achieve. This is good practice. Far too many Web sites include buttons whose effect is unclear until after you have clicked them. You owe it to your visitors to tell them what to expect. Try to remember these two golden rules:

- Never include a link of any kind without an explanation of what it will do, and

- Never use the words "click here" on a Web page unless they constitute a working link.

There is another way of advising a visitor where a link will take him. It uses the **TITLE** attribute which can be applied to almost any HTML element. If we modified the code for our first button to read:

```
<A HREF="earpop_home.html"><IMG SRC="resources/button1.gif"
HEIGHT="50" WIDTH="50" BORDER="0" ALT="This should be a but-
ton!" TITLE="Click this button for Earpop!"></A><BR>
```

the explanatory text would disappear from the page, but would reappear as a "tool tip" when the mouse pointer passed over the button. Try it and see.

Creating a graphical user interface (GUI)

You may not have realised it, but you have just created your first GUI (pronounced "gooey") or Graphical User Interface. We will be looking at GUIs in great detail in the second part of this book, but for now let us define the terminology. Every Web site needs some means by which its visitors can move around — its navigation system. In its simplest form, this might mean a home page listing simple text hyperlinks to other pages on the site. Or it could imply a beautifully designed and fully interactive menu bar with animated buttons linking to other pages.

A GUI is defined as the combination of images on a computer screen which allows the user to access programs or functions by means of a mouse or other input device. Windows® presents the best known GUI. It is based on the philosophy that users are more comfortable clicking images such as buttons and icons, than typing instructions into a command line. Try for yourself. Rather than loading **earpop_home.html** into your browser in the normal way, click your **Start** button, click **Run** and type the following into the **Open** box:

lexplore.exe C:\Web Works\test_pages\earpop_home.html

Which method do you prefer?

We said earlier in this chapter that most computer users are now accustomed to working with a graphical rather than a textual interface. If we are designing our Web pages for the comfort of our readers, it makes sense to use an interface that they are used to. Let us try one more. This time we are going to add a navigation bar across the top of Earpop's home page. We are going to use text, but make it look more like a graphic.

Exercise Four

1. Reload **earpop_home.html** into your text editor.

2. Just below the **<BODY>** tag, add in the following code. Make sure that you leave spaces where we have left them.

```
<DIV ALIGN="Center">
<FONT FACE="Verdana" SIZE="2">
| <A HREF="listing.html">Artists</A>
| <A HREF="http://www.earwax_records.com/listings.html">
Earwax</A>
| <A HREF="images/dead_balloons.jpg">DB Photo</A>
| <A HREF="listings.html#dead_balloons"">DB Facts</A>
| <A HREF="ftp://ftp.earpop.ie/orderform.pdf">Order Form</A>
| <A HREF="mailto:info@earpop.ie">Contact</A> |
</FONT>
<HR WIDTH="560" ALIGN="Center" NOSHADE>
</DIV>
```

Save this and open it in your browser. It should look like Figure 8.4.

We have created a simple but highly effective navigation system for Earpop Records' site. Although it is text-based it has all the characteristics of a GUI and visitors should feel comfortable using it. It is simple and intuitive, and, if we duplicate the same interface at the top of each page on the site, visitors will appreciate the consistent look of our pages.

Work through the code we have used. The links are identical to those that appear on the page below, but lined up along the top, they are more compact and easier to follow. We have used the vertical line character to separate our links and drawn a horizontal rule below them to divide the navigation bar from the rest of the page content. We have also used a different font to make them stand out.

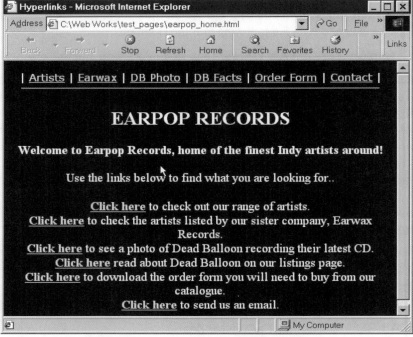

Figure 8.4: A text-based navigation bar for Earpop Records

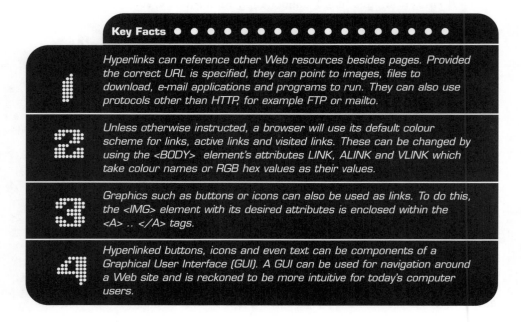

Key Facts

1 *Hyperlinks can reference other Web resources besides pages. Provided the correct URL is specified, they can point to images, files to download, e-mail applications and programs to run. They can also use protocols other than HTTP, for example FTP or mailto.*

2 *Unless otherwise instructed, a browser will use its default colour scheme for links, active links and visited links. These can be changed by using the <BODY> element's attributes LINK, ALINK and VLINK which take colour names or RGB hex values as their values.*

3 *Graphics such as buttons or icons can also be used as links. To do this, the <IMG> element with its desired attributes is enclosed within the <A> .. </A> tags.*

4 *Hyperlinked buttons, icons and even text can be components of a Graphical User Interface (GUI). A GUI can be used for navigation around a Web site and is reckoned to be more intuitive for today's computer users.*

The table below lists all the HTML tags we have used in this chapter:

Opening Tag	Closing Tag	Attributes	Description
<A>	</A>		These tags enclose active content — the text or graphic to be used as a hyperlink.
		HREF="..."	This attribute takes as its value the relative or absolute URL of the Web page or other resource which the hyperlink is to connect to.
<BODY>	</BODY>		New attributes:
		LINK="..."	This attribute specifies the colour in which text hyperlinks are to appear. It takes a value which is either the RGB hex value of a colour or its name.
		ALINK="..."	This attribute specifies the colour in which text hyperlinks are to appear when a mouse pointer rolls over them. It takes a value which is either the RGB hex value of a colour or its name.
		VLINK="..."	This attribute specifies the colour in which visited text hyperlinks are to appear. It takes a value which is either the RGB hex value of a colour or its name.

QUICK REVISION QUESTIONS

1. What is a hyperlink? How does it differ from hypertext?

2. Why does the code which creates a hyperlink always require an absolute or relative URL as the value of its **HREF** attribute?

3. What does FQDN stand for and what are its component parts?

4. How might the FQDN for a site registered outside the US differ from one registered inside the US?

5. What is a Web site's IP address and how is it referenced from the site's written (symbolic) address?

6. What does TCP/IP stand for and what does it do?

7. How would you vary the default colours that a browser uses for the various states of the hyperlinks it is displaying?

8. What is the **<A>** element and what is it used for?

9. What is the main advantage of using graphics such as buttons and icons as hyperlinks?

10. What does GUI stand for and how does it relate to effective Web design?

Chapter 9
Advanced hyperlinks

Brief contents:

1. Creating thumbnail images.

2. How to set up a thumbnail gallery so that visitors can preview your graphics.

3. Using low resolution versions of large graphic files.

4. How to assemble a site navigation system out of button graphics.

5. The concept of client-side imagemaps.

6. How to define active hotspots within an imagemap.

Advanced hyperlinks

In the previous chapter we covered all the essential information you need to create and manage hyperlinks. This is something of a bonus chapter. We will be looking at some of the more complex uses of hyperlinks and how to professionally integrate links into your Web pages. It would be a mistake to attempt this chapter unless you are completely confident in the skills and techniques covered in Chapter 8. If you hesitate at this point, we advise you to go back over that chapter first.

You will have noticed as you worked your way through this book, that we have continually emphasised the importance of design. Web authoring, as we pointed out at the start of the book, involves two distinct skills. You need to be both mechanic and artist. However efficient you are at writing good HTML code, you will never create good Web pages unless you look at them as a designer. A top quality Web site is both a storehouse of useful data and a work of art.

We would also like to introduce a new idea at this point. There is a very valuable rule of thumb which can be applied to all aspects of Web page design. **KISS** reminds you to Keep It Short and Simple (or, as some prefer, Keep It Simple, Stupid!). Since we are now starting to look at more elaborate layouts, we would like you to keep this principle in mind. The best solution to something is very often the simplest solution. We will return to this point later.

We are going to start this chapter by picking up an idea we left dangling in Chapter 8 – the idea of thumbnailing image galleries. We are then going to look in more detail at site navigation, and consider more stylish ways of getting our visitors around our pages. Finally, we are going to look at imagemaps. Let's begin with thumbnails.

Thumbnails

When we considered graphics for the Web back in Chapter 7, we noted the problems with downloading large image files. We also accepted that sometimes there were reasons for including heavyweight graphics on a Web site. An artist's site might include samples of work, a motor racing site might feature photographs of racing cars -– these, and many more, might need a way of storing and downloading large graphic files. It has been suggested that the average Web user grows frustrated if a page takes more than 15 seconds to load. Particularly over a slower modem, 15 seconds would not allow much in the way of page content. There is always the temptation to ignore the visitor and simply insert any images you fancy into your pages, but there is a much better way.

As we noted in Chapter 7, most Web browsers will display an image file just as easily as an HTML file. Look at the two scraps of code below:

```
<IMG SRC="resources/bigfatphoto.jpg">
<A HREF="resources/bigfatphoto.jpg">Look at my photo!</A>
```

Both of these scraps will enable a reader to view the photo, but the first, if inserted into a Web page, will force the image to download and display in the browser. The second, on the other hand, will create a link to that photo, but leave it stored on the server unless the reader chooses to click the link and download the image.

Of course the problem with the second piece of code is that the reader has no way of knowing what **bigfatphoto.jpg** looks like and little incentive to find out. This is where we can use the technique known as thumbnailing. A thumbnail is just a name for a tiny, often low quality, version of an image that is used as a link to the full sized version. Figure 9.1 offers three versions of a thumbnail compared to the original and gives the file size of each. The first two options create identical file sizes, but still cut the download time to one-seventh the download time of the original. The third thumbnail has a very much reduced colour depth and produces a file size of just 539 bytes – one-hundredth the size of the original, but now the quality is suffering. A thumbnail's job is to advertise its big brother. It is necessary to balance file size against the thumbnail's ability to persuade the visitor to click the link.

Thumbnail: 	Full sized image: 
Image reduced to 30% original size. File size = 8KB 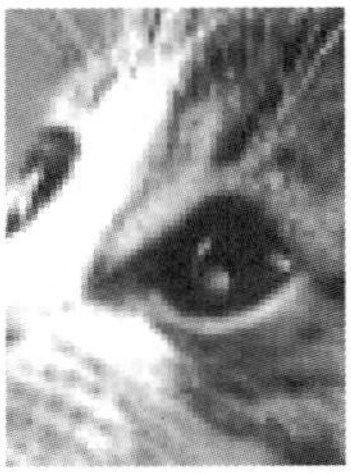	
30% cropped from original to show most appealing detail. File size = 8KB 	
30% original with colour depth reduced to 1-bit. File size = 539 bytes	Original Photographic image. File size = 58KB

Figure 9.1: Thumbnailing images.

To link a thumbnail to its full-sized version, we use the same code we used in the previous chapter. The following exercise provides an example. (Note that in this exercise, we are doing something we have already stated to be a bad idea. We are using HTML code to tell the browser to reduce the size of our original images to create the thumbnails. We are doing this purely for simplicity, because we don't know whether you have access to suitable software for creating thumbnails. On a real Web page, this would be pointless, because the thumbnail you would create would have exactly the same file size as the image you are linking it to! Should you wish to use this technique in your own designs, you will have to use a package like Photoshop® or PaintShop Pro®, or even IrfanView® — which is free — to create your thumbnails.)

Exercise One

1. Check that your have four GIF or JPEG images in your **test_pages/resources** folder and make a careful note of their names and extensions. We will call these **picture1.jpg**, **picture2.jpg** etc. You, of course, must substitute the correct file names and types.

2. Open your text editor and either create a new HTML page or open a template. Insert a page title of "Thumbnails". Pick suitable background and text colours and code them into the **<BODY>** tag. Create and format the headline "Welcome to my THUMBNAIL GALLERY".

3. For each of the four graphics type in the following code – remember to modify it for each image:

4. **<A HREF="resources/picture1.jpg"><IMG SRC="resources/picture1.jpg" WIDTH="100" BORDER="3"></A>**

   Save this file to your **test_pages** folder as **thumbnails.html** and open it in your browser. It should look something like Figure 9.2. If you click any of the thumbnails, the original image will load. Try it to make sure it works.

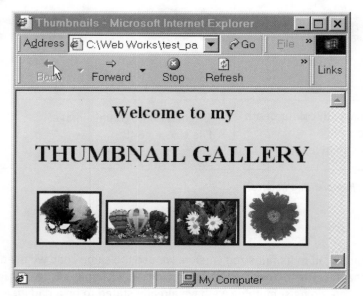

Figure 9.2: A simple thumbnail gallery

If any site you design must include a gallery of images, thumbnailing is certainly the best way of handling things. Remember to keep the images small but representative. (Note that in this page we have not included text to tell the visitor what will happen if he clicks the links. We have also failed to provide a textual alternative for visitors whose browsers can't render images. A perfect thumbnail page would include both of these additions, but we are keeping things simple for this exercise.)

Improving the look of site navigation images

In the previous chapter we created a series of simple buttons and used them in a navigation GUI. Our buttons were just coloured circles and didn't indicate what they linked to. We had to waste page space on text captions explaining what each one did. A far better system would be for each button to incorporate a text label. We would expect a button labelled "Home" to return us to the site's home page, a button labelled "Pictures" to open a picture gallery and so on.

Unfortunately, basic HTML does not include the facility of placing text over images, although more sophisticated Web authoring software such as Macromedia's DreamWeaver® allows you to create text on a separate layer which can overlay an image. On the other hand, most graphics software does allow you to place text on your graphics. Figure 9.3 shows a set of buttons taken from a college Web site.

Figure 9.3: Buttons as hyperlinks

If you are lucky, your graphics software might include a button creation tool. If not, you will find any amount of button clip-art which can be modified to suit your page. You could even draw them, and scan them into your computer. However you do it, you will need a long rectangular button for the next exercise.

Exercise Two

1. Find or create a rectangular button graphic. Using the same graphic for each, create six identical buttons, but label them individually as **"Artists"**, **"EarWax"**, **"DB Photo"**, **"DB Facts"**, **"Order"** and **"Contact"**. Store them in your **test_pages/resources** folder as **artists.gif**, **earwax.gif**, **dbphoto.gif**, **dbfacts.gif**, **order.gif** and **contact.gif**.

2. Open your text editor and reload **earpop_home.html**. Delete all the code between the first pair of **<DIV> .. </DIV>** tags – leave the tags themselves – and replace it with the following code.

   ```
   <A HREF="listing.html"><IMG SRC="resources/artists.gif"
   BORDER="0"></A>

   <A HREF="www.earpop.ie/listing.html"><IMG
   SRC="resources/earwax.gif" BORDER="0"></A>
   ```

```
<A HREF="images/dead_balloons.jpg"><IMG
SRC="resources/dbphoto.gif" BORDER="0"></A>

<A HREF="listing.html#dead_balloons"><IMG
SRC="resources/dbfacts.gif" BORDER="0"></A>

<A HREF="ftp://ftp.earpop.ie/orderform.pdf"><IMG
SRC="resources/order.gif" BORDER="0"></A>

<A HREF="mailto:info@earpop.ie"><IMG SRC="resources/contact.gif"
BORDER="0"></A>
```

Save this file under its original name and open it in your browser. It should look like Figure 9.4 – our version is viewed in the Sun HotJava® browser.

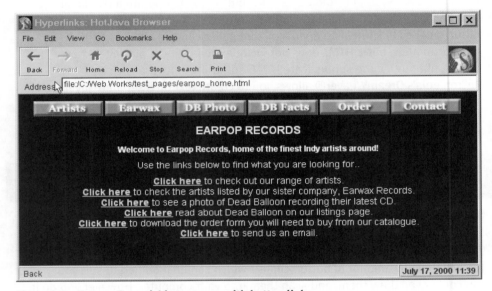

Figure 9.4: Earpop Records' home page with button links.

A series of buttons provides a highly efficient and easily recognised navigation system. Used in the same way on each page, loading times are reduced since once the button graphics have been downloaded for the first page, they are *cached* on the client computer and appear almost instantly when they are used for a further page. Finally, note that we have set the **BORDER** attribute of the button images to "0". If you don't specify this value, the browser will display a border around each of the graphics in the colour you have set your links to – in this case yellow. This would spoil the look of the page.

---

[1] **Cached:** A cache on a computer is a store for temporary data. When an item is cached, it is held, usually in memory but sometimes on the hard drive, for immediate retrieval.

Key Facts ● ● ● ● ● ● ● ● ● ● ● ● ● ● ● ● ● ●

 Thumbnailing refers to a technique where small representations of a graphic are hyperlinked to their full sized originals. A thumbnail gallery is an excellent way of displaying a series of images, since the visitor can click on those thumbnails he or she finds interesting, to download and view the originals in the browser window.

Using small button graphics for site navigation is now common practice. Such buttons should be clearly labelled to avoid any confusion. If the same buttons are used on each page of the site, download times are improved, since the button graphics only need to be downloaded once.

Low resolution images

Although the technique we are discussing in this section is not directly connected with hyperlinks, we are including it here because it relates to graphic file sizes and the idea of thumbnailing. We have suggested that using a thumbnail in place of a full-sized image is often a good idea, but there are circumstances in which it is necessary to include a large, good quality image.

Imagine we were designing a site on the subject of wildlife and needed to include a large image of a pair of seals on one of our pages. We have obtained the photograph. It measures 400 pixels wide and 315 pixels in height, and weighs in at a hefty 78KB. We already know that including this picture will mean a lengthy loading time and that Web users don't like waiting for content. Because our photo is a JPEG rather than a GIF file, we cannot use interlacing, so we need some way of holding our reader's attention while the image loads. From our look at thumbnails earlier in the chapter, we know that there are ways of reducing the file size, but so far these have meant also reducing the size of the graphic, and we want to specify the final image size in our code so that the page formats quickly.

Although the current HTML standard has yet to catch up, the browser manufacturers themselves have provided us with an answer to this problem, by adding a new attribute to the **<IMG>** element. **LOWSRC**, which takes as its value the URL of a second image, allows us to quickly load a low resolution image into the space intended for the high resolution image. It reserves the space on the page, allowing the rest of the page to be formatted around it, then surrenders the space to the final image when it eventually downloads.

 Generally in this book we have avoided using any HTML tags or attributes that are not part of the current standard. However there are one or two exceptions, like LOWSRC, that are so useful that we have included them. We have restricted these to additional code that is supported at least by both the major browsers – Microsoft Internet Explorer® and Netscape®.

Let us see how this works in practice. The following scrap of code:

```
<IMG SRC="resources/highresseal.jpg"
LOWSRC="resources/lowresseal.jpg" HEIGHT="315" WIDTH="400"
ALT="Photograph of a pair of seals.">
```

provides all the alternatives we need. If the browser does not display photographs, the **ALT** text is displayed. If it does, the graphic **lowresseal.jpg** is loaded and replaced after download by the graphic **highresseal.jpg**. Note that it is important that both of these graphics are exactly the same size as specified by the **HEIGHT** and **WIDTH** attributes. Figure 9.5 shows each image loaded into a browser. The file size for **lowresseal.jpg** is just 19KB and will load four times as fast as its big brother. (The browser used is NeoPlanet®.)

Figure 9.5: Low and high resolution versions of the same image

Imagemaps

While we are going to discuss imagemaps as the last item in this chapter, we will be looking at them in much more detail in Part 2 of this book. Imagemaps are now very popular on the Web. They allow you to include an image in your page, then define areas of that image as clickable hyperlinks, or hotspots. As we mentioned earlier, inserting the same imagemap into every page means that download time is saved and navigation becomes much easier for the visitor.

Look back to Figure 9.4. We inserted a series of button graphics and defined each one as a hyperlink. Think how much simpler it would have been if we had included a single graphic showing all the buttons and then defined portions of that image as separate links. An imagemap can be any graphic. A picture of a gorilla could be an image map with its head linking to one page, its arms to another and so on. The problem is that without dragging the mouse pointer across the image to see which areas are active and where the links point to, there is no intuitive way of navigating from such an image.

Clearly, for an imagemap to be effective, it should be designed so that the hotspots are obvious and one way of doing this is to include button graphics in the image. Staying with our old friends at Earpop Records, an imagemap in this format is shown as Figure 9.6. Note that while we have reused our original buttons, the graphic now includes the company logo, a border and a background.

Figure 9.6: An imagemap for Earpop Records

In HTML there are two kinds of imagemaps. The first kind is called a **server-side imagemap**. Here the actual link information is held on the remote server and this tends to lead to a slower response and download time. We are concentrating on **client-side imagemaps**, where all the relevant information is coded into the Web page. This also gives us much greater control over how the imagemap is formatted.

Coding an imagemap is quite a complicated business, so we will work through an example using the graphic shown in Figure 9.6 above. The first thing we need to do is insert the graphic into our page. To do this, we use the normal **<IMG>** element but with an additional attribute **USEMAP** to tell the browser that we are defining the graphic as an imagemap. The **USEMAP** attribute also requires a name as a value. The name will be used as part of the **<MAP>** element later. The map's name could be anything, but it is usually easiest to use the name of the graphic file. The graphic file used as Figure 9.6 is called **earpop_head.jpg** and it is 600 pixels wide and 131 pixels high, so the first scrap of code we require is:

```
<DIV ALIGN="Center"> <!- -This centres our imagemap on the page.- ->
<IMG SRC="resources/earpop_head.jpg" USEMAP="#earpop_head"
BORDER="0" WIDTH="600" HEIGHT="131">
</DIV>
```

This code inserts the graphic, states that it's an imagemap, sets up its position and dimensions and tells the browser to expect further code listing the details of the hotspots. So far so good, but the complications come now that we have to define the hotspots. HTML provides support for three different shapes as hotspots – **rectangles**, **circles** and **polygons** (which are defined as regular or irregular shapes with as many sides as you like). The diagrams below show an example of each.

How's your mathematics? Each of these shapes is defined by its co-ordinates on a 1-pixel-by-1-pixel grid covering the whole image. The top left-hand corner of the imagemap is defined by the **x,y** co-ordinates **0,0**. **x** co-ordinates are measured across the grid from left to right and **y** co-ordinates are measured down the grid from the top. This is easier to illustrate on a diagram.

If you look at Figure 9.7, it shows part of the **earpop_head.jpg** graphic with a pixel scale along the top and down the left-hand side. Unfortunately a single pixel (remember that pixel means picture element and varies with screen resolution) is a very small unit. Our scale shows gradations every 20 pixels. If we wish to define a rectangular hotspot, we can do so by specifying the co-ordinates of its top left and bottom right corners. We have selected the "Earwax button" as the hotspot we wish to use as a hyperlink, and shown the co-ordinates by which that shape can be defined. Using the scale, we can see that the top left corner of the selected area is defined as 185,182 while the bottom right-hand corner is defined as 330,218.

Since defining the position of two corners is not enough to position a circle or a polygon, each of these is defined in a different way as shown in the following table. In all cases, **x** co-ordinates are measured across from the left and **y** co-ordinates are measured down from the top.

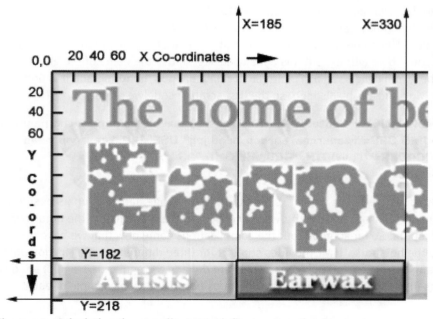

Figure 9.7: Calculating the co-ordinates to define an area of an imagemap

Hotspot Type and Shape:	Format of Co-ordinates:	Explanation:
Rect (Rectangle)	Left-x, top-y, right-x, bottom-y	A rectangle is defined by the x,y co-ordinates of its top left and bottom right corners. Example: COORDS="185,182,330,218"
Circle	Centre-x, Centre-y radius	A circle is defined by the x,y co-ordinates of its centre and the radius in pixels from that centre. Example: COORDS="150,150,20"
Poly (Polygon)	1-x, 1-y, 2-x, . 2-y, 3-x, 3-y etc.	A polygon is defined by listing the x,y co-ordinates of all its corners. Example: COORDS="27,172,156,198,200..."

If we wished only to define the single hotspot identified above, we would then need the following scrap of code:

```
<MAP NAME="earpop_head">
<AREA SHAPE="Rect" COORDS="185,182,330,218"
HREF=http://www.earwax.ie/listing.html  ALT="This is a
rectangle.">
</MAP>
```

In some ways this style of code is similar to that which we use for lists. The **<MAP>** element has opening and closing tags — **<MAP> .. </MAP>** — to identify the start and finish of the list of hotspots. Each hotspot requires its own **<AREA>** element, with the attribute **SHAPE** which takes the value Rect, Circle or Poly. Depending on this value, the **COORDS** attribute takes a sequence of numbers defining the shape's co-ordinates. Finally we use the **HREF** attribute to specify the URL of the resource we are linking to, and the **ALT** attribute to include alternative text. To include further hotspots, you would include further **<AREA>** elements, changing the code as required to suit the shape, co-ordinates and URLs.

When you are defining hotspots that lie very close to, or are even touching each other, you must make sure that the areas you define do not overlap. This can cause a Web browser a whole heap of trouble. There is a lot to be said for designing an imagemap on graph paper before converting it into HTML code.

One final note before we try an exercise on imagemaps. We have mentioned before that some Web users prefer text-only browsers or turn image rendering off. To suit their needs, it is a good idea always to offer an alternative navigation system which does not use imagemaps. The text–based navigation bar we created in Exercise 4 of Chapter 8 would do nicely. Figure 9.8 offers a new design for Earpop's home page. We have included our imagemap, changed the text because we really don't need a third set of hyperlinks, and inserted our text-based navigation bar at the bottom.

Figure 9.8: Earpop's home page with alternative navigation at the bottom.

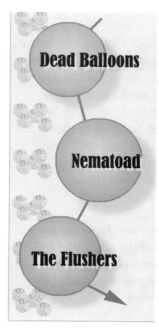

Our final exercise in this Chapter is to create an imagemap for Earpop's artists' page which we have already named **listing.html**. Although we really should use the same imagemap on each page, Earpop has decided that it wants a new look for its artists' page and its designers have come up with the graphic below (Figure 9.9) for us to use as an imagemap.

We can offer you three alternative ways of getting this image into your own computer. If you are an artist, you can draw something similar and scan it into your computer. If you are a digital artist, you can recreate it using whatever graphics software you are happy with. Finally, you can scan it into your computer directly from this page. Whatever you do, you will need a copy of the image stored in your

Figure 9.9: Graphic for Earpop's listings page.

test_pages/resources folder, and it should be called **artistsmap.jpg**. You will also need to measure the graphic in pixels after you have installed it on your own machine, and insert the width in place of "A" and the height in place of "B" in the exercise below.

Exercise Three

1. Create, or load the template for, a new Web page into your text editor.

2. Give the page a title "Earpop Artists", and set the background colour to **#EEEEEE** (this gives a pale grey), the text colour to Navy, the link colour to red and the font to Verdana.

3. Insert the following code into the body section. The first section, marked by the first set of **<DIV .. </DIV>** tags, can be copied from the code you used in **earpop_home.html** and pasted into the new page. This, you will remember, was the code which created our text-based navigation bar. Don't forget to include the correct height and width of your graphic in the relevant **<IMG>** attributes.

```
<DIV ALIGN="Center">
<FONT FACE="Verdana" SIZE="2">
| <A HREF="listing.html">Artists</A>
| <A HREF="http://www.earwax_records.com/listings.html">Earwax</A>
| <A HREF="images/dead_balloons.jpg">DB Photo</A>
| <A HREF="listings.html#dead_balloons">DB Facts</A>
| <A HREF="ftp://ftp.earpop.ie/orderform.pdf">Order Form</A>
| <A HREF="mailto:info@earpop.ie">Contact</A> |
</FONT>
<HR WIDTH="560" ALIGN="Center" NOSHADE>
</DIV>
<DIV ALIGN="Left">
<IMG SRC="resources/artistsmap.jpg" USEMAP="#artists"
BORDER="0" WIDTH="A" HEIGHT="B ">
</DIV>
```

4. Save this file as **listing.html** and check it in your browser. All being well, it should look like Figure 9.10 – we are only showing the top portion of the page.

5. We are now going to create three hotspots to fit the three circles on the image. To do this, we need to find their centres as **x,y** co-ordinates and to measure their radii. We don't need to be terribly accurate as long as our clickable area roughly fits the circles on the page.

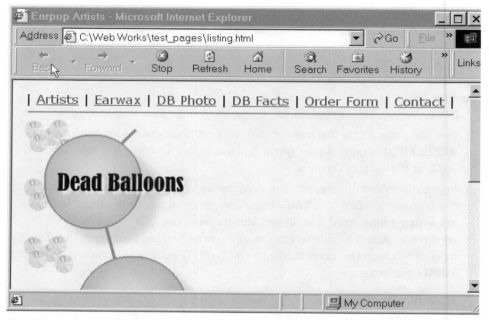

Figure 9.10: Earpop's listing page – top half.

There are several ways of calculating these co-ordinates. If you have a graphics program like Photoshop® or PaintShop Pro®, you can do it by opening the graphic, moving the mouse pointer around the image and reading off the measurements at the bottom of the window. You could make a simple pixel ruler using the graphic itself to estimate the scale. Take a strip of paper and line it up along the long edge of Figure 9.9 as it displays on your screen. You already know its height so calculate your scale from that. A third way would be to use one of the many free programs designed for the purpose — MapThis® is our favourite, although MapEdit® and LiveImage® are just as good.

If none of these methods is viable, you can always estimate. If the size of your graphic is 250 pixels wide by 540 pixels high, as ours is, estimate how far across and down the centre of the first circle comes. For our graphic, we estimate approximately 42% from the left and 23% from the top. 42% of 250 is 112 pixels and 23% of 540 is 124 pixels, so our **x,y** co-ordinates for the centre of the first circle are **112,124**. We also estimate the radius of the circle to be 60 pixels. This means the value of our **COORDS** attribute will be **112,124,60**.

6. Once you have calculated or estimated the values for all three circles, complete the code for the page by adding the following to your existing code within the body section. (We have listed the co-ordinates as **a,b,c d,e,f** etc. but you will substitute your own figures.)

```
<!- - Client-side image map - ->
<MAP NAME=artists>
<AREA SHAPE="Circle" COORDS="a,b,c" HREF="deadballoons.html"
ALT="Circle">
<AREA SHAPE="Circle" COORDS="d,e,f" HREF="nematoad.html"
ALT="Circle">
<AREA SHAPE="Circle" COORDS="g,h,i" HREF="flushers.html"
ALT="Circle">
</MAP>
```

7. Save this again and load or refresh it in your browser. Move your mouse pointer slowly across the graphic, noting where the pointer changes into a moving hand to indicate an active area. How accurate were your calculations? Try modifying your code to make the active areas correspond exactly with the circles.

This has been a long and complex exercise. You will not be surprised to learn that most Web authoring software automates this process for you. In any event, you now know how the process works from the ground up and if you cannot get hold of expensive software, with a little fiddling you can create your own imagemaps.

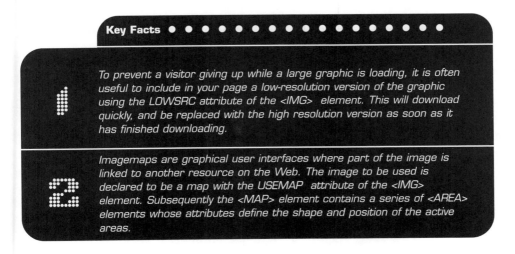

Key Facts ● ● ● ● ● ● ● ● ● ● ● ● ● ● ● ● ● ●

To prevent a visitor giving up while a large graphic is loading, it is often useful to include in your page a low-resolution version of the graphic using the LOWSRC attribute of the <IMG> element. This will download quickly, and be replaced with the high resolution version as soon as it has finished downloading.

Imagemaps are graphical user interfaces where part of the image is linked to another resource on the Web. The image to be used is declared to be a map with the USEMAP attribute of the <IMG> element. Subsequently the <MAP> element contains a series of <AREA> elements whose attributes define the shape and position of the active areas.

The following table lists all the tags that have been used in this chapter.

Opening Tag	Closing Tag	Attributes	Description
<IMG>			New attribute:
		LOWSRC=".."	This attribute takes as its value the URL for a low resolution version of the full-sized image. This version loads quickly and acts as a placeholder.
		USEMAP="#.."	This attribute tells the browser that the graphic it refers to will be used as an imagemap. It takes as its value a unique name (sometimes preceded by the # (hash) symbol to indicate a URL fragment) which will define it to the <MAP> element which follows – see below.
<MAP>	</MAP>		These tags enclose information for a client-side imagemap.
		NAME=".."	This attribute takes as its value the name defined by the USEMAP attribute of the <IMG> element.
<AREA>			This tag is used within the <MAP> .. </MAP> tags to introduce an area which is to be defined as a hyperlink.
		SHAPE=".."	This attribute defines the shape of the area. Valid values are Rect, Circle and Poly.
		COORDS".."	This attribute defines the co-ordinates of the area shape specified by the SHAPE attribute. Valid values depend on the shape being defined. For Rect, the values are the x,y values in pixels of the top left and bottom right corner. For Circle, the values are the x,y value in pixels of the centre of the circle, followed by the radius of the circle

		in pixels. For Poly, the values are the x,y values in pixels of all the corners of the polygon. (See the explanatory table earlier in this chapter.)
	ALT="..."	This attribute takes as its value a text string which is displayed in a browser which does not show graphics.

QUICK REVISION QUESTIONS

1. What are the advantages of using thumbnail images to link to full-sized graphics?

2. If you are using a graphical navigation system, why is it a good idea to use it in the same way on each page of your Web site?

3. What is a low-resolution graphic and how could it be used?

4. What would be the benefit to the visitor to your site of the proper use of low-resolution graphics?

5. What is an imagemap and why is it more efficient than, say, a series of buttons for site navigation?

6. What is the difference between a server-side imagemap and a client-side imagemap?

7. What attribute would you use within the **<IMG>** element to instruct the browser that the graphic in question is to be defined as an imagemap?

8. What element would you use to set up the imagemap?

9. What are the three shapes that can be defined within the **<AREA>** element as active areas? How would you define their positions within the graphic that holds them?

10. Why is it important to offer an alternative means of navigation as well as a graphical one?

Chapter 10
Tables and Frames

Brief contents:

1. Understanding the workings of HTML tables.

2. How to lay out tabulated information on a Web page.

3. How tables can be used in page layouts.

4. How to use a table as a component of effective
   Web page design.

5. How to use a table to create multi-column page layouts.

6. Understanding the concept of framed pages.

7. How to create a simple frameset.

Tables and Frames

Tables are probably the single most useful feature of HTML. If their original purpose was to lay out information in columns and rows, Web designers have now taken them much further. Because tables allow you to position text and images within a structured framework, they are now widely used to create multi-columned page layouts like the pages of a newspaper. We have noted several times in this book that there are difficulties in making text align as we wish it to. Tables allow us to specify an exact grid on a page and force the text to conform to our design. Many of the best sites on the Web are laid out using tables.

Frames, on the other hand, bring mixed blessings. A framing document, known as a frameset, divides the browser window into a series of smaller frames, each of which can display a different Web page. Hyperlinks in one frame can change the contents of another frame. A common use for this is to divide the browser window into two frames – a thin vertical frame on one side of the screen to hold a navigation bar and a wide frame to display the Web pages as they are called. The navigation bar stays on screen all the time, while the contents of the second frame change as links are clicked. Figure 10.1 shows an example of this type of framed layout.

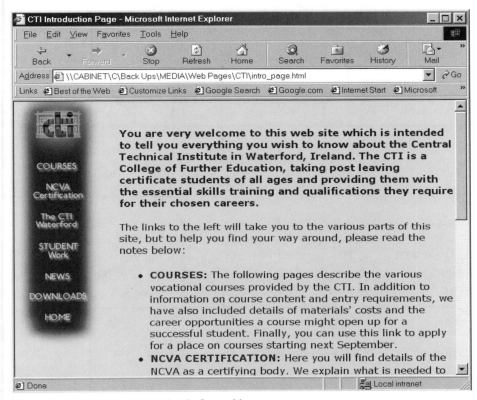

Figure 10.1: Web page using a simple framed layout.

Frames were originally introduced for the Netscape® 2 browser and subsequently became part of the HTML standard. Web authors everywhere grabbed at the idea and frameset-based sites sprang up right across the Web. Unfortunately in many cases they were badly designed and often confused visitors. Many people complained that frames couldn't be printed, that pages became impossible to *bookmark*[1], that the browser's **Back** button wouldn't work properly, and perhaps worst of all, that you could become trapped inside a frameset and unable to move on to a new URL. To a certain extent, frames fell into disrepute, which is a shame because a properly designed and managed frame-based site can be highly effective. Frames can also handle some clever tricks and we will look at one or two of those in the following chapter.

---

[1] **Bookmark:** Most web browsers provide the facility to take a note of a particular page so that you can call it up from a menu without needing to enter the URL. Terminology varies. Internet Explorer® refers to these pages as "favorites", Netscape prefers "bookmarks", and that is the term that is most commonly used.

Tables

As we explained in the introduction, tables have two distinct functions on a Web page. The first, and most obvious, one is to tabulate information. The tag tables at the end of most chapters in this book illustrate this function. Their second use is to format text and images into rows and columns, thus allowing a much greater control over page formatting.

Simple tables set up a matrix of rows and columns then insert data into individual cells. This terminology is important as the elements we are going to use can be quite confusing. Look at the table below:

This is a row		
This is a cell		
	This is a cell	
		This is a column

Tables are set up using the **<TABLE>** element which requires a **</TABLE>** tag to close the section. Within these two tags, any number of table rows can be set up using the **<TR> .. </TR>** tags. Within these again, the number of columns is defined by the number of data cells set up using the **<TD> .. </TD>** tags. All of which can be very confusing and is best explained in a table!

Code:	Explanation:	Result:
<TABLE>	Instructs the browser to set up a table.	
<TR>	Sets up the first row.	
<TD>One</TD>	Inserts "One" into the first cell of the first row.	One
<TD>Two</TD>	Inserts "Two" into the second cell of the first row.	Two
</TR>	Turns off the first row.	
<TR>	Sets up the second row.	
<TD>Three</TD>	Inserts "Three" into the first cell of the second row.	Three
<TD>Four</TD>	Inserts "Four" into the second cell of the second row.	Four
</TR>	Turns off the second row.	
</TABLE>	Turns off the table.	

The **<TABLE>** element also allows us to set the border width for the table using the attribute **BORDER** which takes a value in pixels. Setting this to 0 creates a borderless table which is the feature we shall be using later for text layouts. The **<TD> .. </TD>** tags in the first row can be replaced by **<TH> .. </TH>** tags to create column headings. These appear in bold and are centred in the cell. If we include the **<CAPTION> .. </CAPTION>** tags immediately ofter the opening **<TABLE>** tag, we can give our table a caption which will span the width of the table.

Let's put all this into practice by creating a table for Earpop records that lists the various CDs their artists have produced.

Exercise One

1. In your text editor create a new HTML page or open a template. Set the background colour to black, the text to white and the links to yellow. The following code creates the text-based navigation bar we have been using for Earpop's pages. Type it in or copy and paste it from a previous page:

```
<DIV ALIGN="Center">
<FONT FACE="Verdana" SIZE="2">
 | <A HREF="listing.html">Artists</A>
 | <A HREF="http://www.earwax_records.com/listings.html">
   Earwax</A>
 | <A HREF="images/dead_balloons.jpg">DB Photo</A>
 | <A HREF="listings.html#dead_balloons">DB Facts</A>
 | <A HREF="ftp://ftp.earpop.ie/orderform.pdf">Order Form</A>
 | <A HREF="mailto:info@earpop.ie">Contact</A> |
</FONT>
<HR WIDTH="560" ALIGN="Center" NOSHADE>
</DIV>
```

2. At this point you might save the page as **earpop_template.html**. We will be using this basic layout again so it will save time in the future.

3. Now add in the following code (we don't need to remind you that it goes in the Body section):

```
<P>
<TABLE BORDER="2" ALIGN="Center" CELLPADDING="5">
<CAPTION><H3>Earpop's current artists and
recordings.</H3></CAPTION>
<TR>
<TH>Artist</TH>
<TH>Recordings</TH>
<TH>Order Number</TH>
```

```
</TR>
<TR>
<TD>Dead Balloons</TD>
<TD>I am a genius<BR>Lipposuction</TD>
<TD>EPW356<BR>EPW765</TD>
</TR>
<TR>
<TD>Nematoad</TD>
<TD>All the young frogs</TD>
<TD>EPW549</TD
</TR>
<TR>
< TD>The Flushers</TD>
<TD>Flush me away<BR>Raincheck</TD>
<TD>EPW316<BR>EPW732</TD>
</TR>
</TABLE>
```

4. Save this file to your **test_pages** folder as **earpop_recordings.html** and open it in your browser. It should look like Figure 10.2.

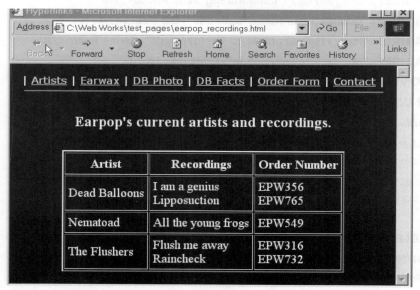

Figure 10.2: Earpop's recordings formatted as a simple table.

The actual mechanics of the table are simple enough. If you check the code against the resulting page, it is easy to see how the table contents have been generated. We have included two additional attributes in the **<TABLE>** element to improve the layout. As before, we have used the **ALIGN** attribute to centre the table. We have also included the **CELLPADDING** attribute with a value of 5. This sets a space in pixels between the cell borders and the cell content. Without it, some tables can look very cramped.

If you think about the code we have used to create this table, you will realise that it can only create a table with the same number of cells in each row. Dead Balloons and The Flushers have both issued two recordings, but we have had to stuff them into the same cell to balance up the table. Ideally they should have a cell each – as should their order numbers, but we would still require a single cell for the name of the band and this would need to span the combined height of both the boxes in the next column.

HTML provides us with a way of doing this using the **ROWSPAN** and **COLSPAN** attributes of the **<TD>** element. **ROWSPAN** allows us to stretch a cell down a series of rows while **COLSPAN** allows us to stretch a cell across a series of columns. Look at Figure 10.3. and compare it with the table in Figure 10.2. In Figure 10.3, the total number of columns used is three, while the total number of rows used is seven, but in the first column there are only five rows. Two cells in that column, the ones containing the words "Dead Balloons" and "The Flushers", are stretched over two rows. Look at the top row: the cell which contains the words "Earpop's current artists and recordings" is stretched across all three columns.

Earpop's current artists and recordings.		
Artist	**Recordings**	**Order Number**
Dead Balloons	I am a genius	EPW356
	Lipposuction	EPW765
Nematoad	All the young frogs	EPW549
The Flushers	Flush me away	EPW316
	Raincheck	EPW732

Figure 10.3: Recordings table using spanned cells.

The code scrap:

```
<TD COLSPAN="3"><H3>Earpop's current artists and
recordings.</H3></TD>
```

stretches the top cell across all three columns. When using **COLSPAN** or **ROWSPAN** elements, it is very important to "add up" the number of cells in each column or row to ensure they match the total number in the table. If, as in this table, there is a total of seven rows, the addition would look like this:

\<TD\>	**Earpop's current artists..**	**1 +**	
\<TH\>	**Artists**	**1 +**	
\<TD\>	**Dead Balloons**	**2 +**	**(ROWSPAN="2")**
\<TD\>	**Nematoad**	**1 +**	
\<TD\>	**The Flushers**	**2**	**(ROWSPAN="2")**
	TOTAL	**7**	

To see how this table would be set up in HTML, work through the following exercise.

Exercise Two

1. Reopen the **earpop_recordings.html** file in your text editor and modify the code as follows:

```
<P>
<TABLE BORDER="2" ALIGN="Center" CELLPADDING="5">
<TR>
  <TD COLSPAN="3"><H3>Earpop's current artists and
      recordings.</H3></TD>
</TR>
<TR>
  <TH>Artist</TH>
  <TH>Recordings</TH>
  <TH>Order Number</TH>
</TR>
<TR>
  <TD ROWSPAN="2">Dead Balloons</TD>
      <TD>I am a genius</TD>
  <TD>EPW356</TD>
</TR>
<TR>
  <TD>Lipposuction</TD>
  <TD>EPW765</TD>
</TR>
<TR>
  <TD>Nematoad</TD>
  <TD>All the young frogs</TD>
  <TD>EPW549</TD
</TR>
<TR>
  <TD ROWSPAN="2">The Flushers</TD>
  <TD>Flush me away</TD>
  <TD>EPW316</TD>
</TR>
<TR>
  <TD>Raincheck</TD>
```

```
<TD>EPW732</TD>
</TR>
</TABLE>
```

(Note: Be extremely careful when making these changes. Some of them are difficult to spot so work through the code line by line comparing old with new.)

Save this over your old file and open it or refresh it in your browser. If everything has worked as it should, the new table will look like Figure 10.3.

Look carefully at what we have done. The caption for the table is now included in the table itself. We have used the code **<TD COLSPAN="3">** to stretch it across three columns. Both Dead Balloons and The Flushers have a double height cell using the code **<TD ROWSPAN="2">**. Compare this with the previous table and you will agree that our second effort looks much more professional.

Key Facts ● ● ● ● ● ● ● ● ● ● ● ● ● ● ● ● ● ● ●

Tables and Frames are HTML elements which provide Web authors with useful tools for creating interesting page layouts. Frames, however, can cause serious problems if they are badly coded and have therefore fallen out of favour.

Tables are created using the <TABLE> .. </TABLE> tags. Nested within these, a series of <TR> .. </TR> tags enclose a single row, and within these again, a series of <TD> .. </TD> tags enclose actual cell content. The table's appearance can also be modified using additional attributes such as ALIGN and CELLPADDING.

Where it is desirable to stretch a cell across several columns or down beside several rows, the <TD> element can take the COLSPAN or ROWSPAN attributes which take as their values the number of columns or rows to span over.

Here is a neat little trick you can use to create coloured lines for your pages. Create a table that contains just one cell, setting the table WIDTH and HEIGHT attributes to the dimensions of the line you require. Remember to set CELLPADDING and BORDER to zero. Create a single pixel GIF file of the colour you require and insert it into the cell. Use the image's HEIGHT and WIDTH attributes to match those of the table, and there you are.

Remember that table content is not restricted to text. Images can also be included as can multimedia elements. One improvement we might have considered for our Earpop recording artists table would be to turn all the album titles into hyperlinks which connected to individual album pages.

Using tables to lay out Web pages

We know from our previous attempts to lay out text that it is often difficult to specify exactly how text will behave. The problem is made worse, because different browsers are inclined to render text in slightly different ways. To a large extent, this problem can be overcome by using tables to control the placement of text. This comes at a price, however. By laying out our text in a table, we complicate the code considerably and complicated code often leads to errors.

Let us begin with a simple exercise to see how a multi-column layout can be created.

Exercise Three

1. Create a new HTML page or open your basic (not Earpop) template. Within the Body section, insert the following code:

   ```
   <DIV ALIGN="Center">
   <H2>A simple layout using a table</H2></DIV>
   <TABLE ALIGN="Center" BORDER="0" WIDTH="650"
      CELLPADDING="10">
   <TR>
   <TD> We know from our previous attempts to lay out text that it is
   often difficult to specify exactly how text will behave. The problem is
   made worse, because different browsers are inclined to render text in
   slightly different ways. To a large extent, this problem can be
   overcome by using tables to control the placement of text. This comes
   at a price, however. By laying out our text in a table, we complicate
   the code considerably and complicated code often leads to errors.
   </TD>
   <TD>We know from ... leads to errors.</TD>
   <TD>We know from ... leads to errors.</TD>
   </TR>
   </TABLE>
   ```

   (Note: The same paragraph is enclosed in each set of **<TD> .. </TD>** tags. We suggest you just type it once and **copy/paste** it into the second and third cells.

2. Save this to your **test_pages** folder as **tablelayouts1.html** and look at it in your browser. This code has created a very simple three-column layout with a page heading. Let's make some changes to see what effects we can achieve. Remember, after making each change below to save the file and refresh it in your browser.

3. Change each of the three **<TD>** elements so that they read respectively:

   ```
   <TD WIDTH="150">
   <TD WIDTH="350">
   <TD WIDTH="150">
   ```

4. So, we can change the width of the columns to suit our design, but notice that the middle column has dropped the text to centre it in the cell. We normally want our text to start at the top of a column, so add a new attribute to each of the three **<TD>** elements – **VALIGN="Top"**. Save the file and look again. The text is now correctly positioned at the top of the column. (It is often a good idea to include this attribute when using a table to lay out text.)

5. Remove the **WIDTH** attributes from all three **<TD>** elements and replace all the text in the second **<TD>** element with one of your images. (As usual, we will refer to this as **picture1.jpg**, but you will insert the correct name and extension.) Use the following code:

<IMG SRC="resources/picture1.jpg">

6. We now have a layout which includes both text and a graphic. Finally add the **ALIGN** attribute to the first **<TD>** element, setting its value to right. Save the file once more and refresh it in your browser. You will see that the text in both outer columns is now aligned down the sides of the graphic.

This exercise has included most of the elements and attributes we can use to lay out our text, but applying them to a page layout is sometimes quite tricky. It is usually a good idea to start from a paper sketch showing the various page elements in position. We'll work through an example to show what we mean. Let's assume we have been commissioned to design a Web site for a company called **John Phelan Power Tools**. If you want to follow it using your own computer, you will need to find suitable graphics to fit. We will start by drawing up a rough plan of how we hope our final page might look.

	This cell will contain our main heading – a graphic logo for John Phelan Power Tools	
This cell will contain text hyperlinks to our four main product areas illustrated opposite.*	This cell will contain text – information about JPPT, company history, current products etc.	This cell will contain an image of an air compressor.
		This cell will contain an image of a rotary sander.
	This cell will contain a price list and ordering information on our four main products.	This cell will contain an image of a belt sander.
		This cell will contain an image of a cordless drill.

*Note: we will be using a two-tone vertical colour strip as our background image.

Now that we have our rough plan, we need to calculate some sizes. The images we will be using are 150 pixels wide so this gives us the width of our right-hand column. We will allow a width of 140 pixels for the left-hand column. This will give us enough space for our textual hyperlinks. We want the whole table to fit easily into a browser window on the lowest resolution monitor our visitors are likely to be using. Let's assume that would be 640 pixels. To give ourselves a slight margin, we will set our overall table width at 600 pixels, and taking away the widths of our outer columns, this sets our centre column at 310 pixels. Height is not important since our table will stretch to fit the contents.

Looking at our layout, we can see that we will need to use several **ROWSPAN** and **COLSPAN** attributes. We will need a total of five **<TR>** table row elements, and a maximum of three **<TD>** table cell elements. Now we can proceed to write the code required to create our layout. Read carefully through the following, we have used the comment tag **<!- - .. - ->** to include notes to explain some parts of the code:

<HTML>
<HEAD>
<TITLE>John Phelan Power Tools</TITLE>
</HEAD>
<BODY BACKGROUND="resources/phelanbackground.jpg" LINK="Yellow">
    <!- -phelanbackground.jpg is our 2-colour background strip. The left-hand colour is grey, so we have set the links colour to yellow to provide a good contrast.- ->
<TABLE WIDTH="600" ALIGN="LEFT" BORDER="0" CELLPADDING="0">
    <!- -We have used the table element to set up an overall table width of 600 pixels.- ->
<TR>
  <TD WIDTH="140"> </TD>
    <!- -This is the first cell in the first row. By setting its width to 140 pixels, we ensure that the whole of the left-hand column is 140 pixels wide. The cell itself is empty, but we have included the ** ** non-breaking space character. This prevents the cell from "collapsing".- ->
  <TD COLSPAN="2"><IMG SRC="resources/phelanheader.jpg">
    <!- -This is the second cell in the first row in which we place our logo graphic **phelanheader.jpg**. We want this to span across the second and third columns, so **COLSPAN** is set to 2.- ->
</TR>
<TR>
  <TD ROWSPAN="4" ALIGN="Center" VALIGN="Top">
    <!- -This is the first cell in the second row in which we want to place our navigation links. We have set **ROWSPAN** to 4 (check the plan above) so that the cell's height spans all the other rows in the table. We have also centred the links and aligned them to the top of the cell.- ->
  <FONT COLOR="Yellow"><B>SITE INDEX</B><P>

```
<!- -We need a heading for our navigation links, and since we have already
set our link colour to yellow, we use the <FONT> element to set the same
colour for the heading.- ->
<A HREF="compressors.html">Compressors</A><P>
<A HREF="rotarysanders.html">Rotary<BR>Sanders</A><P>
<A HREF="beltsanders.html">Belt<BR>Sanders</A><P>
<A HREF="cordlessdrills.html">Cordless<BR>Drills</A><P>
</TD>
</TR>
<TR>
<TD ROWSPAN="2" WIDTH="310" VALIGN="Top">John Phelan Power
Tools offers the very best quality equipment at the very best prices.
Since our company was founded in 1992, we have formed trading links
with manufacturers in Europe and the Far East to source the best
equipment money can buy<P>
The results of our labours are now available to builders here in Ireland.
When you buy a John Phelan power tool, you know you are getting the
finest equipment in the world.<HR>
<!- -This is the second cell in the second row. If you check the plan again you
will notice that it needs to span two cells in the third column, thus ROWSPAN
is set to 2. Again, we have used the WIDTH attribute to set the width of the
column.- ->
</TD>
<TD WIDTH="150"><IMG SRC="resources/compressor.jpg"></TD>
<!- -This is the third cell in the second row and contains the first of our four
images. Again, we have used the WIDTH attribute to set the width of the
column.- ->
</TR>
<TR>
    <TD><IMG SRC="resources/rotarysander.jpg"></TD>
</TR>
<TR>
<TD ROWSPAN="2" VALIGN="Top"><B>Check out some of our
prices:</B>
    <UL>
        <LI>Compressors from just £159 plus VAT
        <LI>Rotary Sanders from just £39 plus VAT
        <LI>Belt Sanders from just £29 plus VAT
        <LI>Cordless Drills from just £59 plus VAT
    </UL>
<!- -To create our price list, we have used the <UL> unordered list element. Lists
– or even other tables – can be nested within tables.- ->
For full details, click the links in the left-hand column</TD>
<TD WIDTH="150"><IMG SRC="resources/beltsander.jpg"></TD>
</TR>
```

```
<TR>
   <TD><IMG SRC="resources/cordlessdrill.jpg"></TD>
</TR>
</TABLE>
</BODY>
```

This is undoubtedly a complicated piece of code, but it still follows a logical pattern. By working through it carefully, you will understand how each line fits into the overall scheme. A slightly cropped version of the page it produces is shown below as Figure 10.4. Check this against the code to see how each element works.

We strongly suggest that you try a similar table layout using your own graphics and text. You will need to find suitable images, then crop them to size. Use the code provided above, but modify it where necessary. Using a table to lay out a Web page is one of the core skills for any Web author.

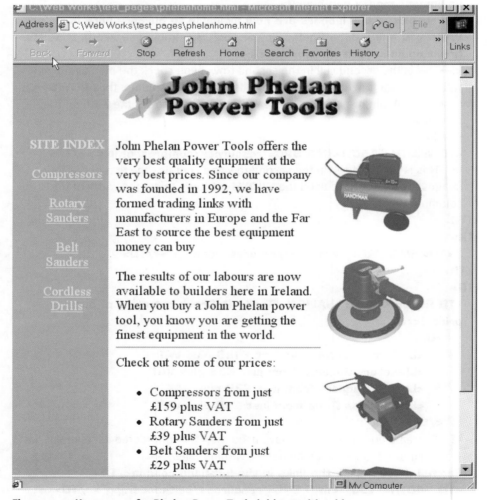

Figure 10.4: Home page for Phelan Power Tools laid out with tables.

Vital

Information

Laying out pages with tables is one of the most complicated parts of Web authoring. A single element out of place and the whole table is thrown out. Unless your table is a very simple one, always draw up a plan first and use it when writing your code.

Finally, remember that tables can be nested – in other words tables can contain other tables. If you use a table to lay out your page, you can easily include a further table to tabulate information or even to create a secondary layout. Simply create a second table within any cell of the first table. The nested table is one of the most useful tools in the Web author's toolbox, and provides for very fine control of content placement.

Frames and framesets

We are going to conclude this chapter by introducing the concept of frames. While the next chapter looks in detail at more complex frame layouts, we are starting the subject here because frames provide many of the same layout possibilities that tables do. They allow us to format our pages with precision, to control the actual placement of page content and to separate different components and manage them individually. But while tables provide us with a definable grid into which we can insert page content, frames permit us to actually subdivide the browser window into a series of physical windows, each of which can display different pages.

A frame is defined as an "independent scrolling region, or window, of a Web page". Frames can have borders, in which case they appear more like a table on screen, or they can be borderless. In Figure 10.4 above we used a borderless table to create the impression that our content has been formatted on the page. Borderless frames give the same impression, with the added bonus that part of the page can be changed while leaving the rest of it static.

To create a framed page, we need to generate a separate document called a frameset. Although the URL for a framed page is its frameset, the frameset itself does not physically appear in the browser window. Instead it is merely a set of instructions to the browser on how to display the frames themselves. Let us assume that we wish to create a simple framed page containing two independent frames. We want a thin frame across the top of the browser window which will contain a navigation bar, and a second frame taking up the rest of the window which will display the pages we call up from the navigation bar. We now need three documents:

The frameset which defines the layout of the whole page.

The page which contains the navigation bar.

The page which will appear in the rest of the browser window.

If this sounds complicated, it will become easier to understand if we work through an exercise to set up a new framed home page for our old friends at Earpop.

Exercise Four

1. The first thing we will do is to create the frameset itself. Create a new HTML page or open a basic template. Give it the title "Earpop's Been Framed!"

2. Framesets do not require the **<BODY> .. </BODY>** tags, so if your template includes these, delete them. In their place, type in the following code:

   <FRAMESET ROWS="75,*" BORDER="0">

   <FRAME SRC="earpop_navigation.html" NAME="top">

   <FRAME SRC="earpop_home.html" NAME="bottom">

   <NOFRAMES><BODY>To view this page you need a browser which supports frames.</BODY></NOFRAMES>

   </FRAMESET>

3. Save this to your **test_pages** folder as **earpop_frames.html**. We will explain what this all means later. Next we need to create our navigation frame. We will use the same text-based system as before. Open **earpop_template.html** in your text editor. You need to change the code slightly as follows:

   <DIV ALIGN="Center">

   <FONT FACE="Verdana" SIZE="2">

   | <A HREF="listing.html" TARGET="bottom">Artists</A>

   | <A HREF="http://www.earwax_records.com/listings.html" TARGET="bottom">Earwax</A>

   | <A HREF="images/dead_balloons.jpg" TARGET="bottom">DB Photo</A>

   | <A HREF="listings.html#dead_balloons" TARGET="bottom">DB Facts</A>

   | <A HREF="ftp://ftp.earpop.com/orderform.pdf" TARGET="bottom">Order Form</A>

   | <A HREF="mailto:info@earpop.com" TARGET="bottom">Contact</A>

   | <A HREF="earpop_home.html" TARGET="bottom">Home</A> |

   <HR WIDTH="620" ALIGN="Center" NOSHADE>

   </DIV>

4. Save this modified file as **earpop_navigation.html** and open **earpop_frames.html** in your browser. It should look like Figure 10.5.

On the face of it, this looks like the page we created before, but it behaves in a very different way. Click the "Artists" link and the artists page opens in the bottom of the window, leaving the navigation bar untouched. Click the "Home" link and the original page reopens. (Apart from the Contact link, the other links won't work – yet!)

Let's look back through the code to see exactly what we have done. Firstly we created our frameset. We used the **ROWS** attribute of the **<FRAMESET>** element

Figure 10.5: Earpop's home page using frames.

to create two horizontal frames. The height of the first frame we specified as 75 pixels. The asterisk (*****) after the comma tells the browser that the second frame should fill the rest of the page. We could have specified the height by coding **ROWS="75,500"**, or created a third horizontal frame, for example **ROWS="75,250,*"**. If we had wanted to create two vertical frames, we would have used the COLS attribute instead, only this time **COLS="75,*"** would have specified the width rather than the height of the frame. We also set the **BORDER** attribute to 0, to make sure that there was no visible border between the two frames.

We then defined the frames themselves with the code scrap:

<FRAME SRC="earpop_navigation.html" NAME="top">

<FRAME SRC="earpop_home.html" NAME="bottom">

This code defined two frames (one for each of the **ROWS** set up earlier). We instructed the browser that when it first opened the frames page, we required the top frame to load **earpop_navigation.html** and the bottom frame to load **earpop_home.html**. Since the contents of either frame might change, we also named the two frames **top** and **bottom** in case we needed to refer to them at a later stage.

<NOFRAMES><P>To view this page you need a browser which supports frames.</NOFRAMES>

Finally we used the **<NOFRAMES>** element to display a text string which would appear in a browser which could not display frames . There are still some around, so it is a good idea always to include a **<NOFRAMES>** element. In the next chapter we will look at a better way to use this element.

To create our **earpop_navigation.html** page, we needed to modify the code we used previously to create our navigation bar. Normally, when you click a hyperlink, the new page replaces the old page in the browser window. In this case we wanted the pages we called for to load in the bottom frame. We had already named this frame as **bottom** in our frameset page, so we added an extra attribute to the **<A>** element. **TARGET** allows us to specify in which frame the new page is to display, so we set its value to **bottom**. Finally, we added one further link to our navigation bar to return us to our original framed page.

Like tables, frames need to be set up with great care. For example, the height of the top frame in our frameset had to be just large enough to display our navigation bar, but not so large as to leave too much space between it and the page content in the bottom frame. We will look at some more advanced uses for frames in the next chapter.

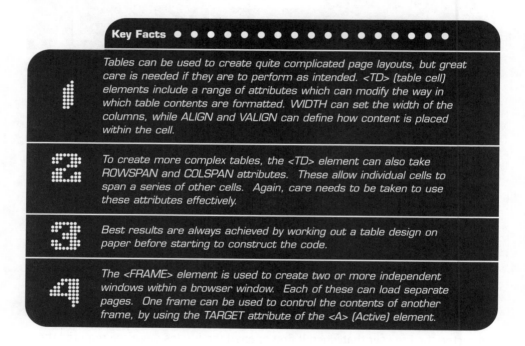

Key Facts

1 Tables can be used to create quite complicated page layouts, but great care is needed if they are to perform as intended. <TD> (table cell) elements include a range of attributes which can modify the way in which table contents are formatted. WIDTH can set the width of the columns, while ALIGN and VALIGN can define how content is placed within the cell.

2 To create more complex tables, the <TD> element can also take ROWSPAN and COLSPAN attributes. These allow individual cells to span a series of other cells. Again, care needs to be taken to use these attributes effectively.

3 Best results are always achieved by working out a table design on paper before starting to construct the code.

4 The <FRAME> element is used to create two or more independent windows within a browser window. Each of these can load separate pages. One frame can be used to control the contents of another frame, by using the TARGET attribute of the <A> (Active) element.

The following table includes all the tags we have used in this chapter.

Opening Tag	Closing Tag	Attributes	Description
<TABLE>	</TABLE>		These tags enclose an HTML table.
		BORDER=".."	This attribute sets the width of the borders in the table. Values are a number of pixels.
		ALIGN=".."	This attribute positions the table on the page. Valid values are: Left, Right and Center.
		CELLPADDING= ".."	This attribute specifies how much space should be left between the border and the cell contents. Valid values are: a number of pixels.
		WIDTH=".."	This attribute specifies the overall width of the table. Valid values are: a number of pixels.
<CAPTION>	</CAPTION>		These tags should follow the opening <TABLE> tag. They enclose a string of text which is centred across or below the top of the table in bold.
<TR>	</TR>		These tags define a table row. They must enclose the <TD> tags below for content to appear in the table row.
<TD>	</TD>		These tags enclose the actual content of a table cell.
		ROWSPAN=".."	This attribute specifies how many rows the cell should span down.
		COLSPAN=".."	This attribute specifies how many columns the cell should span across.

		VALIGN="..."	This attribute specifies how the cell content is aligned vertically. Valid values are: Baseline, Bottom, Middle and Top.
<TH>	</TH>		As <TD> above. These tags operate in the same way as the <TD> .. </TD> tags above, but are used to insert headings into a table. These format the enclosed text in bold and centre it in the cell.
<FRAMESET>	</FRAMESET>		These tags replace the <BODY> .. </BODY> tags in a document and declare it to be a frameset – a page used to define how frames are displayed in a web browser.
		ROWS="..."	This attribute specifies the number and height of horizontal frames to be displayed. Valid values are a series of numbers of pixels separated by commas, each number denoting one frame. An asterisk (*) is used to specify the remaining height of the browser window.
		COLS="..."	This attribute specifies the number and width of vertical frames to be displayed. Valid values are a series of numbers of pixels separated by commas, each number denoting one frame. An asterisk (*) is used to specify the remaining width of the browser window.
		BORDER="..."	This attribute sets the width of the border dividing the individual frames. Values are a number of pixels.

<FRAME>			This tag specifies a frame within a frameset document.
		SRC=".."	This attribute specifies the URL of the document that is initially loaded into the frame.
		NAME=".."	This attribute specifies a name for the frame so that it can be targeted by hyperlinks.
<NO FRAME>	</NOFRAME>		These tags enclose content which is displayed by a browser which cannot render frames.
<A>	</A>		New attribute:
		TARGET=".."	This attribute specifies the name of a frame to be targeted by the hyperlink. Valid values are any names which have previously been specified by the frameset document.

 QUICK REVISION QUESTIONS

1. In HTML, what were tables originally designed to do, and how do Web authors make use of them as design tools?

2. What were the problems with using framed pages that turned many Web users against them?

3. Table terminology can be confusing. What functions do the **<TR>**, **<TH>** and **<TD>** elements perform?

4. Within the **<TABLE>** element, the attributes **BORDER** and **CELLPADDING** can be used to control the way a table is displayed. What does each of these attributes do?

5. How are the **ROWSPAN** and **COLSPAN** attributes of the **<TD>** element used to improve the appearance of tabulated content?

6. What are the benefits of laying out a tabulated page design on paper before attempting to create the HTML code?

7. What is the function of a frameset document?

8. If you wished to create three horizontal frames on a page, specifying the height of the first and third as 200 pixels, what code would you insert into the **\<FRAMESET\>** element?

9. What is the **\<NOFRAMES\>** element used for?

10. How would you ensure that a linked document opens in a particular frame?

Chapter 11
Advanced frame layouts

Brief contents:

1. How to create nested framesets.

2. How frames can be used to create complex page layouts.

3. Controlling the way in which frames are displayed in a Web browser.

4. Targeting hyperlinks to display pages in special ways.

5. How to provide alternative pages for visitors whose browsers don't render frames.

6. How to create and use floating frames.

Advanced frame layouts

In Chapter 10, we introduced the concept of framed documents and worked through a simple example. In this chapter we will extend our use of frames to more complicated page layouts and look at one or two neat little effects we can achieve by using frames.

We noted in Chapter 10 that the use of frames has fallen out of favour and we gave a few reasons for this. We'll start this chapter by adding one more possible disadvantage. It is easy to get so carried away by the possibilities that frames offer, that you clutter up your page with so many little windows, that the main frame — the one used to display the key information — becomes too small to be effective. (We have done this deliberately later in the chapter!) Remember also that in a framed layout, each individual page has to download and this can dramatically affect the time it takes for the page to display.

Add these to the other problems we mentioned, and you might start to feel that the disadvantages of using frames outweigh the possible benefits. We don't accept this. We feel that, properly used, frames can add new dimensions to a Web site. Remember that framed pages can be as complex as tables. Here again there are great benefits from planning the design on paper before starting to code it.

Nested framesets

In our first exercise on frames, we discovered how to divide a page into a series of vertical or horizontal frames, but what if we want to do both? We can create a grid of frames — similar to the grids we were laying out as tables in the previous chapter, by first creating a series of vertical frames, and then sub-dividing them into horizontal frames. The following exercise shows you how to do this.

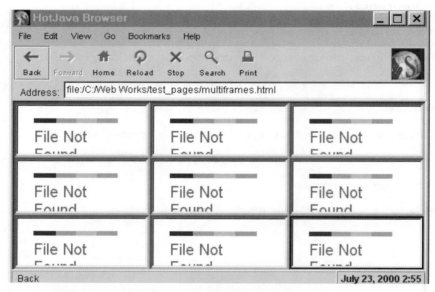

Figure 11.1: Multiple frames displayed in Sun's HotJava Browser

Exercise One

1. Create a new HTML page or open a blank template in your text editor.

2. Remove the **<BODY> .. </BODY>** tags, replacing them with the following code:

```
<FRAMESET COLS="33%,34%,33%">
   <FRAMESET ROWS="33%,34%,33%">
      <FRAME SRC="frame1.hmtl" SCROLLING="No">
      <FRAME SRC="frame2.hmtl" SCROLLING="No">
      <FRAME SRC="frame3.hmtl" SCROLLING="No">
   </FRAMESET>
<FRAMESET ROWS="33%,34%,33%">
      <FRAME SRC="frame4.hmtl" SCROLLING="No">
```

```
    <FRAME SRC="frame5.hmtl" SCROLLING="No">
    <FRAME SRC="frame6.hmtl" SCROLLING="No">
  </FRAMESET>
<FRAMESET ROWS="33%,34%,33%">
    <FRAME SRC="frame7.hmtl" SCROLLING="No">
    <FRAME SRC="frame8.hmtl" SCROLLING="No">
    <FRAME SRC="frame9.hmtl" SCROLLING="No">
  </FRAMESET>
</FRAMESET>
```

Save this file to your **test_pages** folder as **multiframes.html** and look at it in your browser. It should look like Figure 11.1.

Of course your frames are filled with some kind of "File not found" message because the files we specified in the code (**frame1.html, frame2.html** etc.) don't actually exist. We are only interested in the frame layout itself. We have created a 3 x 3 grid of frames by setting up the **COLS** attribute with a value of **33%,34%,33%,** then divided those into three new horizontal frames using the **ROWS="33%,34%,33%"**. Note that we have used percentages of the total browser window here, rather than definite sizes in pixels. This is often useful if you need to specify proportional rather than exact sizes. This means that the frames will remain of equal proportions regardless of the size of the browser window.

For an interesting use of this kind of frameset, look at Figure 11.2.

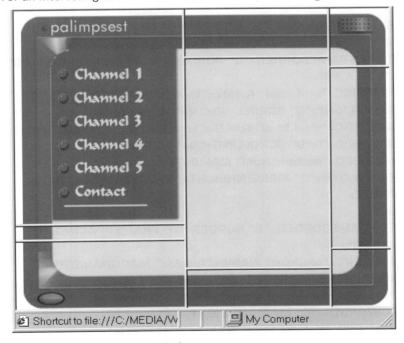

Figure 11.2: Creative use of multiple frames

Figure 11.2 uses 9 frames in a 3 x 3 grid to create the impression of a television screen. We have reduced the size to fit this page. All four corner frames contain a graphic. The frames are sized to fit the graphic and cannot be resized by the visitor. The four frames between the corners are slightly different. They contain only a background image which tiles to fit the size of the browser window. Figure 11.3 shows the background image used to fill the second frame down on the left-hand side. (We have drawn a box around it so that it stands out from the page.)

Figure 11.3: Tile used to create TV frame

Because the side frames use a background image which tiles to fill the frame, it doesn't matter what size the browser window is changed to, the television itself will always be rendered perfectly. The middle frame at start-up uses a simple grey tile. This frame is the target of the hyperlinks shown as channels in the top left-hand frame. Clicking a channel button puts a new image on the telly!

To show how it works, in Figure 11.2 we have added borders to the individual frames. In use, these would be removed to show a perfectly rendered television screen. The code which creates this framed document is given below, followed by Figure 11.4 which shows the final document as it would appear on the Web.

```
<HTML>
<HEAD>
  <TITLE>Television</TITLE>
</HEAD>
<FRAMESET FRAMEBORDER="0" BORDER="0" FRAMESPACING="0"
COLS="212,*,75">
    <FRAMESET FRAMEBORDER="0" BORDER="0" FRAMESPACING="0"
    ROWS="275,*,88">
        <FRAME SRC="topl.html" NAME="Topleft" MARGINWIDTH="0"
        MARGINHEIGHT="0" SCROLLING="No" NORESIZE>
        <FRAME SRC="sidel.html" NAME="Leftside" MARGINWIDTH="0"
        MARGINHEIGHT="0" SCROLLING="No" NORESIZE>
        <FRAME SRC="bottoml.html" NAME="Bottomleft"
        MARGINWIDTH="0" MARGINHEIGHT="0" SCROLLING="NO"
        NORESIZE>
</FRAMESET>
<FRAMESET FRAMEBORDER="0" BORDER="0" FRAMESPACING="0"
ROWS="62,*,50">
        <FRAME SRC="top.html" NAME="Topside" MARGINWIDTH="0"
        MARGINHEIGHT="0" SCROLLING="No" NORESIZE>
        <FRAME SRC="greymiddle.html" NAME="Centre"
        MARGINWIDTH="0" MARGINHEIGHT="0">
        <FRAME SRC="bottom.html" NAME="Bottomside"
        MARGINWIDTH="0" MARGINHEIGHT="0" SCROLLING="No"
```

```
        NORESIZE>
</FRAMESET>
<FRAMESET FRAMEBORDER="0" BORDER="0" FRAMESPACING="0"
ROWS="75,*,75">
        <FRAME SRC="topr.html" NAME="Topright" MARGINWIDTH="0"
        MARGINHEIGHT="0" SCROLLING="No" NORESIZE>
        <FRAME SRC="sider.html" NAME="Rightside" MARGINWIDTH="0"
        MARGINHEIGHT="0" SCROLLING="No" NORESIZE>
        <FRAME SRC="bottomr.html" NAME="Bottomright"
        MARGINWIDTH="0" MARGINHEIGHT="0" SCROLLING="No"
        NORESIZE>
</FRAMESET>
<NOFRAMES>
<BODY>
Viewing this page requires a browser capable of displaying frames.
</BODY>
</NOFRAMES>
</FRAMESET>
</HTML>
```

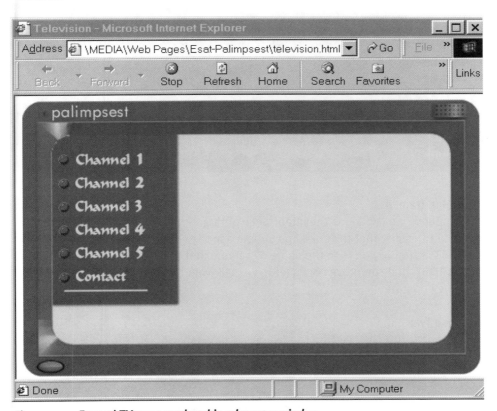

Figure 11.4: Framed TV page rendered in a browser window.

You will notice one or two new attributes included in the code for this page. In addition to the **BORDER** attribute which we used in the previous chapter, we have also included the **FRAMEBORDER** attribute which renders a 3-D border around the frames. These two attributes duplicate each other to a certain extent, but by including both we ensure that most browsers will understand what we want. We have also turned off the **FRAMESPACING** attribute which sets the amount of space between the frames – clearly we want them to fit tightly together.

Within the **<FRAME>** element, we have set the attributes **MARGINHEIGHT** and **MARGINWIDTH** to **0. MARGINHEIGHT** sets the space between a frame's content and its top and bottom borders in pixels, while **MARGINWIDTH** does the same for the left and right borders. Since all our graphics are designed to fill their frames exactly, we don't want any space around them. **SCROLLING="No"** turns off the scroll bars which would otherwise appear automatically if the browser window was sized to render the frames smaller than their contents require, but note that we have left SCROLLING turned on for the centre frame in case the content we load there is longer than the screen size can fit in. Finally, we have used the **NORESIZE** attribute which fixes the size of each frame.

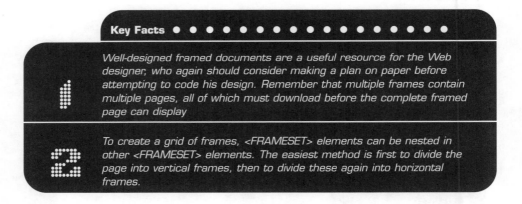

Key Facts

1. Well-designed framed documents are a useful resource for the Web designer, who again should consider making a plan on paper before attempting to code his design. Remember that multiple frames contain multiple pages, all of which must download before the complete framed page can display

2. To create a grid of frames, <FRAMESET> elements can be nested in other <FRAMESET> elements. The easiest method is first to divide the page into vertical frames, then to divide these again into horizontal frames.

Targeting frames

In Chapter 10 we explained the importance of targeting frames from within the **<A>** element to ensure that the linked page opens in the correct frame. Normally the **TARGET** attribute points to the name of a frame, but there are some special values for **TARGET** that can prove very useful. We will work through an exercise to see how they operate.

Exercise Two

1. In your text editor, reopen the file called **navigator.html**. You will remember that this generated a simple navigation bar linked to some of the pages you had previously created. Change the code by inserting a new **TARGET** attribute to the **<A>** element as follows:

<H2><FONT COLOR="Red"> My Navigator</FONT></H2>

<A HREF="earpop_home.html" TARGET="_self"><IMG

```
SRC="resources/button1.gif" HEIGHT="50" WIDTH="50" BORDER="0"
ALT="This should be a button!"></A> Click this button for
Earpop! <BR>

<A HREF="hyperlinks.html" TARGET="_top"><IMG
SRC="resources/button2.gif" HEIGHT="50" WIDTH="50" BORDER="0"
ALT="This should be a button!"></A> Click this button for
Hyperlinks! <BR>

<A HREF="pixel_trick.html" TARGET="_blank"><IMG
SRC="resources/button3.gif" HEIGHT="50" WIDTH="50" BORDER="0"
ALT="This should be a button!"></A> Click this button for Pixel
Trick! <BR>

<A HREF="image_alignment.html" TARGET="_parent"><IMG
SRC="resources/button4.gif" HEIGHT="50" WIDTH="50" BORDER="0"
ALT="This should be a button!"></A>Click this button for Image
Alignment! <BR>
```

Save this over the existing file and open it in your browser. Try clicking each of the links to see what difference the **TARGET** value makes.

Depending on how your browser is configured, you may only notice a difference when you click the third link which opens a new window for the Pixel Trick page. Despite appearances, all of these links are now operating in a different way. The **TARGET** value **_self** is the usual default value where the new page replaces the existing page. **_top** is used for "frame busting". We mentioned earlier that one of the complaints about frames is that it was sometimes difficult to escape from them. If you place a link to a remote page in one of your frames, that link will sometimes open in your frame, leaving your visitors unsure whether they are still at your site or have moved on. The value **_top** ensures that any frames are removed when the link is followed. **_blank** can be very useful. As you saw, it opens the new page in another window, leaving the page you linked from open behind it. This is a good way of linking images from a thumbnail gallery. Finally, the **_parent** value, while seldom used, opens the new page in the parent frame without destroying any other frames that the parent might be nested within. (Don't worry if you don't understand this!)

The NOFRAMES element

We touched on the **<NOFRAMES>** element briefly in the previous chapter. We explained that it should be included in a frameset document to provide content for visitors whose browsers do not support frames, or for those who prefer to turn frame support off. While most Web users these days are able to view frames, it is still a good idea to provide an alternative. While it is acceptable to include a scrap of code like:

```
<NOFRAMES>
<BODY>To view this page you need a browser which supports
frames.
```

```
</BODY>
</NOFRAMES>
```

which simply displays the text in the browser window, a much better idea –
although a time-consuming one – is to create an alternative page which does not
require frames and link to it from your frameset. You would then include a scrap of
code such as:

```
<NOFRAMES>
<BODY>If your browser does not support frames <A
HREF="framefreepage.html">CLICK HERE.</A>
</BODY>
</NOFRAMES>
```

The visitor is encouraged to click the link and stay on your site.

Floating Frames

Our final section in this chapter looks at one of those contentious areas where the
major browser manufacturers have decided to take different paths. Microsoft®
introduced the concept of the floating frame and it was subsequently incorporated
into the current HTML standard. Netscape® decided on a different route to the
same end and introduced the **<LAYER>** element which offers similar features. We
are not including a section on this because it is not part of the HTML standard and
is not likely to be included in future standards. We also need to keep in mind that
while Netscape browsers do not properly support floating frames, they do
understand them and render their contents. Internet Explorer® on the other hand
does render them properly, as do the many browsers based on IE technology,
including NeoPlanet®, Polyview® and even *iPanic ®'*.

A floating frame is defined by the **<IFRAME>** element, and, apart from the
name, acts more like a graphic than a frame. It is intended to create an
independent window on a Web page around which text can flow. A floating frame
can be positioned anywhere within the **<BODY>** element and does not require a
frameset document. Most of the attributes you have previously used with the
<IMG> element work identically for the **<IFRAME>** element, but unlike **<IMG>**,
floating frames need to be closed with the **</IFRAME>** tag.

To see how floating frames should be used, let's work through an exercise.

Exercise Three

1. In your text editor, reopen the file called **aligning_text.html**. You will
   remember that this contains three short paragraphs which we tried indenting
   in various ways.

2. Give the page a new title: "Floating Frames", and insert the following code
   before the first word of the first paragraph:

```
<IFRAME NAME="Floater" SRC="ul_list.html" WIDTH="300"
HEIGHT="220" ALIGN="Left">
```

---

[1] **iPanic:** by the way, is a strange little browser designed for people who are surfing the Net when they
shouldn't be! Click the "Panic" button and your browser instantly transforms into a Word document, thus
fooling your boss who is walking past at the time.

If you can read this, then your browser does not support floating frames!

</IFRAME>

3. Save this as **iframes.html** and open it in your browser. It should look like Figure 11.5.

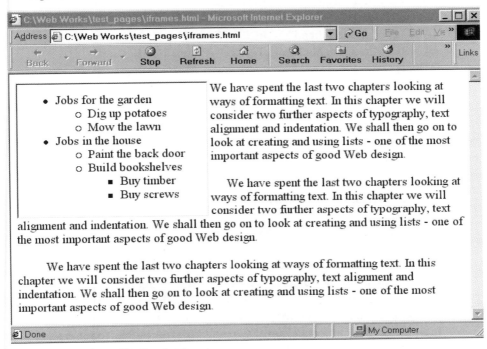

Figure 11.5: Using a floating frame

The code we have used to create this floating frame holds no surprises. We have set the **HEIGHT** and **WIDTH** attributes to match the frame's contents and aligned the text using the **ALIGN** attribute. Note however that the **<IFRAME>** element has a **NAME** attribute and this means that we can target it in the same way that we can target an ordinary frame defined by a frameset.

Floating frames can be used to create some neat effects. Work carefully through the code below to see how a floating frame could be used in a practical application.

```
<HTML>
<HEAD><TITLE>The Flushers</TITLE>
</HEAD>
<BODY BGCOLOR="Black" Text="White" LINK="Yellow"
VLINK="White">
<IFRAME NAME="Float1" SRC="hootyryan.html" WIDTH="300"
HEIGHT="500" ALIGN="Right">
Get a browser that displays floating frames and see what you are
missing!
</IFRAME>
```

```
<DIV ALIGN="Left">
<H2>THE FLUSHERS</H2>
<H3>Check out The Flushers...</H3><BR>
Click on the name of the musician and his details will appear in the
frame to the right! <P>
<A HREF="hootyryan.html" TARGET="Float1"><B>Hooty
Ryan</B><P>
<A HREF="sneezer.html" TARGET="Float1"><B>Sneezer</B><P>
<A HREF="babaoreilly.html" TARGET="Float1"><B>Baba
O'Reilly</B><P>
</DIV>
</BODY>
</HTML>
```

We then need to create a small Web page for each musician. Here is the code for
hootyryan.html:

```
<HTML>
<HEAD><TITLE>The Flushers</TITLE>
</HEAD>
<BODY BGCOLOR="Yellow" Text="Navy">
<IMG SRC="resources/hooty.jpg" ALIGN="Right">
<B>HOOTY RYAN</B><BR>
Plays keyboards, synthesiser, washboard and pedal steel guitar.
Sings background vocals. Born in Tramore, December 1980.
Previous bands: Doctor Mojo, Bullwinkle and The Peddlars of Guilt.
Took up singing at school until warned to stop by his teachers.
Bought his first keyboard at 13 and taught himself to play. Met
Sneezer at college in Tralee and formed The Flushers a year later.
Influences: Brian Eno, Orbital and The Inkspots.
</BODY>
</HTML>
```

Can you follow the code? The first piece of code creates a Web page named
flushers.html with a floating frame that is targeted by the hyperlinks. As the links
are clicked, the relevant musician's details appear in the floating frame. The result
looks like Figure 11.6.

THE FLUSHERS

Check out The Flushers...

Click on the name of the musician and his details will appear in the frame to the right!

Hooty Ryan

Sneezer

Baba O'Reilly

HOOTY RYAN Plays keyboards, synthesiser, washboard and pedal steel guitar. Sings background vocals. Born in Tramore, December 1980. Previous bands: Doctor Mojo, Bullwinkle and The Peddlars of Guilt. Took up singing at school until warned to stop by his teachers. Bought his first keyboard at 13 and taught himself to play. Met Sneezer at college in Tralee and formed The Flushers a year later. Influences: Brian Eno, Orbital and The Inkspots.

Done   My Computer

Figure 11.6: The Flushers' page using a floating frame.

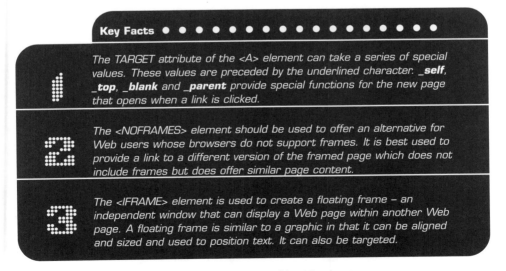

Key Facts ● ● ● ● ● ● ● ● ● ● ● ● ● ● ● ● ● ●

1 *The TARGET attribute of the <A> element can take a series of special values. These values are preceded by the underlined character: **_self**, **_top**, **_blank** and **_parent** provide special functions for the new page that opens when a link is clicked.*

2 *The <NOFRAMES> element should be used to offer an alternative for Web users whose browsers do not support frames. It is best used to provide a link to a different version of the framed page which does not include frames but does offer similar page content.*

3 *The <IFRAME> element is used to create a floating frame – an independent window that can display a Web page within another Web page. A floating frame is similar to a graphic in that it can be aligned and sized and used to position text. It can also be targeted.*

The following table lists all the HTML tags used in this chapter.

Opening Tag	Closing Tag	Attributes	Description
<FRAME>			New attributes:
		SCROLLING=".."	This attribute defines whether scroll bars appear within a frame. The value Yes forces scroll bars, No prevents them from appearing, while Auto lets the browser apply them when content is longer than the window.
		MARGINWIDTH=".."	This attribute sets the space between a frame's content and the left and right borders. Valid values are a number of pixels.
		MARGINHEIGHT=".."	This attribute sets the space between a frame's content and the top and bottom borders. Valid values are a number of pixels.
		NORESIZE=".."	This attribute defines whether or not the user can resize the frame. Valid values are: Yes and No.
<FRAMESET>	</FRAMESET>		New attributes:
		FRAMEBORDER=".."	This attribute defines whether or not the frame should have borders. Valid values are: Yes and No.
		FRAMESPACING=".."	This attribute specifies the space to be left between frames. Valid values are a number of pixels.
<A>	</A>		New values for attribute:
		TARGET=".."	_self: displays the page in the frame containing the hyperlink which opened it. _parent: displays the page in the parent frame.

			_top: displays the page in a full browser window and removes any pre-existing frames. _blank: displays the page in a new window
<IFRAME>	</IFRAME>		These tags create a floating frame – an independent window in a Web page.
		NAME=".."	This attribute specifies a name for the floating frame which can be targeted by a hyperlink.
		SRC=".."	This attribute takes as its value the URL of an HTML page to display when the floating frame is first created.
		WIDTH=".."	This attribute sets the width of the floating frame. Valid values are a number of pixels.
		HEIGHT=".."	This attribute sets the height of the floating frame. Valid values are a number of pixels.
		ALIGN=".."	This attribute defines how the floating frame is aligned within the page. Valid values are: Bottom, Left, Middle, Right and Top.

 QUICK REVISION QUESTIONS

1. A framed page can often take longer to download than one without frames. Why is this?

2. What is meant by the term "nested frameset"? How does a nested frameset differ from a normal frameset?

3. What attribute of the **<FRAME>** element would you use to ensure that the frame did not display scroll bars?

4. The **TARGET** attribute of the **<A>** element can take a series of special values. What are they and what effect do they have on the way a linked page is displayed?

5. How could you use the **<NOFRAMES>** element to direct a visitor to an alternative page which did not make use of frames?

6. What is a floating frame and which element is used to create one?

7. What code would you use to target a floating frame?

REVISION PROJECT: Chapters 7 – 11

For your second major project we would like you to create a suitable Web page (or pages) for the Earpop recording artists Nematoad. Be creative, but remember that this page will form part of the Earpop Web site and must be consistent in style and content with the pages we have already created. The following notes might help with your design.

1. You should definitely start by sketching out your ideas on paper.

2. You will need to source some images for this page. You might try scanning in some photographs from a magazine. Remember to size them to fit your design.

3. You could produce a single page for this project, but why not try your hand at creating a framed page or floating frames as described earlier in this chapter?

4. Why not include a logo for Nematoad? You could design this in a graphics package or create something on paper and scan it into your computer.

Chapter 12
Information about information

Brief contents:

1. The concept of meta-information.

2. Understanding the workings of Web search engines.

3. The contents of document headers.

4. How to define a document's base URL.

5. Understanding the workings of <META> tags.

6. How to redirect a browser to a different page.

7. Creating an internal index for a lengthy Web document.

Information about information

This chapter is about the hidden part of the Web page – the data that never appears in the browser window. Most of this hidden content is information about information, or meta-information in computer-speak. A good example of **meta-information** is the index of a book. The index is not part of the information content of a book, but it is a vital component. It provides the reader with essential data on where to find actual information within the book. It also helps to define the scope of the book, in that readers look up a word to see if the book carries information on that topic.

You might note that we have already used meta-information earlier in the book. Do you remember the comment element, **<!- - .. - ->,** that we used to insert notes to ourselves into complicated code? That was an example of meta-information in its simplest form.

By now you have probably realised that we are going to be talking about the **<HEAD>** element. So far all we have done with this element is to use it for inserting a title into the title bar of the Web browser, but the **<HEAD>** element can be a very useful resource for the Web author. It can carry a lot of information about page content, it can define the style in which the page will be displayed, it can even carry a rating for the page to declare whether the content is suitable for children to view. Most important of all perhaps, it carries the data that search engines use to index the page.

Search engines on the Web

Before examining **<HEAD>** contents in detail, we need to take a detour to look at how users find information on the Web. To put it in simple terms, there are three ways in which a visitor can arrive at a particular page.

1. He or she can find a printed reference to a Web address and enter it into the browser's address box. Most organisations now include the address of their Web site in their literature or in their advertising. Books, magazines and newspapers print Web addresses. People pass them on to their friends or colleagues at work. It is even possible to guess them. If a company is called Redsocks Ltd, it is always worth trying www.redsocks.com or, for an Irish company, www.redsocks.ie.

2. He or she can arrive at a page by clicking a hyperlink. The Web consists of billions of pages all tied together by hyperlinks. Insert a hyperlink into a page and with a single click the resource you have linked to opens in the clicker's browser. You don't even need permission to add someone else's URL to your page. Clickable links appear in other places. E-mails can carry them, software manuals include them and many programs now provide the facility of a direct link to the manufacturer's home site.

3. He or she can use a search engine to look up references on a particular topic, then click a link displayed in the search results.

There are two different types of engine on the Internet. Firstly, there are directory listings such as Yahoo!. Directory listings do not scour the Web looking for pages to catalogue. Instead they index pages which are submitted to them, arranging these into a hierarchical list of sites which can be browsed by category or keywords. Secondly, there are the genuine search engines. These use sophisticated data logging programs, often called spiders, which crawl constantly around the web, following links and cataloguing what they find. The difference need not concern a Web author and both types are usually referred to as search engines.

The major engines, Yahoo, AltaVista, Google, FAST Search etc., index billions of pages. They provide an opportunity for any site – however small – to become accessible to Web users. Webmasters are invited to submit a list of "keywords" which the engines subsequently add to their indices. A page devoted to Formula 1 might generate keywords such as motor racing, Ferrari®, Monte Carlo and Grand Prix.

Unless a Web author can afford to advertise his or her site, getting the site listed on the various search engines is the best way to make sure it is accessible to the public. This can be a very time-consuming business. It is possible to visit each of the search engines in turn and work through their submission procedures, but with so many search engines now covering the Web, it is often better to use one of the many programs which automate the process. Blue Ravine Productions' Page Submit® or the Gnet Page Submission System® are two well known methods of ensuring that a site is widely listed. There are many others, some free for download from the Web. We discuss this further in Chapter 22.

For commercial enterprises, getting a good listing on a search engine is a high priority. A search on a keyword might produce pages and pages of listings and unless a site appears within the first few pages, it is unlikely that the searcher will bother with it. Experts recommend submitting a site in as many different ways as possible, and regularly resubmitting it to reflect any changes in site content.

The <HEAD> element

The **<HEAD>** element can contain a wide range of other elements, some of which we will deal with later in the book. We have already made use of **<TITLE>** to give a page a descriptive title. We now need to look at some of the others and understand why they are useful. The first of these is **<BASE>** which is used to define the original location, or base URL, of the document. At present, all the pages you have created are stored in your **test_pages** folder and any images they reference are stored in your **test_pages/resources** folder. To link to these, you have used a relative URL as in the code scrap:

```
<IMG SRC="resources/picture1.jpg">
```

But what happens if the document that contains this code is moved? The following exercise shows the value of specifying a base URL.

Exercise One

1. At the end of Chapter 2, you created a folder called **Cabinet** in your **Web Works** folder. Find the file called **thumbnails.html** in your **test_pages** folder and drag it into the **Cabinet** folder. Now open it in your browser.

2. You will not be surprised to note that all the images have disappeared. The browser is looking for them in a sub-folder of the **Cabinet** folder called **resources** which does not exist! Leaving **thumbnails.html** where it is, open it in your text editor and add the following code into the Head section:

```
<BASE HREF="file:///C:/Web Works/test_pages/thumbnails.html">
```

3. Save the file and reopen or refresh it in your browser. All the images will be back in place. Clean up by moving **thumbnails.html** back into your **test_pages** folder.

By including the **<BASE>** element you have ensured that any links or linked resources which use relative URLs will always work no matter where on your computer you move the page to. We have specified an absolute URL for the page using the **file:///** protocol. Documents can also be moved on the Web itself. Here your base **URL** might be coded like this:

<BASE HREF="http://www.someserver.net/michaelryan/ home.html">

but as long as the **<BASE>** element is properly defined, relative links will work even if the document is moved to a completely different server.

The Head section might also include the **<SCRIPT>** element and the **<STYLE>** element and we shall return to these later in the book, but most of this chapter is devoted to the **<META>** element and that deserves a section to itself!

The <META> element

The **<META>** element contains meta-information which can be extracted by Web servers and search engines to create indices and perform other search and retrieval functions. It must be placed within the **<HEAD>** element. The **<META>** element can perform a number of functions that we need not be concerned with — for example it can define whether text flows from left to right or from right to left. We are interested in using the element to provide information for search engines and other Web management tools.

The **<META>** tag itself requires two attributes. The first specifies the name of some property of your Web page, for example the author or the date it expires, while the second defines the value of that property, for example David Collins or the 30th December 2001. So a **<META>** tag might look like this:

<META NAME="author" CONTENT="David Collins">

In place of the **NAME** attribute, some **<META>** tags take the **HTTP-EQUIV** attribute which calls on an **HTTP** response such as supplying an email address. In theory, you can specify any value for the **NAME** attribute that you like, so the tag:

<META NAME="favourite Colour" CONTENT="Purple">

is perfectly legal. It is also quite pointless since servers only respond to recognised values for the **NAME** attribute.

We are going to use a series of **<META>** tags in the next exercise to create a new all-purpose template for future exercises.

Exercise Two

1. Use your text editor to create a new HTML page containing the following code. Remember when you use it to insert your own details in place of the italicised content.

```
    <HTML>
<HEAD>
<TITLE>***</TITLE>
```

```
<BASE HREF="file:///C:/Web Works/test_pages/***.html">
<META NAME="creation_date" CONTENT="DDD DD MMM YYYY
    HH:MM:SS GMT">
<!- -In the tag above, time and date should be inserted in the format: Fri
    27 Sep 2001 13:42:15 GMT.- ->
<META NAME="author" CONTENT="Your name">
<META NAME="keywords" CONTENT="*** *** ***">
<META HTTP-EQUIV="reply-to" CONTENT="yourname@your email
    address">
</HEAD>
<BODY>
***
</BODY>
</HTML>
```

Save this as **basic_template.html** in your **test_pages** folder.

If you open this page in your browser, all you will see is three asterisks in the title bar and three asterisks in the browser window. All the remaining content is meta-information. It is stored with the page and can be called on when it is needed. To use the template, replace the asterisks and the date symbols with the relevant information.

The actual meta-information you have included in this template is fairly obvious. You can specify the author of the page and the time and date it was created on — right up to the second. Note in particular the **Keywords** value. These are the words that a search engine would use to index your page. Any number of keywords can be included, separated by commas. If you use this facility when submitting your own pages, be selective in your choice of words and try to think what a searcher might be looking for.

The **<META>** element also provides another useful facility — the ability to redirect a browser to another page. If you move your Web site to a different server, you can leave a redirection page on the old server which will display for a specified time, then automatically load a page from your new site. To see this in action, work through the following exercise.

Exercise Three

1. Open the new basic template in your text editor and modify it as follows:

```
<HTML>
<HEAD>
<TITLE>Redirection</TITLE>
<BASE HREF="file:///C:/Web Works/test_pages/redirect.html">
<META NAME="creation_date" CONTENT="DDD DD MMM YYYY
    HH:MM:SS GMT">
```

```
<!- -In the tag above a date should be inserted in the format:    Fri 27
    Sep 2001 13:42:15 GMT.- ->
<META NAME="author" CONTENT="Your name">
<META NAME="keywords" CONTENT="earpop,indy,music">
<META HTTP-EQUIV="reply-to" CONTENT="yourname@your email
    address">
<META HTTP-EQUIV="REFRESH"
CONTENT="10;URL=earpop_home.html">
</HEAD>
<BODY BGCOLOR="Black" Text="White">
<DIV ALIGN="Center">
<H2>EARPOP has moved!<BR>
In a few seconds, you will be transferred to our new site.</H2>
</DIV>
</BODY>
</HTML>
```

2. Save this as **redirect.html** in your **test_pages** folder and open it in your browser.

The tag:

```
<META HTTP-EQUIV="REFRESH" CONTENT="10;URL=earpop_home.
    html">
```

is responsible for this clever trick. **REFRESH** is an HTTP response header which is handled by the browser. The **CONTENT** value **10**, specifies a 10-second delay, after which the new URL is loaded.

This tag is also useful to display a series of pages one after another. If, for example, you wanted to present a series of graphics in succession, each one could use this **<META>** tag to load the next image. This is called client-pull page loading. You might be able to think up some clever uses for this feature. Remember though to leave enough of a delay to allow the visitor to examine each page comfortably.

Creating an internal index

In general we recommend that Web pages should be kept short. If a page is much longer than a screenful, it is usually a good idea to split the content over several pages and hyperlink each one to the next. However there are occasions when this is not practical. Imagine, for example, that you were creating a Web site on horror films and that one of your pages was a review of all the horror films you had seen. It would seem logical to keep all these reviews on a single page but this might make for an extremely long document. A visitor might need to scroll down a long way to find a particular entry.

One way to solve this problem is to create visible meta-information in the form of a page index. This could be placed at the top of the page and contain hyperlinks to section headings further down the page. After each section, we should also insert a hyperlink back to the top of the page to save our visitor the bother of scrolling back up again.

To see how this might operate, work through the following exercise.

Exercise Four

1. Open the basic template in your text editor and modify the code as follows. (Incidentally, this is the last time we will include the full code for this template. After this, you will need to change the information in the **<HEAD>** element for yourself!) We suggest you type the text paragraph that we use in the exercise once and copy/paste it into the other locations it appears in.

```
<HTML>
<HEAD>
<TITLE>Internal Links</TITLE>
<BASE HREF="file:///C:/Web Works/test_pages/anchors.html">
<META NAME="creation_date"
     CONTENT="DDD DD MMM YYYY HH:MM:SS GMT">
<!- -In the tag above a date should be inserted in the format: Fri 27
     Sep 2001 13:42:15 GMT.- ->
<META NAME="author" CONTENT="Your name">
<META NAME="keywords" CONTENT="internal links, anchors">
<META HTTP-EQUIV="reply-to" CONTENT="yourname@your email
   address">
</HEAD>
<BODY>
<DIV ALIGN="Center">
<FONT FACE="Verdana" SIZE="2">
<A NAME="Top"><B>LIST OF CONTENTS</B></A><BR>
| <A HREF="#1960">1960-69</A>
| <A HREF="#1970">1970-79</A>
| <A HREF="#1980">1980-89</A>
| <A HREF="#1990">1990-99</A> |
<HR WIDTH="380" ALIGN="Center" NOSHADE>
</DIV>
</FONT>
<A NAME="1960"><B>The 1960s</B></A><BR>
This is a paragraph of nonsense whose only purpose is to take up lots
of space on this page. It could include a list of fruit such as rhubarb,
kumquats, watermelons and bananas. It might just use a lot of
meaningless words - squifflebody, for example. Or it could just consist
of clumps of letters slslsl dhdurtehdjj dhjorteons. Whatever you
like.<BR>
<A HREF="#Top"><B>Back to the top</B></A>
<P>
```

```
<A NAME="1970"><B>The 1970s</B></A><BR>
This is a paragraph ... you like.<BR>
<A HREF="#Top"><B>Back to the top</B></A>
<P>
<A NAME="1980"><B>The 1980s</B></A><BR>
This is a paragraph ... you like.<BR>
<A HREF="#Top"><B>Back to the top</B></A>
<P>
<A NAME="1990"><B>The 1990s</B></A><BR>
This is a paragraph ... you like.<BR>
<A HREF="#Top"><B>Back to the top</B></A>
</BODY>
</HTML></BODY>
</HTML>
```

2. Save this as **anchors.html** in your **test_pages** folder and open it in your browser. The top section of your page should look like Figure 12.1.

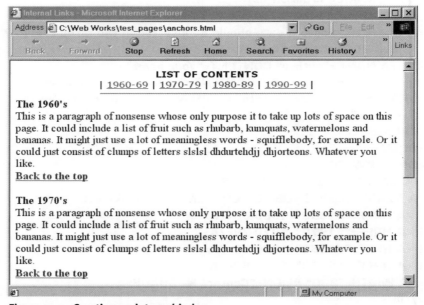

Figure 12.1: Creating an internal index.

To see how this works, reduce the size of your browser window so only the top few lines of the page are visible. Now click the **1980–89** link and the page automatically scrolls to that section. Click the **Back to the top** link and you scroll back up to the List of Contents. This is obviously an artificial use for the technique since our page is fairly short to begin with, but similar code applied to a long document would make navigation a breeze. And simplifying navigation is one of the keys to good Web design.

Look at the code we have used to create this page. We are already familiar with the **<A>** Anchor element, but here we have used it in a slightly different way. Instead of the **HREF** attribute pointing to the URL of a different page, we have pointed it to an anchor on the same page. The code scrap:

<A HREF="#1970">1970-79</A>

gives the **HREF** attribute a value which is a valid relative URL. It says, in effect, jump to an anchor named "1970". Later in the document we define that anchor by naming it with the code scrap:

**<A NAME="1970"><B>The 1970s</B></A>
**

using a further attribute of the **<A>** element, **NAME**.

This style of linking can also be used between pages. Code like:

<A HREF="anotherpage.html#1970">1970-79</A>

is equally valid, provided, of course, that the anchor is named on the new page.

Finally in this chapter, we strongly recommend date stamping all your pages. This is not strictly meta-information but it fits in with the general theme of this chapter. A line at the bottom of each pages which says:

This page was revised on the 13th August 2001.

not only reminds you when you last updated the page, but also tells your visitors that your site is continually being revised.

Key Facts ● ● ● ● ● ● ● ● ● ● ● ● ● ● ● ● ● ● ●

1 Meta-information is information about information. It covers data which does not appear in the browser but is used by authors, servers, search engines and others to comment on, provide access to or index the page which contains it.

2 Search engines are specialised servers on the Web which catalogue and categorise Web pages to produce a searchable database of Web content. Pages can be submitted to a search engine for inclusion in its database. Search engines also "trawl" the Web, following hyperlinks and cataloguing what they find.

3 Most meta-information is contained within the <HEAD> element. The <BASE> element defines the original location for a document, which is useful in case the document is subsequently moved elsewhere. The <META> element lists information which can be used by search engines and Web servers to index the page's content. It can also be used to redirect a browser to another document.

4 The Anchor element <A> can be used to create an internal index for long documents. Links in the index can reference anchors later in the document and move the reader directly to a particular section.

The following table lists all the tags used in this chapter.

Opening Tag	Closing Tag	Attributes	Description
<BASE>			This tag must appear within the <HEAD> element. It defines the original location of the document.
		HREF="..."	This attribute takes as its value the base URL of the document.
<META>			This tag must appear within the <HEAD> element. A series of <META> tags can be included to specify data for search engines or Web servers. Each instance of the tag should include either the NAME or the HTTP-EQUIV attribute, followed by the CONTENT attribute.
		NAME="..."	This attribute associates a name with the meta-information referenced in the CONTENT attribute. Any NAME is valid, but only certain values will be recognised by Web servers.
		HTTP-EQUIV="..."	This attribute "binds" the meta-information in the CONTENT attribute to an HTTP response header. Valid values include REFRESH and Reply-to.
		CONTENT="..."	This attribute contains the actual meta-information
<A>	</A>		New attribute:
		NAME="..."	This attribute names an anchor which can be referenced by the HREF attribute. Valid values are: any text string.

QUICK REVISION QUESTIONS

1. What is meta-information?

2. How is meta-information used by search engines?

3. What is a base URL and why is it important to define it in a Web page?

4. The **<META>** element is used to include meta-information. What code would you use to specify the author of a particular document?

5. Why might you use the **REFRESH** value of the **<META>** element's **HTTP-EQUIV** attribute?

6. What advantage is there in creating an internal index for a Web page?

7. To work properly, an internal index relies on two attributes of the **<A>** element. What are they and how do they connect?

Chapter 13
Multimedia content

Brief contents:

1. The basics of multimedia for the Web.

2. How plug-in applications work with Web browsers to handle multimedia content.

3. The different approaches to multimedia content taken by the browser manufacturers.

4. The different file formats in which audio and video content is available.

5. Understanding the download-and-play approach.

6. How to link Web pages to multimedia files.

7. How to embed multimedia content in Web pages.

8. The difficulties of downloading multimedia files.

Multimedia content

Multimedia is an awkward word. Traditionally, a medium is a means of transferring information, thus the mass media are media which communicate with large numbers of people. The Web is primarily a text-based medium. HTML, in fact, is only capable of directly handling text. All other contents, including simple images, are "pulled in", or included by referencing their URLs. We refer to these contents as binary objects. If we include a binary object such as a video file within a Web document, we add an additional medium. Include a sound file, and we add a third medium. The combination of these media adds up to a multimedia experience, and multimedia is very much the direction in which the Web is going.

You will remember our concerns earlier in the book with limited bandwidth. Downloading fat files such as video objects takes a lot of bandwidth, and current connections over a standard modem are not fast enough to pull-in contents at the speeds required to play them in real time. Newer technologies such as ISDN (Integrated Services Digital Network), ADSL (Asymmetric Digital Subscriber Line) and cable modems offer much greater bandwidth and make real-time playback more of a possibility. The Web is getting faster and as connection speeds increase, they should make true multimedia content viable. Watch this space...

In the early days of the Web, browsers were only able to handle static text and all other content was linked to and managed by helper applications in separate windows. Netscape® pioneered the use of "plug-ins", additional programs which can manage different binary object formats. Figure 13.1 shows the Flash player plug-in, for example. Today's browsers use a wide range of plug-ins which effectively integrate objects into Web pages. Objects such as Flash® files and QuickTime® movies appear to play in the page itself because the plug-ins that handle them operate seamlessly within the browser environment. The table on the following page lists some of the most widely used plug-ins.

Figure 13.1: The Flash plug-in handling a Flash SWF movie file.

The plug-in approach to handling objects comes at a price. Each plug-in has to be installed separately and demands a chunk of RAM to operate. A computer running ten common plug-ins may require as much as an additional 20MB of memory. This hunger for memory means that using plug-ins is often referred to as a "fat-client" approach; the client computer is loaded up with additional software and runs more slowly as a result. An additional problem is that some plug-ins are not available for all computer platforms, so users running Windows 3x, MacOS or UNIX may find themselves unable to view certain objects.

Once a plug-in is installed, adding support for the binary object it handles is simply a matter of including the **<EMBED>** element in the HTML code. To run a RealMedia® video file in a pre-installed Real Player, for example, you might use a code scrap like:

<EMBED SRC="resources/hello.rm" HEIGHT="200" WIDTH="200">

Microsoft® came at the binary objects problem from a different direction, developing what they called ActiveX technology to insert binary objects into Web pages. ActiveX controls are small binary files which are downloaded to a user's system and subsequently accessed from within the Web page itself. Using ActiveX controls requires the **<OBJECT>** element, and the syntax for this is far more complex than that required by the embedding approach.

Faced with these (and other) competing approaches, the Web author might well despair of getting his multimedia content to work! But don't give up; in this chapter we will look at some of the commonest types of multimedia content and explore some of the ways we can include them in our Web pages. And remember there is always the last resort solution; load whatever content you like and let your visitor's browser try to cope with it! We will talk more about this later in the chapter.

Plug-in or helper application:	Details:
Windows MediaPlayer	Supplied as part of the Windows 9x OS, MediaPlayer can integrate with Internet Explorer and Netscape browsers to handle audio and video content such as WAV and AVI files.
WinAmp*	WinAmp is a recent application developed by Nullsoft Inc. Running under Windows, it can operate in any browser environment. WinAmp handles most audio files and is particularly effective with MP3 high quality audio files.
Netscape LiveAudio	The LiveAudio plug-in was included with all versions of the Netscape browser after Netscape 3. It supports AU, AIFF, WAV and MIDI files.
Netscape LiveVideo	Like LiveAudio, LiveVideo is a Netscape plug-in supplied with the browser to support AVI files in Windows.
Apple QuickTime	Apple QuickTime is a cross-browser plug-in which can handle a wide variety of multimedia formats including sound, video, MIDI and even plain text. Developed for the MacOS, Windows users are obliged to install it as an OS service component.

Adobe Acrobat	Not strictly multimedia, the Adobe Acrobat plug-in allows users to view Web documents published in the PDF format.
RealAudio	RealAudio was developed by Real Networks to stream audio from a special server. Content can be handled by the RealAudio or Shockwave plug-ins or Microsoft ActiveX controls.
RealPlayer	The latest development from Real Networks, the RealPlayer plug-in uses the technology described above to handle Real's own proprietary RM video files.
Shockwave	A predecessor of Flash (see below), Macromedia's Shockwave plug-in handles DCR files which are a compressed form of the Macromedia Director format.
Flash	Macromedia's Flash plug-in handles vector-based animations that offer both sound and interaction with the user. Flash files are small and quick to download and have taken the Web by storm.
Microsoft ActiveMovie	Microsoft's own video player can handle both video and audio formats including MPEG, AVI, WAV, AU and AIFF file formats.

*WinAmp is included as an example of independent third-party audio plug-ins. There are many others, particularly with MP3 such a popular audio format on the Web.

Audio content

Opinions differ as to the value of audio on the Web. At one end of the scale, there are those who swear by Web radio and leave their computers permanently churning out the latest rock and pop from around the world. At the other end, there are those who refuse to have anything to do with it and leave their sound volume set to zero. There is a wide range of audio technologies on the Web and the traditional download-and-play types are steadily losing ground to the latest streaming audio which, given a fast connection, can play content in real time.

When we looked at graphics for the Web back in Chapter 7, we discussed the idea of file compression. JPEG and GIF files are compressed using a "lossy" technology which discards some of the detail. Most audio files are compressed in a similar way, losing in particular those parts of the sound spectrum which are inaudible to humans. Clearly, as with images, the more an audio file is compressed, the quicker it is to download. The down side is that sound quality deteriorates in proportion to file size. There is always a balance to be struck between download speed and playback quality.

The following table lists most of the audio formats used on the Web:

File Format:	File extension:	Details:
RealAudio	.ra	Handled by the RealAudio Player plug-in.
Sparc-audio	.au / .snd	Old voice-grade format used mainly on workstations. Plug-ins widely available
Microsoft Waveform	.wav	Waveform format very common on Windows platform. Other platforms can use plug-in players.
Musical Instrument Digital Interface	.mid / .midi	MIDI format is not digitised but synthesised. Poor quality through computer hardware.
Motion Picture Experts Group	.mpg / .mpeg	MPEG format compresses well and provides good quality, now overtaken by...
MPEG Level 3	.mp3	...MP3. Mainly used to transfer sound files over the Web. Handled by widely available plug-ins.
Sound Blaster Instrument	.sbi	Handled by Sound Blaster cards. SBI format uses a single instrument, IBK offers multi-instrument.
Audio Interchange File Format		Common Mac format not widely used over the Web.

We also need to draw a distinction between file types that are used to move music over the Web, MP3's for example, and those that are used to insert audio content into a Web page, such as WAV files. At present, Internet download speeds and the inevitable traffic jams and bottlenecks make it pointless to include large sound files for real-time playback. The best solution, as with large graphic files, is to offer your visitors the choice of downloading stereo-quality audio content which they can then play using their own choice of software. Make sure that you caption the link so that visitors know what to expect.

Click here to hear my latest sampling.

is not as helpful as

Click here to download a 40k sound file of my latest sampling.

If you are offering sound samples, it is also good practice to include a link to a site from which your visitors can download the software to play them. We discuss how to include this type of content in more detail later in the book.

Finally, unless there is a very good reason for doing so, avoid including a compulsory soundtrack in your site. Those who browse with sound switched off – and there are many of them – will never hear it, while those who don't will quickly get irritated by a constantly repeating theme. Background music might be fine in a supermarket, but it's not popular on the Web!

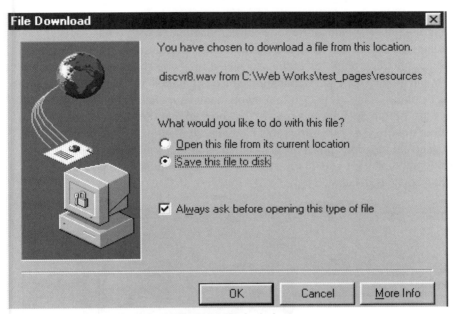

Figure 13.2: Internet Explorer's File Download window

Exercise One

1. For this exercise, we need to assemble a few sound files. Open Windows Explorer and use the Find Files tool to scan your computer for **.wav** audio files. If you're not sure how to do this, look back at Exercise 1 in Chapter 7. (Mac users should open the hard drive and use **Sherlock** to find files whose **kind - is - sound**.) To find out what they contain, double-click them and Windows Media Player or another application should open and play them for you.

2. Select five whose file sizes are larger then 100KB and copy (NOT move) them into your **test_pages/resources** folder. If you can't find large enough files, then copy the largest ones you have. Make a note of their full names on a scrap of paper. We shall refer to these as **sound1.wav, sound2.wav** etc., but you must replace these with the actual file names.

3. Open a basic template in your text editor and type the following code into the Body section:

> **To play the *sound1* file <A HREF="resources/*sound1*.wav">CLICK HERE.</A>
**

4. Repeat the same code for **sound2.wav**, **sound3.wav** etc. Save this file to your **test_pages** folder as **download_sounds.html** and open it in your browser. Click one of the links and, depending on how your computer is set up, it will either play, or you will see a window like Figure 13.2.

What we have done is use the download-and-play approach to inserting audio content. In the File Download window, you, or your Web site visitors, have a choice of saving the file or opening it from its current location. In fact, the latter is misleading, because it will have to be downloaded anyway. If you choose to save it, your computer will prompt for a folder to save it to. If you choose to open it, your browser will look for a helper application which can handle the file type and pass it over to be played back. Note also that if you make your choice then untick the "Always ask before opening this type of file" box, your choice will be repeated every time the browser encounters this file type. Go ahead and tick the "Open file from its current location" box and click OK. The sound file will open in its helper application and play for you. In our case, this means *Winamp*[1] will handle the file and will display as in Figure 13.3.

Figure 13.3: Winamp handling the playback of a .wav file

---

[1] **Winamp:** is a first-class audio player which can handle almost every sound file currently available on the Web. It is free as part of the Netscape Communicator® browser package or can be downloaded as a stand-alone application.

The method described above works well for inserting audio content which the visitor can choose to download and play. Similar code is used across the Web to allow users to download MP3 files, for example. But what if a Web page requires a sound file to play automatically when it opens? What, for example, if the page needs to include spoken instructions? Here we begin to run into browser incompatibility problems.

Background sounds

Internet Explorer, and browsers using the same technology can make use of a proprietary **<BGSOUND>** element to insert a background sound into a Web page, but it will work only with Internet Explorer, NeoPlanet, NetCaptor, Polyview, KatieSoft or other IE-based browsers. To see how this operates, reopen the file **download_sounds.html** in your text editor and add the following tag in the Body section:

<BGSOUND SRC="resources/*sound1*.wav" LOOP="Infinite">

Save the file as **embed_sounds.html,** open it in any of the browsers listed above and the sound will be played continuously for as long as the page is open. The **LOOP** attribute decides how often the sound will be repeated. Set it to a number and the sound will be played that number of times, set it to infinite and it goes on until the page is closed.

If you cannot hear the sound file, check Internet Explorer's settings. Under Internet Options, *click the* Advanced *tab, then scroll down through the list of options to the* Multimedia *section and make sure that* Play sounds *is ticked. If you still can't hear anything, you will need to check that your* soundcard and speakers are working, that Multimedia *has been set up properly and that your speaker volume is turned up.*

If you have Netscape Navigator (or Communicator) installed, try opening the file there and you will hear nothing. Netscape doesn't recognise the **<BGSOUND>** element. For Netscape browsers, you need to use different code. In embed_sounds.html try adding the following code:

<EMBED SRC="resources/*sound1*.wav" HIDDEN="True"
AUTOSTART="TRUE">

Save the file again, open it in a Netscape browser, if you have one installed, and the sound file will start to play. Now open it in Internet Explorer and depending on how your computer is set up, you will either get a warning box saying that you need to download new components from the Internet, or it will play. This is a good example of the need to sometimes include two different pieces of code to cover different browsers. We will be looking at this in more detail later in the book.

By this time you are probably wondering what on earth is going on between the browsers. Since this is the first – but not the last – time we have come up against incompatibility problems, let's take a moment to analyse the situation. Neither the

<BGSOUND> nor the **<EMBED>** elements are actually part of the HTML standard. The former was created by Microsoft® and the latter by Netscape®, and since the two companies are rivals in the browser market, a compromise has yet to be reached. Both browsers see the same code, which should now look like this:

```
<BGSOUND SRC="resources/sound1.wav" LOOP="Infinite">
<EMBED SRC="resources/sound1.wav" HIDDEN="True"
AUTOSTART="TRUE">
```

A Netscape browser ignores the first line completely, since **<BGSOUND>** is not a part of its set of HTML elements. It then responds to the second line of code which it does recognise. Internet Explorer and similar browsers respond correctly to the first line, but also recognise the second line since the **<EMBED>** element is a part of the Windows set. It's hardly surprising that Web authors get grey hairs. So let's make things even worse by looking at the approved HTML standard element.

The <OBJECT> element

While the **<BGSOUND>** element allows us to add a background sound to a page, it is very limited in scope. Microsoft's real alternative to Netscape's **<EMBED>** element is the **<OBJECT>** element we mentioned at the start of the chapter. The **<OBJECT>** element uses ActiveX controls to insert a binary object such as a sound or video file into a Web page. It is approved within the current HTML standard and will eventually become the normal way of building multimedia content into a Web document, but for the moment we are forced to work within Microsoft's implementation of the element.

We will be looking at ActiveX controls in detail in Part 2 of this book, but by way of an introduction, work through the following exercise.

Exercise Two

1. Open a basic template in your text editor. Add the following code to the body section:

```
<OBJECT ID="MediaPlayer1" WIDTH=0 HEIGHT=0
CLASSID="CLSID:22D6F312-B0F6-11D0-94AB-0080C74C7E95">
    <PARAM NAME="AudioStream" VALUE="-1">
    <PARAM NAME="AutoStart" VALUE="-1">
    <PARAM NAME="AutoRewind" VALUE="0">
    <PARAM NAME="BufferingTime" VALUE="5">
    <PARAM NAME="CurrentPosition" VALUE="-1">
    <PARAM NAME="Filename" VALUE="resources/Sound1.wav">
    <PARAM NAME="PlayCount" VALUE="1">
    <PARAM NAME="Rate" VALUE="1">
    <PARAM NAME="Volume" VALUE="-520">
</OBJECT>
```

2. Save the file as **embed_object.html in** your **test_pages** folder and open it in

your browser. You should be presented with a blank page, but your sound file should be playing as soon as the page opens. (You DID replace **sound1.wav** with your own sound file, didn't you?)

You have used the HTML **<OBJECT>** element to include Windows MediaPlayer in your page and passed it your sound file to play. Needless to say, because this page uses Microsoft's ActiveX technology, it won't work on a Netscape browser. We will look at the whole complex subject of the **<OBJECT>** element later in the book.

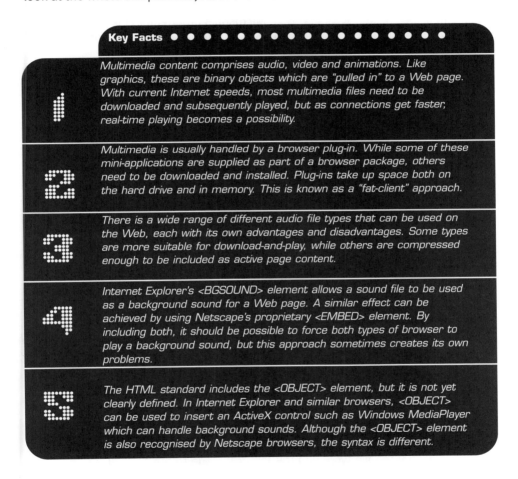

Key Facts ●

1. *Multimedia content comprises audio, video and animations. Like graphics, these are binary objects which are "pulled in" to a Web page. With current Internet speeds, most multimedia files need to be downloaded and subsequently played, but as connections get faster, real-time playing becomes a possibility.*

2. *Multimedia is usually handled by a browser plug-in. While some of these mini-applications are supplied as part of a browser package, others need to be downloaded and installed. Plug-ins take up space both on the hard drive and in memory. This is known as a "fat-client" approach.*

3. *There is a wide range of different audio file types that can be used on the Web, each with its own advantages and disadvantages. Some types are more suitable for download-and-play, while others are compressed enough to be included as active page content.*

4. *Internet Explorer's <BGSOUND> element allows a sound file to be used as a background sound for a Web page. A similar effect can be achieved by using Netscape's proprietary <EMBED> element. By including both, it should be possible to force both types of browser to play a background sound, but this approach sometimes creates its own problems.*

5. *The HTML standard includes the <OBJECT> element, but it is not yet clearly defined. In Internet Explorer and similar browsers, <OBJECT> can be used to insert an ActiveX control such as Windows MediaPlayer which can handle background sounds. Although the <OBJECT> element is also recognised by Netscape browsers, the syntax is different.*

Video Content

In many ways, including video content in Web pages is similar to including audio content, but the scale of the problems is magnified. Video files are enormously larger than audio files and therefore take much longer to download. Streaming high quality video is the ultimate aim of many Web design companies, but the technology to do this is still in the future. One simple set of statistics will reveal the extent of the problem. A 640 x 480 pixel image, using 24-bit colour and playing at 30 frames per second requires a steady stream of data at 27 MegaBytes per second. To put this in simple terms, that is the equivalent of processing the contents of around 20 floppy discs full of information each second. Internet bandwidth is nowhere near adequate for this.

Of course, as with audio, the download-and-play approach is viable – provided users are prepared to wait for large video files to arrive. There are several video formats on the Web. The most common ones are detailed in the following table:

File Format:	File extension:	Details:
Audio Video Interleaved	.avi	Microsoft's proprietary Video for Windows format. AVI is common on the Web and supported by most browsers.
Motion Picture Experts Group	.mpg/ .mpeg	The best format for high-quality video. MPEG can be difficult to work with.
Quicktime	.mov	Apple's® proprietary QuickTime format. Continuously developed and very popular. Supported by most browsers.

Again, let us start with the download-and-play model before looking at other possibilities.

Exercise Three

1. Once more we need to start by tracking down some video files. Start by searching your hard drive for **.avi**, **.mpg**, **.mpeg** and **.mov** files. If you find some, copy one or two examples of each format you have into your **test_pages/resources** folder. If you don't find any samples on your own computer, search through any software CDROMs you can lay your hands on – video content is often included in on-screen manuals or installers. If all else fails, look on the Web for downloadable video files. (As normal, we will refer to these as **video1.av**i, **video1.mov**, **video1.mpg** etc. You will need to insert the names of your own files, but make sure you pick ones of the correct file type.)

2. Open a basic template in your text editor. Assuming that you have got hold of one of each video file type, add the following code to the body section:

    <A HREF="resources/*video1***.avi">CLICK HERE </A>to see how this browser handles an AVI video file.
**

    <A HREF="resources/*video1***.mov">CLICK HERE </A>to see how this browser handles a QuickTime video file.
**

    <A HREF="resources/*video1***.mpg">CLICK HERE </A>to see how this browser handles an MPEG video file.
**

3. Save this as **link_video.html** in your **test_pages** folder and open it in as many browsers as you have installed. Now try clicking the links.

What you have just seen depends on the browser, the installed plug-ins and the platform you are using. As an example, we will describe what happened when we ran through this exercise on a Windows-based PC using Internet Explorer 5.5. Clicking the first link opened the Windows MediaPlayer on top of the existing page which played the AVI file and then remained open until we closed its window. Clicking the second link launched the Apple QuickTime player in a new page which played the QuickTime file, as shown in Figure 13.4. We were obliged to click the **Back** button to return to our original page. The final link played our MPEG file using Windows MediaPlayer as before. Almost all today's browsers handle downloaded video content quite happily.

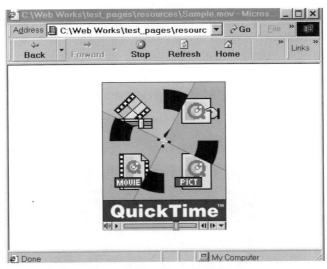

Figure 13.4: The Apple QuickTime Player handling a MOV file.

As with audio files, there is little difficulty with the download-and-play approach. It is when we try pulling video content into the page itself that we have more of a problem.

Embedding video content

Provided your visitors have the relevant plug-ins installed on their systems, displaying embedded video content follows the same basic model as embedding audio described above. Within Netscape, use of the **<EMBED>** element to pull in AVI files will call up the appropriate plug-in. Netscape's own LiveVideo is very simplistic, providing no video or audio controls. Much better is the Apple QuickTime plug-in to handle MOV files. As an example, the following code scrap includes a QuickTime movie into a Web page and sets a range of options for the way in which it is displayed:

```
<EMBED SRC="resources/video1.mov" ALIGN="Left"
   AUTOPLAY="True"
```

```
CONTROLLER="True" VOLUME="200" WIDTH="200" HEIGHT="300">
```

The code above is obvious enough, except for the **CONTROLLER** attribute which determines whether the user sees a set of video and audio controls displayed below the video window. If you have a Netscape browser and the QuickTime plug-in installed, create an HTML page including this code and try it.

Miraculously enough, this code will also work with Internet Explorer, provided that the QuickTime plug-in is installed. Try opening this same page in IE and see what happens. Microsoft's own video player is ActiveMovie, and like the MediaPlayer we looked at earlier, this is designed to be used with the **<OBJECT>** element, but can also be activated by the **<EMBED>** element that we used above. ActiveMovie can handle an extensive range of multimedia formats including MPEG-1 and MPEG-2, AVI and WAV files. The following code scrap uses the **<EMBED>** element and will call up the ActiveMovie plug-in if installed. Otherwise Windows MediaPlayer will be used.

```
<EMBED SRC="resources/video1.avi" AUTOSTART="True"
LOOP="True" HEIGHT="300" WIDTH="200>
```

Again the attributes are self-explanatory. Try using this code in an HTML page to test its result on your own computer.

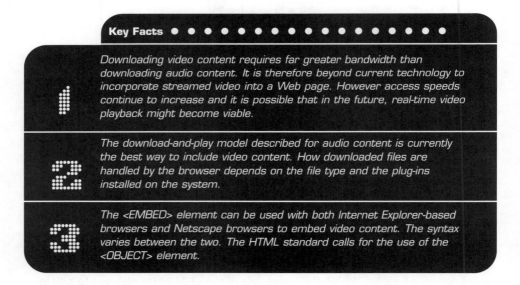

Key Facts

1. Downloading video content requires far greater bandwidth than downloading audio content. It is therefore beyond current technology to incorporate streamed video into a Web page. However access speeds continue to increase and it is possible that in the future, real-time video playback might become viable.

2. The download-and-play model described for audio content is currently the best way to include video content. How downloaded files are handled by the browser depends on the file type and the plug-ins installed on the system.

3. The <EMBED> element can be used with both Internet Explorer-based browsers and Netscape browsers to embed video content. The syntax varies between the two. The HTML standard calls for the use of the <OBJECT> element.

Considering multimedia content

We don't usually close a chapter with a round-up section, but the whole subject of multimedia is so complex that we thought it worth including a few additional notes.

We have no doubt that in the future, Internet access speeds will improve to the point where true video streaming becomes a serious possibility, but at present the only workable method is to offer your visitors the choice of downloading a video file and playing it in their own time. Audio files are smaller, but real-time playback is still well beyond the access capabilities of most Web users. In a nutshell, we strongly recommend the download-and-play approach described above.

Perhaps the key question to ask about multimedia is not "How do I do it?" but "Why should I do it?". Always ask yourself whether your site really needs multimedia content and never include it just because you can.

The following table lists all the HTML tags used in this chapter:

Opening Tag	Closing Tag	Attributes	Description
<EMBED>			Although not part of the HTML standard, this element is widely supported by browsers. It embeds a binary object into a Web page.
		SRC=".."	This attribute specifies the URL for the embedded binary object.
		HEIGHT=".."	This attribute specifies the height of the embedded object. Valid values are: a number of pixels.
		WIDTH=".."	This attribute specifies the width of the embedded object. Valid values are: a number of pixels.
		HIDDEN=".."	This attribute defines whether the object is visible on the page. Valid values are: True and False.
		AUTOPLAY =".."	This attribute in Internet Explorer defines whether the object plays automatically when it is loaded. Valid values are: True and False.
		AUTOSTART ".."	This attribute in a Netscape browser defines whether the object plays automatically when it is loaded. Valid values are: True and False.
		ALIGN=".."	The attribute defines how text is aligned with respect to the embedded object. Valid values are: Absbottom, Absmiddle, Baseline,

			Bottom, Left, Middle, Right, Texttop and Top.
		CONTROLLER ="..."	Where the embedded object is handled by Apple's QuickTime player, this attribute specifies whether the audio and video controls should be visible. Valid values are: True and False.
		LOOP="..."	This attribute specifies how many times the object should be played. Valid values are: a number or Infinite.
<OBJECT>			We will leave discussing the highly complicated syntax of the <OBJECT> element until later in this book.
<BGSOUND>			This tag pulls in an audio file to be played as a background sound to a Web page.
		SRC="..."	This attribute specified the URL of the audio file.
		LOOP="..."	This attribute specifies how many times the object should be played. Valid values are: a number or Infinite.

 QUICK REVISION QUESTIONS

1. In terms of Web page content, what is meant by the term "multimedia"?

2. What is a binary object?

3. How are plug-in applications used by browsers to handle multimedia files?

4. What were the different approaches used by Netscape and Microsoft to include multimedia content in their respective browsers?

5. What are the problems associated with including multimedia content in pages intended for publication on the Web?

6. What is the download-and-play approach to sound and video files?

7. How would you use Microsoft's proprietary **<BGSOUND>** element to add background sound to a Web page?

8. What is the HTML standard's preferred alternative to Microsoft's **<BGSOUND>** and Netscape's **<EMBED>** elements?

9. Like several other plug-ins, Apple's QuickTime player is described as "cross-browser". What does this term mean?

10. What is the key question to ask yourself about including multimedia content?

Chapter 14
Using style sheets

Brief contents:

1. The concept of cascading style sheets.

2. The benefits that style sheets bring to Web design.

3. How to create simple and complex style sheets for your own Web pages.

4 The different ways in which style sheets can be applied to a Web page or to a Web site.

5. How to apply style sheet rules to individual HTML elements within a page.

6. Understanding the concepts of block-level elements and their associated canvas space.

7. How to use style sheets for accurate positioning of Web page content.

8. Recognising HTML core attributes.

Using style sheets

After all the troubles associated with multimedia that we discussed in the previous chapter, this chapter should come as something of a relief. Style sheets, or cascading style sheets to give them their full title, are a real asset to Web designers and their use will eventually replace many of the current HTML tags. In simple terms, style sheets allow Web authors to set up predefined styles for a site which can then be applied to every page or page component within that site. For example, using a style sheet you could specify that every sub-heading within your site was to be a particular colour, font and text size, thus saving yourself the bother of entering all this as code each time. Let us begin by looking at style sheet syntax.

A style sheet is a set of rules bound to a particular HTML element. The syntax is very straightforward. The name of the element is followed by the rules in curly brackets. Here is an example:

H2 {font-size: 16pt; font-family: Verdana; color: black}

We have started by defining the **<H2>** element. We have then defined three "properties" of that element, **font-size, font-family** and **color,** and applied a value to each property. Each rule is separated from the next by a semicolon. Technically, you are "binding" these rules to the **<H2>** element, and every time your insert that element into your Web page it will automatically follow these rules. Well over 50 style sheet rules are included within the current HTML standard. Unfortunately, not all browsers recognise all these rules, so in this chapter we will concentrate on those rules which are widely supported.

There are three points to be borne in mind. First, it is important to realise that a style sheet is not actually a part of HTML itself. It is a separate text document referred to by the HTML code and is therefore linked to or embedded within page content. You will notice that it does not follow standard HTML syntax. Secondly, although it appears to follow the element-attribute-value model we are now so familiar with, this is not the case. Within style sheets, what appear to be attributes are known as properties, and this is how we will refer to them. Finally, although style sheets are taking over across the Web, not all browsers support all the features they offer.

Let's work through a simple example and see how a style sheet operates.

Exercise One

1. Open your text editor and create a style sheet by typing in the following:

   BODY {font-size: 12pt; font-family: Verdana; color: blue; background-color: yellow}

   H2 {font-size: 24pt; font-family: Comic Sans MS; color: red}

2. Save this document in your **test_pages** folder as **simplestyle.css**. Note the extension **.css** which defines the file as a cascading style sheet. Next open a basic template in your text editor and insert the following code within the Head section:

   <LINK REL="Stylesheet" HREF="simplestyle.css" MEDIA="Screen" TYPE="text/css">

3. Within the Body section of the HTML page, type in the following code:

   <H2>This heading inherits its style from a style sheet</H2>

   **So does all this text, since we have defined a style for the Body as a whole.
**

   <H2>Here is another heading - and look! no code...</H2>

   And here is some more text also in the style defined by our style sheet.

4. Save this to your **test_pages** folder as **simple_style.html** and open it in your browser. It should look like Figure 14.1.

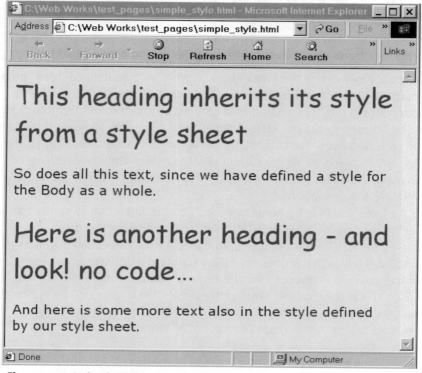

Figure 14.1: A simple Web page using a style sheet

Look first at the style sheet itself. Of course there can only be one **<BODY>** element in a Web page, so this set of rules will apply to all content for which we do not set specific rules. For the **<BODY>**, we have defined four properties, including the background-color property which sets a background colour for the page. Below this, we have specified three properties for any **<H2>** element in the Web page the style sheet controls. These override the **<BODY>** element rules. We could, in fact, specify a further set of rules to apply to a single word within an **<H2>** headline and these would override the **<H2>** rules. This is what is meant by the "cascading" part of cascading style sheets.

Now look at the code used to insert the style sheet into the Web page:

<LINK REL="Stylesheet" HREF="simplestyle.css" MEDIA="Screen" TYPE="text/css">

We have inserted a new element, **<LINK>**, into the **<HEAD>** element, and used the **REL** attribute to specify the relationship between the Web page and the linked document. **HREF**, as usual, specifies the URL of the linked document. As with any other **HREF** attribute, the URL can be absolute or relative. It would be possible to store a style sheet on a server on the other side of the world from the server holding the document itself. A single style sheet can be used by any number of different Web pages. The **MEDIA** attribute defines the media on which the linked information will display, while the **TYPE** attribute defines the type of content, in this case, a **text** document to be used as a **css** – cascading style sheet.

This simple example shows the sheer convenience of a style sheet. Using pure HTML, we would have needed to insert separate pieces of code to define the **<BODY>** element and the style of each of the **<H2>** elements. Even if we were to add a dozen further **<H2>** headlines, every one of them would be automatically formatted using our simple style sheet.

Applying style sheets

Think how easy the use of style sheets would make setting up a Web site for our old friends at Earpop Records. Most of the pages we have created for them so far have been consistent in style. We have used a black background, white text and yellow links. The following style sheet could be used to define all these elements just once:

BODY   {background-color: black; color: white}

A:link   {color: yellow}

Then, whenever we created a new page for EarPop, we would link to this style sheet and most of our text styling would be taken care of.

Linking to a style sheet is probably the easiest way to use the resource, but it does have one possible problem. Since the style sheet is a separate document, it also has to be downloaded. This might delay page rendering time, particularly if the style sheet is stored away from the HTML document that references it. Of course a style sheet is just a text file and should download very quickly, but the point should still be borne in mind.

An alternative to linking to a style sheet is to embed it directly within the HTML page it refers to. To see how this can be done, work through the following exercise.

Exercise Two

1. Open a basic template in your text editor and add the following code within the Head section:

```
<STYLE TYPE="text/css" MEDIA="Screen">

<!- -

BODY        {font-size: 12pt; font-family: Verdana; color: blue;
            background-color: yellow}

H2          {font-size: 24pt; font-family: Comic Sans MS; color: red}

- ->

</STYLE>
```

2. Within the Body section, type in the following code just as before (you might find it easier to copy and paste this from the previous page:

<H2>This heading inherits its style from a style sheet</H2>

**So does all this text, since we have defined a style for the Body as a whole.
**

<H2>Here is another heading - and look! no code...</H2>

And here is some more text also in the style defined by our style sheet.

3. Save this to your **test_pages** folder as **embed_style.html** and open it in your browser. It should look exactly the same as the page you created in Exercise One. Open that page as well, and confirm that the results are identical.

Look back at the code we have used to create this page. Within the **<HEAD>** element, we have included the **<STYLE>** element and specified its type and the media to use, just as we did before. To include the style information itself, we have used the **<!- ->** Comment element. This makes sure that older or less aware browsers won't try to display the information on screen. In this sense, you can consider style information to be meta-information. Hiding it as a comment is always a good idea.

The third way of using a style sheet is to apply it directly to an element within an HTML page. Although this might seem more complicated than defining text using ordinary HTML tags, it is worth remembering that the HTML standard itself is moving towards the use of style sheets and many of the familiar formatting tags will eventually be retired.

To see how inline styling operates, work through the following exercise:

Exercise Three

1. Reopen the file **embed_style.html** in your text editor and modify the following code within the Body section:

<H2>This heading inherits its style from a style sheet</H2>

**So does all this text, since we have defined a style for the Body as a whole.
**

<H2>Here is another heading - and look! no code...</H2>

<DIV STYLE="background-color: green; font-weight: bold; color: black">

But here is some text defined by inline style information.

</DIV>

2. Save this to your **test_pages** folder as **inline_style.html** and open it in your browser. The syntax is similar to other style sheet usage, but has now become the value of the **STYLE** attribute. Note that the inline style has overridden the style embedded in the **<HEAD>** element. This can be very useful.

Cascading style sheets provide a very effective way of applying document- or even site-wide styling. A single style sheet can be referenced by any number of pages to apply identical page rendering to each. This can significantly reduce the amount of time required to code a Web site. Style sheets are a preferred direction for the HTML standard.

Basic style sheets apply a set of rules to every instance of an HTML element. They consist of simple text files defining the properties of an element which are bound to each instance of the element itself. Style sheets are not a part of HTML and need to be downloaded separately.

*A style sheet can be applied to an HTML document in three ways. Firstly, the <LINK> element can be used to link the page to a separate style sheet. Secondly, the <STYLE> element can be used to incorporate style information into the Web page itself. Finally, style information can be applied directly to an element within the **Body** section of the page.*

Applying different styles to instances of the same element

We hope that by now you are convinced of the benefits of using style sheets. You might also have spotted a drawback. If we use a style sheet to apply style information to, for example, the **<H2>** element, what happens if you do not want all your **<H2>** headlines to display in the same way? We already know that inline styling overrules document-wide styling, but if we need to code every exception individually, we are effectively back to using tags. Style sheets provide a solution to this problem by using the **CLASS** and **ID** attributes.

We have not met the **ID** attribute before, but it is a valid attribute for nearly all HTML elements and allows us to give any instance of that element a unique name by which we can then refer to it. For example, the code scrap:

<H2 ID="Heading1">Welcome to Earpop Records.</H2>

assigns the name "Heading1" to this particular heading. Note that "Heading1" does NOT refer to the words "Welcome to Earpop Records.", but to this instance of the **<H2>** heading itself. We can use this ID within our style sheets to refer to one **<H2>** heading while ignoring others. Look at the style sheet below:

```
H2          {font: 24pt; font-family: Comic Sans MS; color: red}
#Heading1   {font: 20pt; color: blue}
BODY        {font: 12pt; font-family: Verdana; color: blue;
            background-color: yellow}
```

As before, we have defined a style for an **<H2>** heading, but we have created an exception for the **<H2>** heading with the **ID** value of "#Heading1". Any **ID** value can be defined like this, provided it is preceded by the # (hash) symbol. But remember that an **ID** value must be unique so can only be used to set the style for a single instance of an element. If we wish to refer to multiple instances of an element, we need to use the **CLASS** attribute.

CLASS works in a similar way to **ID**, but there can be any number of instances of a class. Within HTML the syntax for class is similar to that used for the ID attribute. Thus the code scrap:

<H2 CLASS="Bigblue">Welcome to Earpop Records.</H2>

adds this particular instance of the **<H2>** element to a class whose name is "Bigblue". We can add as many other element instances to this class as we like, and they don't even all have to be **<H2>** headings. The code scrap:

<P CLASS="Bigblue">This could be a paragraph of any length.</P>

adds this instance of the **<P>** element to the "Bigblue" class which now contains both a heading and a paragraph. Within a style sheet, the name of a class must be preceded by a period (full stop), so adding this class to our style sheet, we might have:

```
H2            {font: 24pt; font-family: Comic Sans MS; color: red}
#Heading1     {font: 20pt; color: blue}
.Bigblue      {font: 16pt; colour: navy}
BODY          {font: 12pt; font-family: Verdana; color: blue;
               background-color: yellow}
```

Let's put all this together in the following exercise which creates a style sheet for Earpop records, then applies it to a new Earpop page.

Exercise Four

1. First, we will create a style sheet giving us a range of options for different text and headline styles. In your text editor, type the following:

```
BODY          {background-color: black; color: white; font-family:
               Verdana}

A:link        {color: yellow}

A:active      {color: aqua}

A:visited     {color: aqua}

H2            {color: yellow; text-align: center}

H4            {color: aqua}

.Emphasis     {background-color: yellow; color: blue; text-align: center;
               font-size: medium; border: outset 2pt red}

#Clickbar     {background-color: gray; color: navy; text-align: center;
               font-size: 10pt; border: inset 3pt yellow; width: 200pt}
```

2. Save this to your **test_pages** folder as **Earpop_style.css**. Now open a basic template and add the following code into the Head section:

```
<LINK REL="Stylesheet" HREF="Earpop_style.css" MEDIA="Screen"
TYPE="text/css">
```

3. In the Body section, add the following code:

<H2>EARPOP RECORDS</H2>

<H4>A short but fascinating history</H4>

**Earpop Records was formed in 1997 when musician Geoff Power and businessman Michael Dolan bought up the old Alpha Recording Studios in Parnell Street.
**

<H4>A record label for the independent musician</H4>

**From the very beginning, Earpop made one promise...

**

<P CLASS="Emphasis">Every musician who records for Earpop will be treated with respect.</P>

...and this promise has always been kept.

<P ID="Clickbar">To find out how to sign with Earpop <A HREF="signup.html">CLICK HERE</A></P>

4. Save this to your **test_pages** folder as **earpop_history.html** and open it in your browser. It should look like Figure 14.2

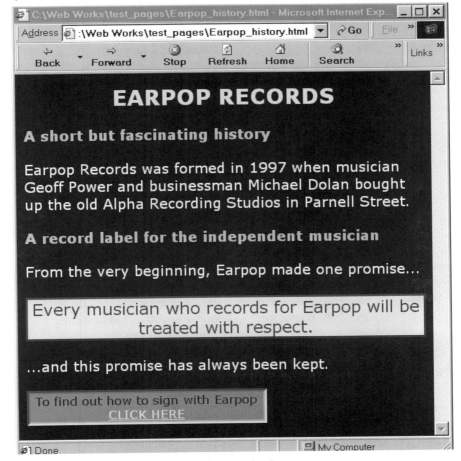

Figure 14.2: Earpop's history page using a style sheet.

Look carefully at both the HTML code and the style sheet rules used to create this page. Most of the style sheet content we have already explained, but we have used two new properties. **text-align** works very much like the **VALIGN** attribute we have met previously and is used to align text within what is referred to as its "canvas space" - in other words, the space it occupies on a page. **Border** is a property which allows us to surround that canvas space with a border. We have used it twice, once within the **Emphasis** (**CLASS**) element, and once within the **Clickbar** (**ID**) element. In each case we have included three values, one for the type of border, one for the border width and one for the border colour. Look closely at the rendering in your own browser to see the effects these values have created.

The table below lists some of the more common style sheet properties for rendering text, page backgrounds and borders. Properties can be applied to any appropriate element, but if you are using a style sheet to set rules for your links, there is a special format. **A:link** refers to a clickable link, **A:active** refers to a link when the mouse pointer passes over it and **A:visited** refers to a link that has already been clicked. Remember when creating a style sheet, that the syntax is always:

Element {property1: value; property2: value}

Property:	Values:	Notes and Examples:
font-family	Name of font or type of font, eg: Serif, Sans-serif, Cursive, Fantasy, Monospace.	Defines a font or family of fonts to be used. You can specify a series of choices, separated by commas. {font-family: Verdana, Arial, Sans-serif}
font-size	Size of font in points or a relative word, eg: xx-small, x-small, small, medium, large, x-large or xx-large	Defines the size of the font. Point sizes are preferred since they give better con-trol. {font-size: 12pt} {font-size: x-large}
font-style	normal, italic or oblique	{font-style: italic}
font-weight	100, 200, 300, 400, 500, 600, 700, 800 or 900	Defines the "weight" or boldness of the font with 900 as the boldest. {font-weight: 400}
font	Any values from the four boxes above	Using the font property allows us to combine a range of font settings into a single rule. {font: Verdana x-large italic 600}

text-decoration	line-through, blink, overline, none, underline	Defines a text effect. (Overline draws a line above the text.) {text-decoration: underline}
color	16 common colour names (red, yellow, blue etc) or colour hex values	Specifies the text colour. {color: red} {color: #FF0088}
text-align	left, right, center, justify	Defines how a block of text is aligned on the page. {text-align: center}
background-color	16 common colour names (red, yellow, blue etc) or colour hex values	Specifies a colour for the background of an element such as a paragraph or a page. {background-color: blue}
background-image	url then the URL of a GIF or JPEG file to be used as a background image, in brackets	Specifies a background image for an element. {background-image: url(resources/picture1.gif)}
background-repeat	repeat, repeat-x, repeat-y, no-repeat	Defines how the background image is tiled on the page. The repeat value tiles the image horizontally and vertically. The repeat-x value tiles the image horizontally only. The repeat-y value tiles the image vertically only. The no-repeat value displays the image once with no tiling. {background-repeat: repeat-x}
background	Any values from the three boxes above	Like Font above, Background allows us to group background properties into a single rule. {background: blue url(pic.gif) repeat x}
border-style	dotted, dashed, solid, double, groove, ridge, inset and outset	Defines the style of a border around an element. Most of these are obvious, but inset and outset are used to create the illusion of an indented or raised box respectively. {border-style: groove}

border-width	thin, medium, thick or a value in pixels such as 20px	Defines the thickness of the border. {border-width: medium}
border-color	16 common colour names (red, yellow, blue etc) or colour hex values	Defines the colour of the border. This property can take four values one after another to specify different colours for all four borders in the order top, right, bottom, left. {border-color: red green blue yellow}
border	Any values from the three boxes above	Border allows us to group border properties into a single rule. {border: dotted 20px green}

Using this table, we can draw up fairly complex style sheets for our pages. Read carefully through the style sheet below and try to visualise the effect that each line will create:

```
BODY     {background-image: url(sand.jpg); background-repeat:
         repeat-y; background-color: yellow; font-family: Comic Sans
         MS; font-size: 12pt}
P        {margin-left: 50pt; color: maroon}
H2       {background-image: url(sand.jpg); background-repeat:
         repeat-x; color: yellow; font-family: Comic Sans MS; font-
         size: 34pt; font-weight: 800; text-align: center}
.Up      {font-size: 14pt; font-weight: 700}
A:Link   {background-color: maroon; color: yellow}
```

Applied to an HTML page containing the following code:

```
<H2>Welcome to HotSauce</H2>
<P>Here at HotSauce we keep you posted on how Irish chefs are
using chillis and other hot and spicy ingredients. We list our
favourite recipes, investigate the <SPAN CLASS="Up">world's
hottest curries</SPAN> and tell you how to sharpen up your own
dishes.</P>
<P>Follow the links below to a world of taste..</P>
<DIV  ALIGN="Center">
<A HREF="sauces.html"> Sauces </A>  
<A HREF="recipes.html"> Recipes </A>  
<A HREF="curries.html"> Curries </A>  
</DIV>
</BODY>
```

... the page produced is rendered in a browser as Figure 14.3.

Figure 14.3: Using a style sheet to position background images.

Note how the same background image has been tiled horizontally behind the heading and vertically to create a margin for the page. For the **<P>** element, the **margin-left** property has been given a value of 50pt to push the text clear of the image. Note also the use of the ** ** character to create a little extra space around the links. Although you can't see them in black and white, the colours used are consistent, with the deep red of the image reflected in the maroon text and the maroon boxes around the links at the bottom.

Using style sheets for page layout

We have discussed page layout several times in this book and now we return to the subject once more. Style sheets give us much greater control over the placement of content. The **margin-left** property used in the previous example shows a further way of indenting text from the edge of the page. Before we look at other ways that style sheets can help with page layouts, we need to take a slight detour to consider some theory.

When we insert page content such as paragraphs of text, headings or lists, each of these elements takes up a block of space on the page. For this reason, they are often referred to as block-level elements. The space each occupies, including the blank area around the actual words, is always rectangular and, as we indicated earlier, is often referred to as canvas space. The diagram below shows how block-level content can be considered:

> This block contains a heading

> This block contains a list.
> 1. Hello
> 2. Goodbye

> This block contains a paragraph of screen text.

Style sheets allow us to specify certain properties for each block-level element, properties that enable us to control very precisely how they are rendered in a browser. Two block-level properties we have already discussed are the **border** and **background-color** properties. Each of the blocks above has a thin black border around it and is filled with a pale grey. For a Web page, we could have used a style sheet rule such as:

{border: solid 1pt black; background-color: gray[1]}

to achieve this result.

We can also define the amount of space between the border of a block-level element and its actual contents using the **padding** property. The style sheet rule:

{padding-top: 1cm; padding-right: 50mm; padding-bottom: 1cm; padding-left: 50mm}

sets different padding values for the sides of the block, and its top and bottom. We have specified these in centimetres, but points (pt) or pixels (px) would also be valid. The **padding** property is useful for creating "white space" around page content.

Height and **width** are also block-level properties used to define the actual size of a block. They can take a value in pixels (px), points (pt) or centimetres (cm). There is also a **margin** property which sets the space between a block's edges and its adjacent elements. Usage is similar to **padding**, so **margin-left** sets the left-hand margin width. We used the margin property in the "HotSauce" example above.

All of these properties give us great control over how text is placed within its canvas space. Consider the style sheet that follows:

P   {height: 200px; width: 200px; padding: 80px 80px 80px 80px; margin-left: 50pt; background-color: black; color:white}

and a Web page linked to it containing only the block-level element **<P>** with, as its contents, the single word "Hello". A browser would render this as Figure 14.4.

Apply this level of control to a complex Web page. By using the **Margin** properties, we can define where content is placed on a page. We can define where content is placed within its canvas space and how large that canvas space is to be.

In 1998, the World Wide Web Consortium (W3C) approved an extension to the style sheet specification. CSS2 introduced a new property, **position**, which allowed block-level elements to be positioned on a page with great accuracy. (Because this is a relatively new development, many older and some current browsers do not

---

[1] **Gray:** note another American spelling!

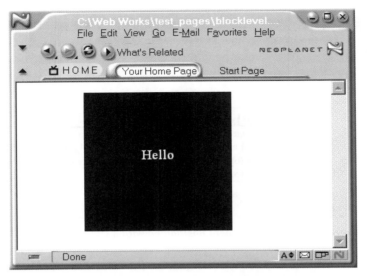

Figure 14.4: Rendering block-level properties in the NeoPlanet browser.

implement this property correctly, so use it with some caution.) The **position** property takes three possible values, but we are only concerned with two of them – **static,** which allows elements to fall into the positions they would under ordinary HTML coding, and **absolute,** which allows us to place elements by defining the position of the top left-hand corner of the element. To do this, we need to assign a value in pixels (px), points (pt) or centimetres/millemetres (cm/mm) to both the **top** property and the **left** property.

To see how this can be used, work through the following exercise.

Exercise Five

1. In your text editor, create a style sheet as follows:

   H2   {position: absolute; left: 120px; top: 50px; background-color: white; border: solid 1pt black}

   DIV   {position: absolute; left: 80px; Top: 80px; background-color: white; border: solid 1pt black}

2. Save this to your **test_pages** folder as **pagelayout.css**. Now open a basic template and add the following code into the Head section:

   <LINK REL="Stylesheet" HREF="pagelayout.css" MEDIA="Screen" TYPE="text/css">

3. In the Body section, add the following code:

   <H2>Here is a headline</H2>

   <DIV>Here is a block of text aligned on the page using the style sheet rules. Because we have wrongly specified the top margin, this paragraph's canvas space sits on top of the headline box.</DIV>

4. Save this to your **test_pages** folder as **pagelayout.html** and open it in your browser. You should see something like Figure 14.5.

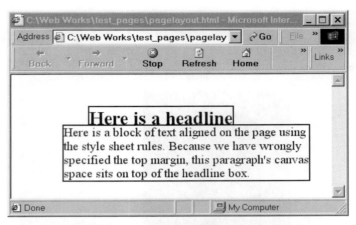

Figure 14.5: Incorrect use of block-element positioning with a style sheet.

The error here is obvious and easily corrected. For the **<DIV>** element, we have specified a position for the top edge of the block which is within the canvas space of the **<H2>** element. To correct the error, reopen the style sheet and change the **top** property of the **<DIV>** element to 100px. Save the style sheet and reload or refresh **pagelayout.html** in your browser. The text block is now positioned correctly below the heading.

We can used the **position** property to create columns and rows, to place graphics and to format lists, and we will be looking at this in more detail when we examine page layouts in Part 2 of this book. The following table lists the style sheet properties we have used in the second part of this chapter.

Property:	Values:	Notes and Examples:
padding-top	Any value in points, pixels or centimetres	Defines the space to be left between the top edge of the block and the block's actual contents. {padding-top: 10px}
padding-right	Any value in points, pixels or centimetres	Defines the space to be left between the right edge of the block and the block's actual contents.
padding-bottom	Any value in points, pixels or centimetres	Defines the space to be left between the bottom edge of the block and the block's actual contents.
padding-left	Any value in points, pixels or centimetres	Defines the space to be left between the left edge of the block and the block's actual contents.

height	Any value in points, pixels or centimetres	Defines the height of the canvas space of a block-level element. {height: 200px}
width	Any value in points, pixels or centimetres	Defines the width of the canvas space of a block-level element.
margin-top	Any value in points, pixels or centimetres	Defines the width of the space between the top edge of a block-level element's canvas space and the adjacent element. {margin-left: 10pt}
margin-right	Any value in points, pixels or centimetres	Defines the width of the space between the right edge of a block-level element's canvas space and the adjacent element.
margin-bottom	Any value in points, pixels or centimetres	Defines the width of the space between the bottom edge of a block-level element's canvas space and the adjacent element.
margin-left	Any value in points, pixels or centimetres	Defines the width of the space between the left edge of a block-level element's canvas space and the adjacent element.
position	static, absolute or relative	Defines how a block-level element is to be positioned on a page. Static leaves the positioning to the HTML code, absolute allows us to place content by specifying the position of the top left corner of the block. We must specify Top and Left below. {position: absolute}
top	Any value in points, pixels or centimetres	Specifies the distance between the top edge of the element and the top edge of the page. {top: 80px}
left	Any value in points, pixels or centimetres	Specifies the distance between the left edge of the element and the left edge of the page. {left: 80px}

In this chapter we have only been able to deal with some of the facilities that cascading style sheets allow us. As we mentioned above, they are seen as the future of Web design, and many of the HTML tags we are familiar with will eventually be removed from the standard in favour of using properties within a style sheet.

Key Facts ●

 Document-wide styling applies to every instance of the defined element. To specify exceptions, the ID and CLASS attributes can be applied to individual elements, then defined within a style sheet. The ID attribute is used to give one instance of an element a unique name, the CLASS attribute to add elements to a class. Within a style sheet, rules can be applied to the ID name by preceding it with the hash (#) symbol and to a CLASS by preceding its name with a period (full stop).

 Within a style sheet individual properties are applied to an element, but in some cases, property rules can be combined into a group. The **font**, **background** and **border** properties group together a series of rules into a single style rule.

 Style sheets offer much greater control over the placement of background images. A background image can be defined for any element's canvas space. It can be placed once, tiled horizontally or vertically in a single row or column, or used to fill the whole space.

 A block-level element is an element which occupies a block of space on a Web page (as opposed to inline elements). The positioning of block-level contents can be accurately controlled from a style sheet. The **height** and **width** properties can define the size of the block, the padding property defines the space between the block's edges and its contents, and the **margin** property defines the space between a block and its adjacent elements. All of these properties take values in pixels, points or centimetres.

The **position** property allows us to place any block-level element precisely on a page by specifying the distance between its top and left edges and the top and left edges of the page itself.

The following table lists all the HTML tags used in this chapter.

Opening Tag	Closing Tag	Attributes	Description
<LINK>			This tag establishes a relationship between the current document and a linked document. It is often used for linking a style sheet.
		REL=".."	This attribute names the relationship. Valid values include: Stylesheet, Index and Alternative.

		HREF="..”	This attribute specifies the URL of the linked document.
		MEDIA="..”	This attribute specifies the destination medium for linked style information. Valid values include: Print and Screen.
		TYPE="..”	This attribute defines the type of content to be linked to. Valid values include: Text/html and Text/css – the latter is used for style sheets.
<SPAN>	</SPAN>		These tags are used to define any amount of text from a single letter up to several paragraphs so that style sheet rules can be applied to it.
<STYLE>	</STYLE>		These tags enclose style information within the <HEAD> element.
		MEDIA="..”	This attribute specifies the destination medium for style information. Valid values include: Print and Screen.
		TYPE="..”	This attribute defines the type of style content and should take the MIME value: Text/css.
CORE ATTRIBUTES: HTML defines four "core" attributes which can be applied to almost every element. We have used three of them in this chapter.		STYLE="..”	This attribute defines an inline style for a particular element. It takes as its value a correctly formatted style sheet rule.
		ID="..”	This attribute specifies a unique name for any one instance of an element. Valid values are: any text string beginning with a letter.
		CLASS="..”	This attribute adds the element that contains it to a class, a group of elements that need not have anything else in common. Valid values are: any text string.

	TITLE="..."	This attribute allows a text string to be associated with an element. Many browsers render this as a "tool tip" - a box of text that appears when a mouse pointer is over the element. Valid values are: any text.

 QUICK REVISION QUESTIONS

1. What benefits does the use of cascading style sheets bring to Web designers?

2. What is a style sheet rule?

3. What are style sheet properties?

4. There are three ways of applying style sheet rules to a Web page. What are they?

5. How can different style sheet rules be applied to different instances of the same element?

6. What are the **ID** and **CLASS** attributes used for?

7. Certain style sheet properties allow a series of individual properties to be grouped into a single rule. Which are they and how are they used?

8. What is a block-level element?

9. How can a style sheet be used to accurately position a block-level element on a Web page?

10. What are the four HTML core attributes and what are they used for?

Chapter 15
Web authoring software

Web authoring software

This chapter is a sort of holiday before we plunge into Part 2 and the serious business of Web site design. We have now covered the fundamentals of HTML and, if you have stuck with us this far, you are competent in creating effective and functional Web pages. Up until now, we have done all our coding in a simple text editor and many professional Web designers will tell you that this is all you will ever need. This chapter considers other ways of creating Web pages and looks at the advantages and disadvantages of using Web authoring software. The good news is that this chapter does not include any assignments, tag tables or revision questions!

The first question to ask is why would a Web designer want to use complicated software, when everything can be done in a simple text editor? Some people might suggest that this is like asking why anyone would want to use a sophisticated word processor such as Microsoft Word® or Corel WordPerfect® rather than Notepad or Apple's SimpleText®, but this is not the same question at all. A word processor provides a range of features that a text editor cannot provide. For example, Word will allow you to create tables, to format text into columns and to insert spreadsheet data – all features which a text editor simply cannot handle. Web authoring software, on the other hand, can only produce code - the same code that you can type into a text editor.

Of course Web authoring software will automate a lot of code production for you. For example, to insert an image into a Web page, you would need to type a line of code such as:

<IMG SRC="resources/mypicture.jpg" WIDTH="200" HEIGHT="300">

A Web authoring package such as AceExpert® might provide a button marked **Insert Image** which would then produce a window like Figure 15.1.

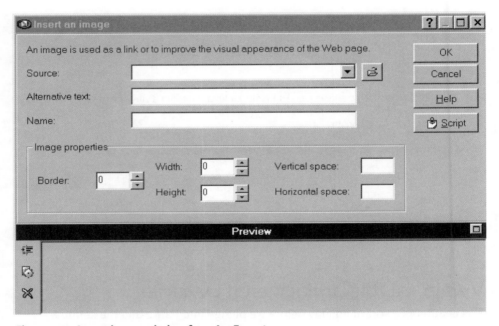

Figure 15.1: Insert image window from AceExpert

But after you have filled in the source, the height and the width, the line of code it produces is:

**<IMG SRC="resources/mypicture.jpg" BORDER=0 WIDTH=200
HEIGHT=300>**

Certainly, you are offered more choices with this approach - the buttons at the lower left provide for image and text alignment, for example, but the basic code it produces is just the same. We should make one point clear from the outset: there is nothing a Web authoring package can do that you cannot do with a simple text editor, provided you know the ins and outs of HTML code.

On the other hand, using Web authoring software does mean that you don't have to work with an HTML text book open at your elbow. It knows all the code and writes it for you, and when the code gets complicated - and we have already seen just how complicated it can get - it can save you a lot of time. For example, a good HTML editor won't forget to drop in the closing tags, it won't forget to wrap URLs in quotation marks and it will remind you to include alternative text for your images. Look back at AceExpert's image window above to see what we mean.

One valid criticism of many Web authoring packages is that they create "bloated" code, by inserting a lot of tags and meta-information that is not strictly necessary. We find it annoying, for example, that packages we have used insist on creating a line of code announcing themselves as the creator of the page. Here's an example from Adobe PageMill®:

<META NAME="GENERATOR" CONTENT="Adobe PageMill 3.0 Win">

This line of code is irrelevant and, in its own small way, takes up bandwidth. Some packages are better than others at writing concise code, but we have yet to find one that can produce tighter HTML than a simple text editor.

We are going to divide Web authoring software into two categories. Firstly we will look at HTML editors and then at fully-featured Web authoring packages. Our first category will include software that displays HTML code on the screen and allows you to write directly into it. Most of these will also provide buttons to automate code production and usually a direct link to your Web browser to see how your page will be rendered. Our second category includes WYSIWYG software, that keeps the code in the background and allows you to manipulate inline and block-level elements directly. Most of these have the facility for modifying the code itself, but this usually requires additional button-clicking.

We cannot hope to cover all the software that is currently available. There are dozens of different products all slightly different in layout, but usually offering much the same in the way of features. Instead we have chosen the packages that we feel provide the best resources and most intuitive operation. Some of these are commercial packages, some are available as shareware from computer magazine cover disks or the Internet, others cost nothing beyond the telephone time it takes to download them. Remember that just because we like a particular package does not mean that you will. If you feel that you want to move on from a text editor, you will need to look for yourself, to try the various demo versions that are widely available, and to decide which suits your own style of authoring.

It is also worth remembering that many modern word processors provide the option of saving work as HTML pages. Microsoft Word® for example offers the ability to save a file in **.html** format. In all honesty, we have to admit that we have yet to find a word processor that produces good HTML code.

One final comment. We can truthfully say that we have never yet created a Web page with any authoring software which has not at some stage required us to get down into the code itself and make changes by hand. Perhaps, at the end of the day, the humble text editor is still the Web author's best friend!

HTML Editors
HTML editors come in all shapes and sizes. Some of them are highly complicated,

others almost ridiculously simple. Although there are variations in the layout, the graphical interface and the number of HTML elements supported, most editors operate in a similar way. In general, on start-up they present the user with either a blank page or a page with the basic HTML tags already in place. To include an HTML element, you position the mouse cursor where you wish to make the entry and click the relevant button or select from a palette. The editor creates the relevant tags but you are required to enter URLs and attribute values. One example of a basic and very easy to use editor is HTML Editor 1.4, which is available as a free download from the Internet. Figure 15.2 shows how it works.

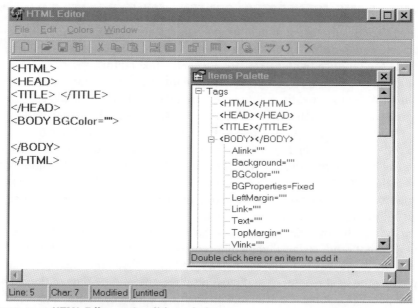

Figure 15.2: HTML Editor 1.4's editing window.

HTML Editor presents the user with a palette of common HTML tags. Double-clicking an item writes the relevant tags into the page. It is arguable that this type of editor actually requires more input than using a basic text editor. Its big advantage is that it does not make mistakes in the code.

Perhaps the neatest and most unusual of the simple HTML editors is NetHTML written by a programmer called Lefteris Haritou and available as a free download. NetHTML is unusual in that it is actually written in HTML rather than one of the genuine programming languages. It therefore opens within a browser and uses client-side scripting to allow you to make changes to an internal Web page. If this sounds confusing, look at Figure 15.3. Internet Explore has opened the file **NetHTML-ie.html** in the same way that it would open any other **.html** file. The file contains the controls to create a Web page in the window at the bottom of the screen which can than be saved as a further HTML file. It can even edit itself, and that's more than any other Web authoring software can do!

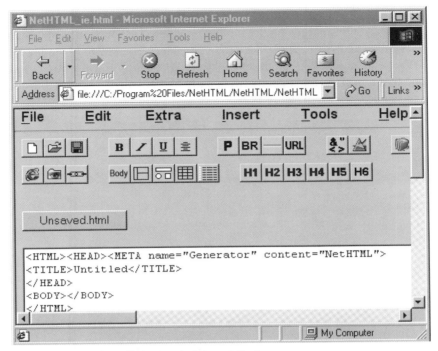

Figure 15.3: The NetHTML editor open in Internet Explorer.

HTML editors can be far more complex than this. Figure 15.4 shows the editing window from AceExpert which offers a much greater choice of HTML elements and supports advanced features like JavaScript and DHTML (Dynamic HTML).

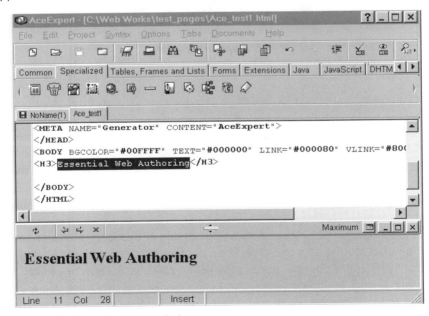

Figure 15.4: AceExpert's editing window

You will see at a glance that this package is a lot more complicated to use than HTML Editor. A series of tabs on the toolbar provide access to groups of buttons. Our illustration shows the Specialized tab open which allows you to modify the **<BODY>** element, insert graphics and links etc. If you look at the buttons, you will see one that depicts a human body (well, parts of it anyway!). Clicking this opens the new window shown in Figure 15.5.

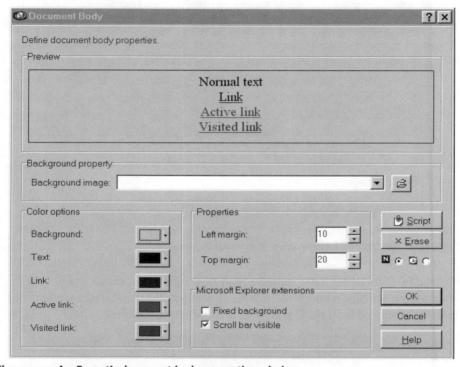

Figure 15.5: AceExpert's document body properties window

Here you have the options to modify all of a document's body attributes including the background colour, text and link colours and the background image. As you make choices, the preview window shows you how your colour scheme will look. Clicking the **OK** button brings up a dialogue box asking you whether you want to replace your existing **<BODY>** element, and clicking **OK** once more writes all the code to your page. An added benefit of this type of editor is a page preview window. Look at the bottom of Figure 15.4 and you will see the partially edited page displayed.

There are a number of HTML editors which operate at this level, although some present a rather more quirky interface. They all require a degree of patience to learn exactly how they operate, but anyone with a good basic knowledge of HTML will be able to work out how to use them. Remember that at this level, you are beginning to sacrifice some degree of control over your code. It is always worth checking pages manually to see whether unnecessary content can be deleted.

The most complicated HTML editors can confuse a beginner with the sheer range of features on offer. Allaire's HomeSite® is a well-respected editor capable of handling every possible HTML entity. Equally complex, but available for free, is 1st Page 2000® whose Expert mode editing window is shown in Figure 15.6. This first class HTML editor operates in four different modes - Easy, Normal, Expert and Hardcore – allowing the user to decide how much clutter appears on screen. Features to note include a window at top left which shows the complete layout of your Web site and a colour palette to the right which lets you pick an exact colour value for any relevant HTML attribute.

Like AceExpert, 1st Page 2000 displays a series of tabs across the toolbar which provide buttons relating to the tab subject. Our illustration shows the Advanced tab selected and the buttons displayed include ones to insert ActiveX controls, and audio and video links. An additional feature of this type of HTML editor is the inclusion of a range of pre-configured scripts to insert active elements like scrolling headlines and background effects. Here we are beginning to venture into the realm of eye-candy!

While the beginner might be confused by the extensive range of buttons on screen, 1st Page 2000 offers a tool tip function. When the mouse pointer is held over a button, a box appears explaining briefly what that button does.

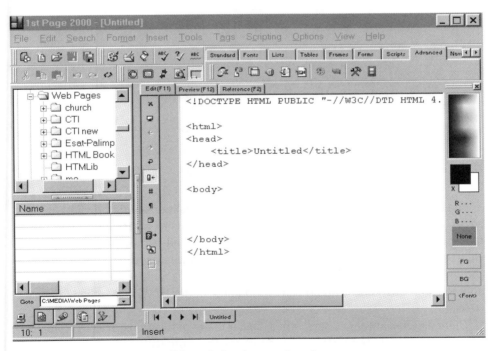

Figure 15.6: 1st Page 2000's editing window in expert mode.

Another editor that deserves a mention is Chami's HTML-Kit, which is another free download. Not only does HTML-kit support every Web technology there is, it also provides a built-in HTML validator which checks every line of your code and not only spots errors, but also suggests ways of improving it. Look at the screenshot in Figure 15.7.

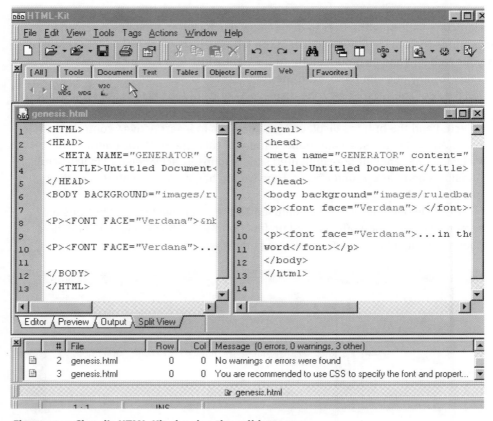

Figure 15.7: Chami's HTML-Kit showing the validator pane.

The bottom pane in Figure 15.7 lists errors or suggestions for improving the code. Note, for example, in Line 3 HTML-Kit suggests using a cascading style sheet rather than HTML tags to specify font properties. The left-hand pane above the validator shows the original code and the right-hand window shows the improved code with preferred syntax and unnecessary blank lines removed. For ease of use and range of functions, it would be hard to find a better HTML editor than Chami's HTML-Kit.

There are many other editors with a similar range of functions. We could, for example, have included HoTMetaL and HotDog Pro, both widely used and very competent. There are two points to keep in mind if you decide that this level of editor is right for you. Firstly, remember that the HTML standard continues to be developed and it is important that your editor is up to date. Old editors write old code which newer versions of browsers might not display properly. Secondly, make sure that the code being produced is concise and understandable. At some stage you will need to get in and make changes by hand, and if the code is beyond you, you will lose control of your pages.

WYSIWYG Web authoring software

You will recall that WYSIWYG is an acronym for What You See Is What You Get. As we mentioned in our introduction, the most sophisticated Web authoring software hides the code completely and lets you work directly on a representation of the Web page itself. These packages work more like desktop publishing software, allowing you to manipulate block-level elements without worrying about the mark-up.

The best known and most widely used Web authoring package is Macromedia's Dreamweaver® shown in Figure 15.8. Perhaps Dreamweaver's greatest benefit is that it allows you to place page content on different layers, each of which can be modified independently. (This approach will be familiar to anyone who has used Adobe PhotoShop® which handles graphics in the same way.) By allowing designers to create independent block-level elements which can be arranged as required, Dreamweaver effectively solves the problems of text alignment which we have returned to time and again in this book.

Anyone moving up to Dreamweaver from a standard HTML editor will find that he or she is confronted by an entirely different approach to Web authoring. Gone is the editing window and toolbar approach. Instead, Dreamweaver presents a range of independent floating palettes which the user can drag around on screen as required.

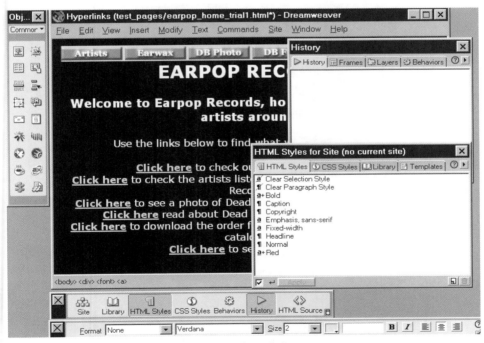

Figure 15.8: Macromedia Dreamweaver's editing windows

Our illustration show's Earpop's home page opened in Dreamweaver. The Objects palette to the left provides a series of tabs with buttons, similar to those provided by the HTML editors we have already looked at. The palette at the bottom is familiar enough, providing basic formatting functions such as font and colour changes. The shorter palette above this controls which other palettes appear on screen. The two palettes which we have dragged on top of Earpop's page itself provide a range of additional functions including the ability to undo mistakes by returning to an earlier stage in the design process, to create and include cascading style sheets, and to create floating layers.

There is no doubt that Dreamweaver is a phenomenally successful package. It is also the software behind many of the Web's most effective sites. One of the reasons for this is that it supports every type of scripting and active content there is, including, not surprisingly, Macromedia's own Flash® content which we have already mentioned and will return to later in this chapter.

Less complex than Dreamweaver, but equally effective in its own way is Adobe PageMill®. PageMill is beginning to show its age and its limitations, and Adobe has moved forward with its new GoLive package which matches most of Dreamweaver's capabilities and adds a few new tricks of its own. Despite this, PageMill is still widely used. It has a simpler and more intuitive interface than Dreamweaver, as shown in Figure 15.9.

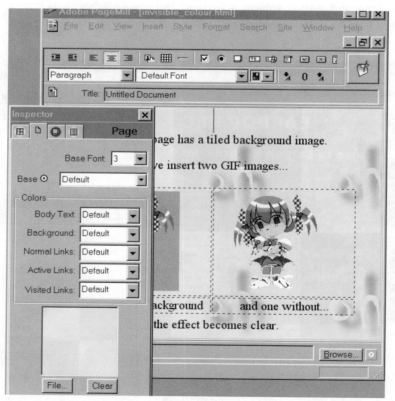

Figure 15.9: Adobe PageMill's editing window.

PageMill provides an editing window and just one floating palette which it calls the Inspector. The Inspector offers tabs to control frames, page properties, forms and objects. All other functions are provided by standard buttons and menus. PageMill can be irritating at times and has a habit of rewriting your code to suit its own preferences, but it is easy to learn and produces fairly concise code.

One of the most widely used packages at present is Microsoft's FrontPage®. The full commercial version of FrontPage is a very large and well-featured piece of software which not only provides a WYSIWYG editor, but also a good Web graphics editor (shown in Figure 15.11) and a utility called FrontPage Explorer which allows you to organise and manage your site locally before uploading it to the Web. One problem with FrontPage Explorer is that it has difficulties with any site configuration other than its own FrontPage Webs. The latest version of FrontPage provides almost every facility imaginable, but is, quite naturally, biased towards Internet Explorer's preferred handling of HTML. Microsoft bundles a cut-down version of the software called FrontPage Express with the latest versions of Internet Explorer. Its editing window is shown in Figure 15.10.

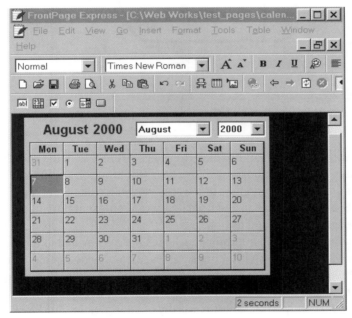

Figure 15.10: FrontPage Express' editing window.

A criticism regularly levelled at FrontPage is that it writes very bloated code, but we have not generally found this to be the case. Certainly its code is very comprehensive, but a little manual editing – and the code itself is easy to access – will chop out unnecessary portions and slim down the final file size.

FrontPage Express is so easily available that it has become one of the most widely used editors in the world. It is a neat and easy-to-operate package which looks and behaves like other Microsoft products – a comfort for those who are nervous of new interfaces. Common functions are provided by easily identified toolbar buttons, while the standard menus give access to an extensive range of advanced features. FrontPage Express supports Java and, of course, Microsoft's own ActiveX components.

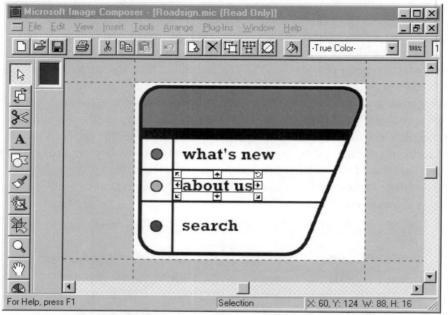

Figure 15.11: Microsoft's Image Composer®.

In the same way that Microsoft bundles FrontPage Express with Internet Explorer, Netscape bundles its own Composer with its Navigator browser. Composer, illustrated in Figure 15.12 below, looks and works very much like FrontPage. It is not a true WYSIWYG editor, as you can see from its screen representation of our HotSauce page, but it is neat and easy to use.

Most of the commercial Web authoring packages are also available for the Mac platform, along with a few specialised ones. Claris, who provide a range of top quality Mac software, offer a well-designed WYSIWYG editor called Home Page® which looks and behaves very like Adobe PageMill but has been optimised for Apple users. One Mac-only HTML editor is worthy of special note. SoftPress' Freeway is a Web authoring application which looks rather like Dreamweaver on screen. It uses a range of floating palettes and creates moveable block-level elements. While Freeway is a much simpler package than Dreamweaver, it is capable of producing highly effective Web pages and writes very tight code. Better still, SoftPress regularly promote new versions of Freeway, by giving older ones away for nothing.

Additional Web authoring software
The packages described above are intended to produce HTML pages for the Web,

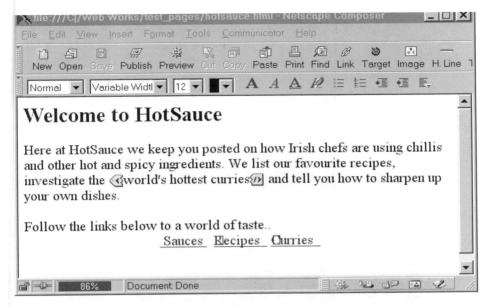

Figure 15.12: Netscape Composer's editing window.

but all of them depend on you as the author to provide the actual content in the form of words, graphics and multimedia. There is an enormous range of programs which can help you to create content, and the Web doesn't mind what you use, as long as the file formats are correct. There is also a wide choice of software to help you to upload and maintain your site when it is ready for publication to the Web. We have referred to a few of these additional applications where appropriate in the text and we will mention several more in the second part of this book. The final section of this chapter we will devote to one or two specialist programs.

We have already looked at animation for the Web in Chapter 7, but one package that we must mention here is Macromedia's Flash®. These days, Flash "movies" are everywhere on the Web. They consist of interactive vector graphics and animations, and are often used for navigation controls or animated logos, with or without synchronised sounds. Their greatest advantages are firstly that compressed Flash files download quickly, and secondly, because they are vector rather than bitmapped graphics, they can be scaled to suit the viewer's screen size. (You will recall that vector graphics define content by means of lines, curves and angles, as opposed to bitmapped graphics which simply apply colours to a grid of pixels.)

The Flash workspace looks intimidating at first, but is actually surprisingly easy to use. Look at the screenshot in Figure 15.13. As well as the usual buttons and menus, there is a Timeline towards the top of the window. Each component of a Flash movie, called a "Symbol", has its own timeline which defines when it appears, when it does something and when it vanishes. Symbols can be graphics, buttons or even movie clips. The lower part of the window is called "The Stage". It is the working area where graphics are assembled and modified.

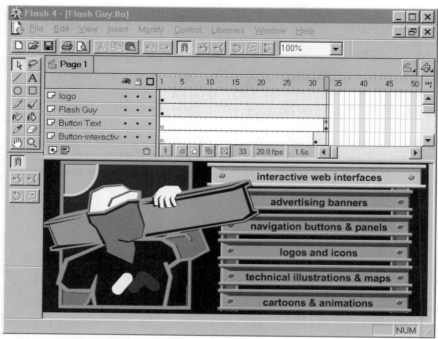

Figure 15.13: Macromedia's Flash animation software.

Like Dreamweaver, Flash offers the ability to work on different layers, so different components of a movie can move independently. Flash movies can be fully interactive with complete control in the hands of the viewer. Clicking areas can start

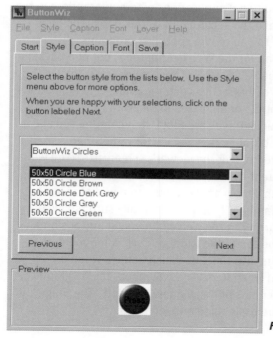

animated sequences, open new boxes or trigger hyperlinks. To view a Flash movie on the Web, you require the Flash movie player which is widely available as a plug-in for most of the popular browsers. Flash files can also be embedded within HTML pages using the **<OBJECT>** element.

A very handy utility which is available as shareware, is Joel Ryan's ButtonWiz shown in Figure 15.14.

ButtonWiz only does one thing, but it does it perfectly. It allows you to create buttons for your Web pages. ButtonWiz offers a wide

Figure 15.14: Joel Ryan's ButtonWiz

choice of styles, sizes and colours. It also allows you to caption your buttons. Many Web sites use buttons of one kind or another, so this little program is a real asset.

Equally useful is David Gauff's Tag Buddy - a utility which looks terrible but proves useful time and again. Essentially, Tag Buddy consists of a set of smaller programs which write specialised tags for you. These tags can then be copied into your own Web pages. Figure 15.15 shows the Image Tag Buddy.

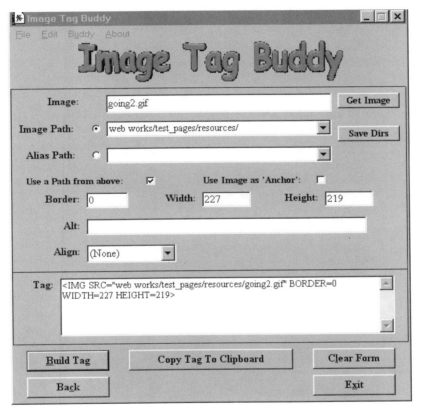

Figure 15.15: David Gauff's Image Tag Buddy.

To use a Tag Buddy, you fill in the details using the boxes or pick-lists at the top of the window, then press the Build Tag button. The complete tag appears in the Tag window where it can be edited if required before copying to the clipboard.

This chapter has covered some of the resources available to Web authors. There are many others equally good that we have not the space to look at. The best way to decide which software to use for your own Web work, is to look around, check the free demonstrations which regularly feature on magazine cover disks, and then make an informed decision on which applications will suit your own way of working.

Part **2**

Designing a site for
the World Wide Web

Chapter 16
Planning your Web site

Brief contents:

1. The importance of thoroughly planning a Web site before starting to construct one.

2. The golden rule – "function dictates design".

3. How to establish a site's objective.

4. How to define a site's target audience.

5. Understanding the idea of Key Messages and how they relate to a Web site's layout.

6. Site structure and hierarchies.

7. The importance of considering page size and shape.

8. How to draw up a design sheet for a Web site.

Planning your Web site

When we first considered the layout of this book, we seriously thought of moving this chapter to the very front. We have lost count of the number of times we have mentioned design concepts in the previous chapters and then left them hanging in the air, waiting for Part Two to bring them all together. In the end we decided to work through the mechanics of HTML and Web coding before looking at design, but we hope that our repeated emphasis on design considerations has kept the subject in front of your eyes.

In one way, Part Two of this book goes right back to the beginning of Web authoring. In this chapter, for example, we shall be starting from scratch. Over the next six chapters, we will be working our way through a logical, step-by-step process intended to provide you with the skills you need to design, create and manage a Web site. If you have followed the chapters and exercises so far, you can consider yourself a competent Web mechanic. Now you need a second qualification as a Web designer.

Some people might be panicking at this point. They will wonder whether they have the artistic or creative abilities to become a designer. There is no doubt that artistic skills are useful to the Web author, but we firmly believe that 90% of good Web design is common sense, the ability to apply sound judgment and to follow basic layout principles. Perhaps the other 10% is inspiration, and if you can bring that to the process, all well and good, but trust us: anyone can become a competent Web designer if they learn the fundamental concepts then use them in their work.

So where do we begin? There is a basic principle which all Web designers should consider tattooing on their foreheads (backwards, perhaps, so that they are reminded of it every time they look in the mirror!). It is this:

Function dictates design.

If you were building a bookshelf, would you nail on a kitchen sink just because you happened to have one to hand? A bookshelf has a function – to hold books, and everything that goes into that bookshelf – the shelves, the uprights, the glue and the screws, should be selected to support that function. Now you might be constrained by the materials available and by the skills you can bring to the project. If you were a craftsman, you might apply elegant mouldings or use beautifully figured timber. But at the end of the day, if the bookshelf doesn't do its job properly, it is a bad piece of work. Exactly the same principles apply to designing a Web site. We will say it again – function dictates design.

From this point on we are going to assume that you have a site to design. It doesn't matter whether you are obliged to do this for your college course, whether you wish to create a site for you own reasons, or whether someone has commissioned you to do so on behalf of some organisation. Whatever your motives, the process is exactly the same. We shall be designing a site of our own over the next few chapters, and as you work along with us, feel free to adapt our suggestions and ideas to suit your own needs. If you still aren't sure what your own site will be about, you are welcome to use our site for practice. At the end of the process, you will be able to go back through the various stages, applying them to your own project.

Start with an objective

Every Web site should have a purpose and that purpose will determine how a site is organised, what it contains and how it is laid out. There are any number of reasons for creating a Web site. At its simplest, one reason might be to test your own abilities and skills – a Web site, if you like, just for the fun of it. On the other hand, you might have something important to say – a political message or information on a subject that interests you. Whether your objective is serious or trivial, the important thing is to keep focused on it. Web sites are dynamic entities, they change and develop over time, but the worst thing you can do is to create one page and then keep nailing other pages onto it.

The following table suggests different objectives for sites, suggestions as to the type of content and related design ideas.

Purpose of site:	Possible content:	Initial design thoughts:
Entertain	Site dedicated to a local, national or international band. Site specialising in a particular type of music or dance. Site listing jokes or strange stories.	Design concepts might be "cool", modern, unusual.
Inform	Site on your local town or region.	Cut back on flashy visual effects in favour of solid but intriguing content.
Educate	Site to help visitors learn about your specialist subject.	Fairly serious and dedicated to the subject matter.
Question or persuade	Site to make your visitors think about an issue. Site to promote your political opinions.	Raise important issues early on the site. Establish your authority as an expert of the points under discussion.
Sell or Promote	Site to auction some of your property. Commercial site selling goods or services. Site advertising your own skills and abilities.	Immediately direct your visitors attention to the benefits and features of the goods or services you are trying to promote.

After you have decided on a purpose for your site, you still have to consider the most appropriate type of site to handle your content. The commonest site type on the Web is the information site. This is a site laid out to provide information to the visitor. There are other types. Some of the most useful resources on the Web are links sites – sites which consist of pages of links to other sites. In some ways these are like indexes to the Web. If you are interested in motorbikes, you can find a links site which lists the URLs of thousands of motorbike sites. This will save you from having to hunt them down one at a time. There are also chat sites, libraries of resources, download sites, help and support sites. You will need to decide which is the most appropriate for your purpose.

We have decided to create a Web site on Japanese manga for no other reason than a lifelong fascination with the artform. Manga are comics and over the years

Japanese artists have created some very beautiful work which we wish to explain and display on our Web site. Unfortunately, the extent of most Western people's exposure to manga is watching Pokémon on television. We feel we have a mission to inform our readers on how much more there is to manga than that! We now have an objective and can start considering our design.

When it comes to designing a Web site, the best way to start is to turn off your computer and sit down with a blank piece of paper. This is how we are going to begin and we suggest you do the same. (Since this chapter is effectively one long exercise, we will not be inserting exercises into the text. Instead we will assume that you will be working through the design process along with us. So, pull out a pad and a pencil and let's get started.)

Figure 16.1 shows our design sheet as it looks so far:

DESIGN FOR MY WEB SITE

1. Objective - inform people about Japanese manga.

Figure 16.1.

Defining a target audience

The next thing we need to consider is who we are aiming our site at. If your site is purely to amuse yourself, you might just as well maintain it on your own computer – there is little point in going to the time and effort of publishing it on the Web. Any other type of site is intended to attract visitors and here we need to think in marketing terms. Marketing specialists talk in terms of target audiences – sections of the public that the products they are promoting are aimed at. Washing powder commercials, for example, are aimed almost exclusively at women because research has shown that most washing powder is bought by women.

Professional marketing uses a concept known as segmentation. It is possible to segment the public in many different ways, by gender, by age, by income, by region, and so on. While we don't need to be too precise as far as our Web site is concerned, we do need to segment to a degree because different segments require different content and style. Think of the Web as a bookshop with millions of titles for sale. Book publishers know that they need to attract readers to their particular titles and they do so by designing covers that appeal to particular segments of the book-buying public. By targeting your audience you stand a better chance of attracting visitors and one measure of the success of your site is how many visitors are persuaded to visit it.

Another consideration when segmenting is the level of Web experience you expect your visitors to possess. In its infancy, the Internet was almost exclusively the province of computer "nerds", but as its appeal and accessibility widened, it attracted users with little or no technical knowledge. Information Technology is a subject that is stuffed with technical terminology that means nothing to the man in the street. If your site is intended for general, rather than specialist, consumption, make sure that the content and navigation mechanics are easy to understand.

After some thought, we have decided to aim our manga site at a mature audience. Clearly we don't care about gender, income or any other factor, but we want to impress our visitors with the artistry and beauty of our chosen subject, and we feel that children will not have the patience or attention span for what we have in mind. So we can extend our design sheet so that it looks like Figure 16.2:

DESIGN FOR MY WEB SITE

1. Objective - inform people about Japanese manga.
2. Target Audience: Teen to adult, no particular gender.

Figure 16.2.

Audience suitability

Now that we have defined our audience, we need to consider how we will make sure our content is suited to them. Some points are obvious. Adults don't like to be talked down to, so we will have to ensure that the tone of our site is friendly and mature. Adults are more critical than children, so we must watch out for bad layout, silly spelling mistakes and active content that doesn't work. Other considerations are more subtle, but equally important. The colour schemes that appeal to adults are more restrained than the bright primary colours that children like. We will need to carefully consider our choice of fonts and text styles. The next chapter contains a detailed look at colour and text schemes, so we'll leave those aspects for the time being, but we can update our design sheet with another important point. It will now look like Figure 16.3.

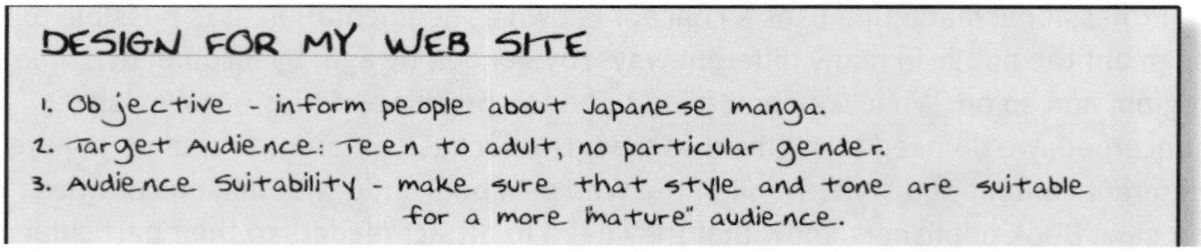

DESIGN FOR MY WEB SITE

1. Objective - inform people about Japanese manga.
2. Target Audience: Teen to adult, no particular gender.
3. Audience Suitability - make sure that style and tone are suitable for a more "mature" audience.

Figure 16.3.

Already we have established a basis for the design of our site. These three notes alone will point us in certain directions as regards both layout and content. Of course our design sheet will also serve as a check list. As we build our site and after our first "draft" is complete, we can refer back to our design sheet and make sure that we are sticking to the rules we have set for ourselves.

Key messages

In advertising there is a tried and trusted formula for measuring the effectiveness of an advertisement. It is contained in the acronym AIDA where:

A = Attention
I = Interest
D = Desire and
A = Action

If an advert is to work, it must first grab the **attention** of the viewer to stop him from turning the page or looking away from the television. Next it must hold his **interest** long enough for him to absorb the sales message. The sales message must be strong enough to make the viewer **desire** the product being advertised. But all of this is wasted, if the viewer's desire is not sufficiently stimulated to persuade him to take **action** – to go out and buy the product. This formula can usefully be applied to the design of a Web site.

When your home page first opens on the visitor's monitor, it has to grab that visitor's attention immediately. If the site is dull and uninteresting (and even more so if it takes too long to download), the chances are that the visitor will give up and go somewhere else. Most Web users are like butterflies: they flit around the Internet, settling on promising sites. You only have a few seconds to convince that butterfly that your site is worth stopping on.

First impressions are fine, but beyond that initial impact must be enough solid content to hold the visitor's interest. If he feels that your site is all show and no substance, he will quickly move on. Once you have claimed your visitor's interest, he will desire more of what you are offering, and then he will take action, he will follow your links, look through your pages and hopefully tell others to come and get it as well.

Consider the concept of key messages. Ask yourself "What am I trying to say in this site?", then make a list of your answers. Look through that list and prioritise it, then make sure that your site answers those questions in the order you have listed them. A good analogy here is a press release. When an organisation issues information to the press, it is always presented with the most important information first and the least important information last. The reason for this structure is that when an editor is fitting that press release into a space in his newspaper or magazine, he will cut it to down to size from the bottom upwards. By starting with the key messages, the Public Relations Officer makes sure that the vital information gets printed.

Every visitor to your site is an editor of sorts. He will go just so far into your site, but you cannot be sure he will read every page you include. If you bury your key messages deep inside, they may never get read.

Applying the key message model to our manga site, we can now update our design sheet so that it looks like Figure 16.4.

DESIGN FOR MY WEB SITE

1. Objective - inform people about Japanese manga.
2. Target Audience: Teen to adult, no particular gender.
3. Audience Suitability - make sure that style and tone are suitable
   for a more "mature" audience.
4. Key Messages: 1. Manga are a genuine artform.
   2. They are not just "comics for kids"
   3. They come in a wide range of styles and formats.
   4. Look at some examples.
   5. You should know a bit about their origins.
   6. Let us know what you think.

Figure 16.4.

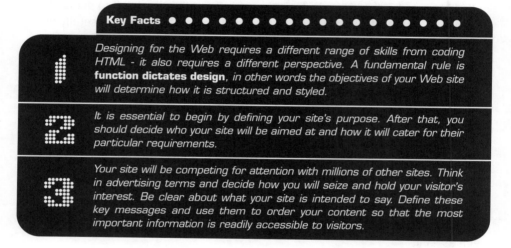

Key Facts ●

1 Designing for the Web requires a different range of skills from coding HTML - it also requires a different perspective. A fundamental rule is **function dictates design**, in other words the objectives of your Web site will determine how it is structured and styled.

2 It is essential to begin by defining your site's purpose. After that, you should decide who your site will be aimed at and how it will cater for their particular requirements.

3 Your site will be competing for attention with millions of other sites. Think in advertising terms and decide how you will seize and hold your visitor's interest. Be clear about what your site is intended to say. Define these key messages and use them to order your content so that the most important information is readily accessible to visitors.

Site structure

We now have enough information to consider the structure of our site. All we know at this stage is that our site will consist of a number of linked pages. We have yet to decide how many pages and how we will link them. The first thing to consider is the site's superstructure. A Web site's superstructure refers to the actual mechanics of organisation and navigation. We need to decide how a visitor will move around the site, how the pages will be organised and what additional information the visitor will need to properly appreciate our site. Navigation is such an important issue that we have given it a chapter to itself, but for now let's agree that each page will feature an identical set of controls. In due course we will decide whether these will comprise an image map, a set of clickable icons or simple text links.

Should we include a table of contents? If our site is "linear", in other words if each page leads directly to the next page, a table of contents might be unnecessary. But if our site is more involved, or if it could in any way confuse our visitor, we should consider including a table of contents, or better yet, a site map. Again we will leave the actual mechanics of this until Chapter 18.

Does our site use specialised terminology and can we expect our visitors to be familiar with that terminology? If our site is on a highly technical topic and it is targeted at other enthusiasts, we might assume that they would be up to speed on the techno-talk, but if we are aiming to extend the interest in our subject to newcomers, it would be sensible to include a glossary. For our manga site, we will be using a number of Japanese words. We considered preparing a translations page, but decided to include these in the text itself.

Now let us consider the structure of our pages. People who are accustomed to getting their information from books are used to thinking in a two-dimensional, linear fashion. Each page in a book is attached both physically and logically to the following page. We can describe this as a "linear hierarchy" and show it graphically in Figure 16.5:

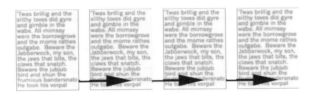

Figure 16.5: A linear hierarchy of text pages.

Computers, on the other hand, are often organised as a "tree hierarchy". (This is not the most appropriate term since they start from a single point and spread out downwards. Perhaps a "root hierarchy" would describe it better.) Most computers have a name of some kind, usually so that they can be identified on a network. Microsoft Windows® uses the name "My Computer", unless the user changes it. Below that name come letters identifying the various drives attached. Most PCs have at least an "A" (floppy) drive and a "C" (hard) drive, and there is often a "D" (CDROM) drive as well. When these drives are mounted, they usually carry folders containing programs or data. Inside those folders might be more folders, which, in turn, might contain still more folders. A small part of the overall hierarchy might look something like Figure 16.6.

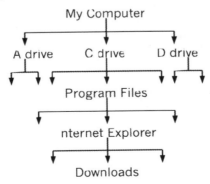

Figure 16.6: A tree hierarchy showing part of a computer's file structure.

We use this hierarchy when we define absolute paths (URLs) on a local computer. The "Downloads" folder in our example can be addressed as file:///C:/program files/internet explorer/downloads.

At first site, this type of hierarchy might seem appropriate for laying out a Web site – indeed it might suit a simple site with very few links involved. We already know that a Web site requires a Home Page – the page that automatically loads when a site is linked to. The page is normally named **home.html** or **index.html**, and from this page, links lead on to other pages. This might suggest a tree hierarchy such as is shown in Figure 16.7:

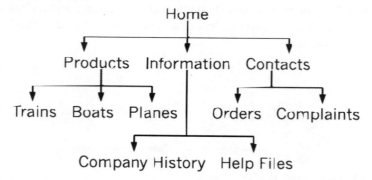

Figure 16.7: A Web site laid out as a tree hierarchy.

In this example there are links from the Home Page to three further pages, Products, Information and Contacts. The Products page contains three further links to the Trains, Boats and Planes pages. All very simple and logical – or so it seems!

The tree hierarchy is a two-dimensional model. You start at the top and travel down or sideways. This type of thinking might prove very useful while the site is being planned. Its major disadvantage is that it cannot cope with the greatest benefit of hypertext links – their ability to operate in three dimensions.

To explain what we mean, take a careful look at Figure 16.8.

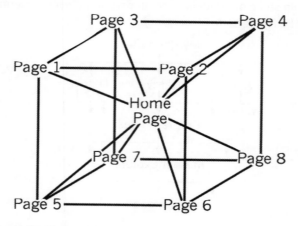

Figure 16.8: A three-dimensional hierarchy

This model looks confusing, but it is difficult to represent three-dimensional layouts on a two-dimensional page. We are attempting to represent a Web site consisting of nine pages, the Home Page and Pages 1 to 8. Each line in the drawing represents a two-way link between two pages. The Home Page is linked to every other page. Page 5, for example, links to the Home Page and Pages 1, 6 and 7. Page 4 links to the Home Page and Pages 2, 3 and 8. This is not intended to model a working site because the layout is too restrictive. We are including it for two reasons. Firstly, it positions the Home Page where it ought to be – right at the centre of the site and linked to every other page. Secondly, it indicates that hyperlinking is a 3D process. Links do not simply move a visitor up and down or across a site. They connect forwards and backwards as well. Let us see what this means in terms of site structure.

Our preferred model for a Web site uses a modified tree structure with different levels of hierarchies. The **Home Page level** is our top level and contains only the Home Page, which links in both directions to every page on the site. Our second level is the **Section Level** and contains a maximum of five pages. These pages, plus the Home Page, are those that can be linked to from every other page and contain information about the sections they introduce. On screen, the links to these six pages comprise the navigation system for the entire site and might appear as a navigation bar or imagemap. We say a maximum of five plus Home, because research has shown that any more than six or seven links can confuse a visitor.

Our third level is the **Content Level**. According to our plan, there can be a maximum of 25 of these pages – five from each Section Level page. These pages contain the "meat" of the site, the actual information. Where a content level page would be too long for convenient reading, it is a good idea to bring in a fourth level, the **Detail Level** which can carry on the theme of the Content Level. This level provides for a maximum of 125 pages – five from each Content Level page. We recommend that your site should be a maximum of four levels deep. If you really need more than this, consider splitting the content into two separate sites. Only as a last resort should you adopt a fifth **Sub-Detail Level**.

Let's look at one part of this structure using the simplified tree hierarchy shown in Figure 16.9. Note that only one set of links is followed all the way down to the bottom.

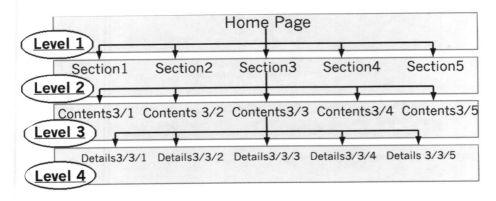

Figure 16.9: Four-level tree hierarchy

While this hierarchical approach is very useful for laying out a site plan, it is almost useless when it comes to plotting links, and links, as we know, are the very heart of a Web site. If we try to use the tree structure above to draw in our links, it will very quickly start to look like a plate of spaghetti with strands going everywhere. Our 3D model above contained just nine pages. Can you imagine how it would look with 50 or 100 pages? Instead, let's leave site plans alone for a moment and agree a set of linking rules instead. We suggest the following.

1. All pages on the site will have a link back to the Home Page.

2. All pages on the site will carry an identical navigation system.

3. Each Section Level page will link a maximum of five Content Level pages.

4. Each Content Level page will link to a maximum of five Detail Level Pages.

5. Each Detail Level page will have a maximum of five links to other relevant pages, with a link back to the relevant Content Level page.

6. We will **never** expect our visitors to use the **Back** button on their browsers.

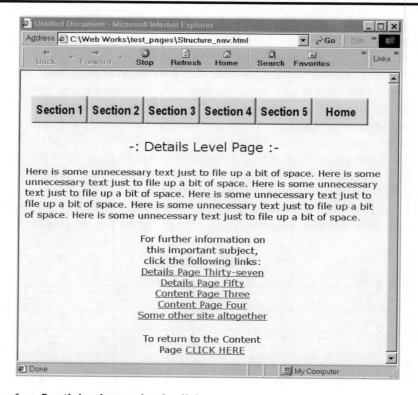

Figure 16.10: Fourth-level page showing links.

The first and most important point is that this linking strategy is both logical and consistent. Let's look at some examples and see how many links we need to click to move around the site. The Home Page and any Section Level page can be reached from any page on the site with just one click of the navigation system. Any Content Level page can be reached in two clicks – one click on the navigation system to reach the relevant Section Level page, and a second click on one of the links on the Section Level page. Any Detail Level page can be reached in a maximum of three clicks – two as before, and a third click on one of the links on the Content Level page. If you are now hopelessly confused, look at Figure 16.10 which shows one of the Detail Level pages on the site.

The navigation bar at the top of the page provides links to the Section Level pages and the Home Page. Within the page itself are five links to connected pages, and a further link at the bottom of the page connects with the Content Level page which links to this page.

We will look at navigation in more detail in the Chapter 18, but for now, let's apply this structure to our manga site. Using a simple tree hierarchy at this stage, we can update our design sheet with a rough plan for our site as shown in Figure 16.11.

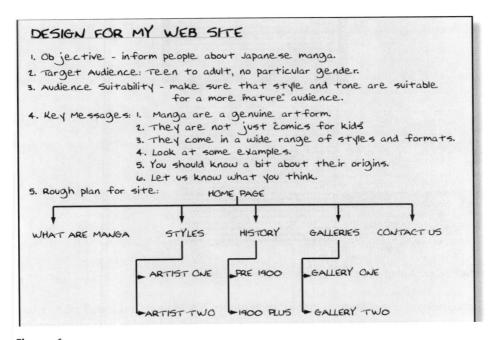

Figure 16.11.

Since our site will be a relatively small one – a total of 12 pages, we will be content with three levels in our hierarchy. Our Home Page and the five Section Level pages ("What are manga", "Styles", "History", "Galleries" and "Contact us") will appear on our navigation system. Links on the Section Level pages will connect to any Content Level pages below them. Of course, with our navigation system appearing on all pages, the Home Page will be accessible from everywhere on the site. With this structure, no page will be more than two clicks away from any other page.

Page level structure

Having agreed a structure, we now need to decide the shape and size of our pages. Firstly, we should give some thought to how long a page should be. It is a fact that most Web users do not like having to scroll up and down pages, so the perfect solution might be to plan our pages so none of them are longer than a single screenful. Look, for example, at Figure 16.12 which shows a long Web page and the amount that can be seen at any one time in a browser's window. Clearly this page is far too long and it would be better to aim for something which would just fit the viewing window. But what constitutes a screenful?

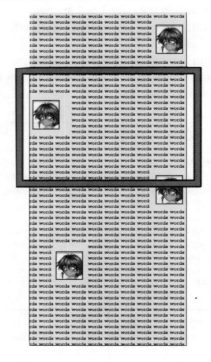

Figure 16.12: A long page related to a browser's viewing window.

Some browsers have larger windows than others. Some users set their text size to large or even extra-large. Different monitor resolutions determine how much can fit on a screen. Turn on more toolbars in a browser and the actual viewing window is reduced in proportion. There are all sorts of variations and combinations of factors which the Web author cannot hope to anticipate. We will have to establish guidelines for page size and hope our choices suit the majority of our visitors.

Secondly, let's consider a shape for our pages. Used full screen, the viewing window of the average browser's proportions are roughly 10:6.5 – 10 wide to 6.5 high. On a monitor whose resolution is set to 640 x 480 pixels, a browser's viewing area would be roughly 620 x 400 pixels. At a resolution of 800 x 600 pixels, the viewing area would increase to 770 x 500 pixels; and at a resolution of 1024 x 768 pixels, to 980 x 640 pixels. The most common monitor resolution at present is reckoned to be 800 x 600 pixels, which suggests that we should base our calculations around a scroll-free page size of 700 x 550 pixels.

On lower resolution monitors, two things might happen to a page designed to that size. If the proportions of all our block level elements are fixed in code, the browser will need to generate scroll bars at both the bottom and on one side of the page for the visitor to see it all. Alternatively, if our design allows the text to flow freely, our layout will be distorted. It will be squashed in from the right-hand side and stretched downwards. On higher resolution monitors, on the other hand, either our pages will appear to the top left of the screen with white space to the left, or they will spread out sideways to fill the screen area, again distorting our layout. On most pages, of course, such distortions won't matter. HTML is intended for flexible layouts which can adapt to different browser window sizes, but lists and tables, for example, do not like being squeezed.

We would recommend working to an overall page size of 700 x 550 pixels, but trying to restrict the width of the actual page content to 600 pixels wherever your design requires the exact placement of content. This will ensure that whatever his monitor resolution, the user will, in most cases, see your design as you intended it to appear. On a page which consists purely of text we do not need to worry, but if (as we intend in our manga site) we require a gallery of images, it might be a good idea to size all our pages to a maximum of 600 pixels in width so that viewers will not need to scroll sideways. (That really annoys people!) If we intend to use tables to provide a multi-column layout, we will make sure that the maximum table width is 600 pixels for the same reason.

As far as length is concerned, we will try not to exceed our 550 pixel limit, but here, as always in Web design, we will be prepared to make exceptions where necessary. If a list of items naturally runs overlength, it would be impractical to break it up. Some *portrait-format*[1] graphics will need to exceed our limit if they are not to be reduced to a size that makes them ineffective. At the top of this section we noted that we were looking for guidelines rather than cast-iron rules. Our only definite rule is that we will ignore our guidelines where content requires it!

Deciding page content

Finally in this chapter, we need to decide exactly what each page will actually contain. Remember that in the Key Messages section earlier in the chapter we stressed the need to post our most important information at the top of the site. This is not to say that the early pages need to be crammed with detail. It is enough for our Home Page, for example, to include our Key Messages in brief, along with links to further information on each subject. In a way, our Home Page is like "teaser" advertising. We want to pull visitors into the depths of our site, so our Home Page will dangle little bits of bait in front of them and entice them to click on in.

---

[1] **Portrait-format:** Graphics are often described as portrait- or landscape-format. The difference is best seen by looking at an ordinary sheet of A4 paper. Hold it with the short side at the top and it is in portrait format, hold it with the long side at the top and it is in landscape format. Clearly a portrait is usually taller than it is wide, whereas a landscape is usually wider than it is tall.

Each level within our site plan requires a slightly different approach to page content.

Top Level: Our Home Page is like the front cover of a magazine. It is intended to attract and entice, to spell out those Key Messages so that the visitor knows what to expect within. It also has to welcome visitors to the site and to make sure they realise how to navigate around the pages.

Section Level: Section Level pages provide more details on the sections they introduce. They break down the contents of the sections and explain how the visitor will find the information he or she is looking for. If the section content is short enough, the hierarchy might stop at this level. For example a contact page should be at Section Level so that it is always accessible from the navigation system. If a contact page contains only a form for visitors to fill in, or a simple e-mail response link, there is no need for any further pages in that section.

Content Level: Content Level pages contain the actual meat and potatoes – the text, graphics and multimedia content that the site is promising.

Detail Level: This level will only exist where there is too much content to fit on the Content Level Pages. Remember that by creating pages on this level, we are increasing the number of clicks required to navigate our site. Where Detail Level pages are needed, the Content Level pages will be modified to become more introductory, leaving this level to present the bulk of the actual contents of the section.

Let's apply this structure to our manga site and see what each page might contain. Look back at the design sheet in Figure 16.11. We have decided that 12 pages will be enough for our site – we can always increase the number if necessary. The table opposite includes the proposed contents for each of our 12 pages. This is a vital part of our plan and we could write it on the back of our design sheet for reference. Remember this is still just a plan – we might need to make major changes as we start to put it into practice.

This chapter has taken us through the first phase of designing our site – there are five more stages of the process in subsequent chapters. So far, we have decided what our site will be about, who it will be aimed at, how large it will be, how it will be structured, and what the individual pages will contain. And we have got this far without even switching our computer on! If you have a site project of your own to complete, now might be a good time go back through this chapter, applying the various stages to your own ideas and drawing up your own plan.

Top Level	**Home Page** Welcome visitors to site. Introduce content and include Key Messages. Discuss site structure and navigation system.						
Section Level	**What are manga?** Define manga as an artform and see how it relates to Japanese culture.	**Style** Talk about different styles of manga and point to the works of the two artists we are presenting at Content level.		**History of Manga** How manga originated from other artforms and point to the detailed history at Content level.		**Manga Galleries** Explain how our galleries are organised and how to use them. Point to the two thumbnail galleries at Content level.	**Contact Page** Details on how to contact us and what we would like to hear from you.
Content Level		Discuss artist 1 with samples of work.	Discuss artist 2 with samples of work.	History up to 1900.	History from 1900 to the present day.	Thumbnail Gallery 1.	Thumbnail Gallery 2.	

Key Facts ● ● ● ● ● ● ● ● ● ● ● ● ● ● ● ● ● ● ●

A site's structure is defined as the way in which the various pages are fitted together. From a planning perspective, a simple tree hierarchy is the easiest to grasp, but keep in mind this model's limitations when it comes to considering hyperlinks.

When designing a site, it is important to consider how the visitor will navigate and to plan the layout to avoid too many clicks between pages. The Home Page should always be accessible from every other page on the site and where possible, every page should be reachable through a maximum of three links.

Before starting any coding, you should decide how many pages your site will contain – you can always modify this afterwards – and how each page will fit into your structure. Draw up a rough site plan showing these pages on the various levels they relate to. This will also help when designing a navigation system. (See Chapter 18.)

It is also important to consider the size and shape of the pages you intend to design. Although HTML is designed to allow text to flow freely and fit the size of the browser's window, there are some elements which cannot be fitted to a window – tables and graphics, for example. Design pages to fit the most widely used monitor resolutions and browser windows, while making allowances for other sizes and configurations.

Your plan should include a rough idea of what each of your site's pages will contain. The tone and style of each page will depend not only on the content, but also on where the page fits into your site structure. Remember the importance of Key Messages.

QUICK REVISION QUESTIONS

1. Why do we draw a distinction between HTML coding and Web design?

2. What do we mean by the phrase "function dictates design"?

3. What is meant by a site's objective?

4. What is meant by a site's target audience? How might you define that audience?

5. What is a Key Message and how does it concern a Web designer?

6. What is meant by a site's superstructure?

7. Why should a Web site have a logical hierarchy? How does a linear hierarchy differ from a tree hierarchy?

8. Why is it important to decide on a "linking strategy" during the design process? What linking rules should be applied to a Web site?

9. Why should a Web designer be concerned with the size and shape of the pages he or she produces? For which sorts of pages would a defined width be critical?

10. What are the benefits of drawing up a table of page contents before starting to code them in HTML?

Chapter 17
Designing a site for impact

Brief contents:

1. The basic design concepts involved in authoring for the Web.

2. The importance of consistency of design across a Web site.

3. How to develop a site-wide colour scheme appropriate to your content.

4. How to create page templates and site style sheets.

5. The importance of balancing the proportions of text and graphic content.

6. How to grab a visitor's attention.

7. The importance of good headlines and subheads.

8. The impact of graphic elements.

Designing a site for impact

In the previous chapter we worked through the first phase of the process of designing a site for the World Wide Web. This chapter picks up where that one left off and looks at the second phase – the actual design of our pages. Note that we have not even considered page design until we have decided on site and page content. Last chapter we memorised one vital rule:

Function dictates design.

Now we are going to add another one:

Content dictates design.

Not only must you consider your site's objectives when you are designing your pages, you must also consider what those pages contain. Let's take a ridiculous example just to illustrate the point. Let us say you were designing a site for a local funeral home. Would you think it appropriate to dress your pages in yellow, green and orange, to *display your text iN a funky font*, and to include animations of dancing skeletons? Of course not. But without going to extremes, there is a definite need for your design to be appropriate to the page contents.

And another one:

Design must be consistent.

In many ways a Web site is like a magazine. When a reader looks at a magazine's front cover, he or she expects it to be a fair reflection of that magazine's contents. If the cover announces features on fashion, music and motor cars, the reader has a right to find all of these inside. But readers' expectations go further than that. The front cover must not only reflect content, it must also reflect the style, tone and approach of the inside pages. If the cover is loud and sensational, it is cheating to fill the interior with long scholarly discussions. If the cover is plastered with full colour photographs, the insides should not consist of pages of text.

A Web site's Home Page has much the same purpose as a magazine's front cover. It sets the tone of the site and promises the visitor more of the same. Design consistency demands that each page is clearly a part of the same site. This is not to say that each page must be identical to all the others. Within a consistent design framework, there is plenty of room for variation. Indeed, a site without any variation can become boring very quickly. In fact the only two items that we urge you to keep exactly the same on every page are the navigation system and where it appears on the page. You owe your visitors that much.

At page level, layout is just as important as it is at site level. Page layout is not concerned with where an individual element is placed. It is very much concerned with the overall structure of the page which depends on the number of elements being used, how text and graphic elements relate and how much white space is included. Layout can be artistic or it can be purely functional, but the test of any layout is how accessible it makes key content to the visitor.

This chapter considers various aspects of page design and suggests how they can be applied within a consistent design framework. As before, we shall be using our proposed site on Japanese manga to illustrate certain points, but if you prefer to work through this chapter applying the various processes to your own design, that is fine with us.

Colour schemes

We have mentioned colour schemes several times in earlier chapters. This section is intended to pull all the information together. Of course, there is no particular reason for starting your design with a colour scheme, and there might be valid reasons for not doing so. You could just as well start from a style of layout. We prefer to begin with colour because once you have decided on a colour scheme so many other design aspects follow automatically.

Remember: content dictates design. It may well be that as soon as you have decided on your content, a colour scheme becomes obvious. If, for example, your site is intended to cover some aspects of natural history, you might decide that a combination of natural colours – greens and browns – would be appropriate. If your site was to be dedicated to a local hurling team, the basis of your colour scheme might be the team colours. These are very obvious examples, but where a colour scheme is less obvious, you will often find that the target audience of the site suggests suitable colours. If a site is aimed at teenagers, modern, exciting colours would be a good choice. If the site is intended for serious, professional people, a more sombre colour scheme might suit. All of these ideas are just starting points for a colour scheme. They are not cast in stone and should be adapted to suit your own design ideas.

Consider also the importance of contrast. Look at the Web page shown in Figure 17.1. Of course this is printed in black and white, but oddly enough this is the one time when greyscale printing can actually help. By reducing colours to greyscale, it is easier to spot contrast.

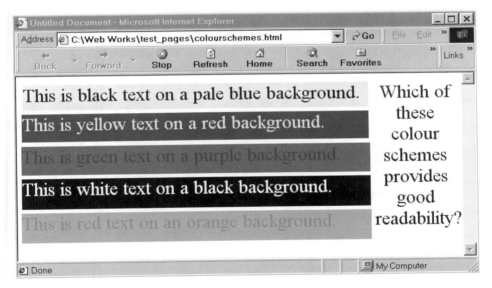

Figure 17.1: Colour contrasts on a Web page.

Of the six colour schemes illustrated (five plus black-on-white in the text to the right), which offers the best readability? The best contrast is provided by plain old black-on-white or white-on-black. Green-on-purple and red-on-orange are almost unreadable. Black-on-pale blue is pretty good, while yellow-on-red might be acceptable for short blocks. Note that we are not asking whether these schemes are effective from an *aesthetic*[1] point of view, only whether they provide good readability.

---

[1] **Aesthetic:** according to the Complete Oxford Dictionary, aesthetic means "concerned with beauty or the appreciation of beauty". It's an awkward word, but we're stuck with it and will be using it quite a bit in this chapter and beyond to refer to whether a page is visually attractive.

Technical Stuff

In case you are wondering how we created these individually coloured blocks, here is the code for the top one:

```
<div id="Layer1" style="position:absolute; left:10px; top:14px;
width:539px; height:41px; z-index:1; background-color: #99FFFF; layer-
background-color: #99FFFF; border: 1px none #000000">
<font size="5">
This is black text on a pale blue background.</font></div>
```

For the subsequent blocks, we changed the value of the <STYLE> element property top *to position each block, and the* background-color *and* layer-background-color *properties to change the background colour. Other blocks also required the COLOR attribute of the <FONT> element to be modified. (Don't worry about the* z-index *property. This determines how block-level elements overlay each other.)*

Readability is an important consideration, particularly since a good Web designer should always be conscious that his or her site might be visited by people with visual disabilities. We shall consider this point further in Chapter 19.

For our manga site, we have decided to use a dark background with high-contrast text and graphic colours. We feel this will look artistic – and our content is concerned with presenting an artform -- and will also provide an effective background for the many graphics we will be including. After experimenting with a range of colour combinations, we have decided to use yellow text on a black background as our primary style. So we will turn over the design sheet we started in the previous chapter and add some more notes on the back as in Figure 17.2.

DESIGN FOR MY WEB SITE
1. Colour scheme for text:
    yellow text on a black background - high contrast!

Figure 17.2

Elements that can be coloured

While background and text colours are perhaps the most visible parts of a colour scheme, we must remember that other elements can also be coloured. Amongst other elements, we can also apply colour to graphic elements, to table borders, to block borders and of course behind individual text blocks as shown in Figure 17.1. We are not restricted to one colour for our text. It can be very effective to apply different colours to different blocks of text or to different sizes of headline. The keyword here is moderation. The use of too many colours in a scheme can be very distracting, unless done for a specific purpose. (The Rainbow text exercise you completed way back in Chapter 4 created a very pleasing effect, but done too often its impact would be lost.)

One means of examining the way in which different shades interact is by using a colour wheel like the one shown in Figure 17.3.

Figure 17.3: The "Webmaster" colour wheel.

While this isn't much use printed in greyscale, the "Webmaster" colour wheel shows all 216 Web-safe colours grouped into blues, reds, yellows etc., with the six greyscale tones in the middle. Similar colour wheels are readily available on the Web for downloading and are a useful tool for any Web designer. Using a wheel, it is simple to pick colours that contrast well, and also those that complement each other. The full range of Web-safe colours is listed by name and Hex value in Appendix 3 of this book.

Web designers often make use of a range of tones of one colour for graphic elements. If, for example, you decided that blue would be a suitable master colour for your site, a highly effective colour scheme might be a navy blue background colour with headlines, text and graphic elements in different shades of light blue. It is simple enough to experiment with colours until you are satisfied with the results. A good way of doing this is to generate a test page and keep changing the colour settings and checking the effect in a browser. The following exercise provides one way of doing this.

Exercise One

1. Open your text editor and create a new Web page by typing in the following code exactly as printed. (Note the in-line style sheet used to colour the table cell backgrounds.)

```
<HTML>
<HEAD>
<TITLE>Colour tests</TITLE>
```

```
<STYLE TYPE="text/css">
<!- -
.cell {color: #0000FF; background-color: #66FFFF}
- ->
</STYLE>
</HEAD>
<BODY BGCOLOR="#0000FF">
<H1 ALIGN="Center"><FONT COLOR="#66FFFF">This is a
headline</FONT></H1>
<H2 ALIGN="Center"><FONT COLOR="#66FFFF">This is a
subhead</FONT></H2>
<P><FONT COLOR="#CCFFFF">This is a block of text. This is a block of
text. This is a block of text. This is a block of text. This is a block of
text. This is a block of text. </FONT></P>
<HR SIZE="4">
<TABLE WIDTH="80%" BORDER="4" ALIGN="Center">
 <TR>
  <TD CLASS="cell">This is table content.</TD>
  <TD CLASS="cell"><FONT COLOR="#0099FF">This is table
content</FONT></TD>
  <TD CLASS="cell"><FONT Color="#330099">This is table
content</FONT></TD>
 </TR>
</TABLE>
</BODY>
</HTML>
```

2. Save this file to your **test_pages** folder as **colour_scheme.html** and open it in your browser. It should look like Figure 17.4.

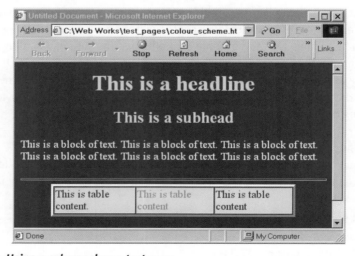

Figure 17.4: Using a colour scheme test page.

256

3. All the colours used on this page are shades of blue. Keeping your text editor and your browser open on the desktop, and saving and refreshing the file as necessary, try other combinations of blues by inserting colour values from the following table into any of the **COLOR** attributes or Cell class properties in the code. (Remember to use zeros and not "O"s in the colour values.)

Colour value:	Name of colour in HTML:
F0F8FF	Aliceblue
00FFFF	Aqua
F0FFFF	Azure
0000FF	Blue
5F9EA0	Cadetblue
483D8B	Darkslateblue
1E90FF	Dodgerblue
87CEFA	Lightskyblue
0000CD	Mediumblue
191970	Midnightblue
9FAFDF	Navyblue
B0E0E6	Powderblue
4169E1	Royalblue

4. Don't be surprised if your text occasionally disappears altogether. Some of these colour shades are so close together that text in one colour may not be distinguishable from the background in another. Keep trying, though, until you are satisfied with your scheme.

As you probably found from this exercise, achieving an effective colour scheme from shades of the same colour is quite tricky. For our manga site we are going to vary our standard yellow-on-black scheme by using white and aqua (pale blue) as highlight colours on headlines and sections of the text. How we will actually apply these variations, we will decide later. In the meantime, let's make a note of this on our design sheet, as in Figure 17.5.

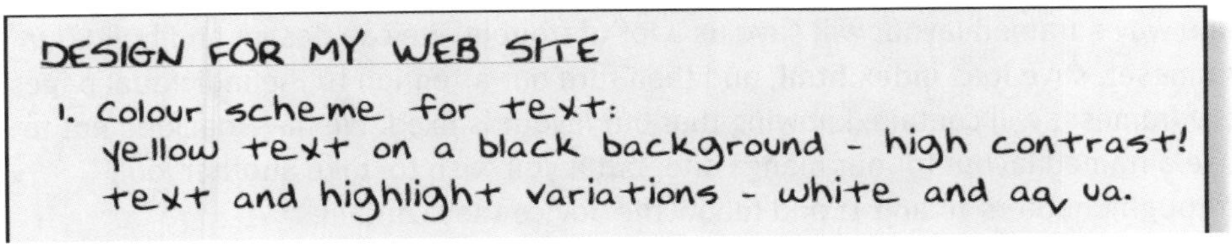

DESIGN FOR MY WEB SITE
1. Colour scheme for text:
   yellow text on a black background - high contrast!
   text and highlight variations - white and aq ua.

Figure 17.5

257

Using page templates

We introduced the concept of page templates some chapters back. The idea is that rather than having to recode each page individually, you create a single template which contains all the common features of the site. You then add content to instances of the template to make individual pages. HTML took this idea a stage further with the introduction of cascading style sheets whose properties can be applied wherever they are required, but even with a style sheet, we still require a template to set up the basic HTML tags.

As you know from Chapter 14, a style sheet contains a list of defined elements and properties that are applied to those elements. At this stage, of course, we cannot be sure which elements we will be using or how we will want them to look. So what we are building is a draft style sheet. We will include all the elements that we think we might use – later we might have to add some others. When we have completed our site building, we will edit the style sheet to remove any elements or properties that we haven't used. Since a style sheet has to be downloaded along with our pages, we want to keep it as short as possible.

This would also be a good time to decide whether our pages are going to be straightforward text and graphics, or whether we will use more complex layouts built with frames or tables. If we decide on a framed layout, we then need to choose where to position our frames and how they should relate to each other. In one way a framed layout will save us a lot of trouble. We can design and build our frameset, save it as **index.html**, and then turn our attention to the individual pages the frameset will contain, knowing that our layout is fixed. We have decided not to use a framed layout for our manga site, but if you wish to, take another look through Chapters 10 and 11 and follow the advice they contain.

As far as tables are concerned, unless we plan to use an identical layout for every page – which isn't very likely – this is not something we can build into our template. We will have to design each page individually. We might use our style sheet for establishing general rules for our tabled layout. For example, we might set up the border and padding properties or specify a background for certain cells, but style sheets can be overused. For simplicity, we have decided to use a linked style sheet rather than embedding style information within our pages. The biggest advantage here is that we need to change an item only once in the style sheet and all our pages will be changed automatically.

Let's begin by creating our page template. In addition to the basic HTML tags, we will put in a link to our style sheet and the meta-information discussed in Chapter 12. Here is our first draft:

```
<HTML>
<HEAD>
<TITLE> ... </TITLE>
<META NAME="creation_date" CONTENT="...">
<META NAME="author" CONTENT="Richard Tammadge">
<META NAME="keywords" CONTENT="manga, comics, japanese,
     artwork">
<LINK REL="Stylesheet" HREF="mangastyle.css" TYPE="text/css"
MEDIA="Screen">
</HEAD>
<BODY>
</BODY>
</HTML>
```

If you are working with us, store this as **mangatemplate.html** in your **web_pages** folder. (Now you know why you created it back in Chapter 2!) If you are working through your own project, give your template a suitable name, but store it in the same place. There are no tags in this code that you haven't met before, but note how some of them have been used. Each page will require its own title, thus the dots. For the time being we have limited our keywords to four obvious ones – we may want to add others as the site progresses. Finally, note that the **<LINK>** element requires us to name our style sheet. We have chosen **mangastyle.css**, but you may wish to use something appropriate to your own site. Let's go ahead and create our style sheet next.

As noted above, at this stage we are still guessing at the style sheet properties we will require, but some we are certain about. We know, for example, that our background colour will be black and our text colour, yellow. We are going to use the Verdana font because it looks modern, but we are going to provide alternatives in case Verdana isn't available on our visitors' computers. Our first draft style sheet will look like this:

```
BODY        {font-family: Verdana, Arial, Helvetica, sans-serif; font-
             size: 12pt; color: yellow; background-color: black}
H1          {font-size: 24pt; color: white}
H2          {font-size: 18pt; color: aqua}
```

.Contrast	{color: white}
.Stress	{font-size: 13pt; color: yellow; font-style: italic}
A:Link	{color: aqua}
A:Active	{color: aqua; text-decoration: underline}
A:Visited	{color: yellow}

We will save this in our **web_pages** folder as **mangastyle.css**. You should be familiar with all the properties we have used. We have created two styles of headline, **H1** and **H2,** and two classes called **Contrast** and **Stress** which we will apply to elements needing some variation or emphasis. Finally, because the default link colours do not show up well on a black background, we have applied new colours to them. Before being clicked, links will be in aqua; as a mouse pointer moves onto them, they will acquire an underline, and once used they will turn yellow.

We need to see how all this will look in a browser, so the next thing to do is to create a test page using our site template. We will add the following content and resave the filled-in template as **manga_test.html**. (Remember to do this. If you just click the Save button, you will overwrite the template itself.)

```
<H1>Big, bold headline. </H1>
Here's a bit of text we have copied and pasted a few times to create a
test paragraph. Here's a bit of text we have copied and pasted a few
times to create a test paragraph. Here's a bit of text we have copied
and pasted a few times to create a test paragraph.
<H2>Smaller subhead</H2>
<P Class="Stress"> Here's a bit of text we have copied and pasted a
few times to create a test paragraph. Here's a bit of text we have
copied and pasted a few times to create a test paragraph.</P>
Here's a bit of text we have copied and pasted a few times to create a
test paragraph. Here's a bit of text we have copied and pasted a few
times to create a test paragraph.
<P Class="Contrast"> Here's a bit of text we have copied and pasted a
few times to create a test paragraph. Here's a bit of text we have
copied and pasted a few times to create a test paragraph.</P>
<P><A HREF="anyold.html">CLICK HERE</A> to go nowhere.
```

After looking at this in our browser we were happy enough with the result, but felt that the text was too big. It is easy enough to make changes in the style sheet, so we have modified the **BODY** properties to reduce the **font-size** value to 10, and the **font-size** property value for the Stress class to 11pt. For consistency, we have also reduced the size values for the headlines defined in **H1** and **H2,** to 18pt and 14pt respectively. If you are working along with us, make these changes to your own style sheet, save it and check the test page in your browser. Our modified test page appears as Figure 17.6.

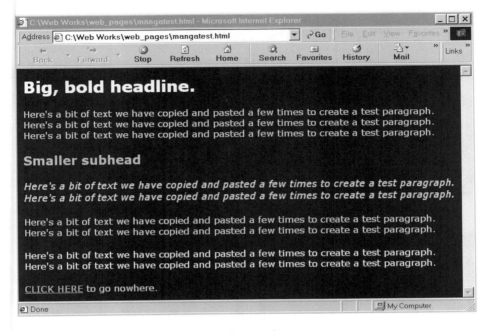

Figure 17.6: A page to test the style sheet for our site.

Balancing text and graphic content

Consideration should always be given to getting the correct balance between text and graphic content. How much of each will largely be determined by the site's purpose, so a site on art, for example, might have a higher proportion of graphics than a site giving instructions on how to write a CV. In advertising, there is a very old guideline which suggests that text and graphics should be mixed in the proportions one-third to two-thirds **or** two-thirds to one-third. This produces a good aesthetic balance from the Web designer's point of view, but must be applied to the **visible** page area and not to the page as a whole.

Look back to Figure 16.12 in the previous chapter which shows an extended Web page scrolling behind a representation of a browser window. You will notice that the proportion of text to graphics depends on where the visible page area is located. To use the two-thirds to one-third guideline, either you must make sure that for most browsers all of your page is visible, or you should design in such a way that the balance remains roughly constant regardless of which part of the page is being viewed.

Figure 17.7 shows a series of different text-to-graphic balances and layouts.

While these things are very much a matter of opinion, we will give you our views on the effectiveness of these examples. See if you agree with us. Example 1 shows too much text for a good balance – particularly with the graphic tucked away into the bottom left-hand corner. In Example 2, the balance is better, but with the page divided into two distinct sections, the graphics tend to dominate. Perhaps this layout would be useful for a site in which displaying graphics was the major objective. Example 3 is much easier on the eye, the graphics are integrated into the text and the balance is about right. Example 4 shows a way of keeping a good balance on a long page. The graphics are confined to strips on either side of the window and the text flows between them.

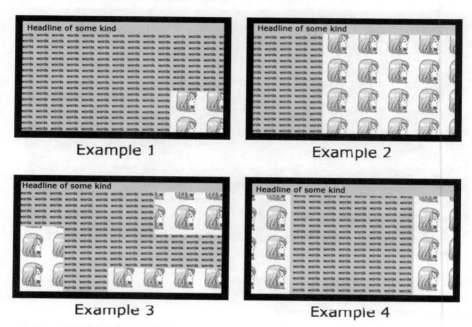

Figure 17.7: Balancing text and graphics.

We stress again that there cannot be any hard and fast rules for balancing the proportions of text and graphics. We have raised the subject because it is something you will need to keep in mind for your own page designs, but content dictates design and you may well find that your choices are limited by the need to display page content in the most visually effective manner.

Grabbing your visitor's attention

The final section in this chapter looks at ways of compelling a visitor to venture into your site. We need to consider the attention-grabbers – headlines, subheads and graphic features. In the section above we considered the balance between text and graphics. No less important is the balance between headlines and body text. Firstly, there is a question of how formal we wish the site to appear. Consider the relative differences between the formats of the Irish Times and the Sun. The Irish Times tends towards long headlines followed by extended passages of text. It is prepared to include complex terminology and sentences often run over several lines. The Sun, on the other hand, prefers a much higher proportion of headlines, although they are usually shorter and snappier. On occasions, headlines take up more space on the front page than any other component. Words, sentences and paragraphs are shorter and easier to browse through. Neither of these styles are better or worse than the other, they are simply intended to appeal to their particular readership.

The Web is, by and large, an action medium. If you buy a newspaper, you take the time to sit down and read it, but most people "browse" the Web, going from site to site as the fancy takes them. It could be argued that Sun-style is more appropriate in this environment, but once again this will depend on the content and target audience of a site. A Web page that comprises a headline followed by a massive block of text can look like hard work. Breaking up the text with subheads makes the page look more accessible. On the other hand, a page which is stuffed full of headlines and subheads, with very little text between them, can look trivial and unprofessional. We recommend short paragraphs – aim for a maximum of 40 to 50 words, with one carefully worded headline, which doesn't need to be at the top of the page. We would also recommend a subhead every two to three paragraphs. These help to break the text up into easily digestible chunks. Figure 17.8 shows an example of this type of format.

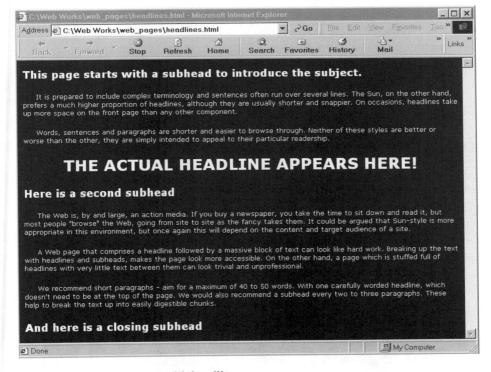

Figure 17.8: Breaking text up with headlines.

The actual wording of headlines and subheads is an art in itself. The best headlines stop the reader in his tracks and compel him to read the story they introduce. A figure that is often quoted is that a Web page has just 15 seconds to make an impact before the visitor loses interest and goes somewhere else. We suspect that even that might be too long and that a site really needs to grab a visitor's attention within five seconds. Clearly this will depend on the visitor's intentions. If he is compelled to visit a site, for example to download essential software, he will be obliged to wait as long as it takes for the relevant links or information to appear. Most sites, however, are not compulsory, and the visitor can choose to stay or go.

The choice of words for a headline depends to a large extent on the audience you are trying to target. "Give them what they want" is a good rule here. If your site is promoting a service or selling something, you might use a sales message as your headline. If you are trying to persuade your visitor to see things from your point of view, your headline might be something challenging or provoking. Keep headlines short and punchy and use subheads to introduce the Key message from the following paragraphs.

Graphics too can be great attention-grabbers, provided they are relevant and not overused. A Web site with too many attention-grabbers can leave a visitor feeling shell-shocked, so use them sparingly. Graphics must conform to the site's overall style and colour scheme. Animated graphics can also be effective, but always remember the download times. Many sites on the Web now use Flash animations on their pages, but these can take an age to load. Even if your visitor is prepared to wait for an animated effect to appear on your Home page, he will rapidly get bored if every other page also takes forever. You can, of course, use one animation on several pages, since it will only have to download once.

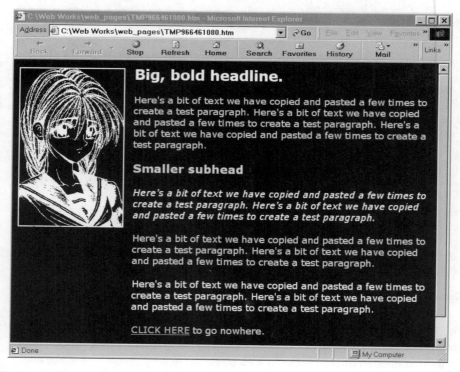

Figure 17.9: Manga site test page with graphic.

With all these things now considered, we can return to our manga site. Remember, we are still in the design phase, so we can afford to experiment with a few different ideas. We have decided to use one particular graphic on all our pages. This will not only fit in with our ideas on design consistency, but it will also give the visitor an immediate visual clue as to our site contents. One of the ideas we eventually rejected is shown in Figure 17.9. Although this is a nice graphic, it lacks impact. We need something more exciting – something to add drama to our pages. We will return to this later in the book.

We should close this chapter by updating our design sheet with notes on how we intend making sure that our site has visual appeal, impact and immediacy. Figure 17.10 brings our design sheet up to date.

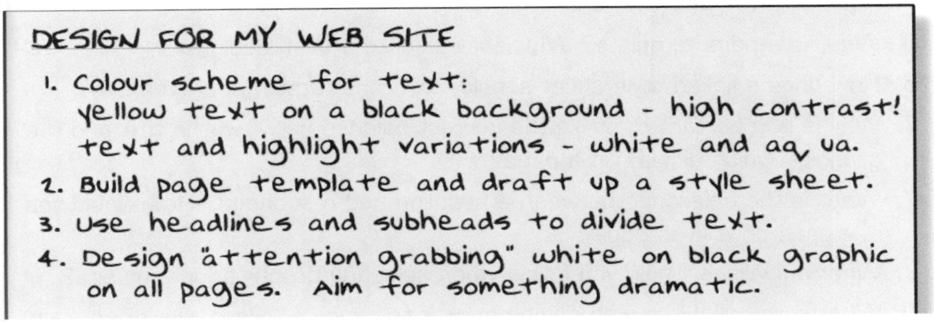

DESIGN FOR MY WEB SITE
1. Colour scheme for text:
   Yellow text on a black background - high contrast!
   text and highlight variations - white and aqua.
2. Build page template and draft up a style sheet.
3. Use headlines and subheads to divide text.
4. Design "attention grabbing" white on black graphic
   on all pages. Aim for something dramatic.

Figure 17.10.

Key Facts ●

1 The construction of a consistently designed Web site is made much easier by the use of a page template and a style sheet. The template should include those elements which are common to all pages. The style sheet will start off as a draft to include as many different style rules as you think you might need. Subsequently, this should be edited down to the minimum required for the site.

2 One important consideration is how to get a good balance between text and graphic content. This balance needs to be applied to the visible page area and not just to the page as a whole. Where possible, graphics should be integrated into the text. They should be relevant and have a purpose within the overall design.

3 A visitor's attention can be grabbed by the use of headlines, subheads and graphics. Again, you need to consider the balance between headlines and body text, as well as matching the style and tone of the headlines to the site's purpose and intended audience.

4 A good model to work from is a tabloid newspaper, unless this does not fit in with the site's objectives for some reason. In general, keep headlines short and to the point, keep paragraphs and sentences small and divide them up with relevant subheads.

QUICK REVISION QUESTIONS

1. What do we mean by the rule "content dictates design"?
2. Web sites require consistency of design. What does this refer to and how would you go about ensuring that your site was consistent in design terms?
3. How could you match your colour scheme to the site's objectives and target audience?
4. In Web terms, what is meant by readability? How would you ensure good readability for your own site?
5. What is a page template? Why is it useful to a Web designer?
6. How does a linked style sheet simplify the construction of a Web site?
7. Why is it important to strike the correct balance between the text and the graphics which display on a page?
8. What is the difference between a headline and a subhead? How would you use each on a Web page?
9. What guidelines would you follow when selecting graphics for your site?
10. What is the problem with adding animations such as Flash movies to your site?

Chapter 18
Interactive content

Interactive Content

So far in this book we have looked mainly at passive and active content. Now we are going one step beyond to look at interactive content. Let's be clear what all these terms mean. Passive content just sits on a page and looks at you – text and graphic images are examples of passive content. Active content does something – animations move, sound and video files play. Interactive content responds to some input from the user. The only interactive content we have met so far are the hyperlinks which move you to another location when clicked. In this chapter we are going to consider more advanced interactive content; content which allows the Web user to influence and control his or her Web experience.

Originally Web content was just for looking at, but the current trend is towards interactivity. Without interaction between user and server, the Web would be little more than an electronic publishing medium. Interactivity allows you to send e-mail, to fill in and transmit forms, to buy products online, to play interactive games and to download files. Perhaps the most significant aspect of such interactions is that they require further processes. If you can remember way back to Chapter 1, we described information exchange over the Internet as requiring four distinct processes – connection, request, response and close. Let's consider the additional processes required by the submission of a simple order form to a Web site.

The programs which handle form data are usually Common Gateway Interface (CGI) applications, although there are other types. Whether the CGI application runs on the Web server itself or on another linked computer doesn't matter. It still introduces a third component into the process. To see how the whole procedure operates, we'll take the list we used in Chapter 1 and extend it like this:

1. **Connection:** the client connects to a Web server.

2. **Request:** the client requests a resource from the Web server. (In this case the form.)

3. **Response:** the server delivers the form that has been requested, or sends an error message explaining why it cannot.

4. **Data transmission:** at the client computer, the Web user adds the required details to the form and transmits them (usually as a straight text file) back to the server.

5. **CGI input:** the server passes the form to the CGI application, which handles the form data according to how it has been programmed.

6. **CGI output:** the CGI application responds to the server with an acknowledgement, a response or a further request as appropriate.

7. **CGI response:** the server delivers the CGI output to the client.

8. **Close:** after the output has been delivered, the connection between client and server shuts down, unless the output requests further data in which case we loop back to 4 above.

The first three processes are the same as before. A form is a document like any other Web document and must be requested and downloaded to the client computer. After this things get more complicated, with data passing from client to server to CGI application and back again.

A process similar to this is required by any interactive content. Interactivity requires that the server does more than merely deliver a resource. Instead it has to run programs as required by the client. This is the real meaning of client/server computing, where the client actually has control, however limited, over the operation of the server. There is no doubt that this development is pointing the way forwards for the Web. Already many companies are offering server-side applications. In the future, you may not need a word processor on your computer. Instead you will connect to a Web-based word processor. You will type up your document, print it wherever the document is required, then log off again.

In this chapter we will look at several different types of interactivity, from including e-mail in your pages through scripting languages which offer a degree of client-side control, right up to server-sider handling of forms. Creating scripts is a subject that is beyond the scope of this book, but you should know a little about the scripting languages available, how they operate and what they can bring to a Web site. We will be looking at one or two simple scripts later in this chapter and using a much more complex one for our navigation bar in Chapter 19. Let's start though by looking at the mailto protocol.

mailto – the e-mail protocol

We have inserted a mailto link once or twice before in this book without looking at the way in which it works. Like HTTP itself, mailto is a protocol which opens a window in which the user can type an e-mail message. Technically, it does this by calling the **Simple Mail Transfer Protocol** (SMTP), which enables a hyperlink to send the e-mail. This assumes that the user has a working e-mail program installed on his computer, otherwise an error message is displayed.

For a Web designer, mailto is the simplest way to interact with visitors. You can invite them to comment on, criticise or even add to your site, and provide them with a mailto link to make it easy for them to respond. Many Web sites feature a line of text such as:

If you have any comments on this site, e-mail me at harryb@hedge.net.

A better way of doing this is covered in Exercise One.

Exercise One

1. Open a basic template in your text editor, and add the following code into the Body section. (Remember to insert your own e-mail address in place of the italics.)

   **I welcome any comments on my site.
**
   <A HREF="mailto:*insert your own e-mail address*">Click here</A> to send me an e-mail.

2. Save this file to your **test_pages** folder as **email.html**, and open it in your browser.

3. Click the link and, if your e-mail application is properly installed, a new window will open with a blank e-mail form ready to be filled in. You should see your own address in the "send to" box. Write yourself a suitable message, connect to the Internet and send it. Depending on your mail server, you should see it appear as an incoming message almost immediately.

Sending messages to yourself is a bit pointless, but it does indicate how basic interactivity works. In this example, of course, no server-side code was involved since all the processes were handled locally. More importantly, this approach provides a very simple way in which you can interact with visitors to your site. If you decide not to include a feedback form in your site, at the very least make sure that you provide an e-mail link so that visitors can send you their opinions. We will be seeing just how important this is in Chapter 21.

Creating simple forms

The **<FORM>** element is the last major element we shall introduce in this book. Because it involves server-side programs, it is different from all of the elements we met in the first part of the book. For a form document to work properly, the relevant data processing extensions must be installed on the server. If they are not, submitting the form will have no effect. As we noted above, data from a form is usually handled by a CGI application. There are many of these and they may work in different ways. The first thing a Web designer must do before he includes a form is to check with his site host, to find out exactly how forms are handled and which attributes are supported. We consider the whole question of site hosting in Chapter 22.

After you have confirmed that your host can handle the form you wish to include, you can proceed to design your form. Forms can be very simple or extremely complicated and this chapter will only look at some relatively simple examples. **<FORM>** is a block-level element and its code can be divided into two sections. The first part of the code defines how data from the form is to be handled. The second part creates the various controls or entry fields that appear in the Web browser. Syntax is identical to other block-level elements, with the **<FORM> ... </FORM>** tags enclosing a series of elements which allow text input. In many ways, setting up a form is similar to setting up a list.

In the following exercises, we shall be setting up forms as separate pages, but note that a form can just as easily be included in another Web document. For example, the log-in and password boxes you will see on some Web sites are usually form controls. To see how a basic form might be coded, work your way through Exercise Two.

Exercise Two

1. Open a basic template in your text editor, and add the following code into the Body section:

```
<HR><FORM ACTION="http://www.earpop.ie/cgi-bin/post-query"
METHOD="POST">
<B>What is your name?</B>
<INPUT TYPE="Text" NAME="CustomerName" SIZE="25"
MAXLENGTH="35">
<BR>
<B>Which CD would you like?</B>
<INPUT TYPE="Text" NAME="CDName" SIZE="25" MAXLENGTH="35">
<BR>
</FORM><HR>
```

2. Save this file to your **test_pages** folder as **form1.html**, and open it in your browser. It should look like Figure 18.1.

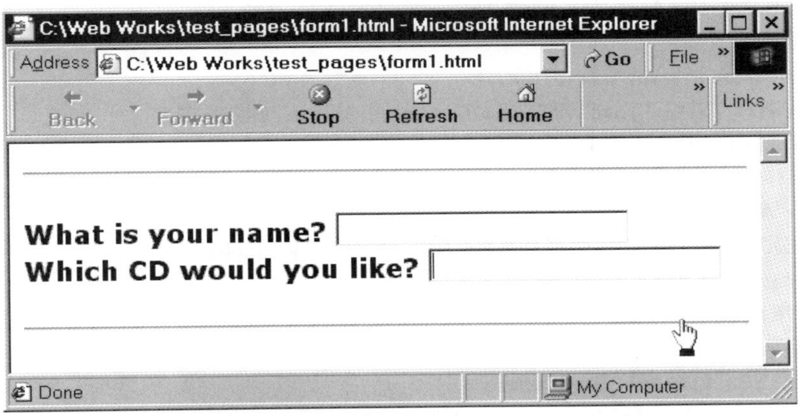

Figure 18.1: Basic input fields in a simple form.

Look at the code used to generate this form. The **<FORM>** element's **ACTION** and **METHOD** attributes specify the address to which the form data will be sent and how it will be sent there. In most cases, **ACTION** points to the URL of the server-side program which will handle the data. Here the program is called **post-query** and resides in the **cgi-bin** folder on our Web site's host server. (This is the way most hosts arrange their CGI applications.) **POST** is the usual value for the **METHOD** attribute. It sends the form data via HTTP to the CGI program. Of course as yet, we have not included any means of instructing the browser to submit the data - we will look at this in our next exercise.

The controls we have included consist of two input fields created by the **<INPUT>** element. **<INPUT>** generates a text entry box, which we have defined with four attributes. The **TYPE** attribute specifies the type of form control. In this case we have given it a value of **TEXT**, which will create a single-line text input field. It is important that every form control is given a unique name, using the **NAME** attribute. The CGI application will reference each control by its name, when it processes the form data. The last two attributes define the size of the control. **SIZE** specifies the width of a **TEXT**-type control in characters – thus the input box here will accept 25 characters without scrolling. Finally **MAXLENGTH** specifies the total number of characters which the box will accept. Be careful to set this value large enough to accommodate the largest possible entry you might expect.

Of course a form also needs a control to send the data. Let's extend the previous exercise to create a more complex form with the necessary **Submit** and **Reset** buttons.

Exercise Three

1. Re-open **form1.html** in your text editor, and modify the code as follows:

```
<BODY BGCOLOR="Black" TEXT="Yellow" FACE="Verdana">
<HR>
<FORM ACTION="http://www.earpop.ie/cgi-bin/post-query"
METHOD="POST">
```

```
<H2>Get the facts on your favourite band...</H2>
<HR>
<B>What is your name?  </B>
<INPUT TYPE="Text" NAME="CustomerName" SIZE="25"
MAXLENGTH="35">
<BR>
<B>What is your full postal address?</B>
<TEXTAREA ROWS="5" COLS="50" NAME="PostalAddress">
Enter your address here.
</TEXTAREA><BR>
<B>Which band are you interested in?</B>
<SELECT NAME="BandName">
   <OPTION VALUE="DB">Dead Balloons
   <OPTION VALUE="NT">Nematoad
   <OPTION VALUE="TF">The Flushers
</SELECT><BR>
<B>Where have you heard this band's music?</B><BR>
Radio <INPUT TYPE="CHECKBOX" NAME="MusicSource" VALUE="Radio">
Television <INPUT TYPE="CHECKBOX" NAME="MusicSource" VALUE="TV">
CD <INPUT TYPE="CHECKBOX" NAME="MusicSource" VALUE="CD">
<P>
<INPUT TYPE="SUBMIT" NAME="SubmitButton" VALUE="Submit">
<INPUT TYPE="RESET" NAME="ResetButton" VALUE="Reset">
</FORM>
<HR>
```

2. Save this file to your **test_pages** folder as **form2.html**, and open it in your browser. It should look like Figure 18.2.

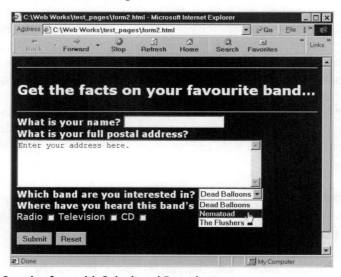

Figure 18.2: Complex form with Submit and Reset buttons.

Although the code used to create this page is more complex, it is easy enough to follow if you work through it carefully. In addition to the controls we used in the first exercise, we have added some new ones. In Exercise One, we used the **<INPUT>** element to create a single-line text input field. Here we required several lines for the visitor to input his or her address, and to do this we have used the **<TEXTAREA>** element. The syntax for this is slightly confusing. The **ROWS** attribute is obvious enough, but the **COLS** attribute takes as its value the width of the text area in characters (letters, numbers and spaces).

The **<SELECT>** element creates a drop-down menu offering the choices we have defined using the **<OPTION>** elements. Note that these – and several other controls – take a **VALUE** attribute. Since the visitor is not actually entering data into these fields, the **VALUE** attribute defines the information which will be passed on to the CGI application for processing. We could have added another attribute to the **<OPTION>** element. The **SELECTED** attribute defines which option is displayed in the menu box when the page first opens. This is useful if you want to provide a default value for this control which the user can change if he or she wishes. Consider the following code scrap:

```
<FORM ACTION="http://www.earpop.ie/cgi-bin/post-query"
METHOD="POST">
Please tell us what you thought of the service we offered:
<SELECT NAME="service">
    <OPTION VALUE="excellent">Excellent
    <OPTION VALUE="good" SELECTED>Good
    <OPTION VALUE="fair">Fair
    <OPTION VALUE="poor">Poor
</SELECT>
</FORM>
```

This would create a selection list with four choices, but the selected choice "Good" would appear in the menu and that is the value that the control would return unless it was altered by the user. Would it have been fair to apply the **SELECTED** attribute to the "Excellent" menu item?

We have also used two other types of **INPUT** controls. With the **TYPE** attribute pointing to CHECKBOX, the **<INPUT>** element generates a small control box which can be checked or ticked. This qualifies the **VALUE** attribute with an **on** or **off** extension, so in the case of our first checkbox, a value of **Radio=on** will be sent to the server. Finally, we have used two preset values for the **TYPE** attribute, SUBMIT and RESET. The effect of these is to create the **Submit** button which, when clicked, will send all the form data to the server, and the **Reset** button which will clear all the fields, allowing the user to start again.

There is one special value for the **TYPE** attribute which is of no use for our purposes, but is widely used on the Web. The value PASSWORD works in every way like the value TEXT, except that the user's entry is obscured by asterisks. If the user enters the password "Fred", all that will show on the screen is ****. This means, of course, that anyone looking over the user's shoulder will not be able to see his or her password.

We also have an alternative to the CHECKBOX value for the **TYPE** attribute, and that is the RADIO value. RADIO boxes behave just like standard CHECKBOXs with two exceptions. Firstly, while CHECKBOXs render as small tickable squares which display a cross when clicked, RADIO boxes render as circles which display a black dot when clicked. More importantly, when several CHECKBOXs are used, the user can check several of them. RADIO boxes on the other hand are mutually exclusive. When the user clicks on one, all the others are unchecked.

Whether to use RADIO or CHECKBOX type input depends on the context. If you were asking a visitor to rate your site as good, moderate or bad. RADIO form controls would clearly be appropriate. Your site could hardly be rated both good and bad. On the other hand, if your site was selling sandwiches, a visitor could require mustard, red sauce, pickle and coleslaw on his meat, so CHECKBOX controls would be suitable. Like the **SELECTED** attribute for the **<OPTION>** element above, both RADIO and CHECKBOX controls can load with a preselected value. In this case the **CHECKED** attribute is used. Figure 18.3 shows both of these form controls displayed in a browser. Note that "Moderate" has been **CHECKED**.

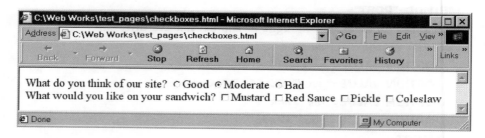

Figure 18.3: Different types of Checkbox form controls.

Like any other Web document a good form needs to be designed, tested and modified. The design we have used for Figure 18.2 is based on the Earpop Records style we have applied to previous documents, but it does look very overcrowded. Like most of us, Web users can get bothered when filling out forms, particularly if accuracy is important. Forms should look simple and be easy to follow. Leave plenty of space between the various input boxes, make sure that connected questions are placed near to each other, and see that each entry field is long enough to take the likely input. Never put more than one form on a page – this is almost certain to confuse your visitors.

As with ordinary pages, all the standard HTML tags work for a form. A form can be laid out using a table to provide greater control over where the text and input fields are placed. Forms can also be linked to a style sheet, and we would recommend doing this so that the form is properly integrated into your site.

As a Web designer, it would be a mistake for you to get too concerned with the server-side operation of form data processing. Normally it is quite safe to leave this to your Web host who will, in due course, submit the processed data back to you so you can respond to it or record it.

Because the text that introduces each form input field is likely to be of different length, your form's appearance might be very ragged, with boxes appearing all over the place. Consider formatting all your form content as preformatted text. (If you've forgotten what this means, look back at Chapter 4.) If your first field is "name:" and your second is "address:", by wrapping all the text in the <PRE> ... </PRE> tags, you can type " name" with three blank spaces in front of the word and the browser will lay out the form so that both input fields start at the same place on the page. Try it and see!

Client/server programming

As we explained in the introduction to this chapter, interactivity on the Web implies proper client/server programming. To understand what this means for the future of the Web, we need to look back a few years. When you connect to the Internet and download pages, a whole series of computers are involved. Firstly, there is your own client machine which is sending requests and rendering downloaded pages. Then there is the server machine which is responding to requests and transmitting pages. Between the two there might be any number of other machines handling the routing and delivery of the pages. Early browsers were little more than simple file viewers. Almost all of the actual computing was handled by the servers. Recently however a whole range of client-side technologies such as ActiveX, JavaScript and DHTML have been developed. These add programming functions to the client machine and reduce the pressure on the server.

Using interactive technologies like these, we can add a wide range of features to Web pages, but there is a downside. Firstly, for a visitor to view or take advantage of Java applets or ActiveX controls, he must have the relevant technology installed and switched on. There have been widespread concerns over the misuse of JavaScript and ActiveX to spread viruses and allow intruders to access other people's computers, so many Web users turn off support for them. Secondly, since we have no way of knowing how a visitor's computer is configured, we cannot guarantee that his browser will render interactive content as we intended. If programming is concentrated server-side, any computing takes place where the data is actually stored. This reduces the chance of problems developing and increases the likelihood of users getting the intended results.

Of course as Web designers there is nothing we can do about server-side programming, beyond finding out what is available from our host server and using it as best we can. For example, the form we designed above relies on a server-side CGI application to handle the data we submit. If it doesn't work, there is little we can do beyond complaining to our Web host. Client-side programming, on the other, hand is completely under our own control. In essence, we write or copy a program, embed it into our Web page and upload it to the server where it sits and waits. When the page is downloaded, the visitor's browser runs the code using its own or a helper application's resources.

So what can we do with client-side programming? By and large scripting languages such as JavaScript and VBScript (Visual Basic Scripting Edition) are used to create small in-line *applets*[1] to perform simple data management functions. They might, for example, check form data before it is sent on to a server, or create animated effects on a Web page. Although both are fairly easy to use – after you have mastered the syntax – they often create problems if badly coded. Bad JavaScript, for example, can easily bring down a browser or even crash the operating system itself.

JavaScript – note that this is not the same as Java, which is a full-blooded programming language – was originally developed by Netscape and was subsequently adopted by most other browser manufacturers. JavaScript is often used to create simple graphic effects like moving elements around on screen, or images that change when a mouse pointer moves over them. As well as generating on-screen effects, JavaScript can be used to create a bridge between straight HTML code and other technologies such as Java applets.

Exercise Four takes you through a very simple JavaScript inclusion.

Exercise Four

1. Open a basic template in your text editor, and add the following code into the Head section:

```
<TITLE>A JavaScript warning!</TITLE>
<SCRIPT LANGUAGE="JavaScript">
<!- -
function Warning()
{
    alert ("Never press that button again!");
}
//- ->
</SCRIPT>
```

2. Now add the following code into the Body section. (Remember to delete the existing **<BODY>** tag.)

```
<BODY BGCOLOR="Black" TEXT="Yellow" FACE="Verdana">
<H2 ALIGN="CENTER">DO NOT PRESS THIS BUTTON!</H2>
<DIV ALIGN="CENTER">
<FORM>
    <INPUT TYPE="BUTTON" VALUE="Don't Press Me"
onClick="Warning()">
</FORM>
</DIV>
```

3. Save this file to your **test_pages** folder as **js_example.html**, and open it in your browser. After you have pressed the button we have told you not to, it should look like Figure 18.4.

---

[1] **Applets:** the word comes from application"lets" – mini-applications with very limited functions.

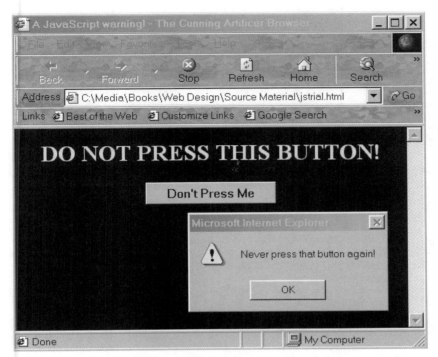

Figure 18.4: A simple example of JavaScript

In this example, form controls have been used to activate a simple JavaScript program which creates a warning box.

VBScript was developed by Microsoft as an alternative to Netscape's JavaScript. Does this sound familiar? In many ways, VBScript is actually a better scripting language, but it is only fully supported in Internet Explorer. For this reason, we would recommend JavaScript if you wish to use a scripting language. It is worth noting that many ready-made JavaScript programs can be downloaded from the Internet for free. If you are interested in including interactive content, use a search engine to hunt down free JavaScript examples and cut and paste them into your own pages.

To include scripts within your pages, you use the **<SCRIPT>** element. This element has three common attributes. **LANGUAGE** takes as its value the scripting language being used, normally JavaScript or VBScript. Often this will be the only attribute used and the script itself will be placed between the **<SCRIPT> ... </SCRIPT>** tags. Sometimes it is useful to store the script in a separate document - if, for example, the same script was being used on several different pages. To do this, include the **SRC** attribute, which should point to the URL of the script file, and the **TYPE** attribute, which defines which type of script is to be run. Values here are usually **text/javascript** or **text/vbscript**. This is very similar to the method we used to link to an external style sheet. An external JavaScript file should have the extension **.js**, while an external VBScript file should have the extension **.vbs**.

Key Facts •

 Interactive content is content which responds to input from the visitor. It includes providing e-mail links for feedback, forms which can return information to the Webmaster, and dynamic effects like alert boxes and rollover images. Interactivity implies genuine client/server computing, where the client takes control over remote programs.

 Interactive content requires more processes than the ordinary request and download cycle. Forms, for example, are downloaded as pages, filled in and returned by the user, but must then be sent on to a processing application which, in due course, returns the data to the Webmaster.

 The simplest form of interactivity is the e-mail link. The **mailto** protocol opens an editing window on the client computer in which the visitor can write his e-mail. An e-mail link gives your visitors the opportunity to comment on your site – a useful source of feedback.

 In-line forms are created using the <FORM> element. A form is only useful provided your Web host offers the relevant CGI application to handle the form data your visitors submit.

 At its best, true client/server programming passes control of server-side programs to the client computer. While early browsers were little more than file viewers, later developments in Web technology brought true interactivity to browsers. Scripting languages like VBScript and JavaScript allow Web designers to incorporate simple programs into their pages, programs which run on input from the client.

Scripts are included in Web pages using the <SCRIPT> element which also defines the scripting language being used. JavaScript is a relatively simple language to use, once you have mastered the syntax, but like all programming, demands great precision. A single error in spelling or punctuation may cause the script to misbehave or fail entirely.

Event handlers

When a visitor interacts with a Web page, he generates an "event" – in other words, he does something. He might click with his mouse button or press a key – in fact even moving a mouse across the screen counts as an event. To make that event run, a script requires binding an attribute of that event to the required script. Such an attribute is called an **event handler attribute**. You have met some of these already. In the previous exercise, the code scrap:

<INPUT TYPE="BUTTON" VALUE="Don't Press Me" onclick="Greet()">

included the event handler attribute **onclick** which bound the **<INPUT>** element to the script called **Greet( )**. Don't be worried about the terminology we have used here. The important thing to remember is that **onclick** is an attribute which takes as its value the name of the script to be run.

There are a fair number of these event handler attributes and they can be used with quite a number of HTML elements, but in practice they are usually included in form control elements such as **<INPUT>, <SELECT>, <TEXTAREA>** and **<BUTTON>** or the active element **<A>**. The table below lists some of the more common event handler attributes and what they mean:

Event handler attribute:	Description of event:
onclick	Occurs when an on-screen element is clicked.
ondblclick	Occurs when an on-screen element is double-clicked.
onload	Occurs when a document finishes loading.
onkeypress	Occurs when a key is pressed and released.
onmousedown	Occurs when a mouse button is pressed.
onmousemove	Occurs when the mouse pointer is moved on screen.
onmouseover	Occurs when the mouse pointer moves over an element.
onmouseout	Occurs when the mouse pointer moves away from an element.
onsubmit	Occurs when a form is submitted – usually by pressing the submit button.

Note: There are other, less common event handler attributes.

Let's work through another quick exercise to see a different event handler attribute in action:

Exercise Five

1. Open a basic template in your text editor, and add the following code into the Head section:

```
<TITLE>Loading an event.</TITLE>
<SCRIPT LANGUAGE="JavaScript">
<!- -
function Stayawake()
{
    alert ("Click this button if you are awake!");
}
//- ->
</SCRIPT>
```

2. Now add the following code into the Body section:

```
<BODY BGCOLOR="Black" TEXT="Yellow" FACE="Verdana"
onload="Stayawake()">
<H2 ALIGN="CENTER">Still awake?</H2>
<DIV ALIGN="CENTER">
Good. Now you can go back to sleep.
</DIV>
```

3. Save this file to your **test_pages** folder as **onload.html**, and open it in your browser. You have generated another interactive warning box, but this one was triggered by the **onload** event handler attribute of the **<BODY>** element.

The scripting examples we have looked at in these exercises have been very simple, but indicate how scripting can be used to build interactivity into a Web page. If you want to go into scripting in more detail, we suggest you buy one of the many books on the subject or check for JavaScript sites on the Web.

Dynamic HTML (DHTML)

Dynamic HTML (DHTML) is a relatively new development. It is intended to extend the functions of standard HTML by allowing a scripting language to access and modify existing HTML elements. This allows new levels of interactivity, since the whole of the page structure and all of its contents come under the control of the visitor. Again, DHTML is too large a subject for this book. The best we can do is to explain how it is intended to work and to offer one or two examples. It is important, though, since all the indications are that more and more DHTML will be used on the Web, making Web browsing a truly interactive experience.

To see what this means in practice, lets take a simple example of how page content can be modified by visitor interaction. Work through the following exercise:

Exercise Six

1. Open a basic template in your text editor, and add the following code into the Head section:

```
<TITLE>Updating a form.</TITLE>
<SCRIPT LANGUAGE="JavaScript">
<!- -
function TalkBack()
{
        myname = document.logform.username.value;
    if (myname !=" ") document.logform.response.value="Hi"+myname+",
welcome to my site!";
    else document.logform.response.value="Go on! Please tell me your
name.";
}
//- ->
</SCRIPT>
```

2. Now add the following code into the Body section:

```
<BODY BGCOLOR="Black" TEXT="Yellow" FACE="Verdana">
<FORM NAME="logform">
<H2 ALIGN="CENTER">LOG IN HERE!</H2>
<DIV ALIGN="CENTER">
<B>Enter your name here.</B>
<INPUT TYPE="TEXT" NAME="username" SIZE="20"><BR><BR>
<INPUT TYPE="BUTTON" VALUE="Click here to log in!"
onclick="TalkBack()">
<BR><BR>
<INPUT TYPE="TEXT" NAME="response" SIZE="35">
</DIV>
```

3. Save this file to your **test_pages** folder as **dhtml_example.html**, and open it in your browser. The initial page should look like Figure 18.5. Enter your name and click the Log-in button; the display will change to Figure 18.6. Delete your name and click again and a new message is displayed. Whatever changes you make to the log-in text, these are taken up by the script and used to modify the on-screen display.

Figure 18.5: Using DHTML – the initial log-in screen.

Figure 18.6: Using DHTML – the page modified by user interaction.

Using DHTML and JavaScript, we have created a genuinely interactive page. You can make changes on screen and the display will be updated to reflect those changes. While this is a very simple example, it does show the potential of DHTML to dramatically change the way the Web works.

Without getting too technical, let's look at the code we have written and work out what is happening. Within the document's Head section we have defined a function called TalkBack. (This is our own name, we could just as well have called it BlueCheese.) This function makes use of a text string called **myname** which is defined as the value that is entered into an input box called **username**. The code scrap:

> **if (myname !="") document.logform.response.value="Hi "+myname+", welcome to my site!";**

> **else document.logform.response.value="Go on! Please tell me your name.";**

actually means: "If something is entered as **myname**, write the message 'Hi **myname**, welcome to my site!' into the text box called **response**. If not, write the message 'Go on! Please tell me your name.' instead.

Within the Body section we have created a form much as we did in previous exercises. We named the form **logform,** to provide a reference for the JavaScript. The major difference in this exercise is that we have included the event handler attribute **onclick** which triggers our **TalkBack** script. Otherwise, everything is standard HTML.

In Chapter 19, we will be using JavaScript to create rollover buttons – buttons which display a new graphic when the mouse pointer rolls over them. This common effect involves some fairly elaborate code. To create image rollovers, a designer has to make two versions of each graphic – one to appear when the page loads, and one to appear when the mouse pointer rolls across it. Our final example shows DHTML can work with a style sheet to create a similar effect, but with much less coding and fiddling around with graphics. Work through Exercise Six.

Exercise Seven

1. Open a basic template in your text editor, and add the following code into the Head section:

```
<TITLE>DHTML Rollovers.</TITLE>
<STYLE TYPE="text/css">
<!- -
A          {color: blue; font-size: large}
.rollover   {color: red; font-size: xlarge}
- ->
</STYLE>
```

2. Now add the following code into the Body section:

```
<BODY BGCOLOR="Yellow" TEXT="Navy" FACE="Verdana">
<H2 ALIGN="CENTER">DHTML Rollover links.</H2>
<A HREF="a.html" onmouseover="this.className='rollover'"
onmouseout="this.className=" ">CLICK RIGHT HERE </A>to go
absolutely nowhere!<P>
<A HREF="b.html" onmouseover="this.className='rollover' "
onmouseout="this.className=" ">CLICK RIGHT HERE </A>not to go
anywhere!
```

3. Save this file to your **test_pages** folder as **dhtml_rollovers.html**, and open it in your browser. It should look like Figure 18.7. Roll your mouse across the links and see what happens. (Don't bother clicking them!)

Figure 18.7: Rollover effects using DHTML.

By now you should be fairly familiar with this code. Within the Head section, we have created a standard style sheet defining the properties of the **<A>** element and a class called **rollover**. The syntax for the event handler attributes is slightly more complex than usual, but in simple terms the **onmouseover** and **onmouseout** attributes trigger two different sets of style sheet rules, depending on whether the mouse pointer is over the link or not.

This chapter has inevitably been long and complicated. If you've got this far with us, you probably deserve a break! All we have been able to do in the limited space available is to tell you a bit about interactive page content and how it can be generated from client-side scripting. You are welcome to include any of this code in your own projects, but we suggest you try modifying it to suit your own pages. The great thing about JavaScript and interactive content in general is that you, as a Web author, are totally in control. You can try things, and if they don't work get back into the code and hack it about until they do.

One final point we must emphasise. HTML is fairly forgiving. If you make mistakes in your syntax – and you would not believe how many mistakes we have made preparing the various examples and exercises for this book – most browsers can usually work out what you mean and display the page correctly. The same is definitely not true with scripting languages. Not only must every letter be in the right case and every punctuation mark be spot on within the script code itself, but the standard HTML it is working with must also be 100% accurate. We are prepared to make a large bet that you have already found this out for yourself!

Key Facts

*Event handlers are specialised attributes which bind an event such as a mouse button being clicked to a particular script. They take the form **on** plus a description of the event, for example **onmouseover**. Event handler attributes can be used with many HTML elements, but are most commonly used with form control elements such as <INPUT> or <SELECT>.*

Dynamic HTML (DHTML) is intended to extend the function of existing HTML elements to allow them to trigger and respond to scripting. It is possible that DHTML will replace more and more standard HTML as interactivity becomes more common.

DHTML interacts with a script to modify page content to reflect changes made by the user. It can also make use of style sheet properties to apply changes to a page, depending on a user's behaviour.

Tricks Of The Trade

JavaScript and VBScript scripts are common on the Web. If you find an interactive effect that you like, open the source code for the page in your editor and take a look. There is nothing to stop you from copying the code, modifying it to suit your own needs and pasting it into your Web pages.

You might have thought you'd seen the end of tag tables. We promise this is the last one before the all-embracing HTML element table that is Appendix 2. Here, for the last time, is a list of all the tags used on this chapter.

Opening Tag	Closing Tag	Attributes	Description
<A>	</A>		New value:
		HREF=".."	The value: mailto:a valid e-mail address, opens an editing window for the user's default e-mail program.
<FORM>	</FORM>		These tags create an in-line form on a Web page.
		ACTION=".."	This attribute takes as its value the URL of a server-side program which will process the form data that is submitted.
		METHOD=".."	This attribute defines how the data will be submitted to the server-side program. The usual value is POST which sends the data via HTTP.
		NAME=".."	This attribute specifies the name of the form which can then be used by client-side programs. Valid values are: any text string (one word).
<INPUT>			This tag specifies an input control for a form.
		TYPE=".."	This attribute defines the type of input control. Valid values are: BUTTON - which indicates a button, CHECKBOX – which creates a small checkable field to be ticked or left blank by the user, RADIO – which creates a similar box, (note that any number of checkboxes can be ticked, but

Opening Tag	Closing Tag	Attributes	Description
			only one radiobox can be ticked), RESET – which creates a button which either clears the controls of any text that has been entered or resets them to their default values, SUBMIT – which creates a button which sends the form data to the program specified by the <FORM> element's ACTION attribute, TEXT (the default value) – which creates a one-line text input field, PASSWORD – operates in the same way as the TEXT value except that the user's entry is obscured by asterisks.
		NAME=".."	This attribute specifies the name of the control which can then be referenced by a scripting language. Valid values are: any text string (one word)
		SIZE=".."	Used with a TYPE="TEXT" control this attribute specifies the width of the input field in characters. Valid values are: a number of characters.
		MAXLENGTH =".."	Used with a TYPE="TEXT" control this attribute specifies the total number of characters which can be entered into the input field. Valid values are: a number of characters.
		VALUE=".."	Used with a TYPE="TEXT" control this attribute specifies the default value for the control – the words that appear after the page has loaded which may subsequently be replaced by the

Opening Tag	Closing Tag	Attributes	Description
			user. Used with a TYPE="CHECKBOX" or "RADIO" control, this attribute specifies the value that is returned to the data processing program if the control is clicked. Valid values are: any text string (one word).
		CHECKED	When used with CHECKBOX or RADIO controls, defines the box which is selected when the page first displays.
<TEXTAREA>	</TEXTAREA>		These tags create a multiple line input control within a form.
		ROWS=".."	This attribute specifies the number of rows of text the form control should allow. Valid values are: a number of lines.
		COLS=".."	This attribute specifies the width of the form control in characters. Valid values are: a number of characters.
		NAME=".."	This attribute specifies the name of the control which can then be referenced by a scripting language. Valid values are: any text string (one word).
<SELECT>	</SELECT>		These tags define a selection list within a form.
		NAME=".."	This attribute specifies the name of the control which can then be referenced by a scripting language. Valid values are: any text string (one word).
<OPTION>			This tag introduces an option within a selection list defined by the <SELECT> element above.

Opening Tag	Closing Tag	Attributes	Description
		VALUE=".."	This attribute specifies the value to be returned to the data processing program when the option is selected. Valid values are: any text string (one word).
		SELECTED	Defines the option which will display in the selection list when the page first opens.
<SCRIPT>	</SCRIPT>		These tags enclose a script inserted in a Web page – usually in the Head section.
		LANGUAGE =".."	This attribute defines the scripting language being used. Valid values include: Javascript and VBScript.

 ## QUICK REVISION QUESTIONS

1. What is meant by interactive content and why is it of interest to the Web author?

2. What is a CGI application and how is it connected to interactive page content?

3. What is the mailto protocol? Why is it useful to Web designers?

4. How is a form inserted into a Web page? How can a Web designer ensure that data submitted from that form is processed by the host server?

5. When a form is designed, it requires controls. What is a control and what choice of controls is available to the designer?

6. What is meant by client/server programming and why is it important to the future direction of the Web?

7. What is a scripting language, and how is it used in Web authoring?

8. What is an event handler attribute? What sort of events do they handle?

9. What do the letters DHTML stand for? What does DHTML bring to Web design?

10. Why is accuracy vital when creating scripts for the Web?

Chapter 19
Navigation

Brief contents:

1. The different navigation methods a Web site can employ.

2. The importance of logical and intuitive site navigation systems.

3. How to implement a textual or graphic navigation bar.

4. How to avoid stranding your visitors up dead ends or through teleports.

5. The importance of site maps.

6. How to "slice" imagemaps to speed downloading and create rollover effects.

Navigation

Site navigation is one of those areas that looks easy, but gets more complicated the deeper you go. It includes all the different ways of moving around a site. We can list these as follows:

1. Text hyperlinks within individual pages.
2. Graphic links such as buttons and icons.
3. Hidden hyperlinks.
4. A navigation bar which appears on every page.
5. A clickable site map – a page which shows the complete layout of the site and includes clickable links.
6. Links generated by active content such as JavaScript or DHTML.
7. The browser's own navigation controls, such as the **Back** button.

Most of these we have discussed at different places in the book, but let's bring them together here. Text (or more accurately "textual") hyperlinks were the first links we looked at. You will recall that any number of words can be enclosed within the **<A>** Anchor element and linked to any URL locally or across the Web. Graphic links we also looked at. An image of any size can be inserted into a page and linked with the **<A>** element in the same way that text can. Both of these types can be used to create in-line links from page to page. By default, text links will be underlined and rendered in blue to make them stand out from ordinary text.

All hyperlinks are "unidirectional" – that is they can only move your visitor in one direction, from the source to the target. To get back again, the visitor must use a second unidirectional link. Whether a link's anchor is textual or graphical, HTML treats it in exactly the same way, but the link itself can have one of four results.

1. It can move the visitor from one location to another within a document.

2. It can move the visitor from one document to another document.

3. It can link to an object such as a graphic or a sound file.

4. It can link to an external program (client- or server-side).

There are occasions when it's useful to create hidden links – links that work like ordinary ones, but are not obvious to the visitor. These can help to test a site, can be included in on-line games or active content, can be passed on to special visitors to give them access to parts of your site hidden from the ordinary public, and can be used to create occasional surprises for your visitors. (Note that they are not very well hidden, since anyone with some knowledge of HTML can look at your source code and spot them at once.)

To see how hidden links can be created and used, work through the following exercise:

Exercise One

1. Use your graphics software to create a .GIF image, 20 pixels square and solid black. Save this to your **test_pages/resources** folder as **blackbox.gif**.

2. Using a standard HTML template, add the following code into the Head and Body sections, exactly as printed:

```
<HTML>
<HEAD>
<TITLE>Hidden Links</TITLE>
<STYLE TYPE="text/css">
<!- -
.nolink {color: white; text-decoration: none}
- ->
</STYLE>
```

```
</HEAD>
<BODY LINK="#ffff00" VLINK="#ffff00" BGCOLOR="#000000">
<DIV ALIGN="Center"><H3><A HREF="earpop_home.html"><IMG
SRC="resources/blackbox.gif" WIDTH="20" HEIGHT="20"
ALIGN="BOTTOM" BORDER="0"></A><FONT COLOR="#ffffff">Find the
hidden link on this page...</FONT></H3></DIV>
<P><FONT COLOR="#ffffff">There is a </FONT><A
HREF="earpop_home.html">link</A><FONT COLOR="#ffffff">
here.</FONT></P>
<P><FONT COLOR="#ffffff">There is also a </FONT><U><A
HREF="earpop_home.html"><SPAN CLASS="nolink">link</SPAN>
</A></U><FONT COLOR="#ffffff"> here. But you can't see it!
<P>OK, try clicking just to the left of the word "FIND".</FONT>
</BODY>
</HTML>
```

3. Save this file to your **test_pages** folder as **hidden_links.html**, and open it in your browser. It should look like Figure 19.1.

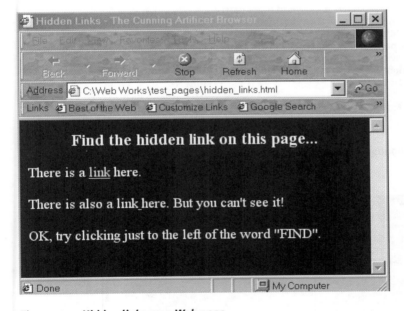

Figure 19.1: Hidden links on a Web page.

We have hidden two hyperlinks in this page. The first link is the square black graphic we have positioned just in front of the headline. Since it is the same colour as the background, it is invisible, but it works in the same way that any other linked graphic would. The second link (the word "link" in the third line) should have appeared just as the link in the line above does, but we have used an embedded style sheet to change its properties back to those of the rest of the text.

Navigation bars

Navigation bars are perhaps the best way to conduct visitors around your site. They are easy to operate – even for inexperienced Web users -- and add considerably to the look of a site. There are several ways that navigation bars can be constructed, and several ways that they can be used within your pages. We have looked at examples earlier in the book and Figure 19.2 shows three ways in which a navigation bar can be used within a page. Read the text in the Figure for further information. None of these three is visually exciting, but they are practical and easy to operate, and those should be the first criteria for a navigation bar. A more stylish bar is shown as Figure 19.3.

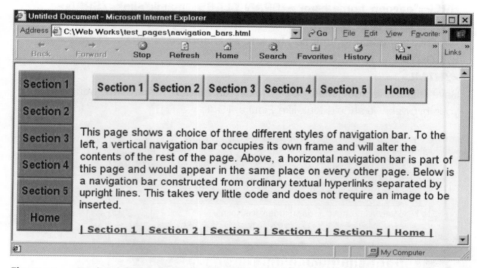

Figure 19.2: Navigation bar styles and positions

Figure 19.3: An example of a stylised navigation bar

Whether you can create a stylish navigation bar or will have to be content with a sensible one will largely depend on your artistic ability. By all means try for something slick, but don't forget that you are designing a tool, and the first requirement for a tool is that it works properly! Remember also that if a navigation bar is to look right on your pages, it must conform to your design. This means thinking about the colours used, the fonts in which you label the buttons and the size and shape of the graphic itself.

A graphic navigation bar is an imagemap and we discussed these in some detail in Chapter 9. We also showed you how to define the area to be used as a hotspot by calculating its co-ordinates in pixels. Not surprisingly, most Web authoring software offers much quicker ways of doing this. Usually the user draws an active area onto an image, leaving the software to calculate the co-ordinates and produce the code. In addition to the full packages, there are a number of small utilities which can do this for you. These can often be found on computer magazine cover disks or can be downloaded from the Internet.

For our manga site, we have decided to use a graphical navigation bar which incorporates small comic figures. Our background colour is black, so our navigation bar will also have a black background to blend seamlessly into the page. We can update our design sheet to include a note to this effect – as in Figure 19.4.

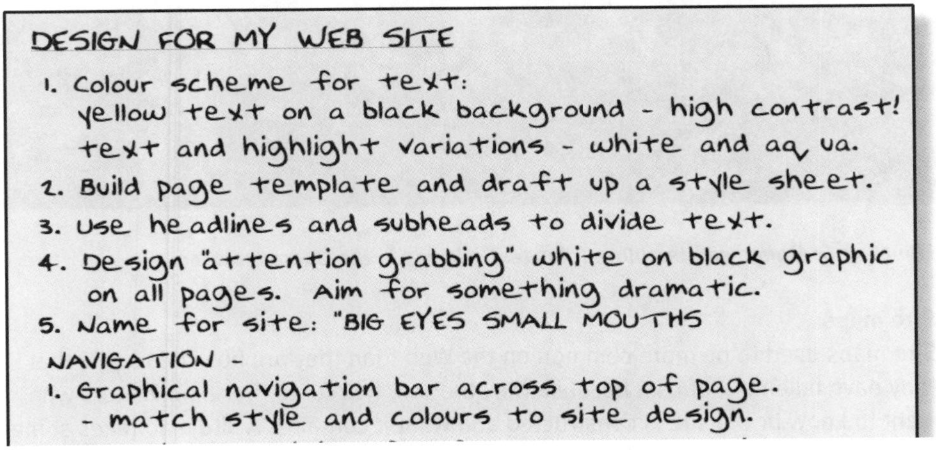

DESIGN FOR MY WEB SITE

1. Colour scheme for text:
   yellow text on a black background - high contrast!
   text and highlight variations - white and aq ua.
2. Build page template and draft up a style sheet.
3. Use headlines and subheads to divide text.
4. Design "attention grabbing" white on black graphic
   on all pages. Aim for something dramatic.
5. Name for site: "BIG EYES SMALL MOUTHS

NAVIGATION -
1. Graphical navigation bar across top of page.
   - match style and colours to site design.

Figure 19.4.

Figure 19.5 shows the navigation bar we have designed for our site. We just wish you could see it in full colour! The lettering is gold and the girl's hair is purple. We also decided on a name for our site – "Big eyes, small mouths", which is how characters are drawn manga-style, and we have incorporated that into our navigation bar.

Figure 19.5: Manga site's logo and navigation bar.

When we install this navigation bar into our template, we shall plot rectangular hot spots for our links just large enough to enclose the captions. With this code inserted into our template, we can be sure that our navigation system will look and work in exactly the same way for every page on our site. Figure 19.6 shows our modified template page open in a browser.

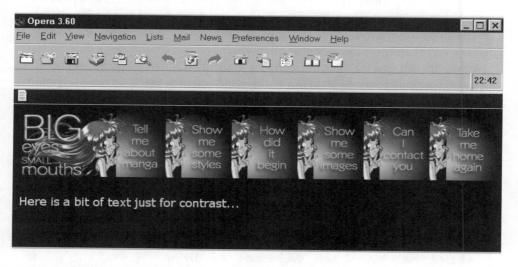

Figure 19.6: Manga site template (plus text) viewed in the Opera browser.

Site maps

Site maps used to be more common on the Web than they are now. It is a pity that they have fallen out of use, because they are very helpful to first-time visitors who want to know how a site is constructed and what it contains. A site map takes some of the pressure off your navigation bar, but it doesn't replace it. It is essential to include a link to it on your Home Page, and useful to link to it from every other page.

Site maps can be graphic or textual, but if textual, they should not just be an index. A site map doesn't only show what a site contains, it also shows the relationship between the various pages and how a visitor can navigate between them. In this sense, it resembles a real map. Using our manga site as an example, a simple textual map might look like Figure 19.7. This is a simplified map and does not show all the links in the site since this would make the map too confusing. On the other hand, it is an active map; clicking on any of the page titles will download the relevant page. Note that this map does not follow the tree hierarchy model discussed in Chapter 16. We have placed the Home Page in the centre of the map, with links going off in all directions. If we had placed the Home Page at the top, the linking would have looked very confused. You might have noticed that we have not included a site map page in our design. This is because we intend placing a version of it on our Home Page itself. If your site is relatively small, like ours, this is a good place for it.

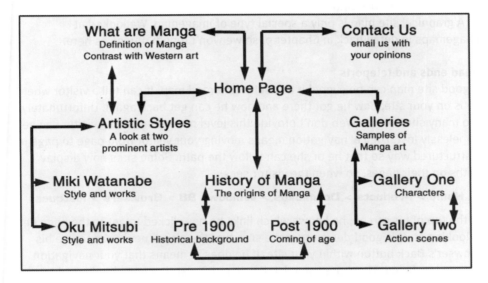

Figure 19.7: .Site map of manga site

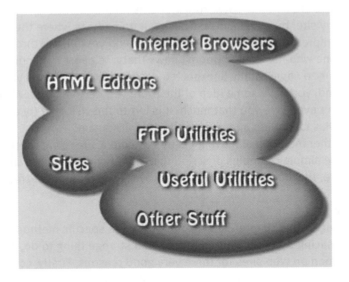

Figure 19.8: A graphical site map for "The Web Pool".

Site maps can also be graphical and since ours will be a site devoted to art, we reckon our site map should show this. We will keep ours in reserve for the moment, so let's take, for example, a site providing advice on Web authoring software, called The Web Pool. The name itself suggests a style for a graphical site map. It also suggests a colour scheme for the site as a whole. We could play around with the pool idea and design in shades of blue. An appropriate site map might look something like Figure 19.8.

A graphical site map is only a special type of imagemap. We looked at imagemaps in detail back in Chapter 9, so we won't repeat ourselves here.

Dead ends and teleports

A good site map can be every bit as useful as a road map. It can tell a visitor where he is on your site, how he got there and how he can get back again. Unfortunately, too many sites on the Web don't provide this level of support, and a visitor can get hopelessly lost. Logical navigation means moving your visitor from page to page in a structured way so that he or she can follow the path. Some sites now display paths on their pages, so when the visitor sees:

Home > Products > Downloads > Windows 98 > Browsers > Netquest

at the top of his screen, he knows which links he has clicked to get to the page he is looking at. It is good design to make sure that the visitor never has to use his browser's **Back** button within your site. If he does, it means that your navigation system has failed. There are two mistakes in particular that you should avoid.

Firstly, never lead your visitor up a dead end. The classic dead end, which is found far too often on the Web, is a series of links which land your visitor on a page from which there are no links back. Your visitor is forced to back up which is irritating on any site, but can be disastrous on a framed site where the **Back** button often brings unforeseen results. Secondly, never send your visitor through a teleport. Anyone who has played Doom knows that a teleport transports you without warning to some totally unexpected destination and strands you there. With a dead end, you have some idea of the route you have taken; a Web site teleport doesn't even give you that much. It is left to the visitor to try and work out where he has landed up and to pick his way back again.

There are other methods of moving visitors around a site using scripting. We looked at some simple examples of scripting in the previous chapter and, as we explained there, this book is not intended to cover the vast topic of creating scripts.

Image slicing

The final section of this chapter is concerned with one specific method of rendering imagemaps – slicing them up. This might sound a strange thing to do, but image slicing is common on Web sites for three very good reasons. Firstly, consider the very common site layout which has fixed content across the top and down the left hand side of every page. A rough design is shown in Figure 19.9.

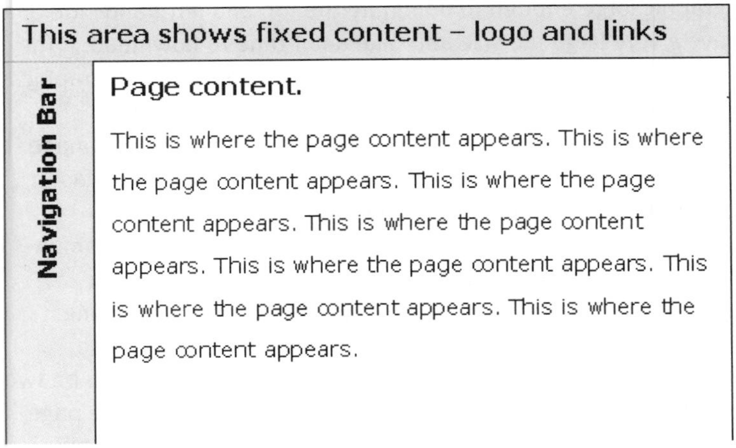

This area shows fixed content – logo and links	
Navigation Bar	**Page content.** This is where the page content appears. This is where the page content appears. This is where the page content appears. This is where the page content appears. This is where the page content appears. This is where the page content appears. This is where the page content appears.

Figure 19.9: Page design showing fixed content top and left

If the shaded, fixed content area in Figure 19.9 is to consist of a single graphic incorporating the site's name, logo and navigation system – a very common format on the Web – this creates problems within HTML, which considers all graphics to be rectangular and tries to wrap text around them. The result of placing this graphic on a page would be to push all the page content in the white area to the left or below the graphic. We have seen ways of solving this problem using layers, but these usually involve complicated coding. If, on the other hand, this image was sliced into three as shown in Figure 19.10, a simple table could then be created with two rows and two columns to contain the three graphic slices and the page content. By reducing the **<TABLE>** element's **BORDER, CELLPADDING** and **CELLSPACING** attributes to zero, the three graphic elements would be seamlessly joined up again.

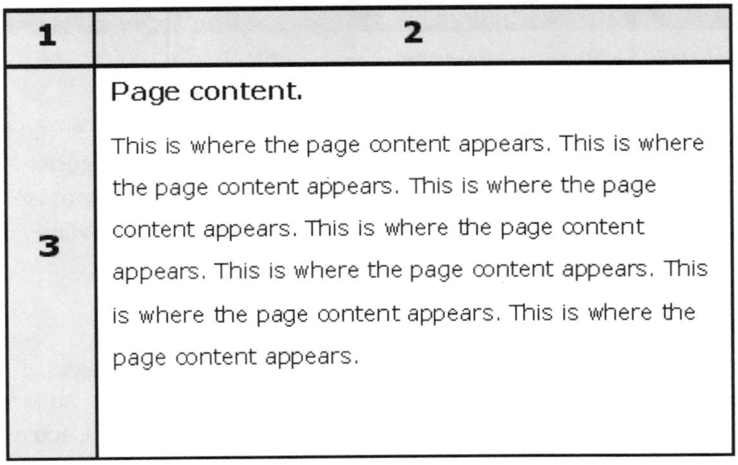

1	**2**	
3	**Page content.** This is where the page content appears. This is where the page content appears. This is where the page content appears. This is where the page content appears. This is where the page content appears. This is where the page content appears. This is where the page content appears.	

Figure 19.10 Graphic slices joined within a table.

Secondly, a single graphic large enough to dominate the top and left-hand side of a Web page would have a very large file size and take a fair time to download. If the image was sliced into smaller pieces and downloaded as a series of small graphics, again joined up by a table, each section would appear as soon as it had downloaded, giving the viewer something to see on screen. (The complete image would actually take longer to download like this, but it would appear to be faster because something could be seen happening in the browser!)

Finally, we mentioned interactive events in the previous section. One common effect on the Web is for a hotspot on an imagemap to change when a mouse pointer passes over it, or when it is clicked. HTML provides for this by defining event handler attributes such as **onmouseover** and **onmousedown,** which we looked at in Chapter 18. For this to occur within an imagemap, there need to be two versions of the graphic available – the one that appears on screen when the page loads, and the one it changes to when the event occurs. If a single large graphic is used, the whole thing has to change to a second large graphic, thus doubling the download time. If on the other hand, the graphic has been sliced, the individual slice that is activated can change to another slice leaving the rest of the graphic unchanged. Better still, this means that each hotspot can be a separate slice and change individually. To see how this operates, look at Figure 19.11.

Figure 19.11: Image slicing to support an interactive event.

We have used the navigation bar designed for our manga site, but we have sliced it into six smaller graphics, one of which is shown slightly separated in the Figure. Each of those six graphics has an alternative which appears when the hot spot is clicked. The top line shows the sliced graphic as it first appears, the bottom line shows how it appears when the "How did it begin" hotspot is clicked.

Work through Exercise Two to see how graphic slicing can be used.

Exercise Two

1. Use your graphics software to create five .GIF images, each 50 pixels square and solid blue. On each graphic, add a number from 1 to 5 in white. Centre the number and make it as large as will comfortably fit within the square. Save these to your **test_pages/resources** folder as **bluebox1.gif**, **bluebox2.gif** etc. Now create five further graphics identical to the first five,

except coloured red. Try to keep the numbers exactly the same size and in exactly the same position as on the blue squares. Save these to your **test_pages/resources** folder as **redbox1.gif**, **redbox2.gif** etc.

2. Create a new page in your text editor and type the following code exactly as printed. (You cannot afford to make a single mistake in this code so type it, check it and recheck it! Where a line finishes and the next line is indented, it is a continuation of the previous line, so you should press the Spacebar but otherwise keep on typing. Do NOT hit the Enter key unless the next line starts at the far left.)

```
<HTML>
<HEAD>
<TITLE>Rollovers</TITLE>
<SCRIPT language="JavaScript">
<!- -
function MM_swapImgRestore() { //v3.0
  var i,x,a=document.MM_sr;
    for(i=0;a&&i<a.length&&(x=a[i])&&x.oSrc;i++) x.src=x.oSrc;
}


function MM_preloadImages() { //v3.0
  var d=document; if(d.images){ if(!d.MM_p) d.MM_p=new Array();
  var i,j=d.MM_p.length,a=MM_preloadImages.arguments; for(i=0;
    i<a.length; i++)
  if (a[i].indexOf("#")!=0){ d.MM_p[j]=new Image;
    d.MM_p[j++].src=a[i];}}
}


function MM_findObj(n, d) { //v3.0
  var p,i,x;  if(!d) d=document;
  if((p=n.indexOf("?"))>0&&parent.frames.length)
{ d=parent.frames[n.substring(p+1)].document; n=n.substring(0,p);}
if(!(x=d[n])&&d.all) x=d.all[n]; for (i=0;!x&&i<d.forms.length;i++)
  x=d.forms[i][n];
for(i=0;!x&&d.layers&&i<d.layers.length;i++)
  x=MM_findObj(n,d.layers[i].document); return x;
}


function MM_swapImage() { //v3.0
  var i,j=0,x,a=MM_swapImage.arguments; document.MM_sr=new
  Array;
  for(i=0;i<(a.length-2);i+=3)
if ((x=MM_findObj(a[i]))!=null){document.MM_sr[j++]=x; if(!x.oSrc)
  x.oSrc=x.src; x.src=a[i+2];}
}
```

```
//- ->
</SCRIPT>
</HEAD>

<BODY bgcolor="#FFFFFF"
onLoad="MM_preloadImages('resources/redbox1.gif','resources/redbox
2.gif','resources/redbox3.gif','resources/redbox4.gif','resources/redbox
5.gif')">
<TABLE width="250" cellpadding="0" cellspacing="0" border="0">
  <TR>
    <TD><A href="a.html" onmouseout="MM_swapImgRestore()"
onmouseover="MM_swapImage('Image1',' ','resources/redbox1.gif',1)"
><IMG name="Image1" border="0" src="resources/bluebox1.gif"
width="50" height="50"></A></TD>
    <TD><A href="b.html" onmouseout="MM_swapImgRestore()"
onmouseover="MM_swapImage('Image2',' ','resources/redbox2.gif',1)"
><IMG name="Image2" border="0" src="resources/bluebox2.gif"
width="50" height="50"></A></TD>
    <TD><A href="c.html" onmouseout="MM_swapImgRestore()"
onmouseover="MM_swapImage('Image3',' ','resources/redbox3.gif',1)"
><IMG name="Image3" border="0" src="resources/bluebox3.gif"
width="50" height="50"></A></TD>
    <TD><A href="d.html" onmouseout="MM_swapImgRestore()"
onmouseover="MM_swapImage('Image4',' ','resources/redbox4.gif',1)"
><IMG name="Image4" border="0" src="resources/bluebox4.gif"
width="50" height="50"></A></TD>
    <TD><A href="e.html" onmouseout="MM_swapImgRestore()"
onmouseover="MM_swapImage('Image5',' ','resources/redbox5.gif',1)"
><IMG name="Image5" border="0" src="resources/bluebox5.gif"
width="50" height="50"></A></TD>
  </TR>
</TABLE>
</BODY>
</HTML>
```

3. Save this to your **test_pages** folder as **mousedown.html** and open it in your browser. If your browser can handle JavaScript you should see something like Figure 19.12. Try passing your mouse over one of the numbers (don't bother clicking them) and see what happens. You must admit, that's a pretty impressive effect!

This type of event is usually called a rollover, since it is triggered by the mouse rolling over a hot spot. The JavaScript script you have typed in is complicated, but don't worry about this. As we explained in the previous chapter, scripts like this are

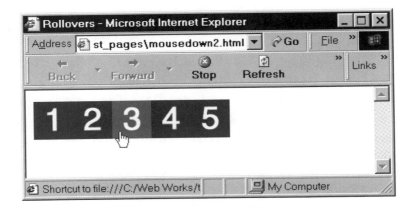

Figure 19.12: A sliced image used with an interactive event.

freely available on the Web. Unless you want to learn JavaScript, the simplest solution is to download the script that handles the effect you want, modify it to use your own images and paste it into your Web page.

To understand how this particular script works, look first at the code within the Body section. In the **<BODY>** element, you have used the **onload** attribute to preload the browser with a series of images which are not yet called for by the page code. This ensures that your alternative (rollover) images are downloaded with the page and ready for action. After that, you have set up a single row, five-column table in the usual way. The code scrap:

<TABLE width="250" cellpadding="0" cellspacing="0" border="0">

creates the table exactly wide enough to accommodate your five graphics in a row and makes sure that no space appears between them. To a visitor, your five squares look like a single long graphic with numbers printed on it.

Now look at the code scrap:

**<TD><A href="a.html" onmouseout="MM_swapImgRestore()"
onmouseover="MM_swapImage('Image1',' ','resources/redbox1.gif',1)"
><IMG name="Image1" border="0" src="resources/bluebox1.gif"
width="50" height="50"></A></TD>**

This appears very complicated at first sight, but examine it logically and you will recognise most of the attributes. The attributes **onmouseout** and **onmouseover** are event handler attributes that we met in the previous chapter. We have used them to trigger the JavaScript program in the Head section, which defines what will happen as the mouse pointer moves on and off the active area (hotspot). You have sourced the image **bluebox1.gif** in the same way as you have done before and defined how it will appear. (As a bonus, this script and code can be modified to suit any imagemap with rollovers that you might want to create. You will need to edit it with great care, though!)

Finally, let's apply some of this to our manga site. We can update our design sheet as shown in Figure 19.13.

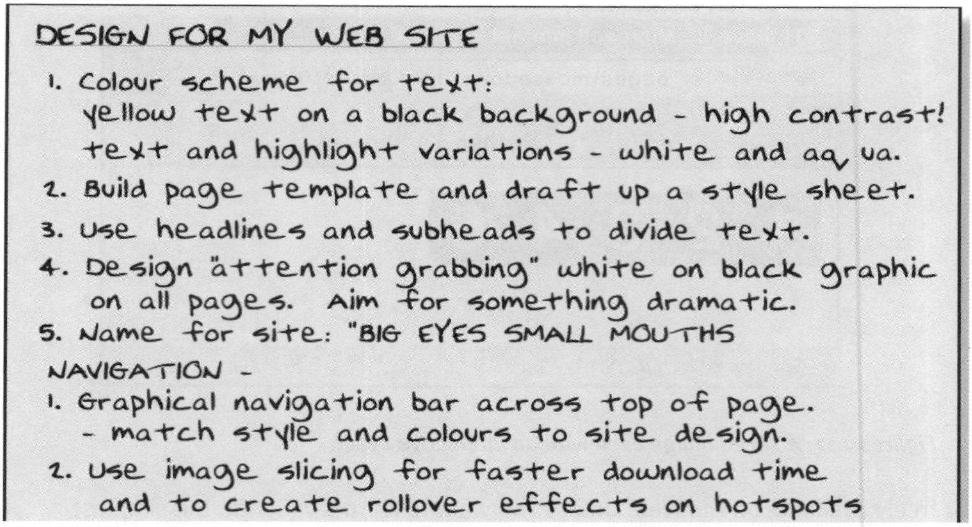

DESIGN FOR MY WEB SITE
1. Colour scheme for text:
   yellow text on a black background - high contrast!
   text and highlight variations - white and aqua.
2. Build page template and draft up a style sheet.
3. Use headlines and subheads to divide text.
4. Design "attention grabbing" white on black graphic
   on all pages. Aim for something dramatic.
5. Name for site: "BIG EYES SMALL MOUTHS
NAVIGATION -
1. Graphical navigation bar across top of page.
   - match style and colours to site design.
2. Use image slicing for faster download time
   and to create rollover effects on hotspots

Figure 19.13.

At the end of Chapter 17, we looked at a possible page graphic for our manga site.
We have now decided to use a combined navigation bar and manga graphic on all
our pages, and have come up with a design we are happy with. We are also going
to slice the graphic so each of our navigation buttons shows the rollover effect from
Figure 19.11 (p. 298). Figure 19.14 shows the complete graphic sliced into segments
– we have separated them slightly so that you can see them more easily. The text
area is not part of the graphic, but is simply the background colour of the table
itself. For simplicity, we have called the seven images across the top row

Figure 19.14: The sliced navigation and graphic image for our manga site.

topleft.jpg, nav01.jpg, nav02.jpg, nav03.jpg etc. The image to the left is simply called **left.jpg**. You can find them referred to in the code below.

Figure 19.15 shows the alternative image which will replace each of our navigation "buttons" when the mouse pointer rolls over them.

Figure 19.15: Our alternative button image.

Finally, this is how our page template code has been amended to include all these changes. (Again, this includes a whole chunk of JavaScript which you need not concern yourself with.) If you are working with us, but do not intend using rollover events, you can delete all the JavaScript in the head enclosed in the **<SCRIPT>** ... **</SCRIPT>** elements, and change each of the **<TD>** elements to include only the original graphic, like this: **<IMG border="0" src="resources/nav01.jpg" width="91" height="96">** Below the code listing, Figure 19.16 shows how our template page will now look in a browser.

```
<HTML>
<HEAD>
<TITLE> </TITLE>
<META NAME="creation_date" CONTENT="..">
<META NAME="author" CONTENT="Richard Tammadge">
<META NAME="keywords" CONTENT="manga comics japanese
artwork">
<LINK REL="STYLESHEET" HREF="mangastyle.css" TYPE="text/css">
<META HTTP-EQUIV="Content-Type" CONTENT="text/html;
CHARSET=iso-8859-1">
<SCRIPT language="JavaScript">
<!- -
function MM_swapImgRestore() { //v3.0
  var i,x,a=document.MM_sr;
    for(i=0;a&&i<a.length&&(x=a[i])&&x.oSrc;i++) x.src=x.oSrc;
}

function MM_preloadImages() { //v3.0
  var d=document; if(d.images){ if(!d.MM_p) d.MM_p=new Array();
    var i,j=d.MM_p.length,a=MM_preloadImages.arguments; for(i=0;
    i<a.length; i++)
    if (a[i].indexOf("#")!=0){ d.MM_p[j]=new Image;
    d.MM_p[j++].src=a[i];}}
```

```
}
function MM_findObj(n, d) { //v3.0
  var p,i,x;  if(!d) d=document;
    if((p=n.indexOf("?"))>0&&parent.frames.length) {
    d=parent.frames[n.substring(p+1)].document; n=n.substring(0,p);}
  if(!(x=d[n])&&d.all) x=d.all[n]; for (i=0;!x&&i<d.forms.length;i++)
    x=d.forms[i][n];
  for(i=0;!x&&d.layers&&i<d.layers.length;i++)
    x=MM_findObj(n,d.layers[i].document); return x;
}

function MM_swapImage() { //v3.0
  var i,j=0,x,a=MM_swapImage.arguments; document.MM_sr=new
    Array; for(i=0;i<(a.length-2);i+=3)
  if ((x=MM_findObj(a[i]))!=null){document.MM_sr[j++]=x; if(!x.oSrc)
    x.oSrc=x.src; x.src=a[i+2];}
}
//- ->
</SCRIPT>
</HEAD>

<BODY onLoad="MM_preloadImages('resources/alternate.jpg')">
<TABLE Width="800" Border="0" Cellspacing="0" Cellpadding="0"
Bgcolor="#000000">
  <TR>
    <TD width="132"><IMG SRC="resources/topleft.jpg" width="132"
height="96"></TD>
<TD width="91"><A HREF="#" onMouseOut="MM_swapImgRestore()"
onMouseOver="MM_swapImage('Image2','','resources/alternate.jpg',
1)"><IMG name="Image2" border="0" src="resources/nav01.jpg"
width="91" height="96"></A></TD>
<TD width="94"><A HREF="#" onMouseOut="MM_swapImgRestore()"
onMouseOver="MM_swapImage('Image3','','resources/alternate.jpg',
1)"><IMG name="Image3" border="0" src="resources/nav02.jpg"
width="94" height="96"></A></TD>
<TD width="91"><A HREF="#" onMouseOut="MM_swapImgRestore()"
onMouseOver="MM_swapImage('Image4','','resources/alternate.jpg',
1)"><IMG name="Image4" border="0" src="resources/nav03.jpg"
width="91" height="96"></A></TD>
<TD width="94"><A HREF="#" onMouseOut="MM_swapImgRestore()"
onMouseOver="MM_swapImage('Image5','','resources/alternate.jpg',
1)"><IMG name="Image5" border="0" src="resources/nav04.jpg"
width="94" height="96"></A></TD>
```

```
<TD width="92"><A HREF="#" onMouseOut="MM_swapImgRestore()"
onMouseOver="MM_swapImage('Image6',",'resources/alternate.jpg',
1)"><IMG name="Image6" border="0" src="resources/nav05.jpg"
width="92" height="96"></A></TD>
<TD width="206"><a href="#" onMouseOut="MM_swapImgRestore()"
onMouseOver="MM_swapImage('Image7',",'resources/alternate.jpg',
1)"><IMG name="Image7" border="0" src="resources/nav06.jpg"
width="87" height="96"></A></TD>
  </TR>
  <TR>
<TD width="132"><IMG src="resources/left.jpg" width="132"
height="429"></TD>
<TD colspan="6" valign="top">
    <BLOCKQUOTE>
     <P> </P>
     <P>Here is some sample text to show how the page will look.
     <P>We hope you will agree that this site design is beginning to
take shape!
    </BLOCKQUOTE>
   </TD>
  </TR>
 </TABLE>
 </BODY>
 </HTML>
```

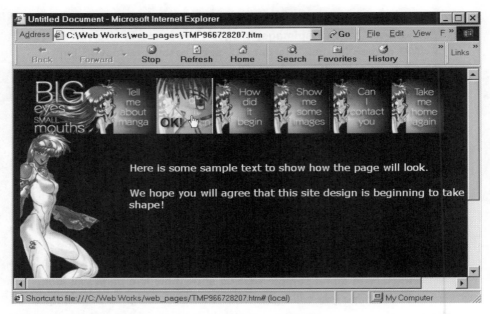

Figure 19.16: Manga site template page shown in a browser.

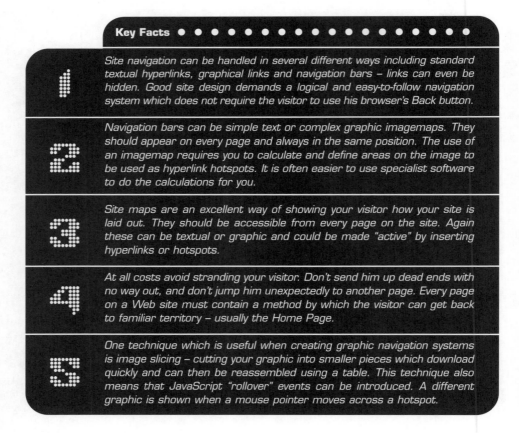

QUICK REVISION QUESTIONS

1. Why is it important for a Web site's navigation system to be intuitive?
2. Are there any advantages in using a textual navigation bar rather than a graphic one?
3. What is a hot spot? What code would you use to define one?
4. What is a site map and why is it so useful?
5. What are dead ends and teleports?
6. What is meant by image slicing and why is it a useful technique?

Chapter 20
Considering your Visitors

Brief contents:

1. Understanding some of the difficulties a visitor to your Web site might encounter.

2. Accessibility issues including site visibility, download times and browser rendering.

3. The ways in which different browsers on different computer platforms render page content.

4. Browser-specific variations in HTML rendering.

5. Understanding the range of different configurations in which Web users set up their hardware and software.

6. The problems of providing pages for non-graphical browsers and browsers which don't support frames.

7. Methods of improving accessibility for visitors with seeing or hearing disabilities.

8. The importance of providing "voluntary content".

Considering your visitors

So far in our design process, we have been mainly interested in creating something functional and interesting. In this chapter we are going to look at Web design and site engineering from a different point of view – that of our potential visitors.

If your site is not intended for others to see, it really has no purpose on the Web. Perhaps in its early days, the Internet was a closed shop, but today it is open to everybody from computer geniuses to small children. Of course some sites are aimed at specific groups of people, but never, we hope, at restricted groups. For your site to prosper, you must aim to extend its audience and attract new viewers. The Web should be a public library and not a private club.

The individuals who first designed the World Wide Web were – and still are – very keen that it should be accessible to all. Of course, there are areas which are restricted; secure sites where you can enter personal details such as your address and credit card number, and be reasonably certain that such information is kept private. But these sites are the backrooms, the rest of the house is open to everyone. The whole idea of hypertext links relies on co-operation. You are entitled to link your pages to anybody else's pages – and they are equally entitled to link back to you. (As a matter of courtesy, you should only link to another site's Home Page. Linking to pages further in – so-called "deep linking" – is frowned on.)

From a designer's point of view, it is safest to assume that anything you post on the Web will be up for public scrutiny. You are therefore competing with highly paid professional site designers. This is not something to worry about – after all you have access to the same code that they do – but it should inspire you to create the very best pages you are capable of. To be effective, a page does not have to complicated or to incorporate dozens of interactive events. Often simplicity and quality of content is all the visitor is looking for, and if you can provide that at a reasonable download speed, then you are up there with the best of them.

Let's start this chapter by considering how accessible your site really is.

Site accessibility

Broadly speaking, we can divide a site's visitors into two categories. There are those that arrive with a specific purpose in mind, and those that are just browsing. In the first category are people who visit a manufacturer's site to download the latest hardware drivers, or those who visit a government site to get the exact words their TD used in a political speech. In the second category are those who look up a reference in a search engine and follow one of a dozen responses to see what they can find, or those who stumble across a site by accident as they follow a twisting trail of hyperlinks across the Web.

Let's assume that your site is not yet compulsory viewing, and concentrate on the second category. If your site has been set up according to the suggestions we made in earlier chapters, a visitor who arrives at your Home Page will have his interest sparked by your design and your use of intriguing key messages. We can hope that from the point of view of content, he or she will be satisfied. Unfortunately, quality of content is only half the story. The other half is accessibility and here matters are largely out of your hands.

A site's accessibility involves three distinct issues – visibility on the Web, download speed and how well it is rendered on a visitor's computer. Let's consider these in turn. Firstly, there is the question of how easy the site is to find. A site designer or administrator – we should use the accepted term "webmaster" – needs to consider how well his or her site is signposted from search engines, directory listings and direct links. We will consider these matters in detail in Chapter 22.

The second consideration – and possibly the most important one – is the speed at which pages download to the visitor's browser. Although there is a theoretical maximum speed at which data can flow across the Internet, in practice this speed is never attained. Access time on the Web is a function not only of the transmission speed of digital information, but also of the carrying capacity of the Internet's hardware – the variable usually described as "bandwidth". In simple terms, the more traffic there is down the wires, the slower that traffic moves.

Think of an Internet connection as a long pipe between the visitor's computer and the server that holds the page requested. Here is a list of just some of the delays that could occur:

1. The remote server might be extremely busy and unable to handle requests.

2. The remote server might be an older machine with a slow processor or insufficient memory.

3. The remote server's connection to the Internet might be slow or badly configured.

4. Connections across the Internet itself might be busy or part of the infrastructure might be down.

5. One of the router servers in the pipe might be busy or broken down.

6. The local loop, the telephone wires back to the visitor's modem, might be damaged or overloaded.

7. The visitor's modem might be a slower type or badly configured.

8. The visitor's own computer might have a slow processor or insufficient memory.

When you look at that list, it's a wonder that anything ever gets through! The pipe analogy is quite useful. If you constrict a pipe, less water can run through it. Even with the Internet's ability to send data down several channels simultaneously, there are still bottlenecks, and one slow section will slow down the whole delivery.

There is nothing you can do about this, of course. If the connection is slow, a visitor is very likely to give up on your site and go somewhere else. Unfortunately, after a couple of failed attempts, he may very well write your site off as a waste of his time and never return. If you know a page will be slow to download, it is a good idea to alert your visitors to this fact. Since text arrives and is rendered before other content, a simple message such as:

Please wait for this page to download fully.

will encourage your visitor to be patient. If you are using active content such as a Flash movie, this message can be programmed into the movie itself and will disappear when the animation proper starts playing.

We have already looked at download times in relation to graphic and multimedia content, and by now you are aware of the importance of keeping file sizes small. Of course, there are limits to the control you have over this process. A graphic file, for example, cannot be compressed beyond a certain limit without losing quality. The balance you have to try for is the best possible content at the fastest possible download speed.

Browser incompatibility

So we have no control over Internet speeds, and we also have no control over the platform, software and configuration of the visitor's own computer. We are told that 95% of the world's computer users are running Windows-based machines of some variety. Of the other operating systems, we know that the MacOS is the most popular with LINUX gaining ground rapidly. By and large, a particular make of browser will render pages in a very similar way regardless of the platform it is running on, but remember that browsers rely on plug-in "helper" applications to handle some content. Some plug-ins are not available for certain platforms which means that the content they are intended to handle will be saved to the hard drive rather than displayed.

Our third accessibility issue is whether the browser accurately renders the page once it has downloaded. We have already looked at some of the difficulties surrounding browser incompatibility. We know that different browsers handle HTML in slightly different ways, which leads to Web pages being rendered in slightly different ways. We also know that some browsers support proprietary HTML elements which are ignored by other browsers, and that some browsers don't support standard HTML elements that others do. Frankly, the whole thing is a bit of a mess. If we play the percentages, we only need concern ourselves with the two major browsers, since Microsoft's Internet Explorer® and Netscape® dominate the field, with over 90% of the market between them. There are other, equally good browsers. Opera®, for example is fast and highly efficient, Sun Microsystems' HotJava® is particularly good at handling active content written in Java, and there are many others.

In Chapter 21 we will look at site testing in different browsers. For now, it is enough to remember that there are differences between the ways in which browsers render pages. We should also remember that many people are very slow to upgrade to a newer version of a browser if the old one is working to their satisfaction. This tendency has been called "techno-inertia" and is largely the fault of the software manufacturers themselves. So often, installing new software creates terrible problems with countless restarts, previously installed software ceasing to work, and even machines crashing. It is hardly surprising that less confident computer users will stick with what they've got. Many people soldier on with older browsers which simply cannot handle the latest HTML standard.

There are also configuration differences. Most browsers are highly configurable to suit their user's preferences. Figure 20.1 shows some of the configuration options available in Internet Explorer 5.5.

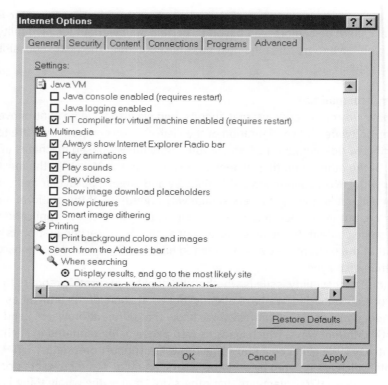

Figure 20.1: Internet Explorer 5.5's configuration options.

Note that the user can switch off animations, sounds, videos and even pictures. This is one reason for including alternative text in your HTML code. Then, at least, the no-graphics browser will see something. We will pick this point up again in the next section.

A further complication comes from all the different types and sizes of monitor that are currently available. Although the older 14" monitors are seldom supplied with new computers, there are still millions of them in daily use. A 14" monitor cannot realistically cope with a resolution greater than 800 x 600 pixels, and many of them are still used with the old 640 x 480 pixel resolution. At the other end of the scale, modern 21" monitors are effective at 1280 x 1024 pixel resolution or even greater. At this resolution a monitor can show more than twice as much content as the 640 x 480 standard. Catering for both extremes is impossible. Once again, we are forced to compromise. It is assumed that the most common monitor resolution at present is 800 x 600 pixels, and provided your pages work at that resolution, you have done all that can reasonably be expected.

Shuffle all these alternatives together and you will see that the number of different set-ups available to the Web user is almost unlimited. There is no conceivable way of ensuring that your pages work properly in all these configurations. The best you, or any Web author, can do is to follow the middle path, trying to make sure that your pages suit the majority of Web users. Inevitably, there will be rogue set-ups that mess up your hard work!

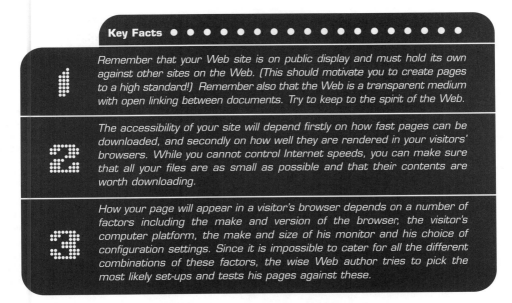

Key Facts ●

1 Remember that your Web site is on public display and must hold its own against other sites on the Web. (This should motivate you to create pages to a high standard!) Remember also that the Web is a transparent medium with open linking between documents. Try to keep to the spirit of the Web.

2 The accessibility of your site will depend firstly on how fast pages can be downloaded, and secondly on how well they are rendered in your visitors' browsers. While you cannot control Internet speeds, you can make sure that all your files are as small as possible and that their contents are worth downloading.

3 How your page will appear in a visitor's browser depends on a number of factors including the make and version of the browser, the visitor's computer platform, the make and size of his monitor and his choice of configuration settings. Since it is impossible to cater for all the different combinations of these factors, the wise Web author tries to pick the most likely set-ups and tests his pages against these.

Non-graphical browsers and browsers that do not support frames

Most people who use the Web are looking for a graphical, even multimedia experience, but there are those who are only interested in the information available. These people have the option of browsing with image rendering turned off. In our opinion, the Web without graphics is a bit like watching television with the picture turned off, but there is no denying how fast access becomes.

Look back to Figure 19.14 in the previous chapter. Figure 20.2 shows the same Web page, but with image rendering turned off.

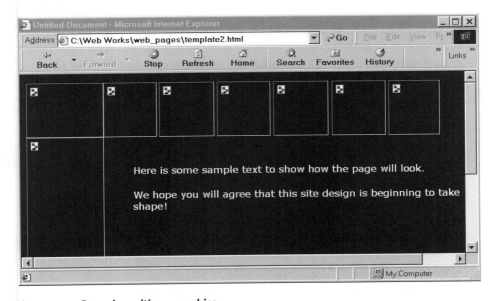

Figure 20.2: Browsing with no graphics.

And, just in case you are wondering how a page would look in a browser which doesn't display graphics at all, Figure 20.3 shows the same page in the Lynx browser – one of the orginal text-only browsers, difficult to use and dull to look at, but very fast indeed!

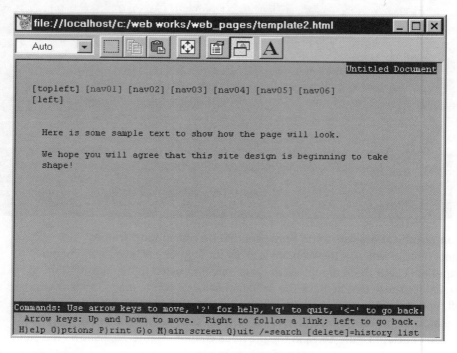

Figure 20.3: The same page in Lynx – a text-only browser.

Note that not only have all our beautifully designed graphics disappeared, but in the browser with graphic rendering turned off, our navigation bar is no longer useable. (Lynx is clever enough to replace the graphic links with text ones.) Some people have suggested that Web designers should cater for the minority who browse like this by offering an alternative page designed with no graphics and all the links presented in text. We are not sure that we agree. How people choose to use the Web is entirely up to them, but if they decide to browse without graphics, should they expect special treatment? After all, the television companies do not subtitle all their programmes for the benefit of those who turn their TV sound off. You must decide whether you are prepared for all the additional work.

We have more sympathy for those Web users whose browsers do not support frames. You will remember back in Chapter 10 we used a code scrap like the following to advise such people that they needed a frame-enabled browser to see our page:

```
<FRAMESET ROWS="75,*" BORDER="0">
<FRAME SRC="earpop_navigation.html" NAME="top">
<FRAME SRC="earpop_home.html" NAME="bottom">
```

```
<NOFRAMES><BODY>To view this page you need a browser which
supports frames.</BODY></NOFRAMES>
</FRAMESET>
```

We could have taken this a stage further by creating a separate page which did not use frames and modifying our Frameset document code like this:

```
<FRAMESET ROWS="75,*" BORDER="0">
<FRAME SRC="earpop_navigation.html" NAME="top">
<FRAME SRC="earpop_home.html" NAME="bottom">
<NOFRAMES><BODY>To see a version of this page which does not use
frames, <A HREF="framefree.html">CLICK HERE</A>.
</BODY></NOFRAMES>
</FRAMESET>
```

A browser which is not capable of rendering frames would ignore almost all this code, responding only to the scrap:

```
<BODY>To see a version of this page which does not use frames,
<A HREF="framefree.html">CLICK HERE</A>.
</BODY>
```

which would create a plain white page with only the text and the link visible. Unfortunately, if you wished to create a frame-free version of your site, this would mean building alternative pages for every framed document on your site, and you might feel that this would be too much trouble. Certainly, we would consider it a low priority.

Catering for "non-standard" visitors

One criticism regularly levelled at the Web is that it is aimed at an exclusive group. Clearly, to access the Web, you need a computer with an Internet connection, and this does discriminate against people in poorer, under-resourced countries. At one time, Web users were almost always young males, but this has changed and Web content is now aimed at both sexes and all ages. And quite right, too!

One major discrimination does remain however, and that is language. The vast majority of Web sites are written in American English – indeed, as we have noted several times, HTML itself requires American English. Of course Web sites are written in other languages, but even these often provide alternative pages in English. As the Web continues to expand, it is quite possible that English will become the only viable language for international communication. Web designers who work in other languages are already finding that the appeal of their sites is limited unless they include an English version. As to whether this is a good thing or not, we make no comment. Certainly, there will always be speciality sites – there are several sites dedicated to the Irish language, for example, but the Web mainstream increasingly demands English.

Some languages are well represented on the Web. Japan, for example, has a very active Web community. It is worth noting that languages which use non-standard

ASCII characters cannot be properly rendered in a Web browser unless a special character set (font) is installed. Without this, Japanese characters are displayed using ASCII characters like o _ - $ ^ =. To their credit, Microsoft tries to support a wide range of different character sets and these can be downloaded for free from their Web site.

We noted in Chapter 4 that HTML includes support for special character entities to provide letters with fadas and accents, and non-English letterforms. There are also entities for Latin and Greek characters, arrows, mathematical symbols and geometric shapes. If you need the full listing, it can be downloaded from the World Wide Web Consortium's own Web site at http://www.w3.org.

There is one group of possible visitors who do deserve special attention and that is those with visual and aural disabilities. If the Web is to function as an open community, we need to make provision for people who are partially sighted or have hearing difficulties. Since the Web is mainly a visual medium, we need not be so concerned with the latter group, beyond ensuring that if any important information is presented as a sound track, the same information is displayed on screen.

Web users with seeing difficulties can make use of the range of accessibility features built into their software. Windows, for example, provides a screen magnifier which enlarges selected portions of the display for easier reading. Within Internet Explorer, the text size specified for a page can be overridden by the user. Compare the standard rendering of our manga site's Home Page in Figure 19.14 in the last chapter, with Figure 20.4 below. Here the text size has been set to the maximum. (If you wish to try this, open Internet Explorer and go **View > Text Size**. In Netscape Navigator, go **View > Increase Font**.)

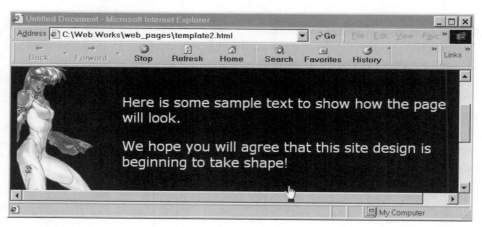

Figure 20.4: Text size set to maximum in Internet Explorer.

With most browsers and operating systems providing similar functions, there is no reason for you to create pages with over-sized text, unless your site is specifically aimed at people with sight problems. You should, of course, be concerned with readability – and not just for your visually impaired visitors. Since we have already stressed the importance of a high contrast display, we will not dwell on the point here.

One feature we have seen on a number of sites recently is an advice page for the visually impaired. It is quite possible that some people with seeing difficulties might not be aware of the facilities available to them, and an advice page would alert them to the accessibility resources available to them. Such a page is an example of social awareness and we have taken up this idea for the revision project at the end of this chapter.

Some browsers allow a user to define his or her own style sheet which will override any style definitions within a downloaded page. Exercise One takes you through the process of creating such a style sheet and implementing it in Internet Explorer. Remember to change the browser's settings back to normal afterwards, or the style sheet will continue to operate as the page default.

Exercise One

1. In your text editor, create a cascading style sheet which provides for high contrast between text and background and large text sizes. The following code is suggested, but feel free to modify it as you see fit:

   BODY   **{background-color: white; color: black; font-family:**
                Sans-serif; font-size: x-large; font-style: normal}
   H1, H2, H3   {font-size: 150%}

2. Save this as **access.css** in your **test_pages** folder.

3. Open Internet Explorer and click **Tools > Internet Options**. [Older versions of Internet Explorer have Internet Options on different menus, so you might need to look elsewhere.] On the **General** tab click the **Accessibility** button, and modify the settings on the window that opens so that it looks like Figure 20.5 below. Click **OK** and **OK** to get back to the browser window.

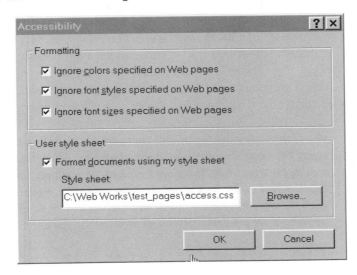

Figure 20.5: Setting Internet Explorer's Accessibility options.

4. Now open the **earpop_home.html** page in your reconfigured browser. It will look something like Figure 20.6. Try a few other pages and note the effect. Of course this style sheet does not cover all the options, only the **<BODY>** and **<H1>**, **<H2>** and **<H3>** elements. To create an all-embracing style sheet would take a lot longer.

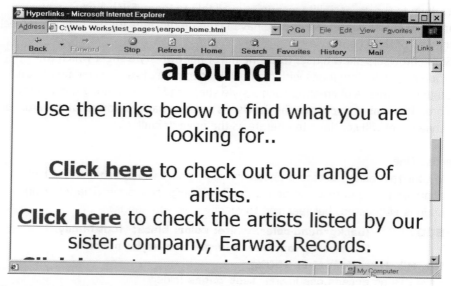

Figure 20.6: A page rendered using the access.css style sheet.

Voluntary content

Finally in this chapter we are returning to a concept we introduced in our look at multimedia content. There are some sites on the Web which just don't want you to leave. Crafty Web designers have found ways of using scripting to lock you into their sites while trying to sell you things. Some of the tricks you will encounter include reconfiguring your browser window to remove your control bar, thus hiding the Back button; ensuring that every time you close a site window, another one opens; or generating a large number of small browser windows on your screen, each echoing their message. This is irresponsible Web programming at its worst, and does nothing but annoy the visitor. It also guarantees that the visitor will never return.

One of the most annoying tricks advertisers on the Web employ is to create little pop-up browser windows which open while the page you are waiting for downloads. These are known as "interstitials" and often infuriate Web users. They waste precious bandwidth, clutter up the screen and very seldom achieve a result. Web authors should never force content on visitors. We are deliberately not covering this type of scripting.

A Web site should be an open house, not a prison camp. As a Web designer, you lay out your stall, arranging your contents in the most attractive and enticing way that you can, but you never drag a visitor inside or lock the door behind him. We would like to stress the importance of "voluntary content". Avoid forcing your visitors to do anything. Never compel them to view your images, listen to your sound tracks or watch your video samples. If you wish to include such content, link to it and make sure that your link is captioned in such a way that your visitor knows exactly what will happen if he or she clicks it.

<A HREF="resources/sound.wav">Click here </A>to hear the sound of my dog barking.

is responsible coding.

<A HREF="resources/sound.wav">Click here </A>for a treat.

is not.

Remember always that your visitors are people like yourself. They are not sheep to be herded around your site. People can be awkward, troublesome and contrary, and very seldom do what you would like them to. They are also your best critics and in the next chapter we will be looking at ways of getting feedback from visitors to help improve our sites.

Let's finish with a checklist of points to be borne in mind if your site is to be visitor-friendly.

1. Ensure that all your files are as small as possible. This might mean reducing the quality of sound and video files down to the acceptable minimum and reducing the size and *colour depth*[1] of images.

2. Ensure that your HTML code includes only essential lines. If you are working with Web authoring software, edit it by hand and remove any unnecessary code that the package has dropped in.

3. Test your pages in as many browsers as you can lay your hands on, but always in the latest versions of Netscape and Internet Explorer.

4. If possible, check your pages on Windows, MacOS and LINUX-based computers. If this is not possible, remember that Windows is the most popular operating system by a long way, and is therefore the key platform to satisfy.

5. Remember to include alternative text for any non-text page content. Most elements that insert content, <IMG> and <EMBED> for example, support the ALT attribute which allows you to add a text string like this:

   <IMG SRC="resources/lion.jpg" ALT="You're missing a picture of a lion!">

6. Ensure that your pages look good and that your text is readable at an 800 x 600 pixel monitor resolution. If they also work well at other resolutions, this would be better still.

7. Be conscious of the needs of visitors with poor eyesight. Make sure that your text contrasts well with your backgrounds.

---

[1] **Colour depth**: the colour depth of an image refers to the minimum number of colours that can be used to create that image. Most graphics software includes a utility to allow you to reduce colour depth.

Key Facts ●

 Some browsers do not support graphics or frames, and some Web users turn off support for graphics and frames. Since the Web is primarily a visual medium, we do not suggest you provide text-only pages, but it is good practice to provide a warning on framed pages that content will not be visible unless the browser is frame-enabled. You might also consider providing alternative pages that do not require frames.

 Most Web sites are written in American English, and even those that aren't often provide an English alternative. Sites written in other languages cannot expect the same level of interest. Languages which use non-ASCII characters will not display properly in a browser unless a special character set has been downloaded and installed. HTML special character entities provide a good selection of non-standard letterforms.

 The needs of visually and aurally impaired visitors should always be considered. Special help is often provided within a computer's operating system, and browsers can be configured for extra large text. From the design side, it is important that text is readable and this implies high contrast between the words and the page background.

Never attempt to bully your visitors. Multimedia content should always be offered to rather than forced on a Web user.

QUICK REVISION QUESTIONS

1. What is meant by the concept of site accessibility?
2. Which factors could interfere with the download speed of a Web document?
3. In Web terms, what is meant by bandwidth?
4. There is a wide range of different platform and browser configurations. How can a Web designer ensure that his or her pages work in the majority of possible configurations?
5. What is meant by the term browser compatibility? Why is it important to Web designers?
6. How should a Web designer provide for visitors whose browsers do not support frames?
7. Why are most Web sites written in American English?
8. What provisions might a Web designer make for visually impaired visitors?
9. What is meant by voluntary content? How might a Web designer offer voluntary content on his site?
10. Why is it important to keep files sizes down to an absolute minimum?

REVISION PROJECT: Chapters 16 – 20

Using the guidelines we have laid down in the last five chapters, we would like you to create an advice page for the visually impaired to be included in your Web site. Carefully designed and coded, the page should provide information on three different topics:

- **The use of features available within a computer's operating system to improve screen readability.**
- **The use of features built into a Web browser to enlarge text size.**
- **The need for Web authors to provide pages with good readability and high contrast.**

The following notes might help.

1. If you have not experimented with the accessibility features built into Windows, you will need to research them now. Try checking the Windows Help file on the **Start** button. Accessibility features are not installed automatically, so you might need to install them from the Windows distribution. To do this, go **Start > Settings > Control Panel > Add/Remove Programs > Windows Setup** and look at the Accessibility components.

2. Try various text size settings within any browsers you have available. We have noted in this chapter that some browsers also allow your to define your own style sheet which can override any styles within downloaded pages. You might consider including instructions on how to create a high readability style sheet.

3. Create a simple text page, and experiment with different text sizes and colours, against different background. You might also check Chapter 16 for additional information.

4. The page you will create should be aimed specifically at visually impaired viewers. Try for large text and very high readability.

Chapter 21
Finishing and testing your site

Brief contents:

1. Turning site plans into HTML pages.

2. Sketching page roughs as guides to layout.

3. The page creation process.

4. Checking and modifying page layouts.

5. Validating HTML code.

6. Checking pages in different makes and versions of common Web browsers.

7. Audience approval.

8. The test – modify – retest cycle.

Finishing and testing your site

We started the second part of this book by working through a Web site design process, using the example of a site on Japanese manga. In this chapter we are going to return to our site design and look at implementing the plans we made. We are going to consider how to turn our design notes into working pages, how to make sure that our HTML code is valid, how to check audience reaction to our pages and how to make changes efficiently. This is a short chapter, but a vital one.

Let's start off by reminding ourselves how far we had got with our design process. These are the design sheets as we left them (we've stuck them both together for simplicity):

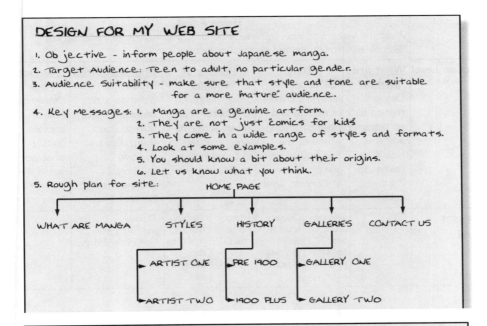

DESIGN FOR MY WEB SITE

1. Objective - inform people about Japanese manga.
2. Target Audience: Teen to adult, no particular gender.
3. Audience Suitability - make sure that style and tone are suitable
   for a more "mature" audience.
4. Key Messages: 1. Manga are a genuine artform.
   2. They are not just "comics for kids"
   3. They come in a wide range of styles and formats.
   4. Look at some examples.
   5. You should know a bit about their origins.
   6. Let us know what you think.
5. Rough plan for site:

HOME PAGE

WHAT ARE MANGA   STYLES   HISTORY   GALLERIES   CONTACT US

ARTIST ONE   PRE 1900   GALLERY ONE

ARTIST TWO   1900 PLUS   GALLERY TWO

DESIGN FOR MY WEB SITE

1. Colour scheme for text:
   Yellow text on a black background - high contrast!
   text and highlight variations - white and aqua.
2. Build page template and draft up a style sheet.
3. Use headlines and subheads to divide text.
4. Design "attention grabbing" white on black graphic
   on all pages. Aim for something dramatic.
5. Name for site: "BIG EYES SMALL MOUTHS"

NAVIGATION -
1. Graphical navigation bar across top of page.
   - match style and colours to site design.
2. Use image slicing for faster download time
   and to create rollover effects on hotspots

Figure 21.1: Design sheets for manga Web site.

Our notes cover most of the important design aspects of our site such as intended audience, content, colour scheme, structure etc., but they are not intended to restrict us. We have deliberately included some rough ideas such as "use image slicing" which are meant to remind us of techniques rather than content. We also have a site plan which looks like this:

Top Level	**Home Page** Welcome visitors to site. Introduce content and include Key Messages. Discuss site structure and navigation system.				
Section Level	**What are manga?** Define manga as an artform and see how it relates to Japanese culture.	**Style** Talk about different styles of manga and point to the works of the two artists we are presenting at Content level.	**History of Manga** How manga originated from other artforms and point to the detailed history at Content level.	**Manga Galleries** Explain how our galleries are organised and how to use them. Point to the two thumbnail galleries at Content level.	**Contact Page** Details on how to contact us and what we would like to hear from you.
Content Level		Discuss artist 1 with samples of work. / Discuss artist 2 with samples of work.	History up to 1900. / History from 1900 to the present day.	Thumb-nail Gallery 1. / Thumb-nail Gallery 2.	

This tells us what each page is intended to contain, although we may need to modify it as we start laying down actual content. On paper we now have everything we need to put together our pages, so let's make a start on creating our Web site.

Converting plans into pages

One of the greatest mistakes a Web author can make is to get caught up in the details of page formatting when he or she should be concentrating on page content. You now know dozens of ways of making your pages look nice, but **content is king**. A visitor might pause and admire your graphics, your layout and your colour scheme for a few moments, but then he starts looking for the substance rather than the window dressing.

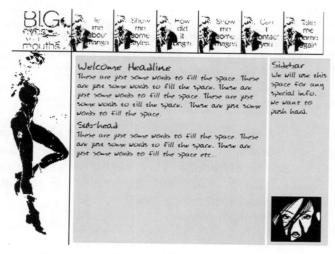

Figure 21.2: Rough plan for manga site's Home Page.

Ideally each page will have a sketched plan. This can be very rough, but it should indicate how the various elements will be placed on the page. Figure 21.2 shows the rough plan we have knocked up for the Home Page of our manga site. From this you can see that in addition to the table layout required for our image-sliced navigation bar, we will also need to define two further areas – one for our main page content and one for a sidebar.

If your site – like ours – will use the same layout for most pages, there is no need to create a rough plan for every one. If, on the other hand, you intend to make every page look different, you should rough out your ideas for each page. (We have already discussed the concept of site consistency, so we won't go through it again here.) In our case, we will need a different layout for our thumbnail galleries and for our contact page, which will consist of a form with form controls to allow our visitors to input their ideas and comments on our site. Work through your site plan and sketch out designs for any page that differs significantly from your main layout.

We believe that most page construction should start with the text. This isn't always the case; for example two of the pages noted in our plan are thumbnail galleries where the placement of graphics would be our starting point. For most pages however the text is the key content and this is where to begin. We have developed a technique for building pages which we think you should consider. We are not forcing it on you, because all Web designers work in different ways. You might prefer another style of working, but this technique has served us well and does have two great advantages. Firstly, it directs your focus onto the textual content and secondly, it builds pages in a very logical and controlled way. Here is our work plan:

1. Before you do anything else, make sure that you have assembled all the resources you need for your Web page.

2. Check that your graphics are set to the right size and colour depth (you can always modify them later if you need to). If you are including audio or video content, make sure that the files are compressed and saved in the right format. If you have set up your workspace as we suggested in Chapter 2, you will already have a folder called **Web Works/cabinet**. This is intended to store all of these resources until you need them.

3. Make sure that your folders are prepared. We suggest that all your completed Web pages should be placed in the **web_pages folder**, with all included content such as graphics and multimedia stored in the **web_pages/resources** folder.

4. If you are using a style sheet, ensure it is located in the folder you will be storing your completed pages in.

5. Leave your templates, style sheets and other Web resources on one side and open a blank page in your text editor. Working from your design notes and the rough sketch of your page, type in all the words you want to use. Remember to include headlines, captions, table cell contents, footnotes, comments, text links ... everything. But don't even consider trying to format them or lay them out in any way.

6. Read through your text, checking the spelling, the punctuation and the grammar. In our opinion there is nothing less professional than a Web page full of spelling errors. If you know your spelling is weak, use a computer-based spell checker or even a dictionary. Web grammar is nothing like as formal as normal written English, but sentences still have to make sense. The best trick we know is to speak each sentence out loud. If it sounds right, it probably is right; if it doesn't, correct it.

7. Save the file to a convenient folder on your hard drive – **Web Works/cabinet** is a good choice, but don't close the file, leave it open on your desktop.

8. Now open a second copy of your text editor and either load the relevant HTML template or create a blank HTML file. If you are using a template, the initial work has already been done. If not, make sure that the key HTML opening and closing tags are in place.

9. Now is also the time to insert the relevant information into your meta-tags. If you are using a style sheet, make sure that the correct reference is included in the Head section.

10. If you are using any HTML layout elements like <DIV>, <TABLE> or <FORM>, or if you intend laying out information in a list, type in the tags for these elements now. Remember to turn off those elements that need it by including the closing tag. If you are not sure which tags to use, check the complete reference table in Appendix 2. Don't type any content into these elements, just the tags.

11. Check through the page and verify the tags you have used. Check that all HTML elements and attributes are properly spelled – remember to watch for American English spellings.

12. Make sure that all the tags have opening and closing brackets. Check that tags that work in pairs, for example <DIV> and </DIV>, have both opening and closing tags.

13. Now work between the two text editor windows you have open. **Select** and **Cut** (not Copy) each piece of text from your content window and **Paste** it into your HTML window, making absolutely certain that you place each piece correctly. By doing this you make sure that none of your text has been missed. Watch for errors like:
<DIV ALIGN="CENTER"Here is some text></DIV>
You may need to add in some text or to change the text you have written. Don't be afraid to make even major changes at this point.

14. Save the page under its correct name (don't forget the .html extension) in the correct folder. The text editor page which previously contained all your typing should now be empty. Close it, but don't Save the file. In this way your original typed text will remain on disk, should you need to refer to it again.

15. Leaving your text editor HTML window open, open your page in a Web browser. Make sure that all the text has appeared as it is supposed to. This is a good

time to check spelling and punctuation once again. Watch out for things like missing full stops – these are easily overlooked when selecting and copying text from place to place.

16. From now on save your HTML page after every change you make and refresh it in your browser window. Remember that if you alter one thing, this will often change other things as well. Graphics, for example, will push text around. You may need to modify your layout to accommodate this.

17. The next stage is to insert all the non-text content into the page. To include an item, move or copy it into the resources folder and insert the correct HTML tags into your page. Since every non-text inclusion will be stored in this folder, the URL for each will always be **resources/itemforinclusion**. In most cases, we recommend doing this one item at a time, but if an element uses more than one graphic – in a navigation bar, for example, you might prefer to move all the related items in one go. Save the page and refresh the browser after each change. You will often find that inserting items requires you to make changes to your text and layout tags.

18. Now proceed to format your text and headlines. You will need to consider HTML tags and attributes, and, if you are using one, any rules set up in your style sheet. It pays to open your style sheet in another text editor window – you will need to go through the save and refresh cycle here as well. Insert any text formatting elements and modify their attributes as needed. If you find you are making the same changes to several elements, consider changing or adding rules to your style sheet. Insert any horizontal rules that you require.

19. Keep checking your changes in your browser. Don't add unnecessary formatting and remember that the page must work as a whole. Bear in mind the need to balance textual and graphic content, and above all else, ensure that the page remains readable.

20. Now add in the hyperlinks by wrapping any required text or images in the <A> ... </A> tags. Carefully check any URLs you type in. Consider whether they need to be absolute, in which case remember to include the protocol and the complete address, or relative, in which case they must point to the exact location of the resource to be linked to. We recommend placing all your HTML files in the same folder. They can then be linked to by name without needing any additional path.

21. Make one final check in your browser to make certain that everything is as you want it to be. Close down all your open windows, and reopen the page in your browser. Ask yourself one final question: Is this the page I intended to create? If you are happy, then Phase 1 is complete.

Checking and verifying your HTML code

If you have followed the plan above, you now have a page that you are happy with aesthetically. The next phase of the process is to validate the HTML code. There are several ways of doing this. There are a number of software validators which can be found on the Web or on computer magazine cover CD ROMs. Several HTML editors and Web authoring applications incorporate HTML validators. One of them that we mentioned earlier in the book is built into Chami's HTML-kit. There are also sites on the Web that can check your code remotely. Even if you use one of these, we still recommend checking your own code for errors. The work plan listed above has several checks built into it, but nothing beats closing down your page and coming back to it later specifically to validate the code.

There are whole ranges of checks that should be applied. In particular you should make sure that:

1. You have used the right tag for the job.

2. All HTML tags and attributes are properly spelled. We'll say it again: watch out for American English spellings.

3. All HTML tags use the correct syntax. Watch out for attribute values which do not have quotation marks at each end and tag angle brackets in the wrong place or missed entirely.

4. All URLs, absolute and relative, point to the correct address. In particular, watch out for URLs which are valid on your own computer. A link such as:

   HREF="resources/mypicture.jpg"

   is a valid link, while one like:

   HREF="file:///c:/web_pages/resources/mypicture.jpg"

   is not because once the page has been uploaded to a Web server, the folder path included will not apply.

5. Every HTML opening tag which requires a closing tag has got one.

6. All nested tags are in the correct order – remember "last on – first off".

Next we need to validate all our links. If any of your links connect to pages on the Web, you will need a connection to the Internet, otherwise do it locally. Click each link on your page and make sure the result is what you intended. (Obviously, if you have created links to pages that have not yet been created, there is no point checking them until the linked pages exist.) If you are using framed pages, watch out in particular that the linked pages open in the correct frame. If not, you will need to change your **TARGET** attribute's value.

Finally, check through all the code to see if anything can be deleted. Make sure that your style sheet, if you are using one, does not contain rules for elements or classes that you have not used. Check that you have not included unnecessary attributes. Streamline your code as much as possible, but remember to check the result in a browser to ensure you haven't removed anything important.

Checking your page in different browsers

Earlier in the book we stressed the importance of checking that your page will work consistently across a range of browsers. How thoroughly you can do this will depend on the number of browsers you have access to, but at the very minimum, you must test your work in Microsoft's Internet Explorer® and Netscape®. Since these two browsers render pages differently, you can expect to see some slight differences in the results, but your pages must look right in both. If one of these browsers cannot display the page as it is supposed to, the chances are that you have used browser-specific tags. In this case, unless you are prepared to restrict access to your site to one group of browser-users and alienate the others, you will need to go back into your page and modify the HTML. This is a real nuisance, but it won't happen very often.

There is also the question of whether you should check your page in earlier versions of a browser. When a manufacturer releases a new version of a browser, large numbers of users inevitably stay with the older version. They may do this because they are happy with the browser they are using or because they know that new releases are often full of bugs that only get spotted and sorted out later.

Testing your page on the very latest release and ignoring the earlier version, which almost certainly has a larger base of users, is not sensible. On the other hand, we do not believe that a Web author has any responsibility to support ancient software which is long past its sell-by date. Then again, there is the question of how many previous releases of a browser should be checked. Apart from anything else, old browsers cannot handle much of the current HTML standard. Our recommendation is to check your page in the current release and also in the previous release, but not to go further back than that.

All this means that your minimum test set consists of the current and previous versions of Internet Explorer and the current and previous versions of Netscape Navigator. But this is an absolute minimum. We do suggest that you install as many other browsers as you can get your hands on and try your pages in them. But if a page works well in the big two, we would not recommend modifying your code just because it fails to render in one of the less popular browsers. Some of them are distinctly cranky!

Figure 21.3: Different browser renderings of the same page.

Figure 21.3 shows the same page rendered in four different browser windows. All of them have been reduced to fit this book, but they have all been reduced by exactly the same amount. In each case the browsers are using their default settings. We have not modified their options in any way, and this, of course, is how most users would operate. Clockwise from top left the browsers are Internet Explorer, Opera, Netscape Navigator and HotJava.

You will remember that we created the page shown using a style sheet. Neither Opera nor HotJava has made use of that style sheet. Instead they have rendered only the text content. They have also used very different font faces and text sizes. Internet Explorer's and Navigator's renderings look the same, but if you examine them closely, you will notice small differences. Look, for example, at the length of the background image behind the headline and the thickness of the line beneath the links at the bottom.

There is an alternative to installing a series of browsers to test your pages and that is to use a browser "emulator" – a piece of software that can display your pages in a series of emulated browsers and browser versions. At present, the only browser emulator available is Browserola® from Codo Software. Figure 21.4 shows the Browserola window in which Internet Explorer 1.0 using HTML standard 2.0 has been selected.

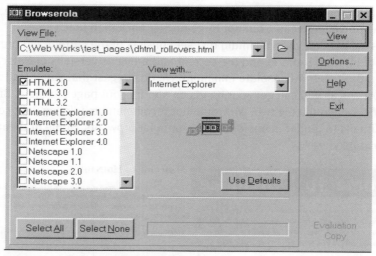

Figure 21.4: The Browserola browser emulator.

Audience reaction

However pleased you are with the pages you have created, sooner or later you will have to try them out on someone else. Your site is for public consumption – that's why you're posting it on the Web, so it's a good idea to get some feedback while you can still make changes locally. If you are working in a group, it is an excellent idea to ask the opinions of other members of the group – the more the better, as you can average out their comments and discard the extremes. If you are working alone, ask friends or family for their views. It is often difficult for a designer to have an impartial view of his or her own work.

Try to get positive rather than negative feedback. Don't ask people **if** they dislike something. Instead ask them **why** they dislike something and how they think it could be improved. Ask them what else they would like to see on your site, whether they find the navigation system easy to use and how it could be changed to suit them. Note their answers down on paper.

When you have gathered enough opinions, try to organise them logically. If no-one likes your colour scheme, it is safe to assume that it doesn't work. Change it. If, on the other hand, half your critics think something should be red and the other half think it should be blue, you haven't really got a consensus of opinion to work from, so it might be safer to stick with your original.

Try to think of Web design as a dynamic process. Adopt the idea that a Web page is never completely finished; that it is in a permanent state of revision. Content might get out of date and need revising. Colour schemes might lose their appeal, and need improving. You might find better graphics than those you originally employed.

In design terms, this is called the **test – modify – retest cycle**, and it never really ends. Even when your pages are live on the Web, you will still need to update and improve them as we shall see in Chapter 23.

Key Facts ●

1 Only after all your design work has been completed should you start actually coding your pages. Working from your design sheet and site plan create a rough sketch of each page's layout.

2 Take a logical approach to writing your Web pages. Don't get bogged down in layout and text formatting at the expense of creating good content. It is a good idea to start by putting down the text, then inserting it into a page template. Graphical and multimedia elements can then be added. Finally, create the hyperlinks. Remember to check your page in a browser regularly.

3 After a Web page has been completed, it is vital to verify the HTML code to make sure it works as intended. Software HTML validators can be used, but it always pays to check through your code line by line. It is also important to check that all hyperlinks work properly.

4 Pages should be looked at in different makes and versions of Web browsers to make sure that the page renders properly. At a minimum, check your page in the current and previous versions of Internet Explorer and Netscape.

5 Finally, you should get the opinions of other people as to how your pages could be improved. Ask as many people as possible and sort their opinions so that you can see exactly where changes are necessary. Remember that Web pages are never completely finished.

QUICK REVISION QUESTIONS

1. Why is it sensible to work from rough sketches when creating Web pages?
2. Why is it generally a good idea to start the page creation process by typing up the text elements of the page?
3. What is meant by HTML syntax?
4. What is meant by validating HTML code? How might you go about it?
5. What is the major benefit of streamlining HTML code?
6. Why is it important to check your Web pages in different makes and versions of the more popular browsers?
7. How could you check audience approval of your Web page designs?

Chapter 22
Uploading your site to the World Wide Web

Brief contents:

1. A look at Web server technology.

2. Finding a suitable Web host.

3. Using FTP (File Transfer Protocol) clients.

4. Uploading a site to a host server.

5. Publicising a site on the Web's search engines.

6. Other site promotion techniques.

7. A quick look at e-commerce.

8. Upgrading and maintaining your site.

Uploading your site to the World Wide Web

Your site has been designed, your pages created, your code has been checked, and, of course you have already confirmed that all your hyperlinks are valid. (Since the structure of both relative and absolute links will be mirrored on your Web site, if they work locally, they will work remotely as well.) Now you are ready to move your site from your own local computer to a server somewhere on the Internet. To do this, you need to take on a third range of skills. We hope by now you are qualified as a Web mechanic and a Web designer. For the final stage of the site creation process, you will need to become a Webmaster - the person who manages and maintains a site on the World Wide Web.

If you have set up your folders as we suggested, you will now have a local file structure something like Figure 22.1. (This is shown using Windows icons. If you are working on an Apple or UNIX computer, the layout will be different, but the file names will be the same.)

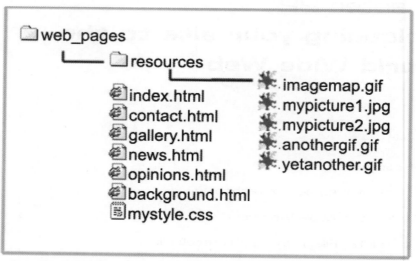

Figure 22.1: File and folder structure for a Web site.

In simple terms, uploading a site means duplicating this exact structure of folders and pages on a remote Web server, but using the *root folder* or *directory*[1] we are allocated in place of our own **web_pages** folder.

Choosing a Web server

Strictly speaking, a Web server is a computer program whose job is to deliver Web documents on demand. Usually we are not so strict and use the term Web server to mean the computer that hosts a site and the software required to store and deliver it. The major Web servers are hardwired to the Internet and are thus on call 24 hours a day, but smaller servers can be connected over the Public Switched Telephone Network (PSTN) when their owners feel like it. (It is even possible that your own computer contains Web server software. Programs like Microsoft FrontPage® install it automatically.) Major communications links on the Internet are known as the backbone. The backbone connects Network Service Providers (NSPs) across the world. When would-be visitors to your site make a dial-up connection to the Internet, they do not connect to the backbone directly. This is the function of their Internet Service Providers (ISPs) who lease a permanent connection to the local NSP.

What all this means is that a visitor's route to your site might go from his own computer to an ISP, from an ISP to an NSP and thus onto the backbone, along the backbone to another NSP and finally to the Web server where your site is actually

---

[1] **Root directory:** Your Web pages will be stored in a folder or folders on a Web server. The starting folder, the one which contains your Home Page, is called the root directory and the URLs of all your other pages and included content will be relative to this folder.

stored. As you have probably guessed, we are back to access speed once more and that is the first factor we need to consider when deciding on a suitable host for our site.

It is easy to state that our first criterion when choosing a Web host should be the speed at which the server can deliver documents, but this can be difficult to check. Speed is a function of several factors. As well as the efficiency of the pipe we described earlier, it also involves the server's own processor, memory and hard drive configurations, the amount of traffic the server is handling and the bandwidth of its local connection. Speed will also change during the day, as traffic to the server increases and decreases. It is important to note that geography is not always a significant factor. Depending on bandwidth and traffic, a high-speed server in Japan might deliver documents faster than a slower one in the nearest city. "Shop local" might be very good for your corner store, but it is a mistake on the Internet.

Unless you can find out the IP addresses of other sites held on the same server, it is very difficult to test server speed. Even downloading from the host's own site may not produce an accurate assessment. It is quite possible that the host's Web site may not be stored on the server used for hosting other people's sites. It is also wise to treat with some suspicion any claims a host makes in its advertising. You will often see phrases like "stored on our own fast server", which means nothing without factoring in traffic loads. To sum up, it is almost impossible to assess server speed. We recommend asking around to find out who is offering a good service. You might find useful information in computer magazines or in Web discussion forums. In general it is a good plan to place your site with one of the larger hosts. They tend to offer faster servers and better bandwidth.

A second factor to be considered is cost. Most ISPs now offer free Web hosting, but there are drawbacks. Sometimes the Web space offered is limited and the access speed is poor. A further problem might be the address a host offers your site. Most organisations want an impressive Web address like **www.myname.com**. All too often ISPs offer something like **www.myisp.net/~myname** - which is a lot less impressive. If you want to stick with your own ISP, there are ways round this. Several Web enterprises offer redirection names which connect visitors to a different site. You might, for example, be able to register a name like **flyto.myname** which you can then publish as your address. Unfortunately, the extra loop in the connection can slow down access time.

There are any number of specialised Web hosts on the Internet. Some offer free hosting if you are prepared to carry advertising banners on your site. The downside is that banner ads can slow up download times and often irritate visitors. If you are prepared to pay for your site, you can dispense with the banners. Prices for site hosting begin at just a few dollars, but you can expect to pay a lot more for a big chunk of Web space on a fast server. Whichever host you choose, you will be sharing it with a number of other Web sites. If any of them become very popular, the bandwidth available to your visitors will be reduced and download times will increase.

Thirdly, you will need to find out what a Web host is offering in the way of support. Some hosts offer a much better package than others. If you wish to include forms in your pages, you must make sure that your host provides the CGI applications to handle form data. Hosts may offer a helpline to their customers, but often technical support is by way of e-mail or pages of frequently asked questions (FAQs). A good Web host will respond promptly to your problems, but larger hosts might be looking after hundreds of sites and you cannot expect to get priority treatment.

All of this makes selecting a host a difficult operation. Before choosing a host, it is important to read carefully through their rules and regulations. Some hosts make it very difficult for you to move your site elsewhere. Others are very restrictive in the type of site content they allow. We recommend that you look at as many hosts as possible and find out exactly what they are offering. Work through the following checklist for each host, and get answers to as many of the questions as possible:

Check:	Notes:
Speed?	Does the host offer good download speeds at all times of the day?
Cost?	How much does it cost to rent space?
Free?	What does "free" imply? Will you have to carry advertising? How much will that slow down access speed?
Web space?	How much Web space is being offered? Can you get more if you need it? Will extra space cost more money?
CGI applications?	Does the host support common CGI applications? Can it handle your form data?
Technical support?	What kind of support is offered? Does the host respond to e-mail promptly?
Restrictions?	Are there any restrictions on the type of content accepted?
Regulations?	Is your site likely to infringe any of the host's rules and can you operate comfortably within them?

Once you have decided on a host, you will need to sign up. This usually involves filling in an extensive on-line form and, unless it is a free site, providing credit card details. Figure 22.2 shows the first part of the sign-up procedure with Freeservers.com.

Part of the procedure will involve your reading through a host's extensive terms and conditions. Do not - as many people do - simply ignore them. It is important to know what obligations you are taking on by signing up. Better still, print them out and read them in your own time.

After the form is completed and submitted, your details will be checked by the hosting company and you will be notified that your site is active, usually by e-mail. You now have an address on the World Wide Web. Check the information that comes back from your host. You will need details such as your site address, your username and your password every time you wish to manage your site. Check also whether there are any special naming conventions you should be aware of. Your

Home Page, for example, will usually be called **home.html** or **index.html**, and it is important that you follow your host's naming conventions if browsers are to access your site properly. Your next job is uploading your pages.

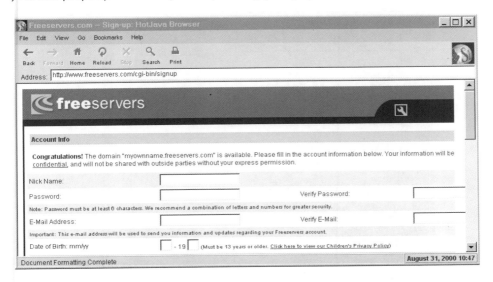

Figure 22.2: Part of Freeservers' sign-up form.

Uploading your site

To transfer your pages to your host's server you will need to use FTP, the File Transfer Protocol. We have met this before in the book. FTP is one of the simplest and most efficient protocols on the Internet, and is used extensively for moving files across the Web. To use FTP, you will require another piece of software, called an FTP client. FTP clients are easy enough to come by. Some Web authoring software, Microsoft FrontPage® for example, includes an FTP client so check to see whether you already have one installed. If not, you will need to buy or download one.

There are some perfectly adequate free FTP clients on the Web, but it might be worth investing in a good one since you will be using it regularly to upgrade your site. WS FTP Pro from Ipswitch® is a well-respected program that many Webmasters swear by. Newer on the scene, but offering more features, is Transoft Ltd's FTP Control®. There are many others so look around and find one that suits you.

To use an FTP client, first make sure that you have the information supplied by your host to hand. You will need your site address, your username and your password. Connect to the Internet and fire up your FTP client. You will be prompted for your site details and when these have been filled in, the client will try to establish a connection to your site. Figure 22.3 shows the connection window from WS FTP Pro.

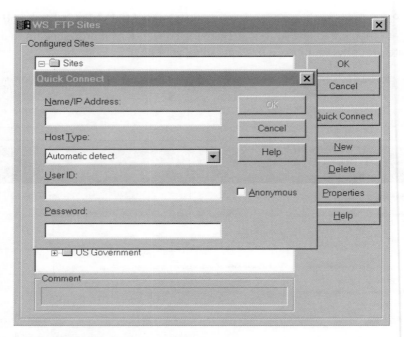

Figure 22.3: WS FTP Pro's connection window.

After connection, your FTP client will usually display a double window, one side showing the files stored on your own computer and the other one showing the files stored on your Web server. Initially, this will probably be empty although some hosts place a welcome page there. Figure 22.4 shows WS FTP Pro's transfer window.

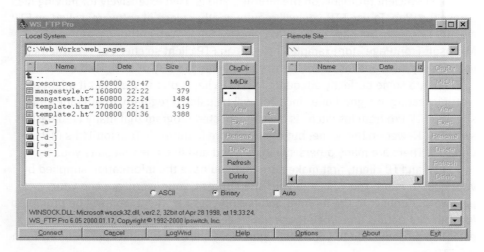

Figure 22.4: WS FTP Pro's file transfer window.

Depending on how your FTP client works, you can now either drag files from one window to the other, or select them and click on a transfer button. Both techniques will copy the files, leaving the originals where they were. In Figure 22.4, note the two arrows between the windows which upload or download files. With WS FTP Pro, you can either drag or click. and while the files are being uploaded, you will see a record of the transfer scrolling up at the bottom of the window.

At the start of the chapter we stated that you needed to duplicate your folder/directory structure on the remote server. This means that if, for example, your images are stored in a folder called **resources** on your local computer, you will need to create a folder called **resources** on the Web server. (In Figure 22.4, note the greyed out **MkDir** (Make Directory) button beside the remote window.) Remember that your pages use relative URLs like **resources/mypicture.jpg** to reference your graphics. If your pages are to perform properly on the Web, these URLs must work on the remote server.

Once you have duplicated your folder structure and copied all of your files across, your Web site is installed on the server, but don't be in too much of a hurry to close your FTP client. Leave it running while you fire up your browser and access your site. Make sure that all your pages and hyperlinks work properly. If they don't, you may have errors in your pages which you will need to correct before uploading them again. It is also worth checking in the FTP client to make sure that all the pages and resources have been uploaded properly. Comparing the file sizes of both your local and remote versions will tell you if part of a page or graphic has been lost in transit. We will look at upgrading and repairing your site in more detail later in this chapter.

If your site is operating properly, close down your FTP client and your browser. We recommend checking your site several times over the next few days. This will give you a chance to verify access speed at different times. You might also spot errors in the way the pages display or decide that the download speed of a certain resource means that it should be replaced or resized. If possible, try accessing your site in different browsers and from different computers. The more information you can assemble on how the site performs, the easier you will make necessary upgrades and maintentance.

Key Facts •

1 When a site is finished and tested it needs to be uploaded to the Web. The best way to do this is to duplicate your local file and folder structure on a Web server. A Web server is the combination of a remote computer and the software required to deliver pages to a browser.

2 Selecting a suitable host for your site involves assessing as best you can a number of factors. You should consider the access speed of the server, the cost of the Web space, how much space is on offer and the level of support that is provided. These are not always easy questions to answer.

3 Once you have decided on a host, you should visit their Web site to sign up. This means filling in a form and waiting for the host to accept your site. Be sure to read the rules and regulations to know exactly what you can and cannot do with your site.

Sites are uploaded to the Web using FTP, the File Transfer Protocol. You will need access to an FTP client. From within the FTP client, you log on to your site and transfer the files, making sure to create any folders you need. Remember, your aim is to duplicate the folder structure on your local computer. Once the site has been uploaded, check it in a browser.

Publicising your site through search engines

Now your site is on the Web, you can consider yourself a genuine Webmaster. Unfortunately only you and possibly a few friends or relatives know that it exists, and that's how it will remain unless you take steps to publicise it. If we knew a quick and cheap way of getting people to visit a site, we'd sell it to one of the big **.com** companies and make a fortune. As many Web entrepreneurs have found to their cost, it is one thing getting a site on the Web, it is quite another to get customers to visit it. Some **.com** companies have crashed despite spending millions of pounds on promotion. Remember the marketing rules we discussed in Chapter 17? Attention, interest and desire are important, but unless visitors take action, a commercial site will inevitably fail.

How you promote your site will, to a large extent, depend on the audience it is aimed at. If your site is meant for a very specific group of people, then it might be enough to make sure that members of that group are alerted and this could be done by word of mouth, by newsletter or by posting information in one of the Web's discussion forums or Usenet newsgroups.

We hope, however, that your site is aimed at a wider audience and that you intend attracting as many people as possible to look at the pages you have worked on. Unless you have a large marketing budget and can afford mass media advertising for your site, your ability to promote it will be limited, but there is still quite a lot you can do.

Firstly, you can make sure that your site is listed in the various search engines and page directories which are widely used to track down information. We discussed search engines, when we looked at meta-information earlier in the book. You already know that most search engines catalogue the keywords you place in the Head section of your pages. (You did make sure that all your pages contain relevant keywords, didn't you?) Search engines come and go on the Web, and with so many on offer, it is hard to know which ones to submit information to. Eventually, perhaps, you should submit to all of them, but it is better to start with the most popular ones.

Some authorities suggest checking a database of common search engines, such as the ones maintained by Copernic® or Apple's Sherlock®. These are intelligent search engines which sit on your own computer and make enquiries of other search engines and directory listings on the Web. The engines currently accessed by Copernic are shown in Figure 22.5. But relying on one listing can be dangerous. We note that this listing ignores one search engine which we would certainly recommend to you – Google, currently the fastest one on the Web.

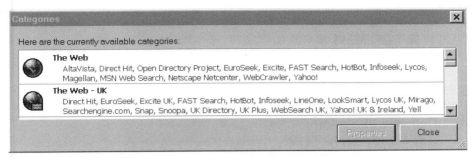

Figure 22.5: The database of search engines referenced by Copernic.

We reckon that the big fourteen at present are:

WebSearch UK	**AltaVista**	**Euroseek**
Excite (and Excite UK)	**FAST Search**	**Google**
HotBot	**Infoseek**	**Lycos (and Lycos UK)**
Magellan	**MSN Web Search (The Microsoft Network)**	
Netscape Netcenter	**WebCrawler**	
Yahoo! (and Yahoo! UK and Ireland)		

In addition to these, many *Web portals*[2] include their own localised search engines, so it is worth submitting to these as well. All these engines have a simple address on the Web. You will find AltaVista at www.altavista.com, Google at www.google.com and so on. The UK engines are usually found at **.co.uk**, so Lycos UK lives at www.lycos.co.uk. In some cases you will find specialised search engines for particular types of content. To track down any of these that are appropriate to your own site, use one of the general search engines, adding "search" as a keyword.

Submitting page information to search engines can be a time-consuming operation. Remember this is **page** not **site** information, so you might need to fill in the same form several times. Many engines offer a submission page which you can fill in on-line. Some of these forms can be quite lengthy and ask a lot of impertinent questions. Unfortunately, if you don't answer the questions, the search engine won't take your submission. Figure 22.6 shows the simple submission page used by FAST Search. Here you just fill in your site details, and FAST Search sends in its spiders to check out and catalogue your site.

If you visit each of the search engines in turn and track down their submission pages – sometimes they are not easy to find – you can at least be certain that your pages will be listed eventually. Unfortunately some engines can take several weeks to get you into their database. There is always the possibility that their spiders will find your site for themselves, but this might take even longer. One solution is to automate the process using one or more of the submission systems which are available.

---

[2] **Web portals:** a portal is an entry point to the Web which usually provides a range of additional services such as personalised pages, a search utility, local news and information and Web-based e-mail. Many ISPs offer this type of service. In Ireland Eircom, Indigo, Ireland-on-line and Oceanfree all provide well-featured Web portals.

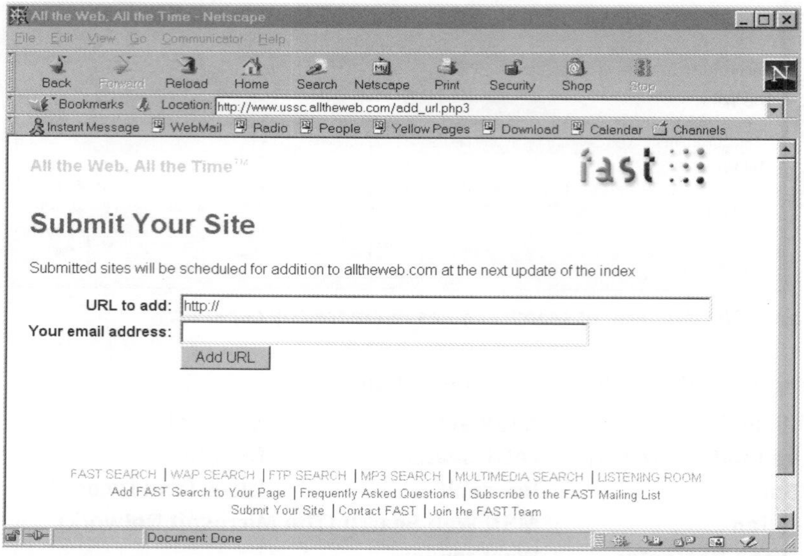

Figure 22.6: The submission page from FAST Search.

There are several very good submission systems. Some of them are free to download from the Internet. Others can be found on computer magazine cover CD ROMs. ADC-Soft's SimpleSubmit® is a free utility. It opens with a submission window in which you type the details of your site. You then select the search engines you wish to submit to, connect to the Internet and the application does all the work for you. It also produces a report to tell you how successful each submission has been. SimpleSubmit's easy-to-use interface is shown in Figure 22.7

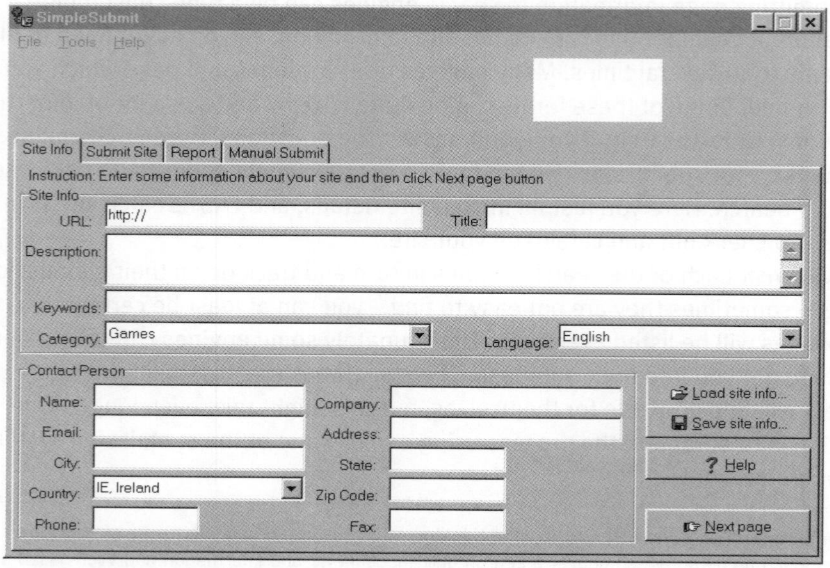

Figure 22.7: The SimpleSubmit page submission system.

Chris Palmer's Page Submit® is also free and works in a very similar way. The GNet Search Engine Submission System is more complicated but possibly more effective. You need to open an account at the GNet portal before you can use it, but after this you fill in and submit the forms as with the other systems. GNet offers several advantages. It keeps you posted of changes to search engines, checks for updates and generally lets you know what is happening on the Web. There are many other options and you will have no difficulty finding one that suits you.

Even if you choose to use one of these automated systems, we strongly recommend submitting your details directly to the key search engines listed above. It is also worth checking the engines now and then to make sure that your site has been listed. Enter your own keywords in the search box and see what comes up. If the search returns thousands of pages, you might have chosen your keywords badly. Rethink your strategy and change your keywords for some that are more exclusive to your own site content. Remember that you will need to upload the changed pages to your Web host and resubmit them to the search engine.

Other ways of promoting your site
Even when your site is listed in the search engines' databases, you should consider other things you can do to spread the word. Unless you have been incredibly original in your choice of a topic, the chances are that there are other sites on the Web with similar content. You could track these down by entering your own keywords in a search engine. Visit some of these sites and if they seem to complement your own, contact their Webmasters and see if they are interested in mutual linking. You would then insert a link to their sites in your pages and they would do the same for you.

It is also worth looking to see if there is a Web ring connected with your topic. A Web ring is a group of sites with something in common. There are Web rings for almost everything anyone could possibly be interested in and adding your site to the relevant ring is very easy to do. Once your site is a member of a Web ring, it will be listed in the ring's own directory of sites. Visit nav.webring.org and take a look around. Figure 22.8 shows the WebRing Home Page with information on how to add your site to an existing ring.

Another way to promote your site is in Web discussion forums and Usenet newsgroups. There are chat sites for most topics somewhere on the Web and tracking them down is again best done through a search engine. Be cautious when trying to plug your site in a forum as they are not really intended for advertising. One or two mentions will probably be tolerated and might bring a lot of visitors to your site, but if you keep pushing, the forum's moderator will probably tell you to stop. There are several newsgroups intended specifically for promoting new sites, so if possible, plug your site in these.

There are other techniques for publicising your site, but most of them involve expense of some kind. You can buy banner advertising on other people's sites or you can organise an e-mail campaign. Both of these might prove unpopular and are unlikely to bring you many visitors unless you have something really unique to offer. Remember that in the end a Web site relies on the goodwill of its visitors. If your site is attractive and interesting, and if it contains new and unusual content, word will soon get round that your site is worth a visit.

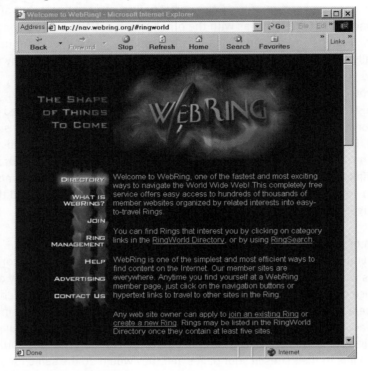

Figure 22.8: WebRing's Home Page at nav.webring.org.

E-commerce

While we do not intend to cover the subject in detail, we should just mention commercial business on the Web. An e-commerce site is just a site with the added ability to take money. At present, everyone seems to be talking about e-commerce and its earning potential. New e-businesses are springing up everywhere and despite some well-publicised disasters, it is clear that business over the Web will be very big in the future. On the other hand, many companies continue to use the Web to promote their normal commercial ventures. These so-called bricks-and-clicks businesses do not rely on the Web as their primary sales medium. They use it more as an extension of their sales catalogue.

Other companies are totally Web-based. They advertise and sell products via the Web and rely on customers on their site to finance their operations. Some products sell easily over the Internet. Books, videos and CDs in particular now have very substantial Web markets. There is no doubt that many more products will be available on the Web in the future. Already you can bank on-line, order your groceries, book holidays and buy legal and medical advice.

It is possible that your site is intended to be an e-commerce site, so we are including one or two notes for your benefit. If you intend selling products, you will need some way of handling secure financial transactions by credit card. Several banks and finance houses have set up systems to help in this area. You can link your site invisibly to one of their secure sites where the financial transaction actually takes place. Be warned though that banks charge a lot for this service.

There are other companies on the Web that offer financial partnerships. In essence, you create the shop, while they provide the till. Normally these companies take a percentage of your sale price. Unfortunately, very few of these organisations cater for the small operator. Unless you are anticipating a large amount of business, they are unlikely to be interested. There are cheaper alternatives on the way, but they have yet to establish a major presence on the Web. PayPal, for example, is a service provided by X.com®. They provide some simple HTML code which you paste into your Web pages. The code creates a button which links to PayPal's secure site. X.com charges only a small percentage of the sale price and expects to take a lot of business away from the costly merchant accounts.

Upgrading and maintaining your site

Earlier in this chapter we stated that a Web site is never really finished. However much work you have put into it, there is always something that can be added or improved in some way. It is important to think of Web pages as dynamic documents – documents which change to reflect new circumstances. If you adopt this attitude, not only does it encourage you to look on your site as a work-in-progress rather than a finished masterpiece, it also reminds you that unless your content changes, your visitors are not likely to keep coming back.

The main reason for upgrading your site is that the Web itself is dynamic and constantly changes around you. Probably the most noticeable change is that Web sites regularly open and close, and those that close often leave a trail of broken hyperlinks behind them. If you try to access a URL that no longer exists, you will usually get a browser window that looks like Figure 22.9.

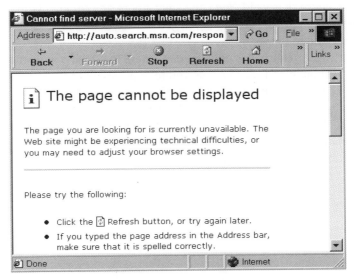

Figure 22.9: "Page cannot be displayed" browser window.

One of the commonest complaints from Web users is that the hyperlinks they are offered don't work. Nine times out of ten this is because the URL the link points to no longer exists. If visitors to your site encounter one or two of these, they are going to get annoyed very quickly. Your job here is to test all your links on a regular basis and make sure they're still valid. Dead links should be removed or replaced with live ones.

Updating your site means bringing your content right up to the minute. If your site is in any way topical, you will need to keep the content up to date. A site on a football team, for example, needs to feature recent results, changes to the players and the latest news from the club. Who wants yesterday's papers? New sites open every day and unless you keep your content fresh, you might well find that another site has overtaken you and is poaching visitors who should be yours!

Even the finest pages need tweaking now and then. You will discover improvements to layout and graphics, better ways to say something and additional elements that will make the site easier to use. HTML coding, like programming itself, seldom offers just one solution to a problem. Often there are several ways to achieve a particular result and the best one is usually the one that requires the least code. Adopt the attitude of a code miser. Congratulate yourself every time you can cut out a few tags or an unnecessary line.

Responding to visitor feedback

Back in Chapter 18 we discussed using forms to generate feedback from your visitors. We also suggested including an e-mail link so that visitors could send you their opinions on your site. If you have installed either or both of these features, you can expect to receive some sort of response – how much will depend on how many people are drawn to your site and whether they can find anything to comment on. Assuming you do receive feedback, your first responsibilty is to check whether that feedback is valid. You can safely ignore any comments that attempt to be offensive or humorous – you may well get some, but any serious submissions should be responded to.

If the feedback is useful, it is only good manners to e-mail a reply thanking your visitor. If it is valuable enough to cause you to make significant changes to your site, it is often worth adding a note to this effect on the site itself. If you have a "What's New" page, this would be a good place to do this. Try to spot trends in the feedback. Make sure you keep records of how many people comment on a particular aspect of your site. If opinion is definitely going in one direction, move with the tide and make those modifications!

Key Facts ●

 Once your site is active, you need to let people know that it exists and what it contains. There are several ways of doing this, but unless you are prepared to pay out for expensive advertising, you are likely to end up using search engines, mutual linking and by publicising your site to interested Internet communities.

 Most search engines provide a facility by which you can add information about your pages to their database. If you have to do this manually at each search engine, this can be a time-consuming business. There are a number of software utilities which can handle page submission for you, but it is still worth registering personally with the major engines.

 If you find other sites on the Web with complementary content to your own, you can often arrange mutual linking. You place a link to their sites on your pages, and they do the same on theirs. Remember to check such links occasionally to ensure they are still live.

 Web rings are groups of sites on a common theme. You can join relevant Web rings and be featured in their directories. It is also worth bringing your site to the attention of relevant discussion forums and Usenet newsgroups.

 E-commerce means trading over the Internet. If you wish to trade from your site, you will need to include the facility to charge visitors' credit cards. This can be expensive as banks and finance merchants charge heavily for the service. New charging systems are being constantly introduced and some of these promise much cheaper rates.

6 It is important to continue monitoring your site for dead links. Respond to any feedback you get from your visitors. If enough people suggest a particular change, it is worth considering making that change whatever your own opinion.

? QUICK REVISION QUESTIONS

1. What is a Webmaster? What are a Webmaster's responsibilities?
2. What factors should you consider when selecting a host for your site?
3. What is FTP and what is it used for?
4. What is an FTP client?
5. Why is it important to duplicate your folder structure exactly on your Host server?
6. How can you get a search engine to list your pages?
7. What is a page submission system?
8. What is meant by mutual linking of sites?
9. What is a Web ring and why is it useful in publicising a site?
10. If you wanted to use your site for e-commerce what additional facility would you need to add to your site?

Chapter 23
...and in conclusion

Brief contents:

10 key points of good Web design

...and in conclusion

That's it really. If you've reached this point fairly and squarely by working through each chapter and undertaking all the assignments, you can take a moment to congratulate yourself. You've come a long way. Of course, you still have a long way to go – if you want to. Beyond this book are all the wonders of client-side scripting, Dynamic HTML and Java. Or there is a different route altogether that takes in computer graphic design, Photoshop, Flash and authoring software like Macromedia UltraDev®.

There are those who predict that HTML itself is doomed and that the future belongs to XML (eXtensible Mark-up Language). XML is a much tighter and more rigidly structured coding system than HTML, but more important to Web designers, it allows you to invent your own tags. You can define your tags using a Data Type Dictionary (DTD) which confirms your vocabulary and syntax so that other people can use them. The bonus is that if you can work in HTML, you're already half way to handling XML.

Whichever way you go from here, we hope that this book has got you started. Web design is a skill that is likely to become ever more useful over the next few years, and you have mastered its fundamentals. Now get out there and Web author...

The final list

To close the book, we want to offer a list of what we consider to be the ten most important points a Web author should remember. And so, for the last time, here we go:

1. Content is what counts. However beautifully designed, your Web site is nothing without interesting, accurate and useful content.

2. Plan, plan and plan before you start coding. Leave your computer switched off and get all your ideas and designs down on paper before doing anything else. Expect to change those plans, but don't start without them.

3. Format your site for impact. Remember the importance of creating a good first impression. Use attention-getters like headlines, colours and graphics to spark your visitors' interest as soon as the first page opens. Think of your key messages and make sure they are visible in the early pages.

4. Use page templates to ensure a consistent design. Templates are not essential, but they make your life a lot easier. If your template contains all the basic tags your pages need, you only need to check them once and after that you know that your code will be correct. If you don't use templates, get in the habit of writing tags in pairs. As soon as you have written an opening tag, immediately put in the closing tag. Then go back and fill in the content.

5. Use style sheets to handle basic layout and formatting. Not only are style sheets the direction that the HTML standard is going in, but they also simplify a lot of your design work. Once you have decided on a particular style, your style sheet can implement that style right across your site and save you coding it into every page.

6. Limit your graphics and multimedia content. Never be tempted to drop in content just because it is available. Everything you add to a page should be functional and significant. Always remember that non-textual content slows up the download speed of your page. Keep it small and relevant and your visitors will thank you.

7. Keep navigation consistent and easy to follow. Whether you use text hyperlinks, an imagemap or a navigation bar, make sure that your visitors can see at a glance how to use it. Put it in the same place on every page. If your site is more than a few pages long, put in a site map and flag it with nice clear links.

8. Check your tags, then check them again. It is so easy to overlook a closing tag or a single angle bracket. Whether you code by hand or using an HTML editor, always check the code yourself. Go through it line by line, making sure that all the tags are as they should be. HTML syntax is important.

9. Consider your visitor's preferences. Don't build your pages so they only work properly in one type of browser or with one particular user configuration. Test your site across as many browsers as possible and consider providing alternatives for visitors who prefer different set-ups.

10. Change and update your site when required. Don't just leave it to gather dust on the Web. Make improvements as you or your visitors spot problems. Keep your content fresh and up to date. Check that your links are all working.

The Appendices

Appendix 1:

A brief history of the Internet.

Appendix 2:

HTML element reference table.

Appendix 3:

Colour names, hex and RGB values.

Appendix 4:

Special character codes.

Appendix 1
A brief history of the Internet

The basic facts of how the Internet and the World Wide Web developed have been printed in so many other books and magazines that we are not going to go into them in any great depth. If you are interested in the detail, we recommend checking the Web itself where you will find dozens of sites dedicated to this very subject. All we are including here is a quick rundown on how the Internet and the World Wide Web came into being.

Let's start by disposing of some of the hype. Forget all the nonsense about cruising the information superhighway or surfing through cyberspace or cherry-picking the info-tree. The reality is that what awaits a beginner to the Web is a confusing and often hostile mess of pick-and-mix data. The footpaths are badly sign-posted, there are any number of highwaymen waiting around corners to relieve you of your purse and you will be travelling on your own for most of the time.

Today's chaotic Web grew out of military order. The origins of the Internet lie back in the late 1960s when the US government was looking to bomb-proof its computers against what was thought to be an inevitable Soviet attack. The Pentagon knew that the electromagnetic pulse produced by a thermonuclear explosion would destroy any traditional computer network, so the Department of Defence's Advanced Research Projects Agency (or Administration according to some authorities) (ARPA) worked out how to create a computer network that allowed information to be routed around any bomb craters in the line. This is illustrated in Figure A1.

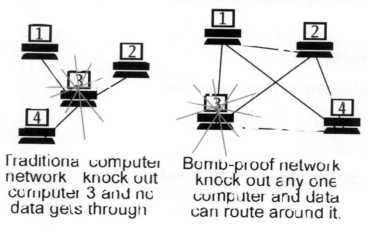

Traditional computer network knock out computer 3 and no data gets through

Bomb-proof network knock out any one computer and data can route around it.

Figure A1: Bomb-proofing a computer network.

At the same time, researchers developed a method of breaking communications down into smaller "packets" which could be sent individually through any convenient connection and reassembled by the target computer. This "packet switching" technology is still the key to the workings of the Internet.

ARPANET

Originally, the ARPANET connected the computer departments of four universities and the data just crawled between them. But over the next few years the system kept getting hijacked by civilian scientists, who thought up better things to do with information technology than use it for storing military secrets. Eventually the military grew so annoyed at losing control of their baby that they went off and built MILNET. This was restricted to military use but it left the fledgling Internet for everybody else.

In 1973 ARPANET went international. Connections were established to University College in London and the Royal Radar Establishment in Norway. Over the next few years, the Internet just got bigger and bigger as more institutions attached their computers to the system. In 1977 the first operational e-mail system was launched. (It's worth remembering that e-mail still makes up the majority of traffic across the net.) Net legend says that it was in 1982 that the word "Internet" was used for the first time, but no-one can say for sure.

NSFNET

In 1984 the National Science Foundation – a US government agency obliged by its charter to offer access to its scientific database to any educational establishment that asked for it – designed the NSFNET. Its regional structure blended perfectly into the existing Internet and provided hundreds of dedicated computers permanently connected to the system. In 1987, the whole network received a major overhaul with faster machines and more efficient telephone connections. Commercial companies, who had been dubious of the benefits at first, began to use the Internet for business communications. E-commerce was born.

During the 1980s the use of e-mail – person-to-person communication over the Internet – became widespread. Colleges began to offer their students e-mail accounts. Transmission Control Protocol/Internet Protocol (TCP/IP), an agreed communications system between remote computers, spread rapidly and became the universal language of the Internet.

In 1988 the first Internet virus, the so-called Internet Worm, was launched in the US. Net users panicked when 6,000 of the then 60,000 host computers were temporarily crippled. An emergency response team was formed to combat the menace, but for the first time the Internet was seen as creating problems as well as solutions. Hysteria about viruses, worms and Trojan horses has never really died down since.

It is important to remember that the Internet at the start of the 1990s was nothing like it is today. There was no graphical interface, no way of viewing images or listening to audio files. All input was by typing directly onto the command line and although the information flow was much faster than in the earliest days, it was still nothing like the speeds we expect today. In a word, the Internet was unfriendly.

The World Wide Web

In Chapter 1, we picked up the story at this point. We described how in 1989 Tim Berners-Lee, while working at the European Laboratory for Particle Physics (CERN) in Geneva, Switzerland, developed a system that allowed physicists to share their research results over the Internet. He and his colleagues at CERN hacked together a simple way to display information on screen and to move from place to place by clicking "hypertext links" – active pieces of text which linked the user to other pieces of information stored on the Internet. But rather than keeping this idea to themselves, or trying to make money from it, Berners-Lee and his team posted the code on the Internet, allowing everyone to make use of it.

Although this code allowed users to combine words, pictures and sounds on pages which would display on the Internet, it was another two years before Marc Andreesen and a team of students at the National Center for Supercomputing Applications (NCSA) in Illinois, USA, developed the first graphical Web browser. Launched in 1993, Mosaic was the ancestor of all of today's browsers.

The relative ease of clicking on links, buttons or images made the Internet accessible to everyone. But it is worth remembering that underneath the Web browser's graphical interface, the Internet still exists and still does the essential work of moving data from place to place.

By 1994, the original four host machines had increased to more than three million across the world, with an estimated thirty million users. The word "phenomenon" began to be used in the press. By 1996, more than 150 countries around the world had Web access.

Almost every day, new uses for the Web are discovered. If the original Internet was seen as an infinite storehouse for information, the second generation of users were taking things much further. In 1997, well over a billion dollars changed hands in the Internet shopping malls. "Vanity sites" – private Web sites created to suit the wishes of individual users – were springing up everywhere. It seemed as if every business in the world, from the tiniest cheese maker in the wilds of Killarney to the biggest multi-national, just had to have a Web site. The age of the Internet had arrived in style.

What the Web can do

The Internet can be described as millions of computers wired together over telephone lines, TV cables and satellite links, with millions more connected whenever their owners choose to dial in. But what can this mass of hardware do? Well, only one thing actually – it can transmit bursts of zeros and ones at incredible speeds. Since most communications – words, pictures and sounds included – can be rendered as patterns of zeros and ones, this means that almost any kind of information can be moved across the net.

Every day millions of couch potatoes, mad scientists, technical wizards, dedicated anarchists, bored students and others dump billions of files onto the Web. Somewhere out there are the speeches of Bill Clinton, advice on how to grow geraniums and triffids, a translation service from Star Fleet English into Klingon, nude photographs of almost everyone you've ever heard of, hate mail to Courtney Love, a group dedicated to speaking like the Swedish Chef from the Muppets, recipes for whale omelette, and the complete works of James Joyce in Urdu. All you have to do is get out there and dig out what you want.

Appendix 2
HTML element reference table

The following table lists the most common HTML elements. While it is based on the HTML 4.0 standard, we have tried to make it as practical as possible by including those elements which are widely supported by browsers, even if they are not part of the strict HTML standard. For the same reason, we have not included certain proprietary elements which are exclusive to one particular make of browser and not supported by others.

For simplicity, we have not included seldom used elements and attributes, or those which have fallen into disuse. Note that the HTML standard is regularly upgraded by the World Wide Web Consortium, which means that new elements are added and old ones removed or replaced. The W3C has expressed an intention to move away from in-line formatting of some content in favour of the use of style sheets. This means that some attributes are "deprecated", or due to be discontinued at some time in the future. Wherever possible, we would encourage you to use style sheets (see Chapter 14) which provide a much greater degree of control than in-line formatting.

Elements are listed alphabetically. For each element, the following information is presented:

1. **The tags used to define the element and the name of the element**. Where both start and end tag are shown, both should be used. For paired tags, content replaces the three dots between the tags.

2. **Description**. A brief description of the purpose of the element.

3. **Attributes**. Common attributes for the element. The next box provides a short description of their effects. Where an attribute requires a value, valid values for that string are given in the box afterwards. Where the attribute is used without a value, we have marked it with "No value required". Remember that attributes MUST be enclosed within the tag brackets.

4. **Notes**. Additional information on the element.

HTML 4.0 introduces several new "common attributes" that apply to a significant number of elements. These are explained in the last section of this appendix.

NOTES: This table is a summary of the HTML elements available under HTML 4.0. More detail on the syntax and use of each element is provided in the chapter which deals with the element. Where such additional information is essential, we have included the number of the relevant chapter in the notes. In general, the syntax for any HTML element is:

<ELEMENT ATTRIBUTE="VALUE">

<!- - ... - -> (Comments)

Description	Used to insert notes or scripts that are not displayed by the browser.
Attributes	No commonly used attributes other than those core attributes and event handler attributes described in the final section of this appendix.
Notes	See Chapters 12 and 18.

<!DOCTYPE> (Document Type)

Description	Defines the document type.
Attributes	No commonly used attributes other than those core attributes and event handler attributes described in the final section of this appendix.
Notes	Used within the <HEAD> element. Should be the first line of all HTML documents. See Chapter 12.

<A> ... </A> (Anchor)

Description	Indicates the part of a document that is a hyperlink or the target destination of a hyperlink.	
Attributes	HREF	Takes as its value the target of the link as an absolute or relative URL. When preceded by the # (hash) symbol, indicates a target location within a document. The URL must specify the protocol to be used – http, ftp, mailto etc.
	COORDS	Used with the SHAPE attribute to define the co-ordinates of a clickable region of an imagemap.
	NAME	Required in an anchor which defines a target location. Valid values are: any text string beginning with a letter, followed by any number of letters, numbers, hyphens or periods (full stops).
	SHAPE	Defines the shape of a clickable region of an image used as an imagemap. Valid values are: CIRCLE, POLYGON and RECT.
	TARGET	Defines the target window for the linked resource. Possible values are: the name of a predefined frame, or special frame values _BLANK, _PARENT, _SELF and _TOP.

Notes	The HREF attribute is required. See Chapters 8 and 9.

\<ADDRESS\> ... \</ADDRESS\>

Description	Text mark-up element to indicate the authorship of a document.
Attributes	None
Notes	

\<AREA\> (Imagemap area)

Description	Used within the \<P\> element to implement a client-side imagemap. Defines a clickable region on an imagemap.	
Attributes	ALT	Takes as its value a text string to be displayed in a browser incapable of displaying images.
	COORDS	Used with the SHAPE attribute to define the co-ordinates of a clickable region.
	HREF	Takes as its value the URL of the target resource of the hyperlink.
	NAME	Defines a name for the clickable region which can then be referred to by scripts. Valid values are: any text string beginning with a letter, followed by any number of letters, numbers, hyphens or periods (full stops).
	SHAPE	Defines the shape of the clickable region. Valid values are: CIRCLE, POLYGON and RECT.
	TARGET	Defines the target window for the linked resource. Possible values are: the name of a predefined frame or special frame values _BLANK, _PARENT, _SELF and _TOP.
Notes	The HREF attribute is required. See Chapter 9.	

\<B\> ... \</B\> (Bold)

Description	Text mark-up element to indicate that the enclosed text should be displayed in bold.
Attributes	No commonly used attributes other than those core attributes and event handler attributes described in the final section of this appendix.
Notes	HTML 4.0 encourages the use of style sheets which give greater control over how an element is displayed. Where appropriate, consider using a style sheet instead.

<BASE> (Base URL)

Description	Indicates the base URL from which all relative URLs are then calculated.	
Attributes	HREF	Takes as its value the original location of the document which contains it.
	TARGET	For framed documents, defines a default target window for all hyperlinks. Valid values are: the name of a predefined frame, or special frame values _BLANK, _PARENT, _SELF and _TOP.
Notes	Should appear in the Head section of a document.	

<BASEFONT> (Base font)

Description	Indicates the default font size, face and colour to be used for the document.	
Attributes	COLOR	Defines the default text colour. Valid values are: name of colour or hexadecimal colour value.
	FACE	Defines the default font name (or names). If the named font is not available on the client system, the browser will use its own default font.
	SIZE	Defines the size of the text. Valid values are: numbers from 1 to 7 (one being the smallest).
Notes	See Chapters 4 and 6 and Appendix 3.	

<BDO> ... </BDO> (Bi-directional override)

Description	Indicates the direction of the text flow.	
Attributes	DIR	Defines the direction. Valid values are: LTR (text flows from left to right) or RTL (text flows from right to left).
Notes	The DIR attribute is required.	

<BGSOUND> (Background sound)

Description	Associates a background sound with a page.	
Attributes	LOOP	Defines how many times the sound is to be played. Valid values are: a number or the keyword INFINITE.
	SRC	Takes as its value the URL of a sound resource which must be a .au, .mid or .wav file type.
	VOLUME	Takes as its value a number between −10,000 and 0 to specify the volume.

Notes	This element is currently only supported by Internet Explorer and browsers based on IE technology. See Chapter 13.

<BIG> ... </BIG> (Big font)

Description	Text mark-up element to indicate that the enclosed text should be displayed in a font larger than the current font.
Attributes	No commonly used attributes other than those core attributes and event handler attributes described in the final section of this appendix.
Notes	Badly defined element, the use of which is discouraged.

<BLOCKQUOTE> ... </BLOCKQUOTE>

Description	Text mark-up element to indicate that the enclosed text should be displayed as a quotation. This usually means indentation from the edge of the page.
Attributes	CITE Takes as its value the URL of a document from which the quote has been taken.
Notes	This element can be used to indent text so is useful for layouts.

<BODY> ... </BODY> (Body of the document)

Description		Indicates the Body section of an HTML document – the content which is displayed by a browser
Attributes	ALINK	Defines the colour of an active link – a link over which the mouse pointer is hovering. Valid values are: the name of a colour or a hexadecimal colour value.
	BACKGROUND	Defines a background image which will be tiled down and across the page. Takes as its value the URL of a graphic file.
	BGCOLOR	Defines the colour of the background. Valid values are: name of colour or hexadecimal colour value.
	LEFTMARGIN	Defines the width of the left-hand margin. Valid values are: a number, which specifies the number of pixels.
	LINK	Defines the colour of a link which has not been clicked. Valid values are: the name of a colour or a hexadecimal colour value.

SCROLL	Defines whether scroll bars are to appear on the page. Valid values are: YES or NO.
TEXT	Defines a text colour for the document. Valid values are: the name of a colour or a hexadecimal colour value.
TOPMARGIN	Defines the width of the top margin. Valid values are: a number, which specifies the number of pixels.
VLINK	Defines the colour of a link which has been clicked. Valid values are: the name of a colour or a hexadecimal colour value.

| **Notes** | Every HTML document should have a BODY element, except frameset documents where it is replaced by the FRAMESET element. |

 (Line break)

Description	Creates a line break in text, restarting the text on the following line.
Attributes	No commonly used attributes other than those core attributes and event handler attributes described in the final section of this appendix.
Notes	

<BUTTON> ... </BUTTON> (Form button)

Description	Creates a clickable region in a form which looks like a button.
Attributes	NAME	Defines the name of a button for scripting purposes or provides a name for submit buttons where there is more than one on a page. Valid values are: a text string beginning with a letter, followed by any number of letters, numbers, hyphens or periods (full stops).
	TYPE	Defines the type of button. Valid values are: BUTTON, RESET or SUBMIT.
	VALUE	Defines the value which is sent to the server when the button is pressed. Valid values are: a text string.
Notes	See Chapter 18.

<CAPTION> ... </CAPTION> (Table caption>

Description	Text mark-up element to indicate that the enclosed text is the caption for a table.	
Attributes	VALIGN	Defines how the caption is aligned in its cell (Internet Explorer only). Valid values are: TOP, BOTTOM, LEFT, RIGHT and CENTER.
Notes	Used within the TABLE element tags. There should be only one caption per table.	

<CITE> ... </CITE> (Citation)

Description	Text mark-up element to indicate that the enclosed text is a citation – usually rendered in italics.
Attributes	No commonly used attributes other than those core attributes and event handler attributes described in the final section of this appendix.
Notes	HTML 4.0 encourages the use of style sheets which give greater control over how an element is displayed. Where appropriate, consider using a style sheet instead.

<CODE> ... </CODE> (Code listing)

Description	Text mark-up element to indicate that the enclosed text is source code from a programming language – usually rendered in a monospaced font.
Attributes	No commonly used attributes other than those core attributes and event handler attributes described in the final section of this appendix.
Notes	HTML 4.0 encourages the use of style sheets which give greater control over how an element is displayed. Where appropriate, consider using a style sheet instead.

<DD> ... </DD> (Definition of an item in a definition list)

Description	Indicates the definition of an item in a list of defined terms.
Attributes	No commonly used attributes other than those core attributes and event handler attributes described in the final section of this appendix.
Notes	The closing tag </DD> is optional. See <DL> below and Chapter 5.

<DIV> ... </DIV> (Division)

Description	Indicates that enclosed content is a single block to be treated as one unit.
Attributes	ALIGN Defines how the content should be aligned. Valid values are: LEFT, RIGHT, CENTER and JUSTIFY.
Notes	Essential element for page layout. Useful for applying style sheet rules to a particular section of text.

<DL> ... </DL> (Definition list)

Description	Indicates a definition list – a list of paired terms and definitions.
Attributes	None
Notes	Items in a definition list require two parts – the term, indicated by the <DT> element, and the definition, indicated by the <DD> element. See Chapter 5.

<DT> (Term in a definition list)

Description	Indicates a term in a list of defined terms.
Attributes	No commonly used attributes other than those core attributes and event handler attributes described in the final section of this appendix.
Notes	See <DL> above and Chapter 5.

<EM> ... </EM> (Emphasis)

Description	Text mark-up element which indicates that the enclosed text should be rendered with emphasis – usually displayed as italic text.
Attributes	No commonly used attributes other than those core attributes and event handler attributes described in the final section of this appendix.
Notes	HTML 4.0 encourages the use of style sheets which give greater control over how an element is displayed. Where appropriate, consider using a style sheet instead.

\<EMBED\> ... \</EMBED\> (Embedded object)

Description	Indicates that the enclosed object is to be embedded in an HTML page.	
Attributes	ALIGN	Defines how adjacent text is to be aligned on the object. Valid values are: ABSBOTTOM, ABSMIDDLE, BASELINE, BOTTOM, LEFT, MIDDLE, RIGHT, TEXTTOP and TOP.
	ALT	Takes as its value a text string to be displayed if the object cannot be supported.
	BORDER	Defines the size of the border around the object. Valid values are: a number, which specifies the number of pixels.
	HEIGHT	Defines the height of the object. Valid values are: a number, which specifies the number of pixels.
	HIDDEN	Defines whether the object is visible on the page. Valid values are: TRUE and FALSE.
	HSPACE	Defines the width of the left and right margins between the object and the surrounding text. Valid values are: a number, which specifies the number of pixels.
	NAME	Defines a name for the object which can then be referenced by client-side scripting. Valid values are: a text string beginning with a letter, followed by any number of letters, numbers, hyphens or periods (full stops).
	SRC	Takes as its value the URL of the object to be embedded.
	TYPE	Defines the MIME type of the object which is then used by the browser to select the correct plug-in to handle it.
	VSPACE	Defines the height of the top and bottom margins between the object and the surrounding text. Valid values are: a number, which specifies the number of pixels
	WIDTH	Defines the width of the object. Valid values are: a number, which specifies the number of pixels
Notes	This element is not part of the HTML 4.0 standard, but is widely supported by browsers. It is usually applied to multimedia content. See Chapter 13.	

<FONT> ... </FONT> (Font definition)

Description	Text mark-up element which indicates the text size, colour and font face for the text it encloses.	
Attributes	COLOR	Defines the default text colour. Valid values are: the name of a colour or a hexadecimal colour value.
	FACE	Defines the default font name (or names). If the named font is not available on the client system, the browser will use its own default font.
	SIZE	Defines the size of the text. Valid values are: numbers from 1 to 7 (1 being the smallest), or sizes relative to the default font from –6 to +6.
Notes	This element is not part of the HTML 4.0 standard but is widely supported by browsers. HTML 4.0 encourages the use of style sheets which give greater control over how an element is displayed. Where appropriate, consider using a style sheet instead. See Chapter 4.	

<FORM> ... </FORM> (Input form)

Description	Indicates a form containing form controls which can be completed and submitted by the user.	
Attributes	ACTION	Takes as its value the URL of a server-side program which will process data submitted by the form.
	LANGUAGE	Where the element is bound to a script, defines the language in which the associated script is written. Valid values are: JAVASCRIPT (or JSCRIPT) and VBSCRIPT (or VBS).
	METHOD	Defines how form data should be transmitted to the server. Valid values are: GET (which appends information to the URL defined by the ACTION attribute) or POST (which transmits data using the HTTP protocol).
	TARGET	In a framed document, defines the frame in which to display the results of a form submission. Valid values are: the name of a predefined frame or special frame values _BLANK, _PARENT, _SELF and _TOP.
Notes	See Chapter 18.	

<FRAME> (Frame)

Description	Indicates a named scrolling window which can display content independent of other windows.	
Attributes	BORDERCOLOR	Defines the colour of the frame's border. Valid values are: name of colour or hexadecimal colour value.
	FRAMEBORDER	Defines whether the frame should have a border. Valid values are: O (no border) and 1 (with border).
	MARGINHEIGHT	Defines the height between the frame's contents and its top and bottom borders. Valid values are: a number, which specifies the number of pixels.
	MARGINWIDTH	Defines the width between the frame's contents and its left and right borders. Valid values are: a number, which specifies the number of pixels.
	NAME	Defines the name of the frame so that it can be targeted by hyperlinks or manipulated by scripting. Valid values are: a text string beginning with a letter, followed by any number of letters, numbers, hyphens or periods (full stops).
	NORESIZE	Prevents the user from resizing the frame in his browser. No value required.
	SCROLLING	Defines whether the frame should display scroll bars. Valid values are: NO (which disables scroll bars), YES (which forces them to appear) and AUTO (which creates them if they are needed).
	SRC	Takes as its value the URL of a file to be loaded into the frame when it first opens. If absent the frame will load an empty page.
Notes	Each frame must be previously named within a Frameset document (see below). Some browsers – particularly older versions – do not support frames. See Chapter 10.	

<FRAMESET> ... </FRAMESET> (Frameset document)

Description	Indicates how a series of frames are to be displayed in a browser.	
Attributes	BORDER	Defines the width of frame borders within the frameset. Valid values are: a number, which specifies the number of pixels, with 0 eliminating borders altogether.
	BORDERCOLOR	Defines the colour of the frames' borders. Valid values are: name of colour or hexadecimal colour value.
	COLS	Defines the number and size of vertical frames within the frameset by listing them from left to right as a series of values separated by commas. Valid values are: fixed widths in pixels (e.g. 200,250,300), percentages of the total width available (e.g. 25%,25%,25%,25%) or an asterisk (*) to indicate the remaining available width. Values can be mixed (e.g. 200,50%,*).
	FRAMEBORDER	Defines whether the frames should have borders. Valid values are: 0 (no border) and 1 (with border).
	FRAMESPACING	Defines the space between frames. Valid values are: a number, which specifies the number of pixels.
	LANGUAGE	Where the element is bound to a script, defines the language in which the associated script is written. Valid values are: JAVASCRIPT (or JSCRIPT) and VBSCRIPT (or VBS).
	ROWS	Defines the number and size of horizontal frames within the frameset by listing them from top to bottom as a series of values separated by commas. Valid values are: fixed widths in pixels (e.g. 200,250,300), percentages of the total width available (e.g. 25%,25%,25%,25%) or an asterisk (*) to indicate the remaining available width. Values can be mixed (e.g. 200,50%,*).
Notes	This element replaces the BODY element in framed documents. See Chapter 10.	

<H1> ... </H1> to <H6> ... </H6> (Heading)

Description	Text mark-up element to indicate that the enclosed text is to be rendered as a heading of the specified size from 1 to 6, with 1 being the largest.	
Attributes	ALIGN	Defines how the heading should be aligned. Valid values are: LEFT, RIGHT, CENTER and JUSTIFY.
	LANGUAGE	Where the element is bound to a script, defines the language in which the associated script is written. Valid values are: JAVASCRIPT (or JSCRIPT) and VBSCRIPT (or VBS).
Notes	It's worth noting that in most browsers, the six heading sizes correspond to the six font sizes supported by the FONT element – but in reverse, so heading size 1 is equivalent to font size 6 etc.	

<HEAD> ... </HEAD> (Head of the document)

Description	Indicates the head section on an HTML document.
Attributes	None
Notes	The head section contains information about the document as well as style sheets rules and scripts. It must contain a TITLE element.

<HR> (Horizontal rule)

Description	Indicates a horizontal line across the page.	
Attributes	ALIGN	Defines how the line should be aligned. Valid values are: LEFT, RIGHT, CENTER and JUSTIFY.
	COLOR	Defines the colour in which the line should be rendered. Valid values are: name of colour or · hexadecimal colour value.
	NOSHADE	Prevents the line from being rendered with shading to suggest a 3D effect. No value required.
	SIZE	Specifies the height (thickness) of the line. Valid values are: a number, which specifies the number of pixels.
	WIDTH	Specifies the width (length) of the line. Valid values are: a number, which specifies the number of pixels or a percentage of screen width.
Notes		

<HTML> ... </HTML> (HTML document)

Description	Identifies the document as an HTML page.
Attributes	None
Notes	HTML tags should enclose the entire document and contain a HEAD element and either a BODY or a FRAMESET element.

<I> ... </I> (Italic)

Description	Text mark-up element to indicate that the enclosed text is to be rendered in italics.
Attributes	None
Notes	HTML 4.0 encourages the use of style sheets which give greater control over how an element is displayed. Where appropriate, consider using a style sheet instead.

<IMG> (Image)

Description	Indicates that a graphic image is to be included in the document.	
Attributes	ALIGN	Defines how adjacent text is to be aligned on the object. Valid values are: ABSBOTTOM, ABSMIDDLE, BASELINE, BOTTOM, LEFT, MIDDLE, RIGHT, TEXTTOP and TOP.
	ALT	Takes as its value a text string to display instead of the image, in browsers which cannot display graphics.
	BORDER	Defines the width of the border around the image. Valid values are: a number, which specifies the number of pixels.
	HEIGHT	Defines the height of the image. Valid values are: a number, which specifies the number of pixels.
	HSPACE	Defines the horizontal space between the image and surrounding text. Valid values are: a number, which specifies the number of pixels.
	LANGUAGE	Where the element is bound to a script, defines the language in which the associated script is written. Valid values are: JAVASCRIPT (or JSCRIPT) and VBSCRIPT (or VBS).
	LOWSRC	Takes as its value the URL of a low resolution version of the image to be displayed while the high resolution version is downloading.

NAME	Defines a name for the image which can then be referenced by client-side scripting. Valid values are: a text string beginning with a letter, followed by any number of letters, numbers, hyphens or periods (full stops).
SRC	Takes as its value the URL of the image.
USEMAP	Defines the image as a client-side imagemap. Takes as its value a map file which associates regions of the image with hyperlinks.
VSPACE	Defines the vertical space between the image and surrounding text. Valid values are: a number, which specifies the number of pixels.
WIDTH	Defines the width of the image. Valid values are: a number, which specifies the number of pixels.

Notes	HEIGHT and WIDTH attributes should always be used as they force the browser to create space for the graphic before it downloads.

<INPUT> (Input form control)

Description	Indicates an input control for a form	
Attributes	ALIGN	If the input control TYPE is set to IMAGE, this defines how adjacent text is to be aligned on the object. Valid values are: ABSBOTTOM, ABSMIDDLE, BASELINE, BOTTOM, LEFT, MIDDLE, RIGHT, TEXTTOP and TOP.
	ALT	If the input control TYPE is set to INPUT, this takes as its value a text string to display instead of the image, in browsers which cannot display graphics.
	CHECKED	No value required. If the input control TYPE is set to CHECKBOX or RADIO, this defines the control which is checked (ticked) when the page first displays.
	LANGUAGE	Where the element is bound to a script, defines the language in which the associated script is written. Valid values are: JAVASCRIPT (or JSCRIPT) and VBSCRIPT (or VBS).
	MAXLENGTH	If the input control TYPE is set to TEXT, this defines the maximum number of characters and spaces which can be entered into the input field. Valid values are: a number, which specifies the number of characters/spaces.

NAME	Defines a name for the image which can then be referenced by client-side scripting. Valid values are: a text string beginning with a letter, followed by any number of letters, numbers, hyphens or periods (full stops).
SIZE	If the input control TYPE is set to TEXT, this defines the width of the input field displayed on the form. Valid values are: a number, which specifies the number of characters/spaces.
SRC	If the input control TYPE is set to IMAGE, this takes as its value the URL of the image to be displayed.
TYPE	Defines the type of input control. Valid values are: BUTTON (which generates a general purpose button), CHECKBOX (which generates a checkbox control), RADIO (which generates a radio button), IMAGE (which displays the image referenced by the SRC attribute), PASSWORD (which generates a text input field which obscures content as it is typed in), RESET (which generates a reset button), SUBMIT (which generates a submit button) and TEXT (which generates a single-line text entry field)
USEMAP	If the input control TYPE is set to IMAGE, this defines the image as a client-side imagemap. Takes as its value a map file which associates regions of the image with hyperlinks.
VALUE	Has two different uses. If the input control TYPE is set to TEXT or PASSWORD, this takes as its value a text string which is displayed in the input field when the page first opens. If the input control TYPE is set to RADIO or CHECKBOX, this takes as its value a text string which is sent to the server when the control is checked.
Notes	The TYPE attribute defines the type of input control. See Chapter 18.

<KBD> ... </KBD> (Keyboard)

Description	Text mark-up element to indicate that the enclosed text is to be rendered as if it were keyboard input – usually displayed using a monospaced font.
Attributes	None
Notes	HTML 4.0 encourages the use of style sheets which give greater control over how an element is displayed. Where appropriate, consider using a style sheet instead.

<LI> (List item)

Description	Indicates a list item in an unordered list, an ordered list, a directory list or a menu list.	
Attributes	TYPE	Defines the type of bullet to be shown in an unordered list or the numbering scheme to be used in an ordered list. Valid values for an unordered list are: CIRCLE, DISC and SQUARE. Valid values for an ordered list are: a, A, i, I or 1.
	VALUE	In an ordered list, defines the number of items. Valid values are: a number.
Notes	See UL, OL, DIR and MENU elements, as well as Chapter 5	

<LINK> (Link to external file)

Description	Indicates a relationship between the current HTML document and an external file.	
Attributes	HREF	Takes as its value the URL of the linked resource.
	MEDIA	Defines the medium in which the style information is intended to be displayed. Valid values include: ALL, PRINT and SCREEN.
	REL	Defines the relationship between the current HTML document and the linked resource. Valid values include: ALTERNATE, CONTENTS, INDEX, SECTION and STYLESHEET.
	TARGET	Defines a target frame or window in which the linked resource will be displayed. Valid values are: the name of a predefined frame, or special frame values _BLANK, _PARENT, _SELF and _TOP.
	TYPE	Defines the type of content to be linked to. Valid values are: text/html and text/css.
Notes	Commonly used to link an HTML page to a style sheet. See Chapter 14.	

<MAP> ... </MAP> (Client-side imagemap)

Description	Indicates a client-side imagemap which associates regions of an image with their destination URLs.
Attributes	NAME Defines the name of the imagemap which is referenced by the USEMAP attribute of the IMG element. Valid values are: a text string beginning with a letter, followed by any number of letters, numbers, hyphens or periods (full stops).
Notes	The map is bound to the image itself, by using the USEMAP attribute of the IMG element. See Chapter 9.

<MENU> ... </MENU> (Menu list)

Description	Older style list element which most browsers will render as an unordered list.
Attributes	No commonly used attributes other than those core attributes and event handler attributes described in the final section of this appendix.
Notes	Use the UL element instead.

<META> (Meta-information)

Description	Indicates information about the HTML document itself which can be used for indexing by search engines.	
Attributes	ONTENT	Defines the actual meta-information whose type is set by the NAME attribute.
	HTTP-EQUIV	Binds the meta-information in the CONTENT attribute to an HTTP response header.
	NAME	Defines a name for the meta-information in the CONTENT attribute.
Notes	Use of the META tag is complicated. See Chapter 12 for sample usage.	

<NOBR> ... </NOBR> (No break)

Description	Forces a browser to display enclosed text without line breaks.
Attributes	No commonly used attributes other than those core attributes and event handler attributes described in the final section of this appendix.
Notes	Used to display a piece of text in a fixed layout. Breaks can be inserted using the WBR element

<NOFRAMES> ... </NOFRAMES> (No frame support information)

Description	Indicates alternative content to display in browsers which do not support frames.
Attributes	No commonly used attributes other than those core attributes and event handler attributes described in the final section of this appendix.
Notes	See Chapter 10.

<NOSCRIPT> ... </NOSCRIPT> (No script support information)

Description	Indicates alternative content to display in browsers which do not support scripting.
Attributes	None
Notes	See Chapter 18.

<OBJECT> ... </OBJECT> (Embedded object)

Description		Indicates an object to be embedded in an HTML document.
Attributes	ALIGN	Defines how the object should be aligned with respect to the surrounding text. Valid values are: BOTTOM, MIDDLE, RIGHT and TOP.
	BORDER	Defines the size of the border around the object. Valid values are: a number, which specifies the number of pixels.
	CLASSID	Takes as its value the URL for an object's implementation. For ActiveX controls this means a long object identifier which cannot be created by the user but must be copied from a reference or from ActiveX control software.
	CODEBASE	Takes as its value a URL to use as a relative base from which to calculate the location of the CLASSID attribute's value. (Compare this to BASEFONT above.)
	CODETYPE	Defines the object's MIME type.
	DATA	Takes as its value the URL of a data file required by the object.
	HEIGHT	Defines the height of the object. Valid values are: a number, which specifies the number of pixels.
	HSPACE	Defines the width of the left and right margins between the object and the surrounding text. Valid values are: a number, which specifies the number of pixels.
	LANGUAGE	Where the element is bound to a script, defines the language in which the associated script is written. Valid values are: JAVASCRIPT (or JSCRIPT) and VBSCRIPT (or VBS).
	TYPE	Defines the MIME type of the data required by the object.

	USEMAP	Takes as its value a map file which associates regions of the image with hyperlinks. This attribute should only be used when the object to be embedded is an image file.
	VSPACE	Defines the height of the top and bottom margins between the object and the surrounding text. Valid values are: a number, which specifies the number of pixels.
	WIDTH	Defines the width of the object. Valid values are: a number, which specifies the number of pixels.
Notes	Used to insert ActiveX controls, but can also be applied to multimedia content, applets or images. OBJECT is not an element which is fully covered in this book. Some additional information is available in Chapter 18.	

\<OL\> ... \</OL\> (Ordered list)

Description	Indicates an ordered (numbered) list of items.	
Attributes	START	Defines the number from which to start numbering items in the list. Valid values are: a number. (Note: even if the TYPE attribute sets the numbering type to letters or Roman numerals, the START attribute still requires a number.)
	TYPE	Defines the type of numbers to be used. Valid Values are: a, A, i, I or 1.
Notes	See Chapter 5.	

\<OPTION\> ... \</OPTION\> (Option in selection list)

Description	Indicates an item in a list defined by the SELECT element.	
Attributes	LANGUAGE	Where the element is bound to a script, defines the language in which the associated script is written. Valid values are: JAVASCRIPT (or JSCRIPT) and VBSCRIPT (or VBS).
	SELECTED	No value required. Indicates the list item which is selected when the page first displays.
	VALUE	Takes as its value a text string which is sent to the server when the item is selected.
Notes	See Chapter 18.	

<P> ... </P> (Paragraph)

Description	Indicates a new paragraph and leaves blank line before it.	
Attributes	ALIGN	Defines how the paragraph should be aligned on the page. Valid values are; CENTER, JUSTIFY, LEFT and RIGHT.
	LANGUAGE	Where the element is bound to a script, defines the language in which the associated script is written. Valid values are: JAVASCRIPT (or JSCRIPT) and VBSCRIPT (or VBS).
Notes	While the closing </P> is optional, it must be included if the element is to be formatted as a block-level element. Using multiple <P> tags to create blank lines is pointless, since browsers will ignore empty P elements.	

<PRE> ... </PRE> (Preformatted text)

Description	Text mark-up element to indicate that the enclosed text is to be rendered as formatted outside a browser, in other words with spaces, returns and tabs preserved. This is usually displayed in a monospaced font.
Attributes	No commonly used attributes other than those core attributes and event handler attributes described in the final section of this appendix.
Notes	See Chapter 4.

<Q> ... </Q> (Quoted text)

Description	Text mark-up element to indicate that the enclosed text is to be rendered as a short inline quotation.	
Attributes	CITE	Takes as its value the URL of a document from which the quote was taken.
Notes	Compare this with the BLOCKQUOTE element above.	

<SAMP> ... </SAMP> (Sample text)

Description	Text mark-up element to indicate that the enclosed text is to be rendered as sample text – usually displayed in a monospaced font.
Attributes	No commonly used attributes other than those core attributes and event handler attributes described in the final section of this appendix.
Notes	As a logical element, SAMP can be used to bind style sheet rules to a section of text – see SPAN below.

`<SCRIPT> ... </SCRIPT>` (Scripting)

Description	Indicates a client-side script for the browser to process.	
Attributes	EVENT	Defines an event which the script should respond to. Takes as its value the name of the relevant event handler attribute. See the last section of this appendix for details.
	FOR	Takes as its value the NAME or ID of the element to which the event defined by the EVENT attribute is applied.
	LANGUAGE	Where the element is bound to a script, defines the language in which the associated script is written. Valid values are: JAVASCRIPT (or JSCRIPT) and VBSCRIPT (or VBS).
	SRC	Where the script is not included in the Head section, takes as its value the URL of a file containing the scripting code.
	TYPE	Takes as its value the MIME type of the scripting language used. Valid values include: text/javascript and text/vbscript.
Notes	Scripts can be loaded in the Head section of a document (and commented out to prevent problems with browsers which can't handle scripts) or loaded from an external file. We recommend the former where possible. See Chapter 18.	

`<SELECT> ... </SELECT>` (Selection list)

Description	Indicates a selection list within a form.	
Attributes	ALIGN	Defines how adjacent text is to be aligned on the selection list. Valid values are: ABSBOTTOM, ABSMIDDLE, BASELINE, BOTTOM, LEFT, MIDDLE, RIGHT, TEXTTOP and TOP.
	LANGUAGE	Where the element is bound to a script, defines the language in which the associated script is written. Valid values are: JAVASCRIPT (or JSCRIPT) and VBSCRIPT (or VBS).
	MULTIPLE	No value required. Specifies that multiple items may be selected from the list.
	NAME	Defines a name for the element which can then be referenced by client-side scripting. Valid values are: a text string beginning with a letter, followed by any number of letters, numbers, hyphens or periods (full stops).

	SIZE	Defines the number of items in the list which are displayed at the same time. Where the MULTIPLE attribute is used, SIZE should take as its value a number, which specifies the number of lines large enough to allow multiple selection of items.
Notes	See Chapter 18.	

\<SMALL> ... \</SMALL> (Small text)

Description	Text mark-up element to indicate that the enclosed text is to be rendered one size smaller than the default font.
Attributes	None
Notes	HTML 4.0 encourages the use of style sheets which give greater control over how an element is displayed. Where appropriate, consider using a style sheet instead.

\<SPAN> ... \</SPAN> (Span of text)

Description	Indicates a section of text to which scripting or style sheet rules can be applied.	
Attributes	LANGUAGE	Where the element is bound to a script, defines the language in which the associated script is written. Valid values are: JAVASCRIPT (or JSCRIPT) and VBSCRIPT (or VBS).
Notes	Useful to apply style sheet rules to sections of text which cannot easily be defined using P or DIV elements. A SPAN element can include anything from an entire page down to a single letter. See Chapter 14.	

\<STRONG> ... \</STRONG> (Strong emphasis)

Description	Text mark-up element to indicate that the enclosed text is to be rendered as strongly emphasised text – usually in a bold font.
Attributes	No commonly used attributes other than those core attributes and event handler attributes described in the final section of this appendix.
Notes	HTML 4.0 encourages the use of style sheets which give greater control over how an element is displayed. Where appropriate, consider using a style sheet instead.

<STYLE> ... </STYLE> (Style information)

Description	Indicates style sheet rules for a document.	
Attributes	MEDIA	Defines the medium in which the style information is intended to be displayed. Valid values include: ALL, PRINT and SCREEN.
	TYPE	Defines the type of style sheet. The usual value is: text/css.
Notes	The STYLE element should only be used in the Head section.	

_{...} (Subscript text)

Description	Text mark-up element to indicate that the enclosed text is to be rendered as subscript.
Attributes	No commonly used attributes other than those core attributes and event handler attributes described in the final section of this appendix.
Notes	See Chapter 4.

^{...} (Superscript text)

Description	Text mark-up element to indicate that the enclosed text is to be rendered as superscript.
Attributes	No commonly used attributes other than those core attributes and event handler attributes described in the final section of this appendix.
Notes	See Chapter 4.

<TABLE> ... </TABLE> (Table)

Description	Indicates a table.	
Attributes	ALIGN	Defines the alignment of the table with respect to the surrounding text. Valid values are: CENTER, LEFT and RIGHT.
	BACKGROUND	Takes as its value the URL of an image file to be used as a tiled background for the table.
	BGCOLOR	Defines the background colour for the table. Valid values are: a named colour or a hexadecimal colour value.
	BORDER	Defines the width of the table's borders. Valid values are: a number, which specifies the number of pixels (0 renders the table borderless for page layouts).

	BORDERCOLOR	Defines the colour of the table's borders. Valid values are: a named colour or a hexadecimal colour value.
	CELLPADDING	Defines the spacing between the edge of a table cell and its contents. Valid values are: a number, which specifies the number of pixels.
	CELLSPACING	Defines the spacing between individual table cells. Valid values are: a number, which specifies the number of pixels.
	FRAME	Defines which edges of a table are to display a border. Valid values are: BELOW (the bottom edge of the table), BORDER or BOX (all edges), HSIDES (top and bottom edges), LHS (left-hand edge), RHS (right-hand edge), VSIDES (left- and right-hand edges) and VOID (no edges).
	HEIGHT	Defines the height of the table. Valid values are: a number, which specifies the number of pixels.
	LANGUAGE	Where the element is bound to a script, defines the language in which the associated script is written. Valid values are: JAVASCRIPT (or JSCRIPT) and VBSCRIPT (or VBS).
	SUMMARY	Takes as its value a text string which defines the table's purpose. This is also used by browsers unable to render the table.
	WIDTH	Defines the width of the table. Valid values are: a number, which specifies the number of pixels.
Notes	Tables are commonly used for page layout as well as to tabulate information. See Chapter 10.	

<TBODY> ... </TBODY> (Table body)

Description	Indicates a group of rows within a table so that common alignment or style sheet rules can be applied to them	
Attributes	ALIGN	Defines the alignment of cell content within the TBODY element. Valid values are: CENTER, JUSTIFY, LEFT and RIGHT.
	BGCOLOR	Defines the background colour for the group of rows. Valid values are: a named colour or a hexadecimal colour value.
	LANGUAGE	Where the element is bound to a script, defines the language in which the associated script is written. Valid values are: JAVASCRIPT (or JSCRIPT) and VBSCRIPT (or VBS).

	VALIGN	Defines the vertical alignment of cell content within the TBODY element. Valid values are: BASELINE. BOTTOM, MIDDLE and TOP.
Notes		This element must be contained within the TABLE element itself.

<TD> ... </TD> (Table data)

Description	Indicates a data cell within a table	
Attributes	ALIGN	Defines the alignment of cell content. Valid values are: CENTER, JUSTIFY, LEFT and RIGHT.
	BACKGROUND	Takes as its value the URL of an image file to be used as a tiled background for the cell.
	BGCOLOR	Defines the background colour for the cell. Valid values are: a named colour or a hexadecimal colour value.
	BORDERCOLOR	Defines the colour of the cell's borders. Valid values are: a named colour or a hexadecimal colour value.
	COLSPAN	Takes as its value a number which defines how many columns wide the cell should be.
	HEIGHT	Defines the height of the cell. Valid values are: a number, which specifies the number of pixels.
	LANGUAGE	Where the element is bound to a script, defines the language in which the associated script is written. Valid values are: JAVASCRIPT (or JSCRIPT) and VBSCRIPT (or VBS).
	NOWRAP	No value required. Specifies that the cell's content should not be automatically wrapped to fit the cell.
	ROWSPAN	Takes as its value a number which defines how many rows high the cell should be.
	VALIGN	Defines the vertical alignment of cell content within the TBODY element. Valid values are: BASELINE. BOTTOM, MIDDLE and TOP.
	WIDTH	Defines the width of the cell. Valid values are: a number, which specifies the number of pixels.
Notes		This element must be contained within the TR (Table Row) element. See Chapter 10.

<TEXTAREA> ... </TEXTAREA> (Text input area)

Description	Indicates a multi-line text input field within a form.
Attributes	COLS — Defines the width of the text area. Valid values are: a number, which specifies the number of characters/spaces.
	LANGUAGE — Where the element is bound to a script, defines the language in which the associated script is written. Valid values are: JAVASCRIPT (or JSCRIPT) and VBSCRIPT (or VBS).
	NAME — Defines a name for the element which can then be referenced by client-side scripting. Valid values are: a text string beginning with a letter, followed by any number of letters, numbers, hyphens or periods (full stops).
	ROWS — Defines the number of rows in the text area. Valid values are: a number, which specifies the number of rows.
	WRAP — Defines how longer text entries are wrapped within the text area. Valid values are: OFF (text is not wrapped), HARD (wraps text and submits line breaks to the server) and SOFT (which wraps text but does not submit line breaks to the server).
Notes	Note the non-standard use of the COLS attribute. See Chapter 18.

<TH> ... </TH> (Table header)

Description	Indicates a header cell for a table.
Attributes	ALIGN — Defines the alignment of cell content. Valid values are: CENTER, JUSTIFY, LEFT and RIGHT.
	BACKGROUND — Takes as its value the URL of an image file to be used as a tiled background for the cell.
	BGCOLOR — Defines the background colour for the cell. Valid values are: a named colour or a hexadecimal colour value.
	BORDERCOLOR — Defines the colour of the cell's borders. Valid values are: a named colour or a hexadecimal colour value.
	COLSPAN — Takes as its value a number which defines how many columns wide the cell should be.

HEIGHT	Defines the height of the cell. Valid values are: a number, which specifies the number of pixels.
LANGUAGE	Where the element is bound to a script, defines the language in which the associated script is written. Valid values are: JAVASCRIPT (or JSCRIPT) and VBSCRIPT (or VBS).
NOWRAP	No value required. Specifies that the cell's content should not be automatically wrapped to fit the cell.
ROWSPAN	Takes as its value a number which defines how many rows high the cell should be.
VALIGN	Defines the vertical alignment of cell content. Valid values are: BASELINE. BOTTOM, MIDDLE and TOP.
WIDTH	Defines the width of the cell. Valid values are: a number, which specifies the number of pixels.

Notes	Must be used within the TR (Table Row) element. Typically, table headers are rendered in bold and centred within their cells.

<TITLE> ... </TITLE> (Document title)

Description	Indicates the title of an HTML document.
Attributes	No commonly used attributes other than those core attributes and event handler attributes described in the final section of this appendix.
Notes	Should occur, once only, in every HTML document and must be placed in the Head section.

<TR> ... </TR> (Table row)

Description		Indicates a row in a table.
Attributes	BGCOLOR	Defines the background colour for the row. Valid values are: a named colour or a hexadecimal colour value.
	BORDERCOLOR	Defines the colour of the row's borders. Valid values are: a named colour or a hexadecimal colour value.
	LANGUAGE	Where the element is bound to a script, defines the language in which the associated script is written. Valid values are: JAVASCRIPT (or JSCRIPT) and VBSCRIPT (or VBS).

	VALIGN	Defines the vertical alignment of cell within the row. Valid values are: BASELINE. BOTTOM, MIDDLE and TOP.
Notes	This element contains the TH and TD elements used to define cell content. See Chapter 10.	

<TT> .. </TT> (Teletype text)

Description	Text mark-up element to indicate that the enclosed text is to be rendered as if it were text from a teletype machine – usually displayed in a monospaced font.
Attributes	No commonly used attributes other than those core attributes and event handler attributes described in the final section of this appendix.
Notes	HTML 4.0 encourages the use of style sheets which give greater control over how an element is displayed. Where appropriate, consider using a style sheet instead.

<U> ... </U> (Underlined text)

Description	Text mark-up element to indicate that the enclosed text is to be underlined.
Attributes	No commonly used attributes other than those core attributes and event handler attributes described in the final section of this appendix.
Notes	Underlining text should be avoided because of confusion with underlined hyperlinks. HTML 4.0 encourages the use of style sheets which give greater control over how an element is displayed. Where appropriate, consider using a style sheet instead. See Chapter 3.

<UL> ... </UL> (Unordered list)

Description	Indicates an unordered list – a list where items are bulleted rather than numbered.	
Attributes	LANGUAGE	Where the element is bound to a script, defines the language in which the associated script is written. Valid values are: JAVASCRIPT (or JSCRIPT) and VBSCRIPT (or VBS).
	TYPE	Defines the style of bullet to be used. Valid values are: CIRCLE, DISC and SQUARE.
Notes	List items are indicated by the LI element.	

<WBR>

Description	Indicates a place where a line break can occur.
Attributes	None.
Notes	This element is used within the NOBR element which prevents a browser from wrapping text.

CORE ATTRIBUTES.

HTML 4.0 defines four core attributes which apply to almost all elements and mean the same wherever they are included.

Attributes	CLASS	Defines a class or classes to which an element belongs. Valid values are: a text string.
	ID	Defines a specific name for an element. Valid values are: a text string beginning with a letter, followed by any number of letters, numbers, hyphens or periods (full stops).
	STYLE	Defines an inline style (rather than a style defined by an external style sheet) for an element. The STYLE attribute should take as its value one or more style sheet rules.
	TITLE	Defines advisory text for an element, which is commonly rendered as a "tool tip" when the mouse pointer is over the element. Valid values are: a text string.
Notes	Core attributes should be used where necessary.	
	The CLASS attribute is commonly used to apply style sheet rules to a particular class of elements. See Chapter 14.	
	Like the CLASS attribute, ID is commonly used to apply style sheet rules or scripting to a particular element.	
	For the STYLE attribute, see Chapter 14.	

EVENT HANDLER ATTRIBUTES.

Event handler attributes can be applied to almost every HTML element. They define an event which will trigger a script. HTML 4.0 defines a wide range of these attributes, most of which are not commonly used. The most useful ones are listed in the table in Chapter 18.

Appendix 3
Colour names, hex and RGB values

The following table lists all the colours supported by the major browsers along with their hexadecimal and RGB values. Most browsers will now correctly render colours that are referenced by name, but there are always exceptions so it is safer to use the hexadecimal value (hex values are explained in Chapter 6). Remember when you use hex values in your code, they must always be preceded by the # (hash) symbol thus: **BGCOLOR="#7FFF00"**.

Alongside the hex value, we list the RGB value of each colour. RGB values define a colour by specifying how much Red, Green and Blue is used to produce it. They consist of three numbers with a value between 0 and 255. The value 0,0,0 (or no Red, no Green and no Blue) produces black, while 255,255,255 (the maximum of each colour) produces white. RGB values are used by graphics software. If you wish to create graphics, then blend them into a Web page, you will probably need to be able to convert between the two formats.

Colour Name	Hex Value	RGB Value
Aliceblue	F0F8FF	240,248,255
Antiquewhite	FAEBD7	250,235,215
Aqua	00FFFF	0,255,255
Aquamarine	7FFFD4	127,255,212
Azure	F0FFFF	240,255,255
Beige	F5F5DC	245,245,220
Bisque	FFE4C4	255,228,196
Black	000000	0,0,0
Blanchedalmond	FFEBCD	255,235,205
Blue	0000FF	0,0,255
Blueviolet	8A2BE2	138,43,226
Brown	A52A2A	165,42,42
Burlywood	DEB887	222,184,135
Cadetblue	5F9EA0	95,158,160
Chartreuse	7FFF00	127,255,0

Colour Name	Hex Value	RGB Value
Chocolate	D2691E	210,105,30
Coral	FF7F50	255,127,80
Cornflowerblue	6495ED	100,149,237
Cornsilk	FFF8DC	255,248,220
Crimson	DC143C	220,20,60
Cyan	00FFFF	0,255,255
Darkblue	00008B	0,0,139
Darkcyan	008B8B	0,139,139
Darkgoldenrod	B8860B	184,134,11
Darkgray	A9A9A9	169,169,169
Darkgreen	006400	0,100,0
Darkkhaki	BDB76B	189,183,107
Darkmagenta	8B008B	139,0,139
Darkolivegreen	556B2F	85,107,47
Darkorange	FF8C00	255,140,0
Darkorchid	9932CC	153,50,204
Darkred	8B0000	139,0,0
Darksalmon	E9967A	233,150,122
Darkseagreen	8FBC8F	143,188,143
Darkslateblue	483D8B	72,61,139
Darkslategray	2F4F4F	47,79,79
Darkturquoise	00CED1	0,206,209
Darkviolet	9400D3	148,0,211
Deeppink	FF1493	255,20,147
Deepskyblue	00BFFF	0,191,255
Dimgray	696969	105,105,105
Dodgerblue	1E90FF	30,144,255
Firebrick	B22222	178,34,34
Floralwhite	FFFAF0	255,250,240
Forestgreen	228B22	34,139,34
Fuchsia	FF00FF	255,0,255
Gainsboro	DCDCDC	220,220,220
Ghostwhite	F8F8FF	248,248,255

Colour Name	Hex Value	RGB Value
Gold	FFD700	255,215,0
Goldenrod	DAA520	218,165,32
Gray	808080	127,127,127
Green	008000	0,128,0
Greenyellow	ADFF2F	173,255,47
Honeydew	F0FFF0	240,255,240
Hotpink	FF69B4	255,105,180
Indianred	CD5C5C	205,92,92
Indigo	4B0082	75,0,130
Ivory	FFFFF0	255,255,240
Khaki	F0E68C	240,230,140
Lavender	E6E6FA	230,230,250
Lavenderblush	FFF0F5	255,240,245
Lawngreen	7CFC00	124,252,0
Lemonchiffon	FFFACD	255,250,205
Lightblue	ADD8E6	173,216,230
Lightcoral	F08080	240,128,128
Lightcyan	E0FFFF	224,255,255
Lightgoldenrodyellow	FAFAD2	250,250,210
Lightgreen	90EE90	144,238,144
Lightgray	D3D3D3	211,211,211
Lightpink	FFB6C1	255,182,193
Lightsalmon	FFA07A	255,160,122
Lightseagreen	20B2AA	32,178,170
Lightskyblue	87CEFA	135,206,250
Lightslategray	778899	119,136,153
Lightsteelblue	B0C4DE	176,196,222
Lightyellow	FFFFE0	255,255,224
Lime	00FF00	0,255,0
Limegreen	32CD32	50,205,50
Linen	FAF0E6	250,240,230
Magenta	FF00FF	255,0,255
Maroon	800000	128,0,0

Colour Name	Hex Value	RGB Value
Mediumaquamarine	66CDAA	102,205,170
Mediumblue	0000CD	0,0,205
Mediumorchid	BA55D3	186,85,211
Mediumpurple	9370DB	147,112,219
Mediumseagreen	3CB371	60,179,113
Mediumslateblue	7B68EE	123,104,238
Mediumspringgreen	00FA9A	0,250,154
Mediumturquoise	48D1CC	72,209,204
Mediumvioletred	C71585	199,21,133
Midnightblue	191970	25,25,112
Mintcream	F5FFFA	245,255,250
Mistyrose	FFE4E1	255,228,225
Moccasin	FFE4B5	255,228,181
Navajowhite	FFDEAD	255,222,173
Navy	000080	0,0,128
Navyblue	9FAFDF	159,175,223
Oldlace	FDF5E6	253,245,230
Olive	808000	128,128,0
Olivedrab	6B8E23	107,142,35
Orange	FFA500	255,165,0
Orangered	FF4500	255,69,0
Orchid	DA70D6	218,112,214
Palegoldenrod	EEE8AA	238,232,170
Palegreen	98FB98	152;251,152
Paleturquoise	AFEEEE	175,238,238
Palevioletred	DB7093	219,112,147
Papayawhip	FFEFD5	255,239,213
Peachpuff	FFDAB9	255,218,185
Peru	CD853F	205,133,63
Pink	FFC0CB	255,192,203
Plum	DDA0DD	221,160,221
Powderblue	B0E0E6	176,224,230
Purple	800080	128,0,128

Colour Name	Hex Value	RGB Value
Red	FF0000	255,0,0
Rosybrown	BC8F8F	188,143,143
Royalblue	4169E1	65,105,225
Saddlebrown	8B4513	139,69,19
Salmon	FA8072	250,128,114
Sandybrown	F4A460	244,164,96
Seagreen	2E8B57	46,139,87
Seashell	FFF5EE	255,245,238
Sienna	A0522D	160,82,45
Silver	C0C0C0	192,192,192
Skyblue	87CEEB	135,206,235
Slateblue	6A5ACD	106,90,205
Slategray	708090	112,128,144
Snow	FFFAFA	255,250,250
Springgreen	00FF7F	0,255,127
Steelblue	4682B4	70,130,180
Tan	D2B48C	210,180,140
Teal	008080	0,128,128
Thistle	D8BFD8	216,191,216
Tomato	FF6347	255,99,71
Turquoise	40E0D0	64,224,208
Violet	EE82EE	238,130,238
Wheat	F5DEB3	245,222,179
White	FFFFFF	255,255,255
Whitesmoke	F5F5F5	245,245,245
Yellow	FFFF00	255,255,0
Yellowgreen	9ACD32	139,205,50

Appendix 4
Special characters

The following table lists HTML character entities. These are special characters which are not part of the standard character set. There are hundreds of these character entities, most of which you will never need. We have included only those which we think will prove useful.

While all of these characters have a numbered entity (for example: **&**), some also have a named entity (for example: **&**) and either of these should produce the correct character in most browsers (in this case, the ampersand **&**). Unfortunately, some browsers assign their own interpretations to these codes. Note that all entities, named or numbered must begin with the ampersand character (**&**) and end with the semicolon (**;**).

To use these characters, simply insert the named or numbered entity into the text as if it were a character. So **© Richard Tammadge** will display as © **Richard Tammadge**.

Description	Named entity	Numbered entity	Displays as:
Space		&#32;	
Number symbol (hash)		&#35;	#
Percent		&#37;	%
Ampersand	&amp;	&#38;	&
At symbol		&#64;	@
Caret		&#94;	^
Tilde		&#126;	~
Trademark symbol	&trade;	™ or ™	™
Pound (punt)	&pound;	&#163;	£
Copyright symbol	&copy;	&#169;	©
Registration mark	&reg;	&#174;	®
One quarter	&frac14;	&#188;	$\frac{1}{4}$
One half	&frac12;	&#189;	$\frac{1}{2}$
Three quarters	&frac34;	&#190;	$\frac{3}{4}$

Description	Named entity	Numbered entity	Displays as:
Uppercase A with acute accent (fada)	&Aacute;	&#193;	Á
Uppercase E with acute accent (fada)	&Eacute;	&#201;	É
Uppercase I with acute accent (fada)	&Iacute;	&#205;	Í
Uppercase O with acute accent (fada)	&Oacute;	&#211;	Ó
Uppercase U with acute accent (fada)	&Uacute;	&#218;	Ú
Lowercase a with acute accent (fada)	&aacute;	&#225	á
Lowercase e with acute accent (fada)	&eacute;	&#233;	é
Lowercase i with acute accent (fada)	&iacute;	&#237;	í
Lowercase o with acute accent (fada)	&oacute;	&#243;	ó
Lowercase u with acute accent (fada)	&uacute;	&#250;	ú
Non-breaking space			
Left angle bracket*	&lsaquo;	&#8249;	<
Right angle bracket*	&rsaquo;	&#8350;	>

* These last two are useful in case you ever need to quote HTML code in your page content. It's no good simply typing in < and >, since a browser will assume you are using HTML tags.

INDEX